BEAT
THE
ODDS

BEAT THE ODDS

▲

CAREER BUOYANCY TACTICS FOR
TODAY'S TURBULENT JOB MARKET

▼

MARTIN YATE

BALLANTINE BOOKS • NEW YORK

Grateful acknowledgment is made to Alfred A. Knopf, Inc. and Raphael Sagalyn, Inc.,
Literary Agency, for permission to reprint excerpts from *The Work of Nations* by
Robert Reich. Copyright © 1991 by Robert B. Reich.

Library of Congress Cataloging-in-Publication Data
Yate, Martin John.
Beat the odds : career buoyancy tactics for today's turbulent
job market / by Martin Yate.
p.   cm.
Includes index.
ISBN: 0-345-38768-6
1. Vocational guidance.   2. Career development.   3. Career
changes.   4. Job hunting.   I. Title.
HF5381.Y37   1995
650.14—dc20   95-6362
CIP

Manufactured in the United States of America
First Edition: May 1995
10 9 8 7 6 5 4 3 2 1

To your security, freedom, and happiness

from the people who
brought you
Beat the Odds

Contents

Acknowledgments

to

the people who brought you
Beat the Odds

My research and production team, David Caruso, Ph.D., Karen Galletti, Michael Savitsky, Stacey Miller, Dan Hoffman, Marie Woodhall, and Joanna Wright, Ph.D. Also John D. (Jack) Mayer, Ph.D., for his guidance on the research.

My thanks to Bob Levine, for all Bob has done to make this book everything it could be, to Stuart Krichevsky for his color commentary, and Sandor Szatmari for telling me it was time.

To Linda Grey, Mathew Shear, Joëlle Delbourgo, and the whole team at Ballantine for "getting it" from the first and getting behind it all the way through. My thanks and gratitude to the eyes and ears of my editor Elizabeth Zack, and to Beth Bortz and Gaia Gerson, who all worked so hard to make this book shine in ways that I could not.

Thank you all for your help and encouragement. *Beat the Odds* wouldn't be here without all your good efforts.

BEAT
THE
ODDS

Introduction:

Understanding the Odds

You were born into the dying days of the industrial age and raised on the work ethic of the Great Depression generation: "Find a job and hang on to it with ten fingers, and should you lose one of those fingers on the job, hang on with nine. Because if you hang in there, you will make it to the American Dream."

Based on this ideology, five generations of professionals sacrificed a life for a corporate career, on the promise of the security that sacrifice would bring. But technology is now allowing business to renege on the promise. The subsequent confluence of job exportation, defense-industry contraction, workplace automation, corporate restructuring, and the continuing dramatic shift to a contingent workforce has led Labor Secretary Robert Reich to comment, that when it comes to steady employment in the nineties, "Nobody is safe."

The truth in today's workplace is that the company will take care of you right up to the time that it can replace you with someone cheaper, or with the technology you, your friends, or your children have developed.

In February 1993, when I got serious about getting *Beat the Odds* out of my head and onto paper, the employment figures showed a record-breaking 385,000 jobs generated—yet 90 percent of them were part-time or temporary low-paying jobs with marginal benefits. The experts said this was an encouraging trend that presaged a surge in full-time employment. I said it was part of a dramatic and irreversible shift toward a massive contingent workforce, reflecting the philosophy of workers as needless liability and overhead. You know who was right. Recently *The Economist* reported that big businesses viewed a long-term employee as an "unwanted liability."

By the turn of the century, upward of 50 percent of the workforce will likely be working on a temporary basis with little or no benefits, and with negligible professional advancement opportunities. I learned everything I needed to know about temp-life from Mitch Fromstein, president of Manpower, a temporary-help company and America's largest employer, when he touchingly observed, "What would they be doing without us? Unemployment lines? Welfare? Suicide?" So, as we reel from the loss of long-term employment security, the backbone of the employment contract and subsequently the backbone of our professional lives and our communities, many Americans will have to adjust to job security the length of a temp contract—a day, a week, a month, or maybe six months if you're lucky. And then what? Unemployment? Welfare? Suicide? *This is the worklife you and I face in the coming years.*

Beat the Odds comes to a workplace shrinking to half its size and to hardworking professionals whose opportunities for success have just halved, and for whom the possibilities of banishment into a *working underclass* have just doubled.

This is not your father's career book. It is here to help you junk the outdated myths of one job, one career, and one loyalty, and replace it with a focus on *your* survival, rather than that of the corporation. I'll show you how we got where we are today, where we are heading tomorrow, and what this means to your ability to achieve the American Dream. I'll show you not only how to weather the maelstrom of change that will be coming in the next twenty years, but also how to prosper.

The reordering of the workplace will see countless professions shrink, and some even disappear. The next twenty years will see this trend expand to include the demise of entire industries. In these pivotal decades it is likely that professions and industries yet unheard of will flourish, only to die and be replaced by others yet undreamed. The questions for each of us confronting the need to earn money over the coming decade is, How will I survive? What will it take to make my career buoyant, and what are my chances of real success?

The shrinking of work opportunities is forcing many downward in search of work, and as they descend, they displace the workers least able to remain competitive. The jobs are disappearing faster than anyone expected, and the competition for the remaining good jobs grows ever stiffer. What's happening? You and I are being made to play a dangerous game of musical chairs, where half of all workers get to join the *new working underclass* on the corporate scrap heap and the rest scramble to avoid the party. We are being made to play this game by companies who were once proud to call themselves American and who now are more conveniently international conglomerates that no longer have need for the services of the people and families who built them or the American culture that nurtured them. "Hey, it's just business, nothing personal"—except that this brazen breaking of the rules that shaped our very culture is throwing millions into a vortex of helplessness.

Psychologist Martin Seligman developed a concept of how we learn to become helpless.[1] He conducted experiments where dogs were taught to jump over a little wall at the sound of a buzzer to escape an electric shock. Then in a different experiment he taught other dogs that a shock would follow the buzzer no matter what they did. Seligman then took a dog who had been through the latter experiment and tried to teach it the "escape" experiment; what he observed was a dog who sat down and whined helplessly. The dog had learned from experience that when the shock was turned on, it had nothing to do with what he did or didn't do, so he learned to be helpless.

Martin Seligman believes that when we experience events that we *feel* we can't control, we end up believing that it doesn't matter what we do. Our motivation to act is decreased. The same philosophy holds true in the new world of work. Many people lose their jobs through no fault of their own, often because of the continued downsizing of employment rosters, regardless of productivity and profits. Far too many of these people walk down the road to learned helplessness at a time when organized, directed action is the only thing that can save them.

Beat the Odds will give you the organized, directed action that can save you, whether you are thinking ahead toward taking a proactive stance in your life, or have already been caught in the downsizings. It is a dramatically different approach to work-life buoyancy with a philosophy of fiscal and professional prudence that increases the odds of your leading a personally fulfilled life, and triples the chances of financial independence in your future.

I am going to help you determine whether to change your employer, your career, your career-management tactics, or all three.

IT'S ALL ABOUT BUOYANCY

The story of *Beat the Odds* is the story of work-life **buoyancy**: making smart decisions and taking organized action to keep that most important of corporations, You, Inc., seaworthy and shipshape.

Achieving buoyancy means that no matter what happens to any particular "core job" in your work life, you have the behavioral competencies to maintain employability and the parallel career activities in place to enhance your solvency. Buoyancy is the state you work toward, first in a particular core career and then for an entire half-century work-life structure.

Once you've read *Beat the Odds*, you will jettison the myopic view of a linear corporate career as the sole pursuit of a professional life, and in its place you will embrace a path that leads to a measure of independence from the no-longer-dependable corporate career track. In this book, I'll show you:

- How to build a viable professional core career in an industry that's healthy.
- How to develop a parallel entrepreneurial career.
- How to turn the career of your wildest dreams into reality.

The book will open with a discussion of how we got where we are today, why we think the way we do about careers, and how we can introduce a revised professional headset for the new world of work.

Beat the Odds (B.T.O.) comes in four parts:

- Part One: The Core Career will show you how to achieve core-career buoyancy.
- Part Two: The Dream Career will show you how to launch and build that successful career of your dreams.
- Part Three: The Entrepreneurial Career will do the same for those entrepreneurial plans that lurk inside you.
- Part Four: Beating the Odds will pull these three separate but parallel careers together into a coherent whole, and make it possible to maintain a vibrant core career while pursuing parallel dream and entrepreneurial careers.

Part One: The Core Career

In this first part of the book I will show you how the current psychology of success in the workplace is outdated and based on bigotry and stereotype, and I'll offer an alternative paradigm.

You will learn how corporate America plans and executes the massive restructurings that are causing millions of Americans to fall through the glass trapdoor into the new working underclass. And you will learn what it takes to make it to the relative safety of the new irreducible corporate core that exists at the heart of every company.

In light of these changes I'll give you a complete appraisal of America's hottest jobs in our healthiest industries. At the end of the core-career section I'll share with you the latest thinking on core-career management in the nineties and beyond, which will include a groundbreaking discussion on the ownership of your intellectual copyright.

Corporate America has made it painfully clear that the fiercely competitive global marketplace means that the unspoken contract of "long-term employment is a given if you give us loyalty and sacrifice" is a thing of the past. These new corporate rules raise the question of the value of your ideas, and their true ownership. In the new world of work this question of intellectual copyright ownership becomes a far more important issue for both employer and employee. Be prepared to render unto Caesar that which is Caesar's, and to keep that which is legally and ethically yours clutched tight to your bosom.

Part Two: The Dream Career

For everyone raised with the professional elitism and isolation ideologies that were once important to the world of work, the second part of the book is going to come as something of a revelation. You will learn something new about how successful dream careerists (sports figures, artists, writers, actors, musicians, and many more) got that way. You will be among the first to share the rewards of our groundbreaking research.

I'll show you how the buoyancy behaviors of buoyant dream careerists closely parallels that of buoyant core careerists: same behaviors but different applications in different contexts. Then I'll take you in for a close-up look at what it really takes to turn four specific dream careers into reality. In each of these four dream-career success blueprints, you will see the ways certain critical buoyancy behaviors come into play in the birthing of any dream career.

By the end of part 2, you will understand how the very behaviors you must develop to survive in your core career can be directly applied to the career of your dreams.

Part Three: The Entrepreneurial Career

Beating the odds of success in the new world of work continues to unfold as you meet the New Entrepreneurs and find they look just like you, with the same hopes, dreams, and fears about stepping out alone. You will see how they overcome these obstacles by reinventing the traditional American entrepreneur.

In this part of the book you will see connectivity as a subplot running throughout the story; the more you connect the dots, the more new vistas and opportunities for buoyancy will open up before you. I will give you a comprehensive review of America's best entrepreneurial opportunities and connect them directly to the core career you work in today.

The connectivity story continues as you study the buoyancy behaviors of successful entrepreneurs. You will see that our research found that the same eight critical buoyancy behaviors of your core career are equally important to your entrepreneurial success; you'll see identical behaviors applied to the different demands of the entrepreneurial life.

Part Four: Beating the Odds

The fourth part of *B.T.O.* pulls each of these separate but parallel paths together into a cohesive plan that is designed to give you a flexible, supportive work-life structure that will keep you buoyant over a typical half-century work life.

As I pull the plots and subplots together, you will see how the *B.T.O.* philosophy for the new world of work can give you a second chance at achieving your dreams for security, freedom, and happiness.

I'll reveal the secret bridges from core-career experiences to successful entrepreneurial and dream careers. You will learn that the lessons of these parallel careers—core, entrepreneurial, and dream—immediately impact each of the other careers. You'll see how an entrepreneurial career can spring from a little innocent core-career moonlighting: The accountant does tax returns on the side, works for her CPA, and eventually opens up her own shop. It can also result from a dream career: She has always read bodice rippers and starts writing her own. It can even spring from a combination of the two: In learning to write, the accountant realizes she can go one better than Lasser and his tax guide, and in the process she writes a perennial how-to best-seller.

A NEW APPROACH

I know that some readers are bound to be skeptical at first. A core career? Obviously. An entrepreneurial career? Why not! But a dream career? Pursued by grown men and women? Grow up!

Conventional wisdom maintains that we pursue careers one at a time, and that there is no time for dreaming. I will prove that this either/or attitude stifles the very creativity necessary for success in any modern career, and that the meaningful pursuit of a dream career is essential to the maintenance of a rewarding life. I am going to show you a new approach to career planning, where everything you do today is an investment in your long-term professional buoyancy and also has an immediate beneficial payback to you *and* your core-career employer.

My philosophy of success is based on three simple principles:

- *Principle 1: You Don't Have to Be a Superstar*

Throughout *Beat The Odds* I'll share eight essential behaviors empirically proven to increase your chances of career buoyancy and work-life success. You need to have all eight of these traits.

While you don't need to be a superstar in all of these areas, you can't just focus on a single behavior either. You will need to achieve a *minimum* level of competency for all eight critical traits.

- *Principle 2: You Are Only As Good As You Think You Are*

Your traits and behaviors will define your work life. A well-developed trait may steer you in one direction or another. But you can't lose sight of the fact that you can do more than that. If you have developed all eight behaviors, there are *many* opportunities for you. Don't box yourself in.

- *Principle 3: You Can Be Whatever You Want to Be*

When you understand and apply the eight behaviors you can learn, change, and grow into anything you want to be. Sure, there may be certain things which are more difficult to change, but I'll show you how to use your strengths as bridges for your weaknesses to cross. Despite the odds, you can start on a path to career buoyancy and work-life success.

What Is Success?

If you achieve success in your career but the rest of your life is a mess, are you successful? I think not. Success is something more than having a career.

So, what is success to you? Is it about how much money you make? Is it about how many people you supervise? Is it the title you hold? Is success defined by your annual performance review? Success is all these things, and none of them. Because even though success may mean doing your job well, in these times it can also be the surest road to failure.

The bottom line is that success is really in your head. It's what you want for your life, what's going to make you feel elated, right, and fulfilled. Success is about choice; it's about getting what you want rather than settling for what's available. It means regaining control over your work life, and it means buoyancy and employability when that huge company you work for deskills or eliminates your job.

Getting to No

After thirty years of positivism, we all know about "getting to yes." It's about reaching agreement, getting things to happen and people to act. In career discussions getting to yes is about negotiating, and it's relevant to things like getting specific job offers and getting raises.

"Getting to No," on the other hand, is about *choice*. It's about you being in control for once in your life: "No, I don't want to do that because I would rather do this instead. I have a choice. I am in control of my destiny, and I will make the choice, not you." Getting to No is a sign that you are flexing your career muscles. Career buoyancy is about Getting to No, because once you are there, you are always in a position of controlling your choices. So if Getting to Yes is about negotiating, then Getting to No is about starting that negotiation from a position of *strength*, by stacking the odds in your favor.

I hope this book catches your spirit and sets your blood tingling, and I believe it will. *Beat the Odds* will show you a unique approach that carves out a clean path to the American Dream in a time of turbulence. So instead of leading a life where *under*achievement is the best you can expect, let *Beat the Odds* empower you with everything you'll need to succeed in an Era of Great Opportunities.

NOTES

1. M. E. P. Seligman. *Helplessness.* San Francisco: W. H. Freeman, 1975.

Part One

THE CORE

CAREER

▼

Chapter 1

Farewell to the Fast Track, and Forget the Race to the Top

Stay at your job, or quit and find a new job: These have been your only options for too long. And, in today's climate, changing jobs just might get you out of the frying pan only to dump you right into the fire. For the first time in industrial history, a recovery from recession has not resulted in a growth of jobs. In the new postindustrial world the maxim is that *more can always be done with less people*, which constantly raises the stress level of all downsizing survivors.

People who have lost their jobs recently are taking longer to find lower-paying jobs[1] with fewer growth opportunities. Used to be it took a couple of months to get a decent mid-level job, and maybe a year at the most exalted levels. Nowadays a year's unemployment is quite common for a third of American workers, and for executives toward the top of the pyramid, the length of the search may drag on for years and perhaps indefinitely.

It gets worse. Eighty percent of two-income families (Americans who are seen as having a superior standard of living) have had no improvement in their standard of living in the last twelve years,[2] and this is despite the fact that many people are working sixty-five-hour weeks. Now, with portable office technology firmly in place, we can expect traditional leisure time to continue to erode and this cycle to tighten in its spin.

Once, you had more than twenty-six hours a week of leisure time; now you barely have fifteen. It is not surprising that Americans are overworked and overstressed. Too many of us live with a constant, low-grade fear of

---

The great challenge is to prepare ourselves to enter these doors [of opportunity].
—Martin Luther King, Jr.

falling into the working underclass. A 1993 survey by North Western Mutual Life, for instance, found that one out of three Americans has a real fear of professional burnout, and an additional one in three had seriously considered quitting a job that year in spite of the job climate. A CNN poll on worker anxiety found that 53 percent of us are worried we will not be able to retire at a reasonable age.

Managers seem to have it the worst. The American Management Association tells us that while middle managers (the 40-to-100K group) make up less than one in ten members of the workforce, they account for *two* in ten of the layoffs. In fact while managerial jobs grew at 5.6 percent through the second half of the eighties, they have shown zero growth since then. What this does to your traditional career future is to remove an additional 2.25 million promotions that you might once reasonably have expected to fuel your professional growth and the subsequent quality of your life.

You live in a world where steady, secure jobs of the old-fashioned kind are going to be harder to come by. And with them will go, to the same degree, your opportunity to reach the American Dream through the traditional routes: the single corporate career, tightly focused to deep knowledge and typecast in a small area of special knowledge. The odds have changed. The days when you could reasonably rely on a job-based career (a job, or a small series of similar jobs, in a single industry) to provide a work life of steady employment and comfortable retirement are gone.

Here's another way to look at the same reality. If current evaluations are proven by time, only 55 percent of *all your colleagues* are likely to remain employed in the American corporate business core in the years to come. So while a successful core career is a great way to reach your American dream, the odds right now are only about fifty-fifty.

LEAVING CORPORATE LOYALTY BEHIND

"Keep the faith, put in the hours and effort, make the sacrifice for the greater good of the team, what's good for the company is good for you" went the litany. Yet the more hardworking and competent professionals following what sounded like good advice hit the skids, the more difficult it was not to face the facts that the implicit laws of the twentieth-century workplace were being thrown out the window.

Business is like riding a bicycle—either you keep moving or you fall down.
—Anonymous

There is a strong perception in the workplace that the leaders of modern corporate America care nothing for the people who build their companies. Successful companies are birthed by good people, who then watch as these same companies literally bite off the hands of those who have nourished them.

When the Goal Was a Sprint to the Top

In the days when we all grew up, and for many years before that, the path to the American Dream was a clearly marked ladder: If you played by the rules, you got to have a middle-class life and the American Dream. The more competitive you wanted to become about it, the more of that American Dream you could get. With education, street smarts, hard work, a little luck, and your best efforts, you could pretty much get where you wanted to go: the place you felt was right for you.

In 1989 I was even planning a book myself based on this premise: Find something you really love, do it well, and just race up that ladder of success. The book was to be called *Race to the Top*. Then the realization dawned that I could not in good conscience write the book. I couldn't because to suggest that someone pursue this course would be ill conceived and quite possibly dangerous.

The Nature of the Beast

In the old story about the rabbit and the scorpion, the scorpion that is crossing a hot, dry desert is stopped by an unexpected stream. By the bank is a nice old rabbit who has spent the entire day working underground; all he wants now is to be left alone to enjoy the sunset. The scorpion asks the rabbit to carry him across the water, but the rabbit declines, saying, "No way. When you get out in the middle, you'll sting me, and I'll drown." The scorpion argues that if he were to sting the rabbit, he, too, would drown; eventually his argument wins over the good-natured rabbit, who sets off to swim across the stream with the scorpion on his back. Halfway across, in the deepest, fastest part of the water, the scorpion stings the rabbit. With his dying breath, the rabbit gasps, "Why did you do it? You will drown, too, now." And the scorpion replies, "I had to. It is in my nature."

Modern American corporations have been built with the sweat and

A man to carry on a successful business must have imagination. He must see things as in a vision, a dream of the whole thing. —Charles M. Schwab

goodwill of American workers. Yet in return for this lifelong loyalty American corporations are now blithely discarding those who have nurtured them, with no real concern for those workers' future. This situation has created an enormous chasm of distrust between workers and employers in the new world of work and will ultimately destroy many corporations, just as corporate behavior is now destroying the lives of many people.

A corporation is an inanimate institution that, through the undying loyalty and sacrifice of many people, takes on a life of its own. In return it provides security and prosperity for those who serve it. Yet like the scorpion, the company is driven by its nature. Although it is given life by the people who work for it, the corporation must obey the primal corporate law: to survive, and to prosper *at all cost.* It adapts as circumstances dictate, so when the opportunity arises to prosper by doing more with less, it does so; to do otherwise would be to harm those who give it life. In these turbulent times if a company doesn't strive for buoyancy, it runs the risk of suddenly floundering.

These changes mean we must now and immediately consign three tenets of industrial-era professionalism to the funeral pyre of outdated ideology.

Tenet 1: If you know your job and do it well, you've got a shot at the top.

Tenet 2: If you play by the rules, you can have a lifetime career and the security that goes with it.

Tenet 3: Loyalty to your employer will have its own rewards.

What Happened?

Let's look back at the eighties for a moment. The 1980–82 recession gave employers an opportunity to tighten their belt, increase productivity, and cut dead wood as they implemented the first wave of workplace-changing technology: the personal computer, the fax, and the modem.

At the same time, management consultants rightly recognized that the best-educated workforce in history was being managed like production-line drones, and that it didn't make sense. The extensive hierarchy built to manage the bulge of baby boomers entering the workforce after the industrial-boom years was no longer needed; with a well-educated and maturing workforce replete with new technology-based productivity tools, it was possible to flatten the hierarchical structure.

Business is a combination of war and sport. —André Maurois

This was well accepted by all. For employers it cuts costs and maintains profitability while staying the same course. And since we each know that incompetence starts one level above us on the professional ladder, everyone was attracted to the idea of putting decision making into the hands of the more competent workers.

But anyone can be in the wrong place at the wrong time—especially if he or she is unprepared. In the last ten years Fortune 500 companies have laid off upward of five million people. These jobs have been outsourced to narrow-band service providers (those who provide single, much-needed services to other companies) or temporary-help companies, exported to cheaper towns and countries, or automated out of existence.

The Future Is Frightfully Clear

It is a trend that will likely continue throughout the decade and beyond as the shakeout caused by the change of eras works itself out. Companies of all shapes and sizes will keep the rein tight on workforce expansion. The trend to downsize is being blamed on fierce competitive markets, on bloated and lazy workforces, but in reality it is happening simply because it is possible.

This elimination of jobs and opportunity must be placed in the context of the next ten years or so, and the workforce changes will have a direct impact on everyone in the world of work today. The Bureau of Labor Statistics tells us in its Fall 1993 *Occupational Outlook* quarterly that fifty million new workers will enter the workforce by 2005. Twenty-eight million of them will be replacing folks leaving the workforce, which is okay. What's worrying me is the other twenty-two million, because for the first time in history, economic expansion is no longer tied to payroll expansion.

The problem is this: The American economy has to generate a hundred thousand jobs a *month* just to suck up these new entrants who are entering and will enter the workforce over the coming years. Unfortunately the track record to date has been increasingly dismal as the new workplace realities take hold. Most of the new jobs are low-level, or temporary jobs with little career future for grown men and women.

There are those, and I'm one of them, who see a contingent workforce ap-

---

I've watched the talented ones who were supposed to change the world make a lifetime commitment to business as usual for the price of a Rolex watch and a new BMW.
—Pearl Cleage

proaching 45 percent in the coming years. That means a big fork in the career road, one that you don't want to take lightly. While a portion of that
contingent workforce will be wealthy, free, and happy, the majority will drop
from corporate security into low-wage, low-opportunity temporary-help jobs
as the door to the irreducible corporate core slams shut behind them.

It is clear that many of today's working professionals have already reached
or passed the high-water mark of their corporate, or core, careers, and not
because they have reached the level of their own incompetence. *It's because the nature of work has changed* that we have an economic climate
where any company wanting to exist tomorrow *must* reinvent itself today.
Out must go the industrial-era structures, management, and principles. In
must come service orientation and "best-in-the-world philosophies" with
their totally new structures and management focus.

The possibilities of technology and new management approaches for
the new corporate structures are opening enormous vistas of opportunity
for corporate behemoths busily reinventing themselves as butterflies. But
vision needs implementation, which requires people with the skills to
leverage the new world of work, and that is where many professionals are
falling short.

We cannot turn back the clock to the industrial era. Like it or not, we
live and must labor in the new world of work. Obviously we must rethink
our perceptions of career strategy and success. We must take responsibility for translating the changes of our era and harnessing them for our purposes, because the truths and rules we grew up with no longer apply.

LOOKING BACK

It has become increasingly clear over the last few years that the old rules
for achieving career success have become faulty to the point of irrelevancy.
Before we can forge a new set of success principles that will help us
weather these winds of change, we first must understand why the old rules
no longer apply.

The rules for success that we live by today are now a hundred years
from when they were set down as goals. The first thing that I and my
team of researchers discovered was that industrial psychology has shaped
our country's view of everything seen as professional and successful be-

*It is not the crook in modern business that we fear but the honest man who does not
know what he is doing. —Owen D. Young*

havior. All current theory and methods in the area of career aptitude and development—which includes much of a billion-dollar career-counseling and career-testing industry—is based on approaches developed in the *teens* and *twenties* of this century. Further, this industrial psychology is the psychology of *employers*, not of employees.

Understanding Why We Think the Way We Do

One of the most influential figures in forming today's beliefs (if we trace the effect of his research on optimum efficiency in the factory of the twenties to modern career thought) was Frederick Taylor, the father of scientific management. Taylor's research concluded that employees were only motivated by extrinsic rewards, such as money. Taylor's work supported the use of productivity incentives, such as piece-rate pay, and efficiency through specialization of job functions.

For factories a certain type of person—obedient, timely, noncreative, and asocial—was found to be the most reliably productive and least disruptive. Taylor brought in time and motion analysts and sought to reduce each job to its most basic and therefore its most efficient components. The decisions and control of the factory workers were placed in the hands of supervisors. A management hierarchy was developed, with knowledge, control, decisions, and power increasing as you went up the ladder.[3] It is on this model of specialization that all of today's success thinking is still based.

As business and government reformed education for the needs of the modern world, the factory floor subsequently became the model for schools as well. Schools existed to support business, and business meant factories. Schools were ideals of rigid, hierarchical control with students being prepared for adult life in the factory—where the most desirable traits were obedience, timeliness, and conformity.

Current Career Thought

One of today's influential career theorists of occupational choice, John Holland, believes that there are six types of people, each with different interests, skills, and personality traits. He also believes that there are six types of jobs. To find job satisfaction, he reasons, match the person's type to the job.

In his view the six types are the following:

The best mental effort in the game of business is concentrated on the major problem of securing the consumer's dollar before the other fellow gets it. —Stuart Chase

   1. *Realistic*—carpenters and people who are practical and conforming
   2. *Investigative*—scientists, who have strong analytical ability
and are critical, independent, and introspective
   3. *Artistic*—creative people, who are characterized as disorderly,
emotional, impractical, and original
   4. *Social*—teachers, psychologists, and social workers, who are
helpful, friendly, insightful, and tactful
   5. *Enterprising*—salespeople and business managers, who are ad-
venturous, domineering, energetic, and sociable
   6. *Conventional*—secretaries and bookkeepers, who are consci-
entious, defensive, efficient, and inflexible

I don't think you can stereotype all mankind by putting them into six
neat little pigeonholes.[4] But something else was off. My researchers and I
came to realize that these theorists were not making claims regarding the
prerequisites for career *success*; their approach to career development was
really just looking at career *satisfaction* in terms of you getting along with
the prevailing culture at the factory or at the office. When you could be
expected to remain at one job for thirty-five years, that made a lot of
sense, but as we know, that isn't the case today.
    Next we found that the approach was not all that objective. In fact
rather than objectivity, we found subjectivity.[5] How were the types developed? Much of the empirical and clinical evidence before us was based on
stereotyping, from a time when stereotyping was the unquestioned nor-
mative behavior of nineteenth-century-raised Caucasian male factory
owners. As a key text on this topic even noted, "We believe that plumbers
are handy, lawyers aggressive, actors self-centered, salesmen persuasive,
accountants precise, scientists unsociable, and the like."[6] It seems incon-
ceivable that the results of this stereotypically based research is still being
used today in many popular testing instruments to guide your career into
the twenty-first century, but that's what's occurring.
    Let's say you are interested in a creative career. You have the talent and
the motivation, you enjoy that type of work, and you are a well-adjusted,
orderly, and stable person. Well, according to the conventional oracles,
you wouldn't like it and therefore wouldn't succeed because you weren't

---

In these times you have to be an optimist to open your eyes in the morning.
—*Carl Sandburg*

disorderly, impractical, emotional, and impulsive enough. Is the inference that you should try to become *more* like the disparaging stereotype in order to succeed at your career? What restrictive and judgmental thinking this is!

It's an Old Theory for Old Jobs

Traditional career theories' adjectives for desirable professional qualities—asocial, obedient, conforming, and adhering to rules—don't describe a happy and fulfilled person as far as I can tell, but more of a workhorse, drone, or android. These words seem to denigrate creativity, at a time when professional creativity is becoming a premium.

Take David, for example, a worker in his late twenties who was employed in a huge printing plant. He had a typical production job. He would get envelopes of materials from different clients, set up the equipment, and go through his printing routine. If asked to describe any accomplishments, he would say about his work, "It's just a job. There's nothing to tell."

However, just last year he told us how frustrated he got with the way the process had been set up. "There had to be a better way," he said. David experimented with different setups until he hit on an idea. Rather than go through the production work client by client, he set up an entirely different system. He would gather all the client materials for the day and categorize them according to size and color. In this way he could then set up the equipment and quickly run through that set of materials. The quality of his work improved since the equipment didn't have to be readjusted constantly.

David went to the trouble of coming up with a better way on his own initiative. No one asked him, or told him, to do this. David showed that he was creative and a nonconformer (some of the stereotypical traits of the artist), while at the same time he showed problem-identification and problem-solving skills that are the hallmark of our most successful professionals, Symbolic Analysts (to be explained later). But according to those who set the rules, since he was a production worker, he was not supposed to think outside the lines.

Yet David is more like the average men and women we know, people

There is no sadder sight than a young pessimist, except an old optimist.
—*Mark Twain*

who really care about the quality of their work as well as the health of their employer.

Today the business press discusses quality circles, involvement teams, and the need for factory workers to run robots and computers; it points out the need for flexible thinking, decision making, and good personal-influence skills, even among people who aren't, according to current industrial psychological models, supposed to need these skills and behaviors. So there is definitely something wrong. But not with David. With our views and theories of what work is, and about what it takes to be successful in different fields.

My team of researchers and I reached the conclusion that the world of work was changing, while the tools to help people deal with that change were not. Business has caught up to the need for reappraisal and reinvention in the new world of work, while the career-planning front is becalmed somewhere in the past.

The Search for What Defines Job Success

It became obvious that because of the changing eras, the tried-and-true tests that help people define their careers—the tools of career guidance that are used by millions of people every year—were no longer completely suitable. And I don't want you to have to settle for advice that might help you get a job today that you can merely tolerate (if you fit some of the prejudicial profiles). In the new world of work, the challenge is to get work today where you can develop the behaviors that will make you employable *tomorrow*.

So our next task in looking backward before leaping forward was to look at job *performance*. Again we looked and we opened up a can of worms. For career success, the authorities argued,

- It's How Smart You Are, Stupid
- No, It's Not
- It Doesn't Matter So Long as You've Got Personality

IT'S HOW SMART YOU ARE, STUPID

One big review of success in entry-level jobs found the best indicator of success was intelligence.[7] Other studies supported this finding for other occupational groups and levels.

Had I been present at the creation of the world, I would have proposed some improvements. —Alfonso X

NO, IT'S NOT

Intelligence doesn't make a bit of difference, others said, if by intelligence we are referring to an evaluation based on traditional intelligence tests. Traditional, or academic, intelligence typically hands us the problem and then forces us to pick the single best answer; this type of intelligence is usually measured by IQ tests, SATs, GMATs, and other kinds of academic-ability tests. While there is a need for academic intelligence—it provides us with valuable analytical training—the successful core careerists of tomorrow, the Symbolic Analysts, also need another kind of intelligence, as does every career-buoyant person, no matter what career he or she is pursuing. This other kind of intelligence that is part of your career buoyancy is *practical* intelligence.[8] Unlike the traditional, academic intelligence we all know about, practical intelligence is the stuff we need in our careers, and in our daily lives.

Practical intelligence lets us identify problems to be solved, to come up with unique solutions, and to implement these solutions. Practical intelligence is a lot harder to measure, and there really aren't good tests for it yet. Practical intelligence identifies problems and ambiguous situations that we encounter in our daily lives. Practical intelligence involves the following abilities:

- To recognize the existence of a problem
- To acquire information
- To solve complex problems with multiple solutions

IT DOESN'T MATTER SO LONG AS YOU'VE GOT PERSONALITY

Of course, there's more to succeeding at your job than academic smarts and problem solving. What about personality? This whole area was a real mess until recently. There were dozens of different traits discussed in the research literature, but no one could prove personality traits or specific behaviors predicted job success.

Then personality theorists began discussing the "Big Five" personality traits. The Big Five took all personality theory and reduced it to five basic clusters:

- Emotional stability
- People orientation

Creation is a drug I can't do without. —Cecil B. DeMille

- Openness to experience
- Being sociable, warm, and friendly
- Conscientiousness: hardworking, plays by the rules[9]

Nothing was really conclusive, though. One major review said that emotional stability and agreeableness weren't all that important to job success; another said these factors were.[10] There was still a lot missing from the picture.

WHAT WE FOUND WRONG WITH EXISTING THEORIES OF WORK

Perhaps this sums up was what was wrong. We found that current theories of career aptitude, satisfaction, and success are

- *Based on averages:* The description of types and of jobs is based on averages—in other words, a theory of scraping by. Nowadays there is no longer that luxury. You deserve—and require—a blueprint based on *success*, not mediocrity.
- *Based on stereotype:* These are stereotypical ideas of what kinds of people are attracted to and suitable for different jobs. We don't agree with stereotyping.
- *For the employer:* According to these theories, the *person* needs to fit the job. Like almost all industrial psychology, theories of work were geared to an *employer's* vision—because employers, with their long-term job security, held the key to that American Dream. But, as we've shown, long-term job security is no longer a viable option. So it's time to focus on the needs of you, the worker.
- *Describing outdated job descriptions:* Thus a job description for an assembly-line operator no longer necessarily applies to work in which people on the line are asked to work in cooperative groups, to make decisions, and to suggest innovations. Employers are making business decisions based on totally different criteria, and this is why so many respected career-guidance instruments are either out of date or don't help you achieve buoyancy.
- *Usually looking at just one little problem:* Very few researchers look at the big picture in psychology anymore. Most studies ask one or

---

Risks, big and small, are the way those of us not born to wealth can pursue it and achieve success. —Clarence Page

two very specific questions. While in a stable society it's true that thinkers must get involved with the minutiae, in the work world it has all changed in the blink of an eye, and we now must focus on the landscape.

How did everything get so out of sync? Well, science usually isn't about new discoveries or explaining novelty. In fact scientists hate novelty.

So, scientists build better mousetraps. They focus on being more precise and accurate in their measurements. For career theory, researchers build better career-interest tests, and they come up with better ways to classify personality. Everyone pats themselves on the back for a job well done, and they ignore the increasing frequency of anomalies. But the frightening realities of modern work life make it most unwise to unquestioningly add layers of new advice onto old career-philosophy structures.

WHAT WE NEED TODAY

Right now many of you are in the worst professional plight of your lives. Everyone working today under the age of fifty must anticipate fierce competition for their jobs from colleagues of their own generation, and from younger, cheaper, possibly better-educated newcomers to the workplace. And the workers who have worked the hardest, sacrificed the most friendships, and burned the most midnight oil, are getting hit the hardest; they have the most difficulty finding new opportunities at similar levels of pay and responsibility because their jobs are being redefined and eliminated. So if you continue to follow advice based on your father's vision of career management—that the path to success comes in settling down fairly early on a single career path—you will be applying advice out of its era. This traditional theory has worked well for many years, but for the new era it is *limited thinking*. What we need is a new approach to careers and work-life buoyancy that literally invests in the *future*. Today's hardworking professionals need a new system of career thought and application that

- Puts your professional survival first
- Says it is *you* who makes the work, not the work that makes you
- Says you are capable of adapting to, and changing, your circumstances

---

It is wise to learn; it is God-like to create. —John Saxe

The more you invest in the approaches I discuss throughout *Beat the Odds*, the more likely you are to move into a lifelong upswing. This B.T.O. philosophy will give you, *at a minimum*:

- Three times the odds of achieving core-career buoyancy
- Three times the odds of attaining financial autonomy
- Three times the odds of attaining your American dream
- Three times the odds of not having to work with jerks
- Three times the odds of having a happy and fulfilling life

Species have always had to adapt to survive, and humankind is the species known for adapting to circumstances best. All you need is a new road map and the rules of the road.

The first rule is that it's now a marathon, a grueling test of willpower and guts with the greatest of prizes: making it in one piece with a grit-eating grin on your face. In a fifty-year work life *strategy*, not speed, will win the day. A long, hard sprint to the top is not what it's about anymore.

NOTES

1. Srully Blotnik's study found 36 percent of job changes were made for less money, and his study was *before* the recession. Current word of mouth has that figure at around 60 percent.

2. Joint Economic Committee of Congress, 1992.

3. Scientific management may not be responsible for this approach toward work; it is really more of a reflection of our society at the turn of the century. We don't hate this guy Taylor, we just use him to illustrate the point.

4. The theory does note that people are a bit more complicated than this, so they are often given two or three "code" types. Jobs are also thought to contain multiple types.

5. Not *all* testing is out of date. We especially like David Campbell's career-interest test, which is really quite helpful in career planning. By the way, he intentionally focused on *positive* behaviors you need for different occupational groups he included in his test! He also based his test on people who were actually working in each occupation and also liked their job. Good work Dave!

6. John Holland, *Making Vocational Choices: A Theory of Vocational Choices and Work Environments*. (Englewood Cliffs, NJ: Prentice-Hall, 1985).

7. E. E. Ghiselli (1973). "The Validity of Aptitude Tests in Personnel Selection." *Personnel Psychology* 26:461–477.

All business proceeds on beliefs, or judgments of probabilities, and not on certainties.
—Charles Eliot

8. U. Neisser, "General, Academic, and Artificial Intelligence." in Lo Resnick (ed.), *The Nature of Intelligence.* (Hillsdale, NJ: Erlbaum, 1976).

9. J. M. Digman, (1990). "Personality Structure: Emergence of the Five-Factor Model." *Annual Review of Psychology* 41:417–440 (1990).

10. No matter how you sliced the data, the relationships weren't terribly impressive. At best some of these traits, such as extraversion, could predict, or explain, only about 10 percent of success. See, for instance: M. B. Barrick and M. K. Mount (1993). "Autonomy as a Moderator of the Relationship Between the Big Five Personality Dimensions and Job Performance." *Journal of Applied Psychology* 78:111–118.

The guy who takes a chance, who walks the line between the unknown, who is unafraid of failure, will succeed. —Gordon Parks

Chapter 2

A Blueprint for the Mechanics of Success in the New World of Work

Gary Null, the nutrition guru, talks of a project he pursued with a university professor and some computer processing power. First they identified a handful of grains and vegetables that provided a perfectly balanced diet, and then they matched them to plants growing in all the different geographic biomes around the world. They loaded their findings into a database and then were able to generate five thousand nutritiously balanced recipes, each with a variant that allowed the dish to be cooked with indigenously grown crops, in any biome, anywhere in the world.

What they had done was to suggest a rational solution to the end of malnutrition in the world. They had discovered a sequence of perfectly balanced, naturally occurring food sources which they then combined into recipes to help every man, woman, and child live a better life.

Gary Null and his colleagues showed how a handful of simple ingredients could be matched to the nutritional needs of anyone, anywhere. In a more humble way *Beat the Odds* works along the same lines.

Take a few simple ingredients:

- Your needs for security, freedom, and happiness
- Eight sensible behaviors
- Core-, dream-, and entrepreneurial-career paths

and, by mixing and matching them, weave a work-life-buoyancy web that supports all your personally defined needs.

Only the gamefish swim upstream. —John Trotwood Moore

Although this new blueprint for success focuses on what is best for *you*, it is *just as good for your employers*. And it is a blueprint that is relevant to working people at a time when our world of work doesn't seem to make sense. In response to this situation, the new mechanics of success must:

- Focus on *you*. If long-term employment is no longer part of the employer-employee contract, the contract can no longer focus solely on what employers want of employees. Rather, the issues of loyalty and the nurturing implicit in loyalty must, I believe, be transferred to a more worthy recipient: you. The blueprint must work to satisfy your needs for security, freedom, and happiness, and those needs that are unique to you.
- Be based on *success*, not averages or hearsay. I want to show you how to succeed in your pursuit of the American Dream, not with just my opinions, but with something rock solid to lean on: the consensus of those who have achieved their goals, those who have made it to the American Dream.
- Be based on *new* job types. The blueprint has to be compatible with the rapidly changing needs of the new world of work. The professional skill sets and behaviors of all jobs have changed, and the entry-level requirements for the jobs with a future have changed dramatically.

I believe in people. More specifically I believe in you. And I believe you can become almost anything you want to be, so long as you learn the new rules and play by them.

THE FOCUS ON YOU: THE ELEMENTAL NEEDS WE ALL SHARE

The psychology of work from the beginning of this century has been more or less the psychology of factory ownership. Our new psychology of work, our blueprint for success, places *you* at the center of the paradigm. You can exercise a measure of control over your living environment, you need no longer fear inevitable job loss, and you can work toward your personal vision of the American Dream.

We All Have Needs

We all have needs and when we give those needs a practical means of fulfillment we feel happy, we feel content with our lives for a while. Coming

The merit of originality is not novelty; it is sincerity. —Thomas Carlyle

to terms with your own unique needs in life and working toward them will be extremely important to your career buoyancy in the coming years.

However, one of the first things you notice about the characteristics of needs is that *they are never completely met.* While you may satisfy one for a time, the need will always creep back up on you. Think about hunger. If you feel hungry, you eat and satisfy the need. Yet within a few hours the gnawing in your stomach will remind you quite emphatically of that very need you just satisfied. Only this time the need is a bit different; perhaps now the urge is for steak instead of tofu and peas.

You are a unique and complex human being with a continually changing web of needs. It's your needs that translate into the initiatives that get things done. Needs set a direction for your development.[1] They get you psyched for any goal-oriented activity, although they don't actually direct you in any way.

Some needs you hold in common with all people, others are part of your personal matrix. Although your personal web of needs is unique to you, there are a handful of needs that most people share:

  • Physical safety and security. You have a need for a roof over your head, food on your table, and affordable health care.
  • A measure of independence, a feeling of some freedom in your life that comes with a level of financial autonomy.
  • A sense of meaning in your life, the feeling that your life is being lived with fulfillment and joy.

In fact, the people whom I regard as buoyant in their work lives are the people who are able consistently to satisfy these needs over the long haul. They are the people who

  • Hold a roof of their choosing over their heads and have the food of their choice on the table
  • Have work that is meaningful and secure
  • Have education and health care for themselves and their loved ones
  • Have passions, hobbies, and interests outside of work, and the freedom to pursue them

---

Do not expect the world to look bright if you habitually wear gray-brown glasses.
—Charles Eliot

- Have lasting friendships and affiliations with others who share their values

In the new world of work I will show you that there can, and should, be harmony between your work and the rest of your life. Harvard University has had an alumni study going on for some fifty years now that examines successful careers, and it shows that the clear winners are not the workaholics, or even the ones with the best grades.[2] Instead the winners consistently have been the men and women who made a life for themselves outside of their core-career work.[3]

Our research echoes this. When we find people who are secure, independent, and happy, we find people who live a balanced life, where they have consciously striven for a modicum of control. When you feel empty and uninspired, when things seem out of whack, the first place to look is to your needs. Maybe your elemental needs for security, freedom, and happiness are not being fulfilled.

THE HEART OF BUOYANCY: THE CRITICAL BEHAVIORS WE NEED FOR SUCCESS

Why do some people just seem more resilient than others when they get tough career breaks? Why does someone like Jill, a corporate controller, land a comparable position within ninety days of being laid off? What is it that allows Paul to run an international division for twenty years, get the sack, take on another presidency from which he soon fires himself, only to land a third hot-seat job with global responsibility within a three-year period?

Paul and Jill are both serious players. They are examples of the kinds of people whose career buoyancy has fascinated me for years, and whom we have been examining in our clinical research. As we studied what it really takes to succeed in the new world of work, our research focused in on the behaviors and opinions of such people. We also examined successful entrepreneurs and dream careerists, separately and then in comparison with the other groups. We asked everyone over a hundred questions to find out what essentially boils down to, "What makes some people in your line of work more buoyant than others? What helps them beat the odds while others just get beaten?"

A friendship founded on business is better than a business founded on friendship.
—John D. Rockefeller

And what we discovered was that successful, buoyant people in all walks of life share a surprising number of hidden affinities with each other. Our research revealed that many of the stereotypes we have been raised with about people and their occupations are clearly as wrong as the stereotypes about gender, race, and nationality.

Throwing Old Stereotypes Out the Window

We all know that artists are flighty and unstable, right? We also know that entrepreneurs are mercurial and that your corporate VP is a terrific worldly intellectual titan. So ingrained are the stereotypes that what was Victorian robber-baron bigotry has become today's incontrovertible facts: we know these things because we've been told them for the past seventy years. But what if we ask today's creative elite to describe the characteristics of successful dream careerists? Would they tell us, "You gotta be maladjusted"? And what if contemporary entrepreneurs were to tell us about other entrepreneurs; would they say, "To succeed as an en-trepreneur, you can't listen to anyone but yourself"? Would aggressive-ness be a key trait for success if we asked buoyant core careerists about others like them?

One of the first experiments we conducted to learn more about career buoyancy was to ask our subjects (already successful people in the three parallel career paths) to evaluate other successful people personally known to them in the same profession.

Dream careerists of many different types suggested that among other traits, their successful colleagues are

- Creative
- Motivated
- Political
- Persevering
- Able to communicate their vision to others

At the same time, buoyant core careerists told us that what they needed to succeed included

- Working well in teams
- The ability to communicate to team members and management

Keep your face to the sunshine and you cannot see the shadow. —Helen Keller

- Motivation
- The ability to identify and solve problems creatively
- Determination

Entrepreneurs listed a series of traits that included

- The ability to keep going
- Creativity
- Motivation
- Communication skills

When we compared them, these answers showed some exciting connections between the behaviors of successful core careerists, entrepreneurs, and their dream-career counterparts.

Dream	Core	Entrepreneur
Creative	Creative	Creative
Motivated	Motivated	Motivated
Political	Able to work well in teams	
Persevering	Persevering	Persevering
Communicative	Communicative	Communicative

Successful core careerists, entrepreneurs, and dream careerists had more in common than anyone had ever thought, and their responses showed that many of the success behaviors of the last seventy years are obviously obsolete. Just as important, though, was that not a single person gave us anything even slightly resembling a negative trait. Not one dream careerist said you needed to be emotionally unstable; no core careerist said aggressiveness was required for success; and not a single entrepreneur told us that you needed to be an egomaniac. Maybe the nineties are a kinder, gentler place after all.

One that deserves to excel should endeavor in those things that are in themselves most excellent. —Epictetus

The Eight Critical Traits of Career Buoyancy

Our research then reviewed all major empirical studies of career success. Next we interviewed hundreds of successful people—corporate professionals, dream careerists, and entrepreneurs—to ask them what leads to success in their field. People told us, in their own words, what constituted buoyancy in their own field. Then they rated the importance of dozens of behaviors and traits for career buoyancy. The following research reflects one of the largest and most comprehensive looks at career success. More importantly, it is also the *only* work we know of that addresses work-life buoyancy.[4] (Of course, this isn't too surprising since work-life buoyancy is a new concept.)

What we discovered from our research were eight connected behaviors, each interacting with the others to create a whole greater than the sum of its parts. These are the behaviors that will help you make it to the new irreducible core, start and run a successful entrepreneurial endeavor, and write that best-selling novel (or whatever is the career of your dreams). In other words, these traits will help you achieve career success on *every one of your career paths.*

The critical eight behaviors are

1. Goal Orientation—working hard to achieve your goals
2. Positive Expectancy—believing in your ability to overcome, and ultimately to succeed
3. Inner Openness—emotional flexibility
4. Personal Influence—communication with a purpose
5. Organized Action—coordinated action efficiently focused on a specific outcome
6. Informed Risk—flexible planning to decrease risk in a constantly changing environment
7. Flexible Thinking—creative adaptability in different contexts
8. Smart Decisions—effective decision making

Let's examine how each of these behaviors earns its place in a work-life buoyancy plan.

1. GOAL ORIENTATION
   Our respondents described it as

One of the strongest characteristics of genius is the power of lighting its own fire.
—*John Watson Foster*

Motivation	Drive	Desire	Achievement	Ambition	Aspirations
	Momentum	Energy	Determination	Realizing Deadlines	
	Being Resolute	Having a Sense of Purpose		Being Firm	
		Having Focus	Being Committed		

What it is:

It's a Destination. The best way to define Goal Orientation is *drive*. Drive means that you are motivated to achieve your goals. To be career buoyant, you first need to know where you want to go—what your goals are—and then you need the motivation to get there. Goal Orientation allows you to see this particular year, and this particular job, in the context of your more-than-fifty-year work life and the end state you envision for yourself. Perhaps more importantly, it charges you up to do what you must do to become buoyant. Goal Orientation gives you the motivation to take action and to make things happen.

If you don't have a goal of where you are going in your work life, how are you ever going to get there? *You're not.* As you read *Beat the Odds*, take the time to let your mind wander and dream of the ways you would like your life to unfold. If you work at it hard enough, then these scattered dreams will gradually combine into a vision of your personal American dream. When you develop a realistic and tangible goal, Goal Orientation will find the tools to give it practical means of expression. Creating goals for your work life means that you will be able to balance priorities and tasks toward achieving those goals, and your dreams. Goal Orientation is your emotional polestar.

It's Getting There. Goal in hand, you have to get up off your buns and get going. You need motivation to make things happen in your life. Motivation is the result of a balance between your skills and your situation. When you can do your job with your eyes closed, your motivation plummets, along with your interest and probably your effectiveness. On the flip side, when you get in over your head, your Goal Orientation slips, and you find yourself doing more talking than actually taking action steps toward your goal.[5]

It appears that in motivation, as in the other eight traits, *balance* in the behavior can be as important as the behavior itself. Too little or too much and you're stymied.

The mode by which the inevitable comes to pass is effort. —Oliver Wendell Holmes

2. POSITIVE EXPECTANCY

Our respondents described it as

> Thinking Positively   Having a Success Orientation   Positive Attitude
> Trusting in the Outcome   Having Faith in a Goal   Belief in Self
> Looking for the Plus Side   Being Capable of Believing   Having a Favorable View
> Making the Best of Assuredness   Confidence   Certainty   Feeling Sure
> Constructiveness   Hopefulness   Anticipate and Expect Success
> Conviction   Can Do/Will Do Orientation

What it is:

It's a Cup Half Full. Positive Expectancy is all about belief in yourself and your potential. The person who succeeds in his or her endeavor is the person who puts the event in its context and applies a positive attitude to the history. I'm not talking here about a smile and a shrug, I'm talking about analyzing what it was that brought you so far in the endeavor (and then doing even more of it in the future) and what it was that stopped you from going farther (and then adapting your approach for the next shot).

It's Learning to Believe in You. Having a positive attitude means that when you fail in some way you are simply experiencing a setback; you are not a failure. *You cannot succeed in any chosen field if you feel yourself unworthy.* Neither can you ever feel happy or fulfilled if your internal dialogues focus solely on the mistakes you have made. Positive expectancy is an attitude that can grow into a behavior. It is easy to feel positive when things are going well, but it takes more effort when the tide of events seems turned against you. A wise old gentleman I used to know said, "All you have to do in life is to look for the pluses in everything that's around you, and when you see a minus, find a way to make it a plus." That's Positive Expectancy in action.

3. INNER OPENNESS

Our respondents described it as

> Responding to Both Positive and Negative Feedback
> Openness to Experience   Tolerance   Open-mindedness   Flexibility
> Having Independent Ideas   The Ability to Learn from Experience   Self-awareness
> Adaptability   Listening Skills   The Ability to Question Beliefs

---

There are glimpses of heaven to us in every act, or thought, or word, that raises us above ourselves. —Arthur P. Stanley

What it is:

It's Knowing Yourself. You are self-aware, knowing your strengths and weaknesses. You take credit for your successes and your strengths, and you recognize your weaknesses, accepting their existence and using that awareness as an opportunity to help you change. Inner Openness means that you know yourself and understand how your style of interaction affects others.

Inner Openness allows people to be honest with themselves. It allows the tone-deaf rock-and-roll singer to say, "Hey, I'll never make it as the front man 'cause I can't hold a tune, but I love to write music, and I love the industry, so I'll focus my core-career search on music publishing and related businesses."

Inner Openness allows you to make the necessary compromises that will ultimately result in career buoyancy. That would-be singer's face may never make it to MTV, but over the years he can make a place in the industry in another capacity and make royalties from his song-writing.

It's Tolerance. Inner Openness helps you stop having knee-jerk reactions to people and events based on a lifetime of social conditioning. Inner Openness allows you to walk a mile in another's shoes and see a familiar situation from a new and different perspective. Inner Openness allows you to build bridges of understanding between you and others—and new perspectives always bolster your flexible-thinking skills.

It's Emotional Agility. When you are open to the world, to events, to those who join you on your work-life journey, you open yourself to new experiences. You gain greater tolerance, and as a result become more emotionally agile. You can handle stressful situations. Complexity doesn't scare you off. You don't need to make everything into a yes-no situation. You can tolerate the ambiguities of life. Inner Openness helps you become more tolerant, tolerance increases your mental flexibility, and together they dramatically improve your connectivity skills and idea-generation abilities.

4. PERSONAL INFLUENCE

Our respondents described it as

Having Clout	*Making an Impact*	*Making Contact*	*Being Enlightening*
Communication Skills	*Having Leverage*	*Charisma*	*Having Pull*
Likability	*Having Sway*	*Ability to Direct Others*	*Being Responsive*

High aims form high characters, and great objects bring out great minds.
—Tryon Edwards

What it is:

It's Persuasion. Personal Influence is communicating with people to influence the way they think about something or the way they act. But I'm not talking about strong-arm tactics, nor about being a negotiator. Personal Influence is about communicating your ideas and your message so that someone else understands it. There is a goal to this communication: to get the other person to understand your point of view. They still might not buy from you, but they will understand your point of view. You have persuaded them to *listen* and to *understand.*

It's Flexible Communication. Some people manage the impressions and the result they achieve with others; they are sensitive to the signals other people give and can figure out how to respond for maximum effect. They understand who they are communicating with, and adjust their style to the needs of the communication.

If you can't adapt your style or your message, it doesn't mean you can't communicate. It just means that you can only communicate with a specific audience, or about specific topics. But if you lack flexibility, you will be less adaptable, and you will lose a bit of career buoyancy as a result.

5. ORGANIZED ACTION

Our respondents described it as

Taking Initiative	*Setting Priorities*	*Developing Practical Methods*
Having a Sense of Order and Balance	*Being Systematic*	*Efficiency*
Focused Effort *Accomplishment*	*Reliability* *Getting Things Done*	*Planning*
Evaluating *Taking Action*	*Having a Game Plan*	*Making It Happen*

What it is:

It's Getting Things Done. Organized Action is easily recognized: You see people accomplishing their objectives. Getting things done is the hallmark of Organized Action.

It's Getting Things Done Efficiently. Put a bunch of chimps in a room with several typewriters, close the door, and it is *possible* that they'll churn out

Wherever I have knocked, a door has opened. Wherever I have wandered, a path has appeared. I have been helped, supported, encouraged, and nurtured by people of all races, creeds, colors, and dreams. —Alice Walker

the Encyclopedia Britannica in a few weeks. Not a good chance of this actually happening, I'll confess, but isn't there at least *some* chance?

Well, there are many ways to get things done, but the buoyant careerists we researched get things done *efficiently*. They don't waste too much time, they don't waste too much energy. Organized Action is *focused* action.

It's Knowing What Works and What Doesn't. Perhaps career-buoyant people can be efficient because they have an intimate knowledge of what works and what doesn't. They have an understanding of the unwritten rules of the game and are able to quickly evaluate alternate ways of accomplishing a task. What they don't know—and it is often a great deal—they can find out. They know how to get the information they don't have, but require, to get the job done.

Organized Action allows you to get things done in the least time possible and with the fewest resources. With Organized Action you break everything down into bite-size pieces that can be completed today. You get things done efficiently, and every action is taken in the interest of the coherent long-term goals.

6. INFORMED RISK
Our respondents described it as

Considering the Risks	Calculating the Risks	Taking Acceptable Risks
Taking Planned Risks	Trusting One's Gut Feeling	Speculating
Balancing Weighing Alternatives	Thinking Ahead	Being Open-minded
Having a Feedback Loop	Having Flexible Plans	

What it is:

It's Weighing the Odds and Then Acting. Informed Risk is facing a fork in the road and estimating from all available knowledge down which road the treasure lies and down which road the dragons lurk. Informed Risk requires that you don't immediately dismiss a course of action just because it is different, has never been done before, or seems that it could fail. Informed Risk means you will consider the pros and cons. If the decision appears way too risky, then you reject it.

Informed Risk is another way of saying you understand the odds. You

---

To do is to be —Rousseau. To be is to do —Sartre. DooBeDooBeDooBeDoo —Sinatra.
—Anonymous

know that in a time when the sum of our knowledge is doubling every ten years, all the facts are never going to be in on any aspect of your work life. So, as risks must be taken in the modern work world, you do your best to inform them with the best practical intelligence you can; you become a student of your world of work.

It's Taking a Chance. The hallmark of the industrial-era employee was conformity. Unfortunately the organization man is still with us today, and you need to fight the urge to conform in order to develop your career buoyancy. I'm not advocating change for its own sake. But there are times when the tried-and-true methods don't work. There are times when "the way things are done around here" isn't the best way to achieve your goals. There are times when you need to take an Informed Risk, which starts by calculating the odds of success of different alternatives and then evaluate new and different possible actions. Informed Risk is having the confidence to suggest a new course of action, to be different when times call for a new approach.

It's Staying on Your Toes—and Adapting. So what happens if your idea turns out not to be terrific? What if it looks like it's going to really mess things up? Do you stick to it, do you stay with tradition and go down in flames with your pride intact? No! That's another hallmark of the industrial-era mind-set. This is the time when your flexibility is brought to bear on the situation. Staying open-minded and open to feedback, you realize that the course of action is less than optimal, so you put a stop to it. You back up and check out what went wrong. So, when the plan doesn't work, or if the situation changes, you just implement Plan B. Plan B was all ready to go; you worked out the details in advance, because you knew that things might not go as you originally planned.

You have to constantly monitor the environment when you take an Informed Risk so that you have a constant flow of new information. Then, when things aren't working out just right, you can change the plan. You increase the odds of success by staying open and flexible.

7. FLEXIBLE THINKING
   Our respondents described it as

The closest to perfection a person ever comes is when he or she fills out a job-application form. —Stanley J. Randall

Creativity	New Ideas	Problem Solving	Originality	New Approaches
Connectivity	Analysis	Reason	Consideration	Reflection
Learning	Thoughtfulness	Openmindedness	Receptivity	
Curiosity	Inquisitiveness	Speculation	Inquiry	

What it is:

It's Having Ideas. Flexible Thinking is creative adaptability in different contexts. You typically hear it described as problem-identification and problem-solving skills, and as analytical and symbolic-analytical skills. Flexible Thinking allows you to take an existing knowledge base and apply it, in the abstract, to another context.

For example, it was the Flexible Thinking skills of one soft-drink marketing executive that landed him the top job at one of the world's leading computer companies. For John Sculley, the ex-Pepsi executive who took over Apple Computer, his lack of basic computer literacy wasn't important when ranked alongside his marketing background in the soft-drink industry and his Flexible Thinking skills that allowed him to adapt that knowledge to a new world. Flexible Thinking approaches allowed him to build bridges of connectivity between the different fields and their ideas, challenges, and needs.

When you connect the dots between seemingly disparate fields of knowledge, that's your Flexible Thinking at work.

It's Idea Fluency. Idea fluency has to do with novel ideas, and the quantity of novel ideas you can generate. You cannot hope to succeed on a single idea; there has to be a flow. Even when you think of one-shot millionaires, a closer look finds that they had many other novel ideas before their one great idea struck a chord and helped them achieve financial success. Idea fluency is having new ideas, and lots of them.

It's Being Curious. You have to be interested in learning, in solving problems, and in exploring the world. Things change so rapidly that you are going to be forced into a lifetime of learning just to stay even. So why not focus it on some activities you would find rewarding? The desire to know and to learn pushes you to adapt to a changing world. Curiosity and a desire to enhance your skills and knowledge base keep you buoyant.

Ability is of little account without opportunity. —Napoleon Bonaparte

It's Intelligence Applied to the Real World. Academic intelligence isn't enough to ensure career buoyancy. Today career buoyancy and career success require *both* academic and practical intelligence[6] for application to real-world problems. This kind of intelligence usually involves the ability to

- Recognize the existence of a problem
- Acquire information
- Solve complex problems with multiple solutions

Combine this rich brew of observation with a purpose—ideas and idea fluency, curiosity, and practical intelligence applied to the real world—and you have the component parts of Flexible Thinking.

8. SMART DECISIONS

Our respondents described it as

Making Up Your Mind	*Reasoned Decisions*	*Practical Know-how*
Common Sense	*Sound Judgment*	*Decisiveness*
Possessing Implicit Knowledge	*Practicality*	*Sensibleness* *Being Savvy*

What it is:

It's Making Up Your Mind. It has been said that the one thing that makes Americans great is an ability to make decisions. My father sees disappointments as setbacks and says that the only people who don't make mistakes are the ones who never make up their minds to do anything.

Career-buoyant people make decisions, and because they are self-aware and learn from their experiences, they estimate the chance of success as being higher than the last time they had to make a decision. And believing that there is a good chance of succeeding, they are more motivated and focused on doing a good job; and because they are connected in this way, they dramatically enhance their chances of successful outcomes.[7]

It's Using Your Mind. You've been asked to develop a plan to increase the market share of your company's key product. So you immediately decide to sell the product in a market that you know very little about. The effort ends up costing the company millions, and you, your core career. Dumb decision. It was a dumb decision because you had no practical know-how or experience in that area. How can you expect to learn anything, how

---

It is only possible to live happily ever after on a day-to-day basis. —*Margaret Bonnanno*

can you expect the odds to be in your favor? Before you can be decisive, you *have* to know the territory. Smart Decisions combine your business savvy with your ability to be decisive. Therefore every decision you make is based on an understanding of your business. Smart Decisions are effective decisions.

The Career-Buoyancy Circle

Here they are again, the eight critical behaviors of success in the new world of work. Perhaps more exciting about these behaviors is that they are *learnable*. In other words, you might not have good Personal Influence skills today, but with a little effort, you can develop Personal Influence skills for tomorrow. The same holds true for each of these behaviors. And because they interact with each other, when you work on one, you work on and improve them *all*.

Goal Orientation	Positive Expectancy	Smart Decisions
Personal Influence	Organized Action	Informed Risk
Flexible Thinking	Inner Openness	

Interacting with each other in a circle of buoyancy, these learnable behaviors create a whole that is greater than the sum of its parts.

Now remember, this isn't just *my* idea of what might work to help you survive in the new workplace. These are the behaviors identified as critical to your success by *already buoyant core careerists, entrepreneurs, and dream careerists.*

DON'T OVERLOOK THE CONNECTIVITY

The ballast that accrues to your career(s) from the circle of buoyancy behaviors comes from their individual benefits and from the *interaction* between the behaviors. For example, our research subjects were unanimous in saying that you aren't going to get anywhere in life without Goal Orientation. But goals in and of themselves don't take you anywhere; reaching your goals will require an Organized Action plan that breaks your goal down into doable steps. What exactly those steps are will require some Smart Decisions about the myriad paths you could take to

---

It is more than probable that the average man could, with no injury to his health, increase his efficiency fifty percent. —Walter Scott

that goal, and it will be your Personal Influence skills that are responsible for implementing the steps of your plan.

It is unlikely it'll be all plain sailing to your goals, so you will need to believe in yourself and your ultimate success (Positive Expectancy). Nevertheless, blind faith will never be enough; to keep yourself on track, you need Inner Openness to remain objective about the causes of setbacks.

There will be times when that Inner Openness tells you that there are oceans between you and your goal on your present course. You will need to pause and take stock of the possibilities (Flexible Thinking) and perhaps consider some options to decrease risk (Informed Risk) where you don't have all the answers.

Each of the eight critical buoyancy behaviors supports the others. Sometimes a work-life challenge will call—say you get laid off. You will need to bring your Flexible Thinking skills to the fore, but they will not be operating in a vacuum; each of the other critical buoyancy behaviors will be *harmoniously coordinating with and supporting the lead behavior.* In the example I've just cited:

> Flexible Thinking *lets you find new solutions to your job-hunt challenge.*

> Inner Openness *lets you know what you have to offer and what you need to work on.*

> Goal Orientation *gives you a sense of direction: three interviews a week.*

> Organized Action *helps you break the task down into doable steps: build a resumé and find three hundred people to contact.*

> Personal Influence *is how you implement that plan: calling, visiting, writing to people.*

> Informed Risk *makes you construct a plan that doesn't put all your eggs in one basket: you don't rely on just the want ads or just networking.*

> Positive Expectancy, *that belief in yourself, keeps you going in the dark before the dawn.*

Loyal and efficient work in a great cause, even though it may not be immediately recognized, ultimately bears fruit. —*Jawaharlal Nehru*

and

Smart Decisions *help you choose the best of the job offers.*

The interaction of these behaviors, in all the contexts of your work life, creates one of the most powerful buoyancy tools in the new world of work. But how do you get the behaviors to work effectively in your life? *With the three principles of success.*

Principle 1: You Don't Have to Be a Superstar. You don't have to be at the top of your class in any of these behaviors, but you must achieve minimum levels of competency in all eight of the critical buoyancy behaviors. Together the eight behaviors form an interactive circle, where each individual behavior interacts with and complements every other behavior.

"You Have Great Ideas, But You Can't Work with People!"
—Principle #1 In Action

Did you ever work with someone who was a real expert on some topic? A real genius? I once worked with a guy who was a brilliant product design engineer. He came up with these really ingenious solutions to important problems. But Matt ended up losing his job in a high-tech shakeout. Why? Matt was brilliant, but he was also a real jerk. He was an individual contributor who came up with great ideas on his own, but he couldn't work with the product development team to get his ideas accepted. He would demean others and their arguments, refuse to accept their input—often sneering, "they're a bunch of idiots"—and revert to technical jargon in response to honest questions.

Matt's career buoyancy was strong in Flexible Thinking, but his Personal Influence and Inner Openness traits were so inadequately developed that they affected his career buoyancy. He was unbalanced—professionally speaking, that is. He just hadn't seen the importance of making an effort in this area; his was one of those arcane techie jobs of that almost distant industrial era when remoteness and superiority were seen as a hallmark of the specialist. No matter how creatively brilliant he was, he couldn't make up for his lousy style. Tolerated during the boom years of the com-

---

Talk about it only enough to do it. Dream about it only enough to feel it. Think about it only enough to understand it. Contemplate it only enough to be it.—Jean Toomer

pany, Matt was allowed to continue on the payroll, but when the tough times came around, Matt went under. And Matt will have a very tough time getting a new job, or keeping one, if he doesn't develop these two critical traits.

It's not that Matt was just at an acceptably *low* level on these traits. He was *way* below the level he needed to be buoyant.

This principle teaches us that when you have a trait that is way above the norm for buoyancy, it is *not* time to slack off. It's time to use that trait in your core career *and* to develop your other, necessary traits. As of press time, Matt is still in denial and unemployed.

Principle 2: You Are Only As Good As You Think You Are. Your strongest traits are your calling card. Your strongest traits will be what people first notice about you, and they will define how you view your own abilities and work-life buoyancy. But you can do more. Use your strengths and remember that your other traits allow you many other opportunities.

"You're the Type of Person Who . . ."—Principle #2 In Action

If you meet the minimum level of competence for all items in the Success Blueprint, you will succeed. For those of you who meet the cut-offs and who also happen to excel in one or two areas, there is some good news—and, maybe, some bad news.

First, the good news. Your strengths are your calling card. It's how people will describe you: "Joe is extremely motivated," "Carol is absolutely brilliant," "Fred is so incredibly decisive." Since the blueprint is focused on positives, this bodes well for you. It is nice to be thought of in any of these ways. These being your strengths, you can lead with them to achieve your dreams.

But there is the potential for bad news, too, if like Matt, you failed to develop your other traits thinking that *one* super strength was enough. You want to make sure that other people will appreciate *all* of your traits, not just your lead traits. You've probably heard some hiring manager say something like this: "Joanna is more of a sales kind of person; I don't think she'd do well in that VP job. It's too analytical." You can develop your other traits, and you can also make sure that other people are aware

---

A man begins cutting his wisdom teeth the first time he bites off more than he can chew. —Herb Caen

of them. It isn't necessary to be restricted in your professional life because of one or two superstrengths.

To manage your professional growth, remember that although people often use key *marker* traits in order to pigeon-hole you, you can actively combat these biases and stereotypes. It can be unfair when you are classified and categorized, because it limits who you really are. But we all do it. Your job is to make sure that someone doesn't do it to you and limit your buoyancy.

And *you* need to be aware of your other strengths as well! Don't pigeonhole yourself. If you develop all eight traits, you will have countless opportunities to achieve security, freedom, and happiness during your long and productive work life.

Lead with your strength—but don't forget about the importance of the rest of the buoyancy traits.

Principle 3: You Can Be Whatever You Want to Be. When you apply the critical eight behaviors to your work life, you can learn, change, and grow into anything you want to be. Sure, there may be certain things that are more difficult to change, but you can use your strengths as bridges for your weaknesses to cross.

"My, How You've Changed"—Principle #3 In Action

In *The Wizard of Oz*, the Tin Man gets a heart, the Scarecrow brains, and the Lion courage. It sounds pretty easy, getting such noble qualities out of a wizard's bag. But you and I know that these three characters had all of these qualities all along. They just needed to become themselves.

That's one way to learn, grow, and change, but there are other ways. And there are other reasons, too. Take Rob, for instance. Passed over for promotion, not once, but three or four times, Rob was angry and upset. He *knew* that he deserved those positions, and that it was just office politics that prevented him from getting ahead. Rob's profile indicated that he did, indeed, have most of the right stuff. But he really lacked one of the eight critical traits: Inner Openness.

Rob was smart, creative, and motivated. But he could never accept criticism or input of any kind. He would run his meetings, asking for members' input and ideas. Then, he would ignore them—all of them. Personality pro-

---

Everything should be made as simple as possible, but not simpler. —Albert Einstein

files supported, in spades, the fact that Rob was extremely closed-minded and intolerant.

Once Rob faced his weaknesses, he was able to work on them. He was able to learn and adapt to the changing times, just as he had done when he first entered the workforce. He found the whole process one of intense renewal, and at the time I am writing this he is considering two job offers in general management.

People can, and do, change and develop. I'm not going to tell you that it's easy, but I do see it happen to career-buoyant men and women everyday. It takes all of the Career Buoyancy traits to change and grow. And it especially takes Inner Openness, and at least *one* Smart Decision to help yourself.

You will see the eight critical buoyancy behaviors illustrated in many different ways, and in many different contexts, throughout the book.

A HEADSET FOR THE CAREER BUOYANT: PARALLEL PATHS TO PURSUE

In the old world a career got you where you wanted to go. In the new world the odds are that everyone can expect more jobs and more career changes than ever before. If we are to believe authorities like Drake Beam and Challenger Gray,[8] and there is every reason to trust their judgment, then you must be prepared for one day having to leave the relative safety of the corporate nest.

In the new world of work you need a new work-life plan, conceived for turbulent times and geared toward maintaining work-life buoyancy over a fifty-year span. Now, while everyone says you'll have at least three careers in your work life anyway, and possibly up to ten, I'm telling you that it *doesn't have to be an eternity of stop-and-start career dislocations.* It doesn't have to be either-or anymore, with one sequential career chain followed to its bitter end before another is traumatically birthed.

The Linear Career

Times have changed. Used to be you would find a profession, start at the bottom, and work your way steadily upward to a point which satisfied your needs for security; and having gotten to that place, it was possible to

---

To err is human, but when the eraser runs out ahead of the pencil, you're overdoing it.
—*J. Jenkins*

literally retire in the job. Freedom and happiness were meant to be found in retirement, which was a reward for the many years of loyal service. It was the old way to the American Dream—and it doesn't work anymore.

The Parallel Careers

This is the basis of the work-life buoyancy philosophy: There is a behavioral connectivity we have discovered among the critical eight behaviors that becomes the bridge between where you are today and where you intend to be tomorrow. This makes it quite possible to pursue more than one career path at a time—and in today's turbulent market, we strongly advise that you do so to achieve work-life buoyancy. We believe you should pursue the following career choices, whether consecutively, in pairs, or all together, for the following reasons:

- A core career—to satisfy physiological and security needs, first and foremost (although the more true freedom and happiness a core career gives you, the better)
- An entrepreneurial career—for more personal freedom, to hone understanding of important business realities, for affiliation with meaningful people and causes outside your traditional core career, and for the development of behaviors critical to your career buoyancy
- A dream career—through hobbies, interests, and passions for no more than their own sake, for the joy and meaning it returns, for the dollars it could return when properly pursued, and for the development of behaviors critical to your core-career buoyancy

Furthermore, when a career path is pursued with serious intent and application of the eight behaviors, your capabilities in each of your other careers *benefits in direct proportion to your developing skill levels.* In other words, do good things for yourself today, and get paid back two or three times tomorrow.

The Work-Life Buoyancy Web

The critical eight traits, used in different applications and in different contexts, are the common threads between the three separate but parallel

The meek shall inherit the earth, but not the mineral rights. —J. Paul Getty

worlds of work. They are part of the weave of a strong, pliant, and supportive structure called the work-life buoyancy web.

In a mature work-life web we find there are the three major sinews of
core, entrepreneurial, and dream careers. Connecting them are the eight
finer (yet equally strong) sinews that are the eight critical behavioral traits.
These eight traits interact with one another and with each of the three
major career sinews simultaneously, in a reciprocal network that works for
the greater good of the whole.

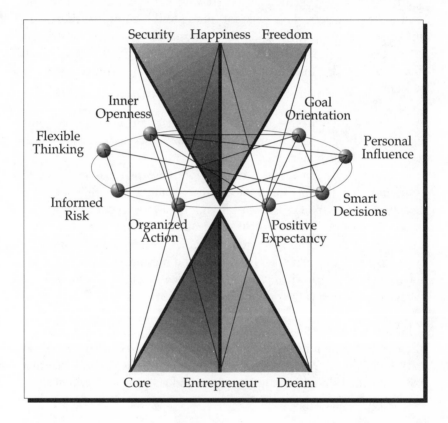

This elegant network of reciprocal strengths exists to satisfy the three
elemental needs of every man and woman working in modern society: the
needs for security, freedom, and happiness.

The technology revolution has made possible a more cost-efficient com-

One always has time enough, if one will apply it well. —Johann Wolfgang von Goethe

pany that requires only a special kind of person at its core; everyone else can be dispensed with. You must recognize that any employer will do without you if he or she can, especially if to do so will cause no hardship to the company and will increase profits. It's nothing personal, it is just the way life is, so you might as well come to terms with it—and work toward diminishing any negative impact this could have on your professional life.

It is because of this state of affairs that I suggest you first concentrate on stabilizing the odds of your financial survival in your *core* career. To do this, you must adopt and develop the critical eight buoyancy behaviors. These are the behaviors most in demand by the best employers in the healthiest industries; these behaviors will land you the jobs of the future, in the industries of tomorrow.

However, because of the practice of "it's just business; it's nothing personal," a separately pursued entrepreneurial career then becomes a sensible option to pursue, for without it you may be unable to achieve a greater measure of financial autonomy in your life. It also makes sense because the behavioral competencies you will develop from the entrepreneurial experience will make you more valuable to core-career employers.

By the same token, a vigorously pursued dream career, while giving you a richer and more satisfying life, will further stimulate a set of behaviors that are found at the heart of the jobs that spell core-career success in America's immediate future and could well open the door for you on the career of your dreams.

This is why pursuing *each* career is an integral part of the work-life buoyancy web.

The New Commandments: How Is Pursuing Three Careers Practical?

It's a new era, and a new era needs new commandments if you are to achieve work-life buoyancy. You must replace concepts like

- Narrow focus
- Either-or thinking

with a different set of values more practical in the new work world:

Ideas are the glory of man alone. No other creature can have them. Only man can get a vision and an inspiration that will lift him above the level of himself and send him forth against all opposition. —Matthew Henson

- An attitude of connectivity
- An attitude of practical know-how

AN ATTITUDE OF CONNECTIVITY

An attitude of connectivity says that instead of looking at how different and specialized your profession is in relation to that of others, you should develop an ability to simplify your job to its essential components: that is, its transferrable behaviors. The payoff with the new attitude of connectivity is that it allows you to discover the essential elements of *all* successful endeavors, in all walks of life.

As you discover commonalities with other people and their occupations, where once there were walls, you will now find bridges and pathways to personal opportunity and fulfillment. It is this connectivity that makes *Beat the Odds* such a practical approach.

As connectivity develops, ideas for dream and entrepreneurial pursuits will bubble out of your head because you realize you have most of what it takes to give it a go already.

AN ATTITUDE OF PRACTICAL KNOW-HOW

Practical know-how (P.K.H.) is knowing how and why things work in a particular way. It is being able to identify the building blocks of change, and apply them in other projects in fresh contexts. P.K.H. allows you to evaluate the pros and cons of a particular argument in the advancement of a work project and then make it happen with the desired result.

Practical know-how is the cog at the heart of every career engine ever driven. Ultimately your whole work life will come either to stutter or to accelerate on the strength of your P.K.H. Practical know-how shows you where to start, and how to continue. P.K.H. is the street smarts of your work life; it informs many of the eight critical buoyancy traits.

The Finely Tuned Work Life

Don't let your life be a series of quickly cobbled-together careers spread over a fifty-year span, when with *Beat the Odds*, you can integrate the careers of your choice into a work-life plan geared toward the prosperity of You, Inc.

You cannot depend on your eyes when your imagination is out of focus.
—Mark Twain

NOTES

1. We pay our respects to several important theorists, including Maslow, F. Herzberg, W. Neff, and D. McClelland. While objective research has often poked holes in many of these theories—mostly Maslow's and Herzberg's—their lists of needs is well thought out.

2. The Grant Study, Harvard University. This topic was further pursued by George Vaillant of Harvard, who was involved with the original study, and is addressed in his *Adaptation to Life* (1978). Little Brown & Co., New York.

3. One psychologist who believes that the needs for belonging and connectedness are just as important as traditional, male-oriented needs for power and control is Carol Gilligan. See *In a Different Voice* (Cambridge: Harvard University Press, 1982).

4. Our career buoyancy research involved three stages, conducted over the course of one year. First, we reviewed all major psychological studies of career development and job performance. Second, we conducted in-depth interviews with dozens of already buoyant careerists in each of the parallel careers. Finally, we conducted a quantitative study of buoyancy traits by contacting some 3,500 people across the United States, through personal contacts, referrals, professional association contacts, and a direct mailing. From this we culled over 300 qualified respondents to our quantitative survey of career buoyancy. These data were analyzed using a principal components analysis, with varimax rotation, yielding eight factors with eigenvalues greater than one.

5. Similar to the concept of *flow*. See J. D. Mayer, et al., M. Csikszentmihalyi, *The Evolving Self* (New York: HarperCollins, 1983).

6. U. Neisser, "General, Academic, and Artificial Intelligence," in L. Resnick (ed.), *The Nature of Intelligence* (Hillsdale, N.J.: Erlbaum, 1976). This work is still relevant to our discussion, even though holes have been poked in it.

7. See J. D. Mayer, et al. "Mood Congruent Judgment Is a General Effect," *Journal of Personality and Social Psychology* 63 (1992): 119–32.

8. Two national outplacement firms.

You see things and you say "Why?"; but I dream things that never were and I say "Why not?"—George Bernard Shaw

Chapter 3

Escaping to the Irreducible Core: Why Layoffs Aren't Going to Stop, and What to Do About It

NO MORE JOB SECURITY

Big firms have decided that job security is more of a liability than an asset.
—*The Economist*

I was reading in *The Wall Street Journal* the other day how Madison Avenue is portraying the modern workplace as hell on earth, to which I say, "Thank God for truth in advertising." They noted *Fortune* magazine with its insecurity campaign that asked, "What's worse: getting laid off on Friday, or being asked to pick up the slack on Monday?" The fear of losing a job, and with it the ability to maintain our standard of living, makes this a universal terror. "You're fired" isn't a phrase heard so much these days—there are about twenty other euphemisms deemed more palatable—but the results are the same: no job and an immediately plummeting self-esteem.

Since the recovery from the 1990 recession began, American corporations have laid off over two million people—only unlike prior recessions, in this one only 14 percent of laid-off workers can expect to be recalled; the others have had their jobs restructured out of existence.

This period of restructuring and the resultant layoffs will likely last through 2005, when we will have retooled the educational system for the

---

When two men in a business always agree, one of them is unnecessary.
—William Wrigley, Jr.

new workplace needs and when that system is spitting out freshly minted, information-era-qualified workers. By 2005 all those people who are now in their twenties, thirties, and forties who do not reinvent themselves today for the future, are likely to be prime targets for another wave of layoffs.

Job Export

You cannot trust America's blue-chip companies any longer. The fact is that with technology, far fewer people are needed to generate enhanced revenue streams. In his book *Work of Nations*, Robert Reich quotes a Colgate Palmolive executive on American corporations' commitment to America: "The United States does not have an automatic call on our resources. There is no mind set that puts this country first."

As I have observed elsewhere in my work, corporations take on a life of their own, and must feed and breathe to live. In many cases where U.S. workers might be earning fifteen dollars an hour to produce a product, the companies in question may be able to get the same production work done for as little as one dollar an hour in any of two dozen rapidly emerging economies around the world.

Also, when we lose, say, a hundred thousand manufacturing jobs to another country, the benefiting country doesn't typically gain a hundred thousand jobs, even at a buck an hour. Because the facilities are frequently custom-built with the latest technologies, the manpower needs in the new facilities will probably account for no more than ten thousand jobs at a couple of bucks an hour.

As jobs' mobility carries them across borders, it will affect paychecks and career buoyancy for all of us. Until recently all jobs have had to be done on site, so pay-scale and benefit variances for similar jobs have been determined by regional cost-of-living differentials. Now, while you certainly have to earn more to live in New York City than you do to live in Bad Axe, Michigan, the variance widens far more dramatically as you cross borders and find yourself in Brazil, or the new eastern-bloc countries with their highly educated and underutilized people. How long can it be till certain exportable jobs achieve a set global value—or until these new global wage scales return to America with our leading corporations to downgrade remuneration in these functional areas? Or failing that, till these kinds of jobs are exported forever?

There is no cure that does not cost. —Ivory Coast saying

Job Outsourcing

Outsourcing is paying another company to produce goods and provide services for the corporation that used to be supplied by payrolled employees. This way the same or better work gets delivered, while the employer sheds the burden of employee responsibility. The overriding corporate philosophy today is "Find out what we do best and do it, and outsource all the other functions to companies for whom such a function is their world-class strength."

Outsourcing is no longer limited to customer service and manufacturing; it applies to just about *every* corporate function. Perhaps it is karma that these prevalent "best in the world" philosophies will effectively hit in-house technology centers worse than any other group, simply because the outsourced vendor-specialist is likely to be better equipped to handle a particular set of business-related technology challenges.

But very often a company will first outsource a particular function, then, as technology allows, cut costs further by automating the process and bringing it back in-house. Barnett Banks of Florida (as of this writing the seventeenth largest bank in the nation) is an interesting case in point. Originally Barnett employees would talk to in-house benefits experts about choosing and then using their benefit programs. This was expensive, and Barnett found it could outsource the whole process, which allowed a saving over the costs of doing the work in-house and a reduction in manpower commitments. Then technology caught up and allowed Barnett to automate the function. They brought it back in-house as an interactive voice-operated system (talking to machines) which halved their costs again and improved the service they provided to their employees.

What we are hearing in this story are the first rumbles of the next technology earthquake that will rock the world of work to its foundations. This quake has been most commonly referred to as *artificial intelligence*.[1]

The Technology Revolution

Artificial intelligence, among its many possibilities, will almost definitely have a major role in the training and retraining all of us will undergo in the next few years; we can expect a boom in self-paced multimedia training tools, for if you aren't computer literate, you will be unable to take ad-

Two birds disputed about a kernel when a third swooped down and carried it off.
—Congolese saying

vantage of much that is available. This new technology will also likely replace jobs in the new Routine Production and In-Person Server occupations (both jobs to be explained in detail later).

It is a sobering picture for all of us, because the technology revolution is indeed creating two significant economic classes. But unlike in the past when hard work, determination, and guts could pull you up, in the next few years the stakes are going to escalate so much that entry will depend on years of initial preparation, retraining, and a basic technological literacy.

Telecommuting: It Isn't What You Think It Is

We are, most of us, working harder today than we were twenty years ago at the birth of the computer revolution. Some experts say we work as much as a month a year more. In the good old days you had to leave the job at some point and go home, but now with faxes, modems, and personal computers, the office goes with you wherever you and seven million other Americans go.

If I have been told once, I have been told a thousand times that this is a great and wondrous thing. I can live at the beach and fax that pesky work right in to the ole office. When we read about it in magazines and watch it on television, it all sounds so, how shall I put it, empowering. The problem is, if you can telecommute to your job, your job security is in jeopardy.

If people can telecommute, so can jobs. You see, if I can do my job anywhere for $x,000 a year, what is to stop my employer looking everywhere for people like me who can work just as hard and just as efficiently and productively for only $y,000 a year? Nothing, absolutely nothing, and the result is the migration of jobs all over the globe.

We hear of 800-number fulfillment and customer-service centers being telecommuted to Ireland and the Philippines and say how terrible that is, but we don't notice that those much-touted "good" jobs of tomorrow, such as software developers, are also being exported to the corners of the earth.

There are reasoned predictions of job losses of up to twenty-five million by the turn of the century from the effects of extant electronic advances and as artificial intelligence is integrated into the workplace.[2] The lesson is simple, as all lessons should be; if you can telecommute on your job, that job is in jeopardy and you must strategize accordingly.

Every intersection in the road of life is an opportunity to make a decision, and at some time I had only to listen. —Duke Ellington

Here Come the Time-and-Motion Men

Nights, twenty-five years ago, I was funding my education at a local auto plant, and I still remember the night the time-and-motion men came. These were horrors from another planet whose fiendish task was to make us work harder through further oversimplifying work we could do with our eyes closed anyway.

They are not called time-and-motion men anymore. Now they are severally disguised as consultants and employee-involvement programs, with the goal not so much to make people work harder as to dispense with those same employees altogether.

Of course the way you hear about the changes your involvement in the process brings will be orchestrated to make them more palatable. A case in point is the laying off of thirteen thousand Proctor and Gamble employees that was announced in 1993.

Ed Artz, chairman of P & G, explained that despite the company's record-setting profit picture, the results of customer surveys indicated that consumers found their brand-name products expensive and were turning to "own brand" labels. So, to maintain profitability, discounts would be needed, and that meant that costs would have to be cut. These cuts were announced not because the company was troubled but because consumers wanted cheaper products, and unless action was taken now, "there might be problems a few years down the road."

A thousand managers in a dozen teams fanned out across the globe seeking input from the newly empowered P & G work groups on ways to improve productivity, and according to Mr. Artz in a *New York Times* interview, "The suggestions bubbled out of the organization." The results were duly tabulated and evaluated. At the same time the employee-involvement project was going on, Proctor and Gamble consulted with the world's leading authorities on corporate reorganization toward their goal of maximizing profitability with a new irreducible core. The beauty of this play is that all the improvements are seen as coming from the employees.

The result was the closing of thirty factories, the consolidation of sixty-five computer systems into three, and the chop for thirteen thousand workers from around the world. Mr. Artz didn't want to do this—it hurts

---

To think that the doors of opportunity will fly open out of a sense of goodwill and brotherhood is naive. —Parren Mitchell

him more than anyone—but at least the company would be able to reduce overhead by 2.5 cents on the dollar, so that prices can be cut without
hurting profits, and the shareholders would be well served, as would
bonuses. All this is true and right; Mr. Artz got happy shareholders and
consumers got cheaper products. But Ed Artz really wasn't doing this because of some economic bogeyman hiding down the road in 1997; *he did
it because it was possible.* As will your employer.[3]

We can expect long-term investments in outsourcing, technology, and
automation to continue because the bottom-line rewards have exceeded
anyone's expectations. This is like the surge that came with the combustion
engine, when one man could suddenly have the power of forty horses. We
are at that time again; a man suddenly has the productive power of fifty
like him. This is good news for people in software and human resources,
and even better news for the entrepreneurial Symbolic Analysts who are
able to identify the opportunities such a confluence brings.

This also signifies to the intelligent observer that while startups are mush-
rooming at an incredible rate, all companies in all industries are striving
to reinvent themselves as nimble global guerrillas with a reduced number
of products and services and a *hugely reduced payroll.*

Every company in America is examining itself as we talk. Its leaders are
asking that in a day when the market and the competition are largely
global, what does their company have that's good enough to survive
world-class competition. Once this is established, the next job is to dis-
pose of those parts of the company that no longer fit the picture by selling
them, closing them down, or spinning them off. As this process continues, each and every business person in America is saying to himself or
herself, "To operate my company, I have a once-in-a-lifetime opportunity
to design a completely new operational structure that is much more sleek
than was ever possible before. There are plenty of jobs I can automate,
including whole functions, such as customer service, sales, design, accounting, engineering, R & D, human resources, and administration.
Hey, since I can automate or outsource just about anything, the only remaining question is, 'What sort of core structure do I need to support my
company's goals?' "

It is exactly this incredible window of opportunity for corporate re-
birth that puts your full-time-single-focus-core-career profession in serious
jeopardy.

The hell with that. —Martin Yate

ESCAPE TO THE IRREDUCIBLE CORE: A LOOK AT THE BASICS AND BARE MINIMUMS OF ENTRY

First and last, the business of business is making money. So the people who make it to the new irreducible core will be those whose advanced information assimilation and connectivity skills allow them to parlay the turning of ideas into money; they are the alchemists of the modern world. Their success will be knowledge based, and a talent for thriving on learning will be an important survival tool. Those with the best academic educations and practical know-how are going to develop a very real advantage.

As corporations identify and shrink to their irreducible core of best-in-the-world talents, products, and people, those who make it and thrive in the core corporation are likely to be well rewarded. They will have the most prestigious and well paying jobs in the new corporate community. Their jobs will be the most challenging and with the broadest scope, and they will receive whatever private-sector-training dollars are available. In turn they will seek out those people most adept at turning ideas into realities.

The Eye of the Needle

Those who are not seen as part of the new core corporation will find their jobs being simplified (deskilled), automated, outsourced, and exported. Anyone who finds himself in a situation where his job is getting simpler, and where he or she is learning nothing new, is being deskilled as a matter of corporate policy. By doing this, your employer is systematically eliminating your job, and, as a by-product, eliminating your ability to find gainful employment elsewhere. Unless you do something now, your productive capabilities will completely atrophy in five years.

Any Bids for Mahogany Row?

The primary career directive for the traditional single career called for chasing up that career ladder just as far and as fast as you could. Those who made it to mahogany row were said to have "arrived," to have "got it made," or to have "made the grade."

Pursuing this traditional course today with the skills and approaches of

---

It's a recession when your neighbor loses his job; it's a depression when you lose your own. —Harry S Truman

yesterday is courting disaster. The ones who are surviving the cuts and making it to the new irreducible core are those whose skills and behaviors are most in tune with corporate needs—the eight critical behaviors we touched on earlier.

The overwhelming first task for professionals today is not to focus on becoming a vice president or a partner by the age of thirty something. Nor is it a longer view of becoming president by age fifty. Such goals are pipe dreams until the stepping-stone of membership in the irreducible core has been successfully passed. The overwhelming first task is achieving buoyancy when everyone's employability is under examination.

We are living through a period where job titles may remain the same while the jobs themselves are altering dramatically with each passing month and year. So it could be suicidal to pursue the traditional corporate-management track based on your observations of the behavior of your role models, because some of those role models are hanging on by their teeth until their linear, narrow, controlling habits and industrial-era behaviors are scrapped by the reinvented corporation.

Know Yourself Through Other Eyes

While you must understand that most employers have already written off your job security as a needless liability, you have to make a renewed and reinvigorated commitment to wherever you are working, knowing full well that the company is highly unlikely to make the same commitment to you. I know this doesn't sound rational, and it certainly isn't reasonable, but right now it's a buyer's market.

You need to make this commitment as a protective measure while you retool and get everyone back on a level playing field again. I will show you a way to make it not only palatable but a veritable pleasure. It will enhance your personal gain as much as your employer's. But instead of rededicating yourself to the *corporation*, it is now time to dedicate yourself to *your career buoyancy* (To quote a commonly used phrase, "Hey, it's only business, nothing personal.") Nevertheless the work you do at work must be the very best you can do because it creates the framework for your life. Employers may come and go, but your employability must always endure for the benefit of you and *your* shareholders: yourself, your

The Wright brothers' design allowed them to survive long enough to learn how to fly.
—*Michael Potts*

family as you define it, and your community. Besides, your employer will continue to be a prime beneficiary of your renewed vigor.

THE NEW JOB DESCRIPTIONS

What you also need to do to make it to the irreducible core is to look at the kind of job you have—and see where it is going to take you tomorrow. This is crucial, as the architects of the new workplace have recategorized all the jobs, literally. In fact, there are only going to be three jobs in the future. I am going to explain them so that once you understand the roles your current job skills fit you for in the new workplace, you will be able to solidify and improve your position as circumstances dictate. Robert Reich, in his seminal *Work of Nations*, talks of the "three jobs of the future," and in so doing gives you the lens with which to examine your professional skills in light of the new workplace. The three job classifications that will comprise the majority of work for Americans in the workplace of the future will be:

1. Routine Production Services
2. In-Person Service
3. Knowledge Workers (also known as Symbolic Analysts)

Can you guess which one makes the bucks?

1. Routine Production Services (R.P.S.)

Production jobs—checking in at the time clock, punching cards, doing the same shtick over and over again for five eight-hour stretches a week for thirty years—these are traditional Routine Production Services jobs. But we mustn't make the mistake of thinking that is all that constitutes R.P.S. jobs. Our brave new high-tech world is also full of these jobs; Reich cites stuffing computer boards and routine software coding as new categories of R.P.S. jobs, and he identifies the factory hands of the future as hordes of data processors:

> The foot soldiers of the information economy are hordes of data processors stationed in back offices at computer terminals linked to world-wide information banks. They routinely enter data into computers or take it out again—records of credit card purchases and payments, credit reports,

---

Self-acceptance means self-discovery. —Richard Perry

checks that have cleared, customer accounts, customer correspondence, pay-roll, hospital billings, patient records, medical claims, court decisions, sub-scriber lists, personnel, library catalogues, and so forth. The information revolution may have rendered some of us more productive, but it has also produced huge piles of raw data which must be processed in much the same monotonous way that assembly-line workers and, before them, textile workers processed piles of other raw materials.[4]

Routine producers typically work in the company of many other peo-ple who do the same thing, usually within large enclosed spaces. They are guided on the job by standard procedures and codified rules, and even their overseers are overseen, in turn, by people who routinely monitor—often with the aid of computers—how much they do and how accurately they do it. Their wages are based either on the amount of time they put in or on the amount of work they do.

Anyone considering a core career in Routine Production Services will want to know that the career ladder consists of supervisory positions and the first couple levels of management ranks. Thus Mr. Reich cites indus-trial-era titles such as foremen, line managers, clerical supervisors, and sec-tion chiefs as defining the upper ranks of this particular career track.

Job performance typically requires that R.P.S.'s be able to read and do basic adding, subtracting and guzintas; and that they can take direction, are reliable, and are loyal. It is this type of work, notes our current Labor Secretary, for which "a standard American education, based on the tradi-tional premises of American education" is normally sufficient.

More bluntly, most of us at best are qualified for no more *than* these jobs. As a nation we are becoming rapidly marooned in the lower-middle classes of core careerdom. Average pay in R.P.S. jobs runs eleven to fifteen dollars per hour, where the pay is usually in direct correlation to the hours worked. The ceiling for those who make it to the top of R.P.S. manage-ment will be earning twenty to twenty-five dollars per hour.

2. In-Person Services (I.P.S.)

I.P.S. jobs comprise approximately 35 percent of the workforce, and the percentage is growing rapidly. These workers also perform simple and frequently repetitive tasks. Pay is also hourly but often has greater in-centives for productivity. More so than R.P.S. jobs, I.P.S. jobs require

A coward is a hero with a wife, kids, and a mortgage. —Marvin Kitman

communication skills and people orientation, because the nature of I.P.S. jobs involves face-to-face interaction.

The *Work of Nations* identifies I.P.S. as:

> In-person servers work alone or in a small team. Included in this category are retail sales workers, waiters and waitresses, hotel workers, janitors, cashiers, hospital attendants and orderlies, nursing-home aides, child-care workers, house cleaners, home health-care aides, taxi drivers, secretaries, hairdressers, auto mechanics, sellers of residential real estate, flight attendants, physical therapists, and—among the fastest growing of all—security guards.
>
> In-person servers are supposed to be as punctual, reliable, and tractable as routine production workers. But many in-person servers share one additional requirement: They must also have a pleasant demeanor. They must smile and exude confidence and good cheer, even when they feel morose. They must be courteous and helpful, even to the most obnoxious of patrons. Above all, they must make others feel happy and at ease.[5]

Upward mobility can be fairly limited. A high school diploma and, at max, some vocational training will gain you entry, and two or three ranks of tightly controlled supervision mark the limits of career growth for I.P.S. careers. The pay averages twelve dollars per hour and is not going to get you on *Lifestyles of the Rich and Famous.*

However, a lot of entrepreneurial successes get launched from this occupational biome,[6] and as long as there is a local market for the service, there should be a good job base and customer base. The I.P.S. sector is expected to sustain runaway growth over the next few years, and will provide the vast majority of work opportunities in the coming years.

3. Knowledge Workers (Symbolic Analysts)

Knowledge Workers have a very special home in the new world of work. The people with these types of skills and supportive behaviors are the ones destined to inherit the new American Dream.

The *Work of Nations* identifies Knowledge Workers (or Symbolic Analysts) as:

> Like routine production services (but unlike in-person services), symbolic analytic services can be traded worldwide and thus must compete with for-

---

He most prevails who nobly dares. —William Broome

eign providers even in the American market. But they do not enter world commerce as standardized things. Traded instead are the manipulations of symbols—data, words, oral and visual representations.

Included in this category are the problem-solving, -identifying and -brokering of many people who call themselves research scientists, design engineers, software engineers, civil engineers, biotechnology engineers, sound engineers, public relations executives, investment bankers, lawyers, real estate developers, and even a few creative accountants. Also included is much of the work done by management consultants, energy consultants, agricultural consultants, armaments consultants, architectural consultants, management information specialists, organization development specialists, strategic planners, corporate headhunters, and systems analysts. Also: advertising executives and marketing strategists, art directors, architects, cinematographers, film editors, production designers, publishers, writers and editors, journalists, musicians, television and film producers, and even university professors.

Symbolic analysts solve, identify, and broker problems by manipulating symbols. They simplify reality into abstract images that can be rearranged, juggled, experimented with, communicated to other specialists, and then eventually, transformed back into reality. The manipulations are done with analytic tools, sharpened by experience. The tools may be mathematical algorithms, legal arguments, financial gimmicks, scientific principles, psychological insights about how to persuade or to amuse, systems of induction or deduction,[7] or any other set of techniques for doing conceptual puzzles.

Some of these manipulations reveal how to more efficiently deploy resources or shift financial assets, or otherwise save time and energy. Other manipulations yield new inventions—technological marvels, innovative legal arguments, new advertising ploys for convincing people that certain amusements have become life necessities. Still other manipulations—of sounds, words, pictures—serve to entertain their recipients, or cause them to reflect more deeply on their lives or on the human condition. Others grab money from people too slow or naive to protect themselves by manipulating in response.

Like routine producers, symbolic analysts rarely come into direct contact with the ultimate beneficiaries of their work. But other aspects of their work life are quite different from that experienced by routine producers. Symbolic analysts often have partners or associates rather than bosses or supervisors. Their incomes may vary from time to time, but are not directly related to how much time they put in or the quantity of work they put out. Income depends, rather, on the quality, originality, cleverness, and occa-

God will not look you over for medals, degrees or diplomas, but for scars.
—Elbert Hubbard

sionally, speed with which they solve, identify, or broker new problems.[8] Their careers are not linear or hierarchical; they rarely proceed along well-defined paths to progressively higher levels of responsibility and income. In fact, symbolic analysts may take on vast responsibilities and command inordinate wealth at rather young ages. Correspondingly, they may lose authority and income if they are no longer able to innovate by building on their cumulative experience, even if they are quite senior.[9]

Symbolic analysts often work alone or in small teams, which may be connected to larger organizations, including worldwide webs. Teamwork is often critical. Since neither problems nor solutions can be defined in advance, frequent and informal conversations help ensure that insights and discoveries are put to their best uses and subjected to quick, critical evaluation."[10]

When not conversing with their teammates, Symbolic Analysts sit before their computer terminals—examining words and numbers, moving them, altering them, trying out new words and numbers, formulating and testing hypotheses, designing or strategizing. They also spend long hours in meetings or on the telephone, and even longer hours in jet planes and hotels, advising, making presentations, giving briefings, and doing deals. Periodically they issue reports, plans, designs, drafts, memoranda, layouts, renderings, scripts, or projections that in turn precipitate more meetings to clarify what has been proposed and to get agreement on how it will be implemented, by whom, and for how much money. Final production is often the easiest part. The bulk of the time and costs come in conceptualizing the problem, devising a solution, and planning its execution.

Most Symbolic Analysts have graduated from four-year colleges or universities; many have graduate degrees as well.

[Note: What Mr. Reich didn't mention was the behaviors behind these essential skill sets of successful Symbolic Analysts in the new world of work.]

Your Name Is on the List

Right about now someone somewhere is analyzing your job in light of these three categorizations. Once you have been pigeonholed with everyone else of your category, they will then decide how they can get the most out of you and/or someone quite like you, only a bit cheaper, or with a bit of technology for a lot cheaper.

Now, as corporate reinvention proceeds, the differences between our old

---

To a sensible man, there is no such thing as chance. —Ludwig Tieck Foriunat.

titles and new responsibilities are going to be cloudy for a while. When the dust settles, terms like *professional* and *managerial* will have largely lost their clout, because not all professionals or managers are Knowledge Workers.

Reich notes that the cranking out of wills, contracts, incorporations, and divorces that make up so much of the legal profession is hardly the work of a Symbolic Analyst or Knowledge Worker. An M.B.A., C.P.A., J.D., or PH.D. after a person's name doesn't mean that the individual who possesses the degree is any good at solving problems. The passing of a set of exams, as required by many of our professions today, needs no more than a good memory and passable writing skills. In fact, as the Labor Secretary has noted, the "professional" sobriquet originally applied to those who had mastered a "particular domain of knowledge," where "the knowledge existed in advance, ready to be mastered."

What the Symbolic Analyst/Knowledge Worker of today needs is an ongoing educational foundation, an attitude of knowledge, and the ability to connect these talents to the needs of the customer, who in turn expects creativity and understanding of the context of the problem as elementary to customizing the solution.

Core-career power and prestige will shift to those with the creative powers and connectivity who can apply their skills to the art of making money, the lifeblood of the corporation. They are the Knowledge Workers, and it is they who are to become the new power elite, not only as core careerists but as entrepreneurs and dream careerists.

Look Yourself in the Face Before It's Too Late

So when it comes to its restructuring, every company will naturally build its irreducible core of invaluable players with Symbonalysts. In every industry, whether it be a company with its roots in Routine Production Services or one with In-Person Services as its base, the people with the exciting growth jobs and money, power, and prestige will all have symbolic analysis skills. They are the people who make the I.P.S.-based and R.P.S.- based companies thrive and prosper.

In career terms you must look for and find yourself; you must recognize your skills for what they are and squarely face the issues this discovery raises. Wherever you stand today, there is plenty of opportunity to develop the new skills you need as you plan and manage your work life.

Have the courage to act instead of react. —Earlene Larson Jenks

As restructuring continues throughout the next ten years at least, layoffs and outsourcings of all types will continue. The corporate plan to ride out the rough weather is to weld a small but highly diverse group of Knowledge Workers into an irreducible corporate core. These people will come from many different job titles and many different beginnings, but they will all share certain common learnable skill sets, characteristics, and behaviors—that will become clearly attributable to the successful Knowledge Worker.

THE KEY TO THE DOOR OF THE SHRINKING CORPORATE CORE

In the old days of the corporate hierarchies the headhunters talked about "career windows" and how you had to keep your earnings in line with your experience in order to continue that upward climb.

Now, while many people working and climbing the hierarchical career ladder in the eighties were receiving merit raises well into the double digits, today, with the help of a technology-depressed labor market, younger and better-educated or recareered people can be found to do the job at much less cost. This state of affairs is to become the norm. You must maintain skill/wage competitiveness with each successive wave of technology and people that enter the marketplace.

If your earnings get out of sync with your market value, you are over-specialized, obsolescent, and probably making too much to pass through the eye of the needle.

Developing Your Own New Corporate Irreducible Core

In the last ten years America's largest companies have shrunk from employing around sixteen million people to today, when the number hovers around eleven million. We are talking here about a reduction in America's core corporate workforces of almost 40 percent. This did not happen in any haphazard fashion, and it is going to continue for some years on a global scale.

A Game for Symbolic Analysts

To help you make sense of the workplace upheavals taking place all around you, I am going to ask you to take part in a little exercise of symbolic analysis. I shall place you in the role of a senior retail executive

---

In Man, Ambition is the common'st thing: / Each one, by nature, loves to be King.
—*Robert Herrick*

charged with restructuring a conglomerate to maximize profit. By learning the ins and outs of restructuring in one particular profession, you can apply the lessons to your own pursuit of access to the irreducible core. As a result you will better understand the mind-set of those who currently control your professional destiny, and will be better able to see trouble coming down the pike.

You are going to play the lead part in the reinvention of a successful retail conglomerate. Based on our extensive survey of current downsizing philosophies and technique, and review of numerous case histories of hierarchical reinventions, I am going to share with you the very best thinking on how to shrink your company.

I'm choosing a retail company because we can all relate to its products. There isn't an adult anywhere who, failing to find that perfect pair of shoes, dress, jeans, dinner jacket, or whatever, hasn't vowed in frustration, "I should really start my own label; *I* know what people really want." Recapture that perhaps fleeting moment when you thought of becoming a fashion mogul: That was the creative you at work, the Symbolic Analyst identifying problems and their resulting opportunities.

So what if you *had* gone ahead with your idea to design and make that retail item? Well, in our game, you did. It is now ten or twenty years later, and you are the head of an important and respected international fashion retailer that carries your name. As the founder and leader of this global enterprise you feel under siege from the storms of change. You feel you have to make changes because not to is to risk extinction, and you see that happening all around you to those once-healthy companies.

Here's the deal: You started with one retail shop selling dresses and ladies' accoutrements. Your sense of color and knowledge of the theories and traditions of fashion allowed you to create a retail empire that is known throughout the world for its quality and style. Your company is now making money, but not all the units have equal potential for profit, and in these tough times it's best to see where the leaks are; you have to plug them immediately or else you'll go down with all hands. Well, if you were smart, you'd get the best advice going, say that of world-class management consultants McKinsey & Co., and follow it. Based on their analysis, here's what you would do to your profitable enterprise and why.

Your company has four divisions:

Never, never, never give up. —Winston Churchill

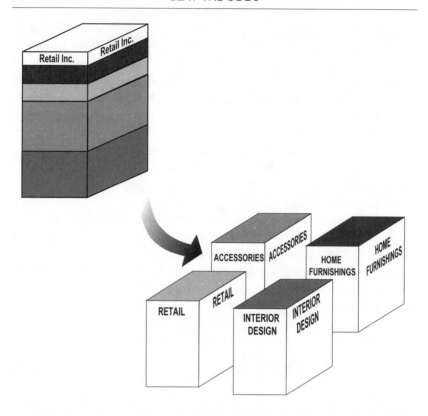

Some of these operations are better bets than others. Your choices are to asset-strip, shut down, or sell different divisions (or operations within those divisions). This may include taking a small but profitable operating department in an unsuccessful division and spinning it off as a new entity under your name while you shut down or sell off the rest of the division. Or it may include plant closings, spin-offs, management buyouts, asset sales, and the automation, outsourcing, and export of jobs on a wholesale basis. The first thing a good management consultant, familiar with the terrain, will tell you is to get an employee-involvement program going as the communications P.R. vehicle, this way many of the early changes can be given the spin of "employee empowerment."

Downsizing intelligently is a delicate task; you have to rethink all your ideas about labor and the structures that led to grand corporate offices.

Order marches with weighty and measured strides; disorder is always in a hurry.
—Napoleon Bonaparte

You are moving directly away from the global Swiss-army-knife conglomerates you have modeled your company on, to something altogether smaller and dramatically more powerful.

You will achieve this by identifying the profitability and potential of each separate operation within your company. This means not only looking at whole divisions but also breaking them down by departments and identifying who the key players are in each operational area. Conceptually every department is viewed as a potential minicorporation, and of each area you ask, "Is there a market for its products and services? Is it reliably profitable?" Could you reconfigure one group you deem profitable with other profitable "minicorporations" within your company to create entirely new entities? Sometimes the answer will be yes, and sometimes no. Of those that are the least profitable and most troublesome, world-class management consultants McKinsey & Co. are likely to say, "These should either be sold or shuttered immediately or stripped of R & D spending and operated for cash until profitable contracts end. Then they, too, should be shut down and sold." McKinsey & Co. might also say that in certain circumstances you may choose to keep them if they can provide a predictable cash flow with "depreciated plant and equipment."[12]

They have also told you that none of this will pull together unless you have developed a comprehensive vision of your corporate future, for this will allow you to make the tough decisions. All in all, McKinsey's message is quite plain: "Shrink smart or die."[13]

Now let's look at each of your four divisions in detail. Each is made up of maybe a thousand workers. A couple of families have three generations working for you, and many have given you ten or twenty years of their lives; there's a rich heritage of shared endeavor here. However, your reorganization consultants tell you that the next three or four years are going to keep you in a state of near pandemonium as you go through the restructuring and that you must be prepared to "make sober, almost cynical, assessment of the viability of each business unit within the company."[14] In other words, you must try to remove the faces and make decisions based on the facts and the new possibilities.

So here we go:

Interior Decoration. This dog hasn't turned a profit in years, despite investments and cost-cutting measures. It takes up valuable retail space in

---

Not failure, but low aim, is crime. —James Russell Lowell

all your stores, and while it gives you a very impressive image, it's a labor-intensive albatross. Your consultant reports, "The business should be closed down and written off. In this case shrinking smart means acting swiftly."

Home Furnishings. Some years you are more profitable than others, but the bottom line is that you are never likely to be world-class. You can't even get your own Interior Design division to actively endorse your product line. Here the consultants will say the company is healthy enough to sell to a major competitor who, by buying the division, will eliminate a competitor in the process, so sell it, and by doing so help both companies.

> *Note:* Whenever there is a merger, people lose jobs, and those on the mergee side traditionally lose by far the greatest percentage. Special attention is usually given to the senior executives of the mergee, so most of them will be okay. It's the guys who are just underneath who have to worry.

Accessories. Hot, hot, *hot* market. Your brand-name accessories are market leaders. In fact you see enormous potential for designing private-label lines of accessories for other retail fashion houses. Here the smart money tells you to form alliances with other companies in your industry to develop world-class capabilities to do the larger private-label work. Joint ventures of other natures might further enhance this already thriving division—perhaps your own brand line of perfume and toiletries, or maybe a men's line where there was none before. A wise move might be to liberate this division and have it operate independently as a wholly owned subsidiary.

Now, while any alliances created here always have the possibility of blossoming into a merger (in which case, see the box above), they also provide you with a wonderful opportunity to build your webs of corporate connectivity.

Retail. Retail made you, and it is still at the core of all your success. With all your desirable mall real estate throughout the world, you are positioned to deliver what you've always done best.

Now you have a new vision of a tightly run, highly profitable, labor-lite corporation that only competes where its odds are the best. Since you know what you want to look like in your new manifestation, you can now go forth and search the ranks of the other divisions and recruit those from

---

Theirs not to make reply, theirs not to reason why, theirs but to do or die.
—Alfred, Lord Tennyson

the appropriate areas and with the skill sets and behaviors that are deemed valuable at the new irreducible corporate core.

You will want to create an irreducible core that will maximize your newly focused retail commitment. This will be made up of current retail personnel and the best minds you can find at all levels in your other three divisions plus any liquid assets you might appropriately siphon off.

The Knowledge Era Satellite/Cloverleaf Corporate Structure

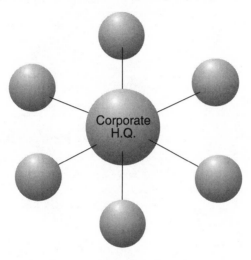

The very structure of your current irreducible core is changing, from a hierarchical pyramid to the cloverleaf and satellite structures that represent the new slimmed-down corporation, with its autonomous and highly mobile units structured to turn on the proverbial dime in response to market demands.

In restructuring this typical mythical retail conglomerate, you have fulfilled your duty to the corporation by making it as healthy as it can be. You set out to do good by the company, and you did; that thousands will lose jobs and perhaps careers as a result of your work is neither here nor there. It's business, nothing personal; you do what you have to do to help the company survive as best it may. That is what everyone is hired to do—and this is the argument being made down the hall behind those closed doors right now. So now that you understand the thinking behind a typical corporate restructuring, you will be more prepared to sense

Discipline is the soul of an army. —George Washington

which way the winds of change are blowing around your own particular high-rise salt mine.

The Industrial Era Hierarchical Pyramid

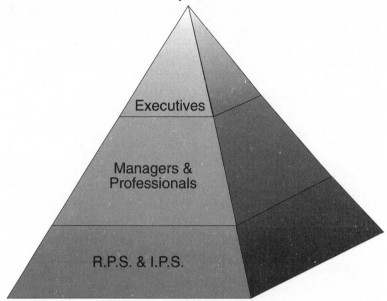

There won't be a last word on the irreducible core for some years to come. As the very nature of business changes, the irreducible core will continue to change, and quite possibly shrink to one-quarter the size it was in 1980. We'll see more and more smaller companies focused on a particular sequence of niche services and products. These post industrial companies will be made up of fewer people, and each of those people will have to learn to perform at a higher level in more areas and with greater connectivity. Gone is the corporate one trick pony.

ON THE LOOKOUT FOR LAYOFFS

Despite the knowledge that layoffs, career plateaus, and downward pressure are in the cards for all core careerists at some point, many otherwise smart people stick their head in the sand like ostriches and hope that by doing so the problem will pass them by. Unfortunately it doesn't, and

A genius? Perhaps, but before I was a genius, I was a drudge. —Ignace Jan Paderewski

those who think "It could never happen to me" are the ones caught least prepared to survive economically or professionally.

Watch Out for These Fourteen Danger Signals

1. Your company is behaving like an ostrich, or like Elmer Fudd on Turkey Day. If it's the first, it is doomed, and so are you. If it's the second, well, at least the company recognizes the stakes and is taking action to survive—but that doesn't necessarily mean you will survive with it.

2. A sea change in your industry, or section of your industry. Most of us understand the concept of rolling recessions, where the recession will roll through industries and geographies in an apparently random fashion, as it did in the early eighties with manufacturing taking the first serious hits, then agriculture, energy, real estate, and ultimately financial services. In a similar way, what we are going through now in our work world is *rolling restructuring*. Where is your industry in the restructuring process? What areas are getting worked on in other companies and why? Then figure out the ramifications for your own company and how this will affect your job.

3. Mysterious suits. There is no such thing as a recession-proof industry, or a company that won't be restructured. Plug in to the company grapevine and find out what all those consultants are really up to.

4. It's merger time. Everything will *not* be the same after the merge. If you are the Martha in the merger, it's disastrous, and while the Georges always receive first consideration, they never get off scotfree, either.

5. A leveraged buyout. Exercise caution if your outfit is involved in a leveraged buyout. Very often buyouts sound tremendously energizing and egalitarian. But what is the agenda for those who actually make it happen? They ultimately want to profit by selling the company again. In other words, it's a business deal where the assets are what must be protected and nurtured, not the people. Additionally, leveraged buyouts can get strapped for cash payments on the principal loans, and we know what happens then: cutbacks to survive in the fierce global economic climate.

6. If you're in Advertising/Public Relations, Human Resources, Support Services, and even R & D, beware: These areas are early targets for cutback, automation, and outsourcing.

7. If you hate your job, are scared, or show either. Your feelings will appear as negativism, and we all know the weak links are the first to go.

The way to go from rags to riches is to start by getting a decent set of rags. —Anonymous

8. If your normal stellar reviews suddenly take an unexpected downturn or if your review is postponed. It's easy to get into denial over this, but dangerous. If there is a sudden negative change, talk to someone about it; don't stay hurt and confused. Register your concerns about the appearance of "areas for improvement" where there were none before; they could be legitimate—but they might not be.

You should be very sensitive to postponed performance reviews if layoffs are in the wind. Those in the know say that it is difficult for a boss to fire you when you have just been given a great review—it increases your ammunition should you seek legal redress. By postponing a review, there's nothing on the record and no corporate guilt.

You owe it to your career and yourself to stop the corporation from rigging your personnel files with malice aforethought. And don't say, "Gee, I work for a Fortune 500 company, they wouldn't do that." The case law and the courts are littered with big-name defendants.

9. You, your group, department, or whatever suddenly appear out of the normal information loop. This could mean that you no longer need to know what is going on because you aren't long for this particular corporate world.

10. If hiring freezes and early-retirement incentives have come and gone. Layoffs are never far behind them. *Never.*

11. Challenging work normally headed your way is now rerouted elsewhere, and you seem to be able to do the job with your eyes closed. This is often a sign that your job is being deskilled.

12. People above and below you are getting the old heave-ho!

13. You are Customer Remote. In the current management culture, customers are everything. The farther away you get from the customer, the more difficult it is to justify the existence of your function.

14. "The layoffs are over." Whenever anyone makes this statement, you can be sure layoffs will continue, as will layoff waves.

The road to riches in the old days was to get a job and hang in there; maybe you might make a few moves, but you were always looking for that place to call home until retirement. Unfortunately the layoffs aren't going to stop, and no matter how good at your job you might be, you can still get sideswiped by the juggernaught of change.

The universe is full of magical things patiently waiting for our wits to grow sharper.
—Eden Phillpotts

The idea that a lifetime of service and dedication is no longer required is simply unacceptable to far too many professionals. They think that as soon as they get another job with a "more stable" or a "better-run" company, things will return to normal and they can get on with their lives as they did before. This will not happen, ever. The old days are gone, and the choice is simple, if brutal. Adapt or die.

Career management is infinitely tougher today than it was just five years ago. Adapting to the realities of a workplace where the number of good jobs is shrinking in opposite proportion to the number of people waiting to fill them requires a complete reappraisal of basic career strategy. However, that reappraisal must first be put in the context of where all the jobs are going to be, which we'll look at next.

NOTES

1. Although it has been referred to in the past as *expert systems*.
2. Respected futurist Joseph Pelton in *Futuretalk* (NJ: Smith Micro, 1991).
3. *Newsweek*, July 6, 1993.
4. Robert Reich, *The Work of Nations* (New York: Random House, 1992), p. 175.
5. Ibid, p. 177.
6. To understand the concept of biomes and biome clusters, visit a zoo and you'll hear about desert biomes and mountain biomes and tropical biomes, and the types of life that adapt to and flourish in a particular biome. When we talk about biomes in *B.T.O.*, we are talking about the quality of life in a particular professional area, for some industrial and occupational biomes are much pleasanter and safer than others. As we developed the book, we analyzed all growing industries and learned for ourselves just where the best steady-employment bets are. We grouped similar environments (biome clusters) together to help establish greater practical job and career connectivity.
7. Among other things, an attitude of practical know-how and street smarts.
8. In other words, connectedness.
9. This was job security going plop.
10. Reich, *Work of Nations*, p. 181.
11. Harvard Business Review. November/December 1992, p. 74.
12. Ibid.
13. Ibid.
14. Ibid.

Ambitious people don't make excuses. —Anonymous

Chapter 4

What's Hot: Understanding Where the Job Opportunities Are for the Next Few Years

What does the new world of work look like? Everywhere we look, we see it. It's the local hospital that employs an abundance of doctors, nurse practitioners, technicians, physical therapists, nurses, maintenance workers, and employees of almost every description; the travel agency down the street that arranges trips around the world for local businesses, retirees with time and cash on their hands, and others; the law firm downtown that handles malpractice suits, bankruptcies, divorces, and corporate acquisitions; and the fast-food restaurant just off the highway that feeds, and employs, just about everybody in the community at one time or another.

Nonetheless jobs today are not lifelong appointments. The only job security that exists now or will exist in the future is that which you can create for yourself. To stay gainfully employed in the years ahead, you will have to focus your energies on finding the hottest jobs with the greatest horizontal and vertical flexibility within the hottest industries. But with all the conflicting information that's out there, how can we determine which industries are relatively safe and which ones are not? Some industries—such as computers and finance—are reputedly growing by leaps and bounds. Yet it seems that every day we read about another computer manufacturer company or bank that's laying off thousands of people.

First we have to look past the headline hype; the breaking stories generally yield more confusion than practical advice. Second we have to see the

---

Most people want to improve themselves, but not many want to work at it. —Anonymous

big picture—not only *which* industries are growing but also *why* they're growing. If we understand the trends that precipitate the rise and fall of industries, we can find out what to avoid and improve our odds.

TRENDS

Three big trends will drive our economy over the next twenty years. They have to do with our aging population, the exponential growth of technology, and the globalization of work—and together, these influences will revolutionize the world of work.

The Aging Population

What's happening to the population? We're becoming older—and richer. With two-income households, and longer life spans, and baby boomers now reaching their prime and the height of their earning potential, our society is positioned to spend more money than ever before on medical care, personal services, recreation, and child care. Other industries that will benefit from the aging population are law, travel, retail, education, and social services.

Technology

The second trend is a Pandora's box. New technology will increase productivity and in turn eliminate millions of jobs. This is a rolling process as technology is applied to more and more complex occupational functions throughout all industrial biomes. On the other hand, automation will also create new work opportunities.

The Globalization of Work

As involvement with international trade becomes routine, it is inevitable that some jobs will be lost because of increased competition. On the other hand, it is likely that many jobs will be gained as new opportunities are created. The greatest danger awaits those Americans qualified for the lowest level R.P.S. jobs, as many of these jobs are by their nature exportable. This is also likely to exert downward pressure on R.P.S. wages for some time to come.

Perseverance is everything. —West African saying

BIOMES AND CLUSTERS

We did our own research to identify the world of work for the future. It has shown us that the new workplace will have, at its core, twenty-two separate industrial biomes, which we have organized into four greater biome clusters. A biome is a healthy professional living environment, where different types of professionals can survive, and some can flourish. We grouped different, yet similar, industries together into biome industries where the work climate is similar and where much of the professional expertise and practical know-how is transferable.

In the new workplace you will not be able to count on one job, one career. Instead the focus will be on finding work in a healthy *biome*—where, if the job itself isn't secure, at least the *environment* is habitable over the long term. You can then move from job to job within a particular biome, or within its cluster (a grouping of similar biomes), thus giving yourself more flexibility.

The four biome clusters into which the twenty-two industrial biomes have been organized are as follows:

1. Information and service brokers
2. Technology
3. Global industries
4. Public service

Biome Cluster 1: Information and Service Brokers

Since it is the largest biome cluster, information and service brokers includes the greatest number of symbonalyst occupations. Due to its size, it also employs the majority of R.P.S. and I.P.S. workers. Its industrial biomes include

- Health care
- Human potential (contains both education and human resources)
- Insurance
- Law

When you reach for the stars, you may not quite get them, but you won't come up with a handful of mud either. —Leo Burnett

- Media/Communications
- Finance
- Food service
- Retail
- Travel

Biome Cluster 2: Technology

This biome cluster includes the industry biomes that, more than any other, will shape our world during the next twenty years. These industry biomes are

- Biotechnology
- Computer
- Engineering
- Telecommunications
- Environment

These areas represent those jobs with the greatest horizontal and vertical flexibility.

Biome Cluster 3: Global Industries

While most of our industry biomes will *join* the worldwide marketplace in the near future, the industrial biome that is already global is

- Manufacturing and Trade

Biome Cluster 4: Public Service

This biome cluster is made up of those industrial biomes that help the country and your community function:

- Federal government and defense
- State and local government
- Social services
- Nonprofit organizations

An unfulfilled vocation drains the color from a man's entire existence.
—Honoré de Balzac

Jobs That Cross Industry Lines

As job security erodes over the coming years, your job's relative flexibility will become increasingly important. The narrower the applications of your job, the more limited your core career opportunities become in the inevitable event of layoffs.

By the same token, the wider the applications of your job, the wider your career horizons become. Some core career jobs have such wide application that they offer almost unlimited flexibility to move from one no-longer-hospitable biome to another that promises greener professional pastures.

These jobs include:

- Sales/marketing
- Public relations
- Accounting

These jobs offer opportunities in all biomes and constitute some of the most flexible options available to modern professionals. We will address the jobs and working environments that make up the new world of work biome by biome, but for simplicity's sake, we will treat these jobs just listed separately and in detail, as if they were a biome unto themselves.

TOMORROW'S OPPORTUNITIES

A closer look at the aforementioned industry clusters will reveal where the hottest opportunities are now and where they're likely to be in the years ahead.

Cluster 1—Information and Service Brokers

Information and service brokers form the backbone of the new service economy. Quite simply this biome cluster includes industries that exist to provide a service, such as health care, or to provide information in some way, such as education.

We've got to stand by ourselves before we can make it. Nobody's going to help us.
—Kareem Abdul Jabbar

HEALTH CARE

Health care is virtually recession-proof; whatever the economic climate, people still get sick. Which is not to say that the industry isn't changing or that it isn't subject to changing further in the future. The health care industry is reinventing itself as steadily as it is growing.

With new, portable medical equipment, the aging population, and the expense of hospital visits, at-home health care will be in the forefront of industry growth over the next decade. (There has also been a boom in preventive medicine that seems bound to continue.)

Visiting nurses, physician assistants, home health aides, outpatient therapists, and others who provide I.P.S. services will not only be in de-mand—in fact theirs will be among the fastest-growing jobs in the econ-omy—but their professional roles will also expand. Highly trained nurses and assistants, especially nurse practitioners, will provide primary care in place of doctors. Home health aides will oversee their patients' nutritional needs, as well as provide companionship and housekeeping services. And therapists will provide at-home services to patients, saving them hospital visits and reducing expenses.

Today one out of every ten people works in health care. In many areas of the country the expanding health care industry has replaced a number of the jobs lost in manufacturing. However, when these production-line workers lost their jobs, it didn't mean they all got new ones as doctors, nurses, and therapists; the new jobs go to the people with the new *skills.*

At-home health care will create many new jobs, but there will also be high growth in more traditional health care settings: hospitals, clinics, pharmacies, medical laboratories, private doctors' offices, HMOs, dentists' offices and labs, and so on. Positions will be available across the country, although the highest concentration will be in California, New York, and the Middle Atlantic states because of the high density of the population in those areas.

Hot jobs in health care include: Medical Assistant, Radiologic Tech-nologist, Medical Record Technician, Physical Therapist, Medical Secre-tary, Occupational Therapist, Physical Therapist, Surgical Technologist, Podiatrist, Dispensing Optician; in nursing: Intensive Care, Medical-Surgical, Rehabilitation, and Geriatric Care Specialist, Health Designer/Architect, Home Health Care Specialist, Managed Health Care Manager,

---

Each generation must, out of relative obscurity, discover its mission, fulfill it, or be-tray it. —Frantz Fanon

Radiologic Technologist, EEG Technologist, Respiratory Therapist, Registered Nurse, Licensed Practical Nurse, Recreational Therapist, Nursing Aide, Psychiatric Aide, Nurse Practitioner, Integrated-Care Deliverer, Nurse Anesthetist, Home Health Nurse; for physicians: Intern, Geriatric Medicine, Preventive Medicine; Family Physician, Geneticist, General Surgeon, Adult and Child Psychiatrist, Health Service Administrator, Health Service Manager, Podiatrist; in dentistry: Orthodontist, Oral and Maxio-Facial Surgeon, Pediatric Dentist, and Prosthodontist.

HUMAN POTENTIAL

Education and human resources combine to form the human potential field. The business side of human resource development includes corporate human resource staffing positions, as well as permanent and contingency placement, and outplacement.

Training people and keeping them gainfully employed will become a bigger challenge—and a more profitable one—in the decade ahead, with the following questions to be answered: How much education and training will they need? What will students of all ages—including members of the workforce—learn, and how will they learn? How often will they need retraining, and how flexible will they have to be?

Education. Educational services, which includes schools, colleges, vocational-training centers, and libraries, is one of the largest sectors in the economy. More than one-quarter of us are involved in it, either as educators or as students. Corporate downsizing and workforce displacement have led to phenomenal expansion in the personnel industry, with temporary agencies fast becoming one of the mainstays of the economy. In-house human resources departments will also become increasingly active in training, dispute resolution, and diversity management. However, the restructuring to smaller corporate cores will have a dramatic and negative impact on all minorities. Ratios may be perfect, but in sheer numbers, whole sections of our minority and special-interest communities are going to be trapped beneath the glass trap door.

Where will you find education and training for the jobs of the future? In the schools, naturally, where a great emphasis will be placed on math and science. Even now there are not enough math and science teachers to fill all the vacancies. Bilingual- and special-education teachers will become key players as schools become global, reflecting the path corporations are taking. Teachers will be in great demand as more and more jobs require at

One can never consent to creep when one feels an impulse to soar. —Helen Keller

least a high school diploma and basic academic skills. This will lend to a long-overdue reinstatement of teachers' social status.

Hot jobs in education include most teaching positions in all disciplines, and especially those in secondary schools, which will open up in the next decade as a large wave of educators reach retirement age. Teacher aides and counselors will also find themselves in great demand along with teachers; principals, too, will reach retirement age in large numbers over the next few years, providing room at the top for dedicated careerists.

Staffing Industry. Employment interviewers, in both temporary and permanent placement agencies, will have diverse qualifications depending on what type of people their agencies provide. Companies that supply administrative people, such as secretaries and word processors, will often hire staff who have minimal education and training; those that provide accountants, engineers, and others with specialized degrees may hire interviewers who themselves have experience in those fields. Many staffing-industry consultants work on some kind of incentive-based pay. They may eventually advance to managerial positions, where opportunities abound in an exceptionally healthy biome. Temp agencies will be called upon to fill companies' increasing needs for contingency workers—but while temporary workers may earn wages equal to those of permanent workers, they rarely receive benefits, such as vacation time, sick days, and health insurance.

Human Resources. Corporate human resources people of all kinds, such as compensation specialists and diversity managers, and particularly in-house trainers, will be called upon to teach employees necessary skills, which may range from reading and writing to staying on top of new technology. Training managers may also educate other managers and employees about sexual harassment, discrimination, diversity, problem solving, and employment law. All trainers require exceptional communication skills.

Hot jobs in human potential include: Human Resources Manager; Employment Interviewer; Training Manager; Alternative-Dispute-Resolution Practitioner; Diversity Manager; Labor Relations Specialist; Benefits and Compensations Specialist; Director of Training; Employee Assistance Program Manager; and specialists in Human Resource Information, Corporate Training, Drug, Gerontology, Day Care Programs; Pension Matters, and Union Negotiations.

Whenever the occasion arose, he rose to the occasion.
—*Jonathan Brown, on Diego Velazquez*

INSURANCE

The insurance industry has traditionally provided retirement and savings programs for many Americans. However, if people continue to invest in mutual funds, this could put the pinch on the insurance industry. But even if that happens, it's only going to be a gnat's bite on an elephant's bottom, for the enormous insurance industry will still be one of the biggest and most stable industrial biomes in the country.

The proliferation of fax machines, entertainment systems, camcorders, and other at-home business and leisure equipment spells good news for this industry: As we buy high-ticket items, we have to insure them. New technology, combined with our increasing expendable income, will provide an endless supply of things that need to be insured.

Other factors behind the insurance industry's growth include women's ever-increasing need for life and disability insurance, brought about by their mass entry into the workforce; the complexity of the modern business world, which has increased demand for such insurance as product liability and pollution liability; and skyrocketing health and legal costs, which is pumping up sales of health and prepaid legal insurance policies.

With more than two million people, the insurance industry is made up of two segments:

- The large insurance carriers that we all know, such as Metlife and Blue Cross and Blue Shield
- Everybody else who works in insurance, including the smaller companies, agents, brokers, and others.

Although most jobs in the industry are created by insurance carriers, the balance is shifting. Until now insurance carriers employed twice as many people as any other segment of the industry. Automation will temper insurance carriers' hiring, because fewer people will be needed to review applications and process claims. By comparison, other insurance people, especially small-company employees who have direct contact with the customer base, are less likely to be affected by automation.

Actuaries, who predict the probability of accidents, deaths, and so on,

---

The Coca-Cola company sold only four hundred Cokes in its first year of business. Dr. Seuss's first book was rejected by twenty-three publishers. Henry Ford went bankrupt twice before hitting it big in the automotive industry.

and what such probabilities will cost the company monetarily, enjoy one of the fastest-growing jobs in the insurance industry, as well as in the whole economy. The Bureau of Labor Statistics expects the number of actuarial positions to grow almost 40 percent by 2005.

Hot jobs in insurance include: Insurance Agent; Broker; Actuary; Computer Science and Systems Analyst; Record Clerk; Billing Clerk; Bookkeeping, Accounting, and Auditing Clerk; Brokerage Clerk; Statement Clerk; File Clerk; Word Processor and Data-Entry Clerk; Librarian; Library Assistant; Order Clerk; Payroll and Timekeeping Clerk; Personnel Clerk; and Secretary.

LAW

Law has always been a glamour profession and will likely remain so. With a bigger world population and increased business activity, especially in international trade, we'll need even more lawyers during the next ten years. But there is likely to be some industry-wide restructuring.

Recently law firms have come under fire for the high cost of their services.[1] Now a whole industry is growing around helping clients get what they pay for. And many of us will soon be buying prepaid legal-service plans, similar to health insurance, to counter the high price tag of counseling.

Whatever changes occur in the industry, law is still hot. The Bureau of Labor Statistics predicts that demand for attorneys will rise 31 percent by the year 2000. But although demand for legal professionals will be extremely high, the competition for those jobs will be fierce.

Today competition in the law field is already intense. Paralegal firms compete with law firms; they charge less, and handle wills, name changes, uncontested divorces, and other routine tasks that have traditionally been the bread and butter of law firms. Lawyers compete with other lawyers to become full partners in law firms. The path to partner now takes at least ten years, and it will grow increasingly difficult to make the cut. And new graduates compete with more established lawyers—many of whom are moving laterally rather than climbing the career ladder—and with other recent graduates for jobs.

Many students are now entering law school with advanced degrees, such as M.B.A.'s and even M.D.'s, to increase their marketability. A law degree can also enhance any entrepreneurial or dream careerist. After all, knowing the rules of the game so intimately can only help your other pro-

Lose not courage, lose not faith, go forward. —Marcus Garvey

fessional careers. Technology degrees are also seen as a strong plus for career changers considering the legal profession.

Turnover in the field is low because of the time and money invested in becoming a legal professional. Also, despite the pressure and long hours—many lawyers work more than fifty hours a week—lawyers, judges, and others in the industry are rewarded with high status and pay.

Hot jobs in law include: Litigator, Specialist in Elder Law, Bankruptcy and Tax Attorney, Judge, and specialists in Intellectual Copyright.

MEDIA/COMMUNICATIONS

The up-and-coming technologies of communication include television, computers, and the telephone. We are already seeing some of the early results—video conferencing, interactive television, and electronic publishing—but these products are only the beginning. Multimedia technology is the face of the future. The next decade will see a reshaping of the entire communication industry as multimedia technology becomes commonplace.

Publishing. Print journalists—writers and reporters—will be most likely to find employment opportunities with small-town newspapers.

One of the fastest-growing fields, not only within publishing but in the entire communications industry, is slated to be electronic publishing. In an era where the manipulation of knowledge is paramount, certain information that perhaps may once only have been enshrined within the covers of a book will now appear in electronic ways that offer more interactively.

Electronic publishing specialists can edit, design, and produce books and magazines entirely on computer, and distribute them through on-line services or on CD-ROM. Creative people with a combination of design and computer skills will be in great demand to fill publishing jobs in the publishing cities of New York, Boston, Chicago, and San Francisco. Of course, if you're really good, you may do these jobs and still live in Bad Axe, Michigan. I myself am based near Manhattan, but my graphics guy operates happily out of Washington.

Television and Radio. More traditional media outlets, and in particular cable television, should also prosper, but mostly because of advertising revenue. Although the audience is growing, cable subscriptions will level off as the market becomes saturated. Most cable jobs will be in sales or technical areas rather than in production/programming—unless, like those

---

Blessed is he who has found his work; let him ask no other blessedness. —Thomas Carlyle

two dauntless entrepreneurs, Wayne and Garth, you're willing to broadcast a show out of your basement.

For the rest of the broadcast sector (radio and network television), smaller television and radio stations, in less important media markets, will provide most of the employment opportunities. Once you've paid your dues at a small station, career progression means moving to one of the larger media markets. This is because traditionally an industry that comprises many small companies in small markets has limited growth opportunity. As a result it has become the norm within the electronic and print media for professionals to move around every couple of years, creating their own career track. Media professionals focus on finding a job in a bigger market rather than getting a better job within the same company.

The growth of cable television, television syndication, movie rentals, theater, and film production has created a need for programming. This translates into more acting, directing, and producing jobs available during the next decade than ever before. But don't quit your day job yet—few jobs in the entertainment industry will go begging, and many more potential celebrities are called than are chosen. Only the most talented, dedicated, hardworking, and tenacious actors, directors, and producers tend to make it in the long haul in an industry with such global appeal.

Hot jobs in media/communications include: Public Relations and Communications Specialist, at both the corporate level and in local media; Technical Newsletters, and small Radio and Television Stations. Electronic Publishing Specialist, Database Manager, Technical Writer; and technically trained communications personnel including Engineer, Systems Analyst, and Technician.

FINANCE

It's finally happening: Baby boomers are learning to save money, and Generation X say they will just as soon as they get some. Their newfound thriftiness, and their realization that it's time to plan for retirement—given that they've reached middle age—is contributing to the overall growth in the finance industry. The winners, besides the boomers, include securities and financial services representatives, sales and marketing specialists, financial planners and analysts, and other investment professionals.

For baby boomers and others with money to invest, what may be better

---

I take a simple view of living. It is keep your eyes open and get on with it.
—Laurence Olivier

than money in the bank? Money in mutual funds. Mutual funds have supplanted banking as the fastest-growing segment of the finance industry; banking, which employs more than two million people, is still the largest, but it isn't growing as quickly as the mutual-funds sector. Even people who normally don't invest in the stock market are flocking from banks to mutual funds because of low-interest-earning savings accounts and certificates of deposit, and a strong securities market.

To further attract new customers, mutual-fund families are beginning to offer products that appeal to specific markets—for example, so-called Green Funds, that invest only in ecologically conscious companies. They are also starting to offer new services to make mutual funds more convenient. For example, electronic transactions (that is, automatic withdrawals from paychecks or bank accounts) are becoming more widespread.

Hot jobs in finance include: Investment Professional, Environmental Accountant, Forensic Accountant, International Tax Accountant and Auditor, Audit Accountant, Financial Planner, Currency Trader, Financial Service Sales Rep, Corporate Controller, Corporate Treasurer, Credit Manager, Auditor, Loan-Workout Specialist, Securities and Financial Services Representative.

FOOD SERVICE

With dual-income households, hardly anyone has time to cook anymore. Food service companies, particularly those establishments that offer delivery, takeout, and drive-through, are all in high gear supplying our three squares a day. Even though we are increasingly becoming a nutrition-conscious culture, fast foods—especially hamburgers, pizza, chicken, and french fries—are still the hottest businesses.

The melting pot of America has given rise to a wonderful diversity of ethnic foods. Current awareness of cholesterol and saturated-fat levels has also been a boon to the ethnic-food market, as more and more people are trying different foods, not only for the taste treat but because many of these prepared foods are low in cholesterol and saturated fats.

Overall, food service is the third-largest industry in the country. According to the Bureau of Labor Statistics, the food service industry is expected to create more new jobs than any other small-business-dominated sector over the next decade.

Most eating and drinking places are small businesses—according to the

The tragedy of life doesn't lie in not reaching your goal. The tragedy lies in having no goal to reach. —*Benjamin E. Mays*

Washington, D.C.–based National Restaurants Association, three out of four restaurants are small businesses—so unfortunately there is not much chance of advancement. Even though restaurants are small operations, there *are* lots of them, so jobs should be plentiful in the decade ahead. Nevertheless an industry dominated by giants like McDonald's and pygmies like the deli down on the corner is not great news for those climbing the career ladder. The limited number of giant conglomerates common in food service means a lack of career-growth opportunities, which is exactly the same problem we face with small business.

Hot jobs in food service include: Chef, Restaurant Site Selector, Training Manager, Convention Services Manager, Front Office Manager, Food and Beverage Manager.

RETAIL

What do we do with our hard-earned money? Well, we spend most of it. Our growing disposable income in the decade ahead will buy us more luxury items, such as cars, compact disc players, large-screen television sets, and laptop computers. And with technology rapidly creating or improving the things that we need (how many apart from me are still buying vinyl records), retail stores will reap the benefits.

The industry is also being fed by the entrance of women into the workforce. Working people require the clothes, uniforms, and accessories of their trade, so apparel stores will therefore see some of the biggest growth in the industry. These same workers will also need reliable cars to get them to and from the office or wherever they work. Thus automotive dealers and service stations will also be among the fastest-growing segments of the industry.

A mature workforce has money to spend at specialty stores—for example, they buy furniture at Ethan Allen rather than Sears. Which is not to say that discounters such as Wal-Mart will be hurting for business; they're growing, with no end in sight.

Drugstores will also be a high-growth area of retail. An aging population will create on ongoing demand for new medicines—which we will see developed in the traditional way by pharmaceutical companies, and also possibly by the biotech industry in the years ahead.

We succeed only as we identify in life, or in war, or in anything else, a single overriding objective, and make all other considerations bend to that one objective.
—Dwight D. Eisenhower

Hot jobs in retail include: Merchandise Manager, Sales Associate, Manager of Mall Marketing, and Promotion.

TRAVEL

Employment of travel agents is expected to grow much faster than the average for all occupations through the year 2005. Many job openings will arise as new agencies open and existing agencies expand, but most will occur as experienced agents transfer to other occupations or leave the labor force.

Spending on travel is expected to increase significantly through the year 2005. As business activity expands, so will business-related travel. Employment of sales and marketing professionals, and others who travel extensively, is expected to experience continued growth. Also, with rising incomes, more people are expected to travel on vacation, and to do so more frequently than in the past. In fact, many people take more than one vacation a year.

Charter flights and larger, more efficient planes have brought air transportation within the budgets of more people. So has the easing of government regulation of air fares and routes, by fostering greater competition among airlines to offer better and more affordable service. In addition, American travel agents organize tours for a growing number of foreign visitors. Although most travel agencies now have automated reservation systems, this has not weakened demand for travel agents.

The travel industry is generally sensitive to economic downturns and political crises, when travel plans are likely to be deferred. Therefore the number of job opportunities fluctuates.

Travel agents held about 115,000 jobs in 1992 and are found in every part of the country. More than nine out of ten salaried agents worked for travel agencies; some worked for membership organizations. Many travel agents are self-employed, so it can also offer an interesting entrepreneurial segue. Nearly one-half of the travel agencies are in suburban areas; about 40 percent are in large cities; and the rest, in small towns and rural areas.

Hot jobs in the travel industry include: Secretary, Tour Guide, Airline Reservation Agent, Rental Car Agent, and Travel Counselor.

Cluster 2—Technology

It is technology that has changed our world and every job in it, and with the explosion of high-tech innovations we're seeing dramatic growth in the

To have a grievance is to have a purpose in life. —Eric Hoffer

biotechnology, computer, telecommunications, and environment industries. Companies that didn't even exist ten years ago—small, pioneering firms— are replacing Fortune 500 companies as the country's top employers.

Yet, while demand for skilled high-tech people is expected to increase by more than 5 percent annually (according to *Staffing Industry Report*), that doesn't necessarily translate into an abundance of jobs.[2] Start-up companies are often "lean and mean," and even the more established companies in such fledgling industries as environment and biotechnology are only just beginning to recruit on college campuses. Even when in full swing as mature companies, these organizations will never reach the size of industrial-era hierarchical conglomerates.

And there's something else to be wary of: Glamorous high-tech jobs aren't immune to automation and export. As we export our technological knowledge to other countries, we will face increased global competition for those jobs. United States companies may find cheaper labor—including engineers, researchers, physicists, and computer programmers—overseas.

However, if you're looking for a glamour job in a cutting-edge industry—and you're willing to acquire the skills, earn a modest starting salary, and intelligently protect your career foundation and market yourself appropriately—chances are you'll be able to carve a professional niche in high technology. You will also arguably have a front-row seat for any coming technology waves that will affect any or all of our professional careers in the future.

BIOTECHNOLOGY

The biotechnology industry, which recently reinvented the tomato by crossing it with a flounder, is a dream come true for clinical researchers, lab assistants, marketers, and a host of other science and engineering professionals. And as it revolutionizes agriculture, health care, and the environmental fields, the biotechnology industry will create new jobs at the rate of more than 10 percent annually.

Genetically engineered foods, medicines, and other products often enhance life, and sometimes are the only chance for saving it. Where would we be without the McGregor Flvr Svr Tm [sic] tomato, one of the latest genetically engineered products?

As I write this, the first genetically engineered tomato, thanks to McGregor's, has been cleared for public consumption. Genetically im-

---

Well done is better than well said. —*Benjamin Franklin*

proved to stay fresher longer, its economic impact can only be appreciated by walking down the tomato-products aisle in your local supermarket (the average supermarket has ten to thirty-five feet devoted to tomato products).

But high research costs, technical barriers, public resistance, and strict government regulations make it difficult—and sometimes impossible—to get a new product on the market. However, in the world of biotech, one new food or medicine is a global market, which means a big score for everyone involved.

And the sales of biotech products are rising dramatically. The United States leads the world in biotechnology research, especially in biomedicine, which comprises about half of the biotechnology industry. Studies are currently under way to develop biomedical vaccines and cures for deadly viruses—including AIDS—cancer, heart problems, Parkinson's disease, and a seemingly endless list of ailments.

The application of biotechnology to our environmental woes is another area that can only grow as we strive to save our planet for our heirs with new environmental regulations and increasing community activism. Bioremediation, an experimental system that uses microorganisms to clean hazardous wastes, looks promising. Patent owners, patent beaters, and smart marketers are going to clean up here. Biological substances that can replace pesticides, herbicides, and fungicides; break down fertilizer; diagnose environmental toxins; and reduce manufacturing pollution are also being developed.

Genetically engineered vegetables, milk, and other food products are beginning to arrive on supermarket shelves amid a great deal of fanfare—and suspicion. Whether or not we should so readily accept the new and improved foods, we are going to see agriculture and biotechnology reinvent each other—and who knows where that could lead? According to some experts, sales of biotech agricultural products could increase between 15 and 20 percent annually. However, all in all, biomedicine dominates, with most new biotech products coming from medicine and diagnostics. Agriculture is the next largest area, and environment comes last. Future sales in these latter nonmedical areas will ultimately depend on the public's acceptance or disapproval of genetically engineered environmental and food products.

In 1970 fewer than 150 people were employed in the biotechnology industry; by 2000 that figure should grow to between 35,000 and 40,000. That's tremendous growth—but then again, it's not very many jobs.

The beginning is the most important part of the work. —Plato

Chemists, physicists, and engineers who want to cross over into the biotech industry are especially welcome, as are doctors, nurses, physical therapists, pharmacists, and other health care professionals; they're needed to help with testing and evaluation. The biotech industry is still in its infancy, with most companies researching products that may not be on the market until well into the twenty-first century. As the industry matures and companies move from research to production, jobs requiring a background in business, patent law, manufacturing, or marketing will increasingly become available for core careerists. A little before this will come the opportunities for founders and stockholders, the recent entrepreneurs of today who will become the leaders of tomorrow.

Hot jobs in biotechnology include: Research Scientist, Biological Scientist, Biotech Salesperson, Computational Chemist, Molecular Biologist, Organic Chemist, Ecologist, Geneticist, Biochemist, Nuclear Medicine Technologist, and Protein Chemist.

COMPUTERS

Computers are everywhere, and they do just about everything—even Windows. But except for the notebook and laptop categories, and such up-and-coming products as CD-ROM and virtual reality, computer hardware is no longer where the industry is at. The focus now is on applied technology for the next decade. These include:

—Software-Related Professional Services
  • Custom programming
  • Integrated systems design

—Information Services
  • Creating information
  • Storing information
  • Manipulating information
  • Payroll
  • Credit reporting

—Hardware Services
  • Rental and leasing
  • Maintenance and repair opportunity

They conquer who believe they can. —John Dryden

Professions such as systems analysts, computer scientists, and operation re-search will see a great deal of growth. But the fastest-growing job in the computer industry—and the one that's getting the most media hype—is that of software developer. As companies use computers more and more, the job of developing appropriate software will continue to be challenging and reward-ing. Which means that those with the right background—a technology degree as foundation combined with practical project-management know-how—may be able to command a six-figure salary.

The industry employs people with a wide range of skills and education, and while size and location of a company often determine pay, the computer industry demands more skills and greater education—and consequently pays more—than other industries.

Work environments in the computer field also vary greatly. Consultants, salespeople, and programmers frequently work at their clients' job sites. Word processors and data-entry professionals, and others whose work can be done at a terminal, may telecommute from home. Computer companies range from gargantuan to small, with the typical computer firm having eighteen employees. The odds are you will work in an entrepreneurial start-up or growth company; expect spartan surroundings and gung-ho attitude. This is maybe not surprising given the fact that 75 percent of all computer-industry people are between twenty-five and forty-four years old.

Hot jobs in computers include: Software Developer, Computer Systems Analyst, Computer Programmer, Consultant, Information Services (I.S.) Manager, Network Administrator, Database Manager, Systems Integrator, Systems Management Specialist, Systems Analyst, Computer Consultant, Information Systems Analyst, Information-Systems Specialist, Computer and Peripheral Equipment Operator.

ENGINEERING

We're living in a technological culture, and we couldn't have technology without engineering. Engineers develop new technology, design software, and rebuild the infrastructure. They are the shapes of the future and the pioneers of our age.

Some engineering jobs are more flexible than others. Some engineers, including mechanical, electrical, electronics, chemical, civil, biomedical,

---

The oldest habit in the world for resisting change is to complain that unless the remedy to the disease should be universally applied, it should not be applied at all. But you must start somewhere. —Winston Churchill

computer software, and environmental, will pretty much be able to write their own tickets in the decade ahead. There is already a shortage of trained chemical engineers. The Bureau of Labor Statistics predicts 25 percent more openings for engineers by the year 2000, and 40 percent job growth for electrical and electronics engineers.

Engineers often reach the senior-management level. Those who do what is referred to as the *dirty work*—that is, clean up environmental disasters—command top pay. Environmental engineers who specialize in hazardous waste currently earn about 25 percent more than other engineers.

Hot jobs in engineering include: Civil Engineer, Computer Scientist, Electrical Engineer, Electronics Engineer, Chemical Engineer, Mechanical Engineer, Biomedical Engineer, Computer Software Engineer, and Environmental Engineer.

TELECOMMUNICATIONS

In the next decade telephone lines will become the new interstates, carrying sound, pictures, and data to anyone, anywhere.

The industry now provides such services as electronic mail; teleconferencing; enhanced facsimile services; voice message services; call forwarding, screening, and tracing; database access; managed network services; 800- and 900-number calling; WATS (wide area telephone service); credit card verification; privately leased lines; and electronic data interchange.

In particular cities and towns, which will become electronic off-ramps (because they will house the fiber-optic networks and have digital switching capabilities), high-wage telecommunications jobs may replace many of the lost manufacturing jobs. Wanted will be individuals who specialize in installing, upgrading, and marketing communication systems. Telecommunications professionals may be able to get on-the-job training, provided they have a background in math, engineering, or science.

Cellular telephones will also greatly contribute to the structure and volume of the market. Wireless specialists will be in demand to build the cellular networks that make portable telephones possible. The imminent advent of interactive TV will change television and retail in as yet unimaginable ways.

Hot jobs in telecommunications include: Corporate Communications Manager, Sales Representative, Systems Analyst, Regulatory Compliance Administrator, and Telecommunications Manager.

The only completely consistent people are the dead. —Aldous Huxley

ENVIRONMENT

Green is the color of a booming industry that includes hazardous-waste cleanup, solid-waste disposal, conservation, fishery and wildlife management, forestry, and recycling of everything from toxic waste to soda bottles.

The irrefutable facts about acid rain, ozone depletion, global warming, the greenhouse effect, lead poisoning, and other recently understood consequences of ill-considered industrial-era actions have led to public support of environmental reclamation and protection. This has led to environmental legislation, which, in turn, has yielded a whole new crop of hot jobs in both private industry and government, including prestigious, high-paying opportunities for civil and chemical engineers, air-quality specialists, recycling coordinators, environmental lawyers and accountants, toxicologists, wetlands ecologists, and industrial environmental managers.

The industry engages a high percentage of independent consultants rather than employees, perhaps reflective of its birth as an industry on the cusp of a new era, which means opportunities in start-up and growth companies, and on-the-job-training for your entrepreneurial career.

Hot jobs in environment include: Environmental Manager, Environmental Engineer, Ecotourism, Environmental Law, Public Relations Professional (for energy companies and other firms that impact on the ecology), Waste Management Expert, Environmental Scientist Specialist/Ecopreneur, Green Marketing Manager, Ecological Scientist/Biologist/Earth Scientist, Fund-raiser, Environmental Lawyer, Environmental Educator and Communicator, Recreation Wildlife and Natural Resource Manager, Geographical Information Systems Specialist, Toxicologist, Air-Quality Specialist, Recycling Coordinator, and Environmental Specialist.

Cluster 3—Global Industries

For those who are willing to travel, learn new languages, and drink bottled water for months at a time, there's a whole new world of opportunity. Manufacturing and trade are now global industries.

Most companies in manufacturing and trade say they are operating in a global marketplace—some because it's true and others because it's convenient. Soon all business entities must learn to adapt to the needs of customers around the world in order to prosper. In the future that is now,

The gods help them that help themselves. —Aesop

the customer, the competitor, and the colleagues—the three C's of global competition—can be located anywhere in the world.

MANUFACTURING AND TRADE

The technological age is making possible everything from CD-ROM to high-definition television sets. It's up to manufacturers to produce the latest machines, medicines, and gadgets. If you want to work in the goods-producing sector, then your task will be to find the companies that are producing the right goods. For example, you probably don't want to work in a plant that manufactures typewriter ribbons, because no one uses them anymore and the companies that make them will be closing down. In the technological age there is a whole world of new products that are being developed, manufactured, and traded, and these are the kind of areas you should look at.

Some experts say that by the late 1990s manufacturers will generate 26 percent of the gross national product. Health care, computers, electronics, chemicals, and printing and publishing industries that serve a global market will spur most of the growth. No matter what, we will *always* need stuff, and when we get too much stuff, we will throw it out and upgrade it, and do it all over again. There will always be jobs in manufacturing. Unfortunately the odds of their appearing in your town are shrinking. R.P.S. jobs can, by their very nature, be located wherever the lowest manufacturing dollar lives.

Technological developments will also result in job loss; if you're not working with a computer, it's very likely you'll be replaced by one.

The global marketplace has rejuvenated manufacturing at the same time as it has devastated some manufacturing industries—for instance, the steel business. But minimills are helping to revitalize the domestic steel industry by bringing steel closer to the customers, and the jobs to different areas of the country.

The future of foreign trade and import-export businesses looks promising. In general, smaller and highly adaptable companies will be in the best position to take advantage of global opportunities, adapt to the changing marketplace, and add value for their customers. Manufacturing companies will be concentrated in the south and the west of the country, because these areas are growing and offering the lowest overhead for business.

Man is what he believes. —Anton Chekhov

Hot jobs in manufacturing include: Information Officer, Quality Control, Manufacturing Engineer, and Statistical Control Specialist.

Cluster 4—Public Service

Federal, state, and local government, the defense department, social services, and nonprofit organizations are the machinery that makes the country run. And that is likely to remain the status quo, even with the end of the cold war and cuts in government spending.

Whatever the economy, there will *always* be a need for public programs and services. The government, as the nation's largest employer, hires people of every occupation. And as an added bonus, public-service jobs usually provide better benefits and more job security than the private sector.

FEDERAL GOVERNMENT AND DEFENSE

Join the navy (or the army, Marine Corps, air force, or Coast Guard) as either a civilian or a uniformed member of the armed forces, and you'll be working for the largest employer in the country: the federal government. More than half of all federal-government employees work for the Department of Defense. Despite cutbacks in defense, you will most likely be able to count on steady employment, good pay, great benefits, challenging assignments, and opportunities to increase your skills and education.

There is also a wide range of fields beyond the armed forces that are defense-related. These include manufacturing of aircraft, missiles, ships, and so on; personnel-supply services; public relations; retail and wholesale trade; and transportation. Generally the higher your level of education and skills, the safer your defense-related job will be in all of these areas. (Symbonalysts score again!)

Other federal-government career opportunities exist in the United States Postal Service and the three government branches:

—The Legislative Branch
- General Accounting Office
- Government Printing Office
- Library of Congress
- Congressional Budget Office

He who considers too much will perform little. —Johann Von Schiller

—The Judicial Branch
  • Supreme Court
  • Court of Appeals
  • State district courts
  • Special courts, such as the Court of Military Appeals

—The Executive Branch
  • Offices and councils that surround the president of the United States, such as the Office of Management and Budget and the National Security Council

Hot jobs in the federal government and defense include: Technician; Repairer; Communications and Intelligence Specialist; officers in administrative, medical and dental specialities; Aircraft Pilot; and Infantry Officer.

STATE AND LOCAL GOVERNMENT

Most public-sector employees work for either their state or their local government. Along with public education, hospitals, and social services, this industry includes transportation, courts, police and fire departments, and the local political machine that exists in every community throughout our country.

Inspectors and compliance officers, correction officers, sheriffs, mayors, and subway operators are just some of the people on the public payroll. Even with budget cuts, states will always need competent people to run them—as will county, municipal, township, school district, and special district governments.

Hot jobs in state and local government include: Government Chief Executive and Legislator; Tax Examiner; Urban and Regional Planner; Judge, Magistrate, and other judicial workers; Police Officer; Firefighter; and Waste Water Treatment Plant Operator.

SOCIAL SERVICES

In the age of machines and computers it's nice to know that people need people more than ever. Social welfare service aides, human services people, and social workers will be some of the most sought-after professionals in the country during the next decade.

Most other social services workers are government employees who provide either at-home or residential care for individuals and families. They

Whatever is worth doing at all is worth doing well. —Lord Chesterfield

also offer counseling, crisis intervention, rehabilitation, and vocational training. Although on average these workers earn less than they might in other industries, social services is projected to be one of the fastest-growing industries. Job opportunities in social services will increase in proportion to the number of elderly, children, mentally ill, disabled, and others who need care or assistance. The major dislocation of our society as we retool for the new world will guarantee growth in these occupational areas.

Some social services agencies focus on welfare relief, such as food stamps and rent assistance, or on protecting children. Others provide meals, household chores, or companionship to the elderly. Still others care for recovering alcoholics and drug addicts.

And along with the federal and state government, the private sector also provides job opportunities for social services workers. These private-sector jobs closely parallel those available from the government. In addition many social service professionals are self-employed, and they typically provide job training or vocational rehabilitation. Some are even volunteers. With an exceptionally high turnover and burnout rate, jobs in the industry open up even more quickly than new ones are created.

Preschool teachers and other child-care providers will be in great demand. Not only will working parents, especially dual-income families and single parents, need care for their infants, preschoolers, and kindergartners, but they will also need before- and after-school care for their older children. Both government and corporations will be called on to contribute an increasing amount of child-care funding as part of the cost of doing business.

While child-care positions should be relatively easy to find, the jobs can be physically and emotionally taxing, because they involve bending, lifting, cleaning, providing discipline, and so on. Turnover is high, and the pay is low, and that's unlikely to change in the near future. But the opportunity for employment—and self-employment—is unparalleled in any other industry.

Hot jobs in social services include: Social Worker, Human Services Worker, Adult Education Teacher, Counselor, and Social Welfare Service Aide.

NONPROFIT ORGANIZATIONS

Nonprofit organizations range from consumer groups through professional associations to museums. Ironically, as budgets are cut, the need for

The soul ever yearns to be doing something. —Cicero

committed Symbonalysts—particularly those who are adept at fund-raising and project management—increases.

Some employers come to nonprofits from other industries after layoffs or after retiring from the corporate rat race. Others choose nonprofit companies because the work is personally meaningful to them.

Hot jobs in nonprofit organizations include: Member Services Director, Fund-Raising/Planned-Giving Manager, and Sales/Marketing/Public Relations Manager.

Jobs That Cross Industry Lines

Occupational biomes that cross industry lines are arguably the most prudent play for people who are planning their careers today, or retooling them for tomorrow. In a horizontal occupational biome it is often easier to move from industry to industry. Hot horizontal occupational biomes include sales/marketing, public relations, accounting, and engineering. Maximum career buoyancy with horizontal occupational biomes is gained by routing your career—say, accounting—in a healthy industrial biome— perhaps health care—and then carefully pursuing your core career.

The buoyancy comes because not only can you move *within*, say, the health care industry, but you can also move in and out of *any other industrial biome.* I am not recommending biome surfing here, but improving your professional flexibility.

SALES/MARKETING

There will always be opportunities for people who can sell, especially in the biomes we mention as hot. Selling is one of the three ways (the other two are saving money and saving time) to affect a company's bottom line. And even in slow economic times, sales and marketing go on—in fact, they become more critical than ever. As we face tougher global competition, competition for customers will escalate. This will create even more jobs for salespeople and marketers. And as more overseas markets are opened, the need for entrepreneurial international sales and marketing people will grow.

Although specialized education and training are not necessary for success, perseverance and emotional security are. The field has its drawbacks: long days, evening work, and frequent rejection. Some jobs have a great

---

Men must be decided on what they will not *do, and then they are able to act with vigor in what they ought to do. —Mencius*

deal of travel, others have a great deal of telephone work, and many have both. Almost all sales jobs are productivity- and therefore commission-based, a drawback for some.

Sales is a wonderful way to break into a field, so if you are moving from a dying industry, sales is a very practical entree into another field.

I have noticed over twenty years of observing the sales profession that most successful people use it as a stepping-stone to other areas of endeavor within a company, or industrial biome, or other entrepreneurial endeavor.

When you strip it of all its posturing and doublespeak, all business comes down to one simple basic building block: Someone sells something to someone else. Consequently the opportunity to understand and apply the sophisticated communication skills required in sales is a skill few truly buoyant professionals can afford to be without.

I have spent time in sales myself. It didn't come naturally to me, but I learned my lessons and have managed to keep my head above water ever since. Everything I ever really needed to know about cash flow I learned as a salesperson. The skills used in sales will firmly underlie your entrepreneurial- and dream-career success.

In fact there is only one other thing as good for your entrepreneurial- and dream-career foundations, and that's accounting. The man or woman who can develop foundations in sales or accounting can achieve his or her destiny.

Hot jobs in sales/marketing include: Industrial and Technical Sales (particularly pharmaceutical and medical equipment sales) and Service Sales Representative.

ACCOUNTING

In business all that really matters is the bottom line, and that is the accountant's jurisdiction. C.P.A.'s and accountants are not only good professional bets to ride out economic downturns and provide an entree to the irreducible core, but accountants will also have plenty of opportunities to provide accounting services to entrepreneurs.

Profit-and-loss statements may not sound glamorous, but accountants—who have also studied languages, international management, tax law, financial planning, and so on—can launch careers in international accounting, tax accounting, auditing, forensic accounting, environmental accounting, and the like.

Whatsoever thy hand findeth to do, do it with thy might. —Ecclesiastes 9:10

Openings for accountants and actuaries will increase dramatically over the next decade, perhaps by more than 20 percent. Earning potential for accountants should skyrocket.

Hot jobs in accounting include: International Accounting, Tax Accounting, Auditing (both financial and operations), Environmental Accountant, Forensic Accountant, and International Tax and Audit Accounting.

PUBLIC RELATIONS

In a world where selling something to someone is at the heart of every business endeavor, image is everything. Public relations specialists work with health care, law, accounting, engineering, consulting, publishing, and many other types of firms to garner the right kind of print- and broadcast-media exposure.

Public relations employs selling and marketing skills; public relations specialists and writers essentially sell editors, reporters, and producers on the idea of writing or producing stories that feature their clients' companies, personnel, and products. And entrepreneurs in the field naturally must be able to sell potential clients on using their P.R. services. Like other salespeople and marketers, public relations professionals have to be resilient enough to handle frequent rejections.

Because public relations professionals work closely with the media, knowledge of the communications industry is a plus. And public relations is a great outlet for the talents of those with a background in television or radio production, broadcast or print journalism, who are temporarily unable to find a job in the media field. Not only does public relations open up additional job possibilities for them, but it also provides ample opportunities to network with media professionals—and it offers communications-related work experience.

Public relations employees may work as research or account assistants, and later advance to positions as account executives or supervisors. And many experienced P.R. specialists eventually start their own firms. The start-up capital for a public relations business is minimal—all that's required is a telephone, a computer, and media-contact lists.

Hot jobs in public relations include: Public Relations Specialist, and Publicity Writer.

What's the difference between a stumbling block and a stepping-stone? The way you approach it. —Anonymous

FOUR GOALS IN THE NEW WORLD OF WORK

"What does the new world of work look like?" I asked at the beginning of this chapter. Well, it is obviously in a state of flux, with an enormous amount of opportunity for the career savvy. Jobs today are not lifelong appointments, just as "finding and doing what you love" no longer guarantees a stable career, even in these most healthy and hospitable biomes we have discussed.

The only job security that exists now, or will exist in your future, is that which you create for yourself as you develop different approaches to encourage security in your core career. Here are four such approaches, set forth for you as goals. Their pursuit will add to the weave of your work-life buoyancy web.

1. Establish a job base in a healthy industrial biome.

2. Develop subject-matter expertise and symbolic-analytical skills to take you to the irreducible core of that biome.

3. Develop subject-matter expertise in an area that provides maximum horizontal movement from biome to biome, and cluster to cluster.

4. Establish empowerment webs in each of these areas.

Now that we have examined the drastic changes taking place all around us, I want to move on and examine the subsequent changes in approach we each must make inside our head.

NOTES

1. We had heard that some offenders were overcharging clients by as much as 60 percent. But this seems so far below the actual number that we have a hard time believing it.

2. *Staffing Industry Report,* September 1994, p. 4.

Our greatest glory is not in never falling but in rising every time we fall. —Confucius

Chapter 5

Making Changes in Your Head: Successful Core Career Behaviors for the New World of Work

Everyone has to work smart to achieve the good life; if you don't work smart, you still have to work just as hard, only for less money. So when it comes down to it, there really isn't much of a choice at all, is there? It's work smart or work dumb.

But what is working smart in the New Workplace? Yes, it's knowing where the hot jobs are in the healthy industries, and it's understanding that even hot jobs in healthy industries aren't that safe in the modern work world. But you gotta be street smart too, so that you understand how employers are reinventing themselves and recognize that those workers identified in some way as Symbolic Analysts (or Knowledge Workers) are likely to be the best paid, with the best futures, in the most secure of work environments. So whatever your profession, you have to understand the need to become and to be known as someone with good symbolic-analytical skills.

Ah, but there's the rub; what is it that makes up "good symbolic analytical skills"?

In identifying the Symbolic Analyst as the *strength of all modern nations,* Robert Reich and others gave us a snapshot of the successful modern professional. In this chapter we will look farther into the behavioral makeup of such people, and the behaviors which make some careers more buoyant in rough weather than others.

Alis volat propriis—he flies with his own wings. —Anonymous

HOW WE FOUND THE BEHAVIORS

We examined everything we could find about survival in the urban world. We read the professional literature, browsed the stacks, perused the CD-ROMs, and mined the on-line databases like Compuserve, the Net, and Lexis/Nexus. We conducted interviews with successful core, dream, and entrepreneurial careerists, and came up with hundreds of traits and behaviors relevant to career success. It was a huge list, which we would proceed to whittle down, by keeping only the behaviors common to success in all three parallel careers.

We then contacted over a thousand buoyant core careerists. We then asked them to tell us, in their own words, what makes someone buoyant in his or her own field, and rated the key behaviors that our research suggested might be important to buoyancy. A pattern in the replies of the core careerists began to emerge that clearly reflected a modern core-career professional far different from his predecessor.

A NEW APPROACH FOR A NEW WORLD

Earlier in the book I shared with you how formidable workplace thinkers such as Robert Reich have recategorized the divisions of labor into just three jobs: (a) In-Person Services; (b) Routine Production Services; and (c) Symbolic Analysts. It was clear that of these three major groups of workers, only the Symbolic Analysts stood any chance of breaking through to their American Dream. So in analyzing only those who are buoyant in the midst of this maelstrom of change, I felt that we would be getting a truly objective look at what it was that constituted a core-career Symbolic Analyst. We finally came up with eight specific behaviors that all the successfully buoyant *core* careerists and their colleagues seemed to share.

1. Goal Orientation: Working hard to achieve your goals
   She knows what she wants and does what it takes to get it.

2. Positive Expectancy: Believing in your ability to overcome, and ultimately to succeed
   He is the master of his destiny and believes in his own abilities.

3. Inner Openness: Emotional flexibility
   He is self-aware and open to divergence and complexity.

He only is a well-made man who has a good determination. —Ralph Waldo Emerson

4. Personal Influence: Communication with a purpose
   He is a natural salesperson.

5. Organized Action: Coordinated action efficiently focused on a specific outcome
   She takes the initiative toward her objective.

6. Informed Risk: Flexible planning to decrease risk in a constantly changing environment
   He looks before he leaps, but he still leaps when he needs to.

7. Flexible Thinking: Creative adaptability in different contexts
   She is an innovator and an effective problem solver.

8. Smart Decisions: Effective decision making
   She knows how to evaluate her options and makes great decisions.

Let me now show you how each of these key traits is critical to your *core*-career buoyancy. I'll tell you more about the trait and show you how some core-buoyant people use these traits. You'll come to see that the interaction, or connectivity, between the critical eight behaviors is as important to your career buoyancy as the behaviors themselves.

Goal Orientation

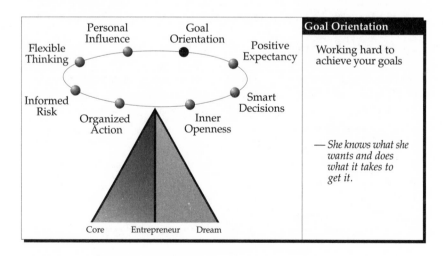

Let us do nothing abjectly, nothing timidly, nothing sluggishly. —Cicero

You're driving in a new area, unsure of where you are. You forgot to get the address, and you have only a vague sense of where you need to get to. But you do know that you're late, so you speed up. After a while you realize that you are probably heading in the wrong direction, so you take another road, driving faster and faster since you are becoming later and later for your appointment. Oops, wrong again! It's not a lot of fun, is it? Hard work alone will not help you achieve career buoyancy; in fact it could take you even farther away from it. You have to have a destination, a goal in mind, and you have to know how to get there first.

Goal Orientation combines your destination, your personal vision of your career, with the drive and determination to achieve it. Goal Orientation is essential to your buoyancy. Without goal orientation you aren't going anywhere.

Goal Orientation isn't about working your butt off for no reason. It starts with knowing where you want to go with your career. It starts with your vision of security, freedom, and happiness. With a destination firmly in mind, do you now have the willpower and the determination to slog through the muck to achieve your vision? That's what Goal Orientation is all about: having a career vision that offers a practical means of fulfillment for your needs and the drive to achieve it.

It doesn't mean that you don't need to put in long days. It *is* going to take determination and drive to become, and stay, buoyant. But your career energy needs to be guided by your personal vision, toward your personal career goals.

On the job with . . . Goal Orientation

She knows what she wants and does what it takes to get it.

A strong Goal Orientation directs our activities and pushes us to achieve.

Rita is focused. I could tell from the tone of her voice, which had a sense of purpose and urgency to it, just how driven she was. Rita had undertaken a mammoth restructuring of her company's selection procedures. She loved this assignment, and both peers and upper management loved the results. As she told me, "I know I may eventually actually lose my job as the company shrinks even further. But I'm not that concerned. Not only did this assignment conclude successfully, but I gained many new skills and updated old ones by doing it. Now I have world-class skills and experience. I am extremely employable."

A decision is the action an executive must take when he has information so incomplete that the answer does not suggest itself. —Arthur W. Radford

Goal Orientation interacts with:

Positive Expectancy

You've heard them before. You know who I'm talking about, and you know what they're going to tell you: "It's just not worth it" or "It'll never work" or the definitive "Why bother?" Sound familiar?

If you know that the situation is hopeless, then these pundits are right: don't bother. But if you believe in the goal, if you have faith that you will succeed, if not now, then at some point, you *will* bother. In fact, you will bother quite a lot. Your Goal Orientation is fired up by a feeling that you will achieve your goal, that it is within your means to succeed. That feeling, that confidence, is your Positive Expectancy pushing and pulling you toward your goals.

Just when your fire appears to be going out, Positive Expectancy is a breeze you can use to fan the flames into a roaring blaze of energy and motivation.

Positive Expectancy

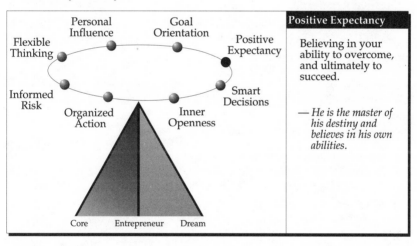

Positive Expectancy is an attitude. It takes criticism and turns it into productive feedback. Positive Expectancy tells you that you will find a way, that you will succeed. Positive Expectancy is *persistence*; it allows you to keep going, even after setbacks. Everything you do that is worth doing has obstacles and

The past is a foreign country; they do things differently there. —Lesley Poles Hartley

setbacks. It may be one step forward and two steps back one day. You will look for support and find none, test your ideas out and have them fail; but if you give up, you go down. You need to expect to succeed, and when you don't, you *have* to bounce back and try, try again. Positive Expectancy analyzes the results and, having made appropriate changes, screams, "Charge! Once more into the breach." Positive Expectancy is the understanding that success can only come as a result of experience, and that all experiences, good and bad, have the power to increase the odds of your ultimate success.

Positive Expectancy allows you to

- Keep going when the going gets tough
- Take credit for your successes
- Take responsibility for your setbacks, and channel your new understanding
- Feel you have free choice and free will
- Become more self-confident
- Leverage changing circumstances to your advantage[1]

Positive Expectancy isn't wearing rose-colored glasses. It doesn't mean you walk around feeling invincible. Positive Expectancy just tips the odds in your favor. You feel that you will succeed, and so you act like a winner, like a career-buoyant person.

On the job with . . . Positive Expectancy

He is the master of his destiny and believes in his own abilities.

James seems always to find a lesson in every storm cloud. He worked on one client meeting for six months and finally managed to get it set up with the division VP. James expects success, and used all of the noes of the last six months to learn how to get the yesses. "No, not in the morning." "No, I don't think that's the future of this company." He takes it all in, and comes back for more.

Other people would have crumbled after the first attempt, or after the third month. But by turning failure into productive feedback, James modified his style and kept chasing his goal. He knew he'd encounter some bumps along the way, but James never doubted that ultimately he would succeed.

If a thing is worth having, it's worth fighting for. —Anonymous

Positive Expectancy interacts with:

Inner Openness

You will sink like a stone unless you stay open to change, unless you listen to life's constant feedback. Inner Openness allows you to channel feedback. Instead of lying down and dying when someone tells you that your presentation at the conference was lousy, Inner Openness and Positive Expectancy interact to turn setbacks into feedback. You alter your presentation, and next time—or twenty times from now—you succeed. You will always succeed when Inner Openness and Positive Expectancy work together.

Inner Openness

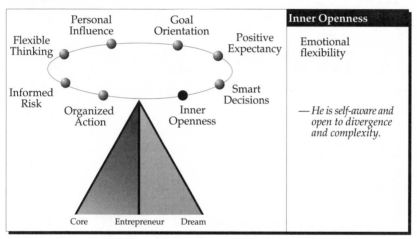

Inner Openness is an attitude of learning, an approach to life that realizes you don't always have all the answers and that you must be open to any input that will improve your understanding.

To be open means that you consider alternative ideas, listen to people, and are aware of your own strengths and weaknesses. Inner Openness lets you handle the complexity of your work life by:

- Getting along with others
- Being aware of personal strengths and weaknesses

An American believes more than anything else in the last four letters of that title: I can. —Anonymous

- Asking for and accepting feedback
- Listening and hearing.

On the job with . . . Inner Openness

He is self-aware and open to divergence and complexity.

Dave is not perfect. He messes up. But when he does, people usually tell him about it. They've learned that when they go to Dave with advice, complaints, and feedback, he listens to them. As one co-worker said, "He doesn't just nod his head up and down, smiling, and not really taking it in like so many people. At times he can get defensive, but then he comes back to me later and thanks me for the suggestion—even when the suggestion is really a major complaint. And he doesn't get mad, he doesn't get even. He just adapts his style next time, if he agrees with me. If he doesn't, he tells me so, and he tells me why. I really respect this guy."

Inner Openness doesn't mean you are just doing as you're told. It means you are open to feedback. With Inner Openness on your side you actually have a team—everyone you work with—helping you to achieve buoyancy in your core career.

 Inner Openness interacts with:

Organized Action

Marie came from the poorer part of town, and at eighteen she was helping support her parents as she started a family of her own. Marie didn't have a good education; she couldn't read or write too well, and she could never land a job paying much more than minimum wage. Marie had the courage to look at her deficiencies, at her lack of an education, and realize she had to backtrack to get some basic skills up to par. So she developed a plan. She got a job in a factory that helped workers with their education, got her high school equivalency diploma, and then her A.A. degree. She improved her jobs within the company as she progressed in her education. Today, thanks to her Inner Openness and an Organized Action plan, she's the office manager for the personnel department.

The man who knows when not to act is wise. To my mind, bravery is forethought.
—Euripides

There are no right and wrong answers anymore. Throughout *Beat the Odds*, I am asking you to reevaluate your ideas of what a career is all about. I am asking you to get away from either-or thinking which artificially limits your options. This is what Inner Openness is all about, and why it is so critical to your core-career buoyancy.

But Inner Openness is more than looking *inside* you. It allows you to look *around* you as well and to open yourself up to the many opportunities in the new world of work. Inner Openness opens you to other people, provides you with the skills to work well with others, and allows you to include others in your fifty-year work life. Without Inner Openness, you will miss out on countless opportunities for achieving security, freedom, and happiness through personal and interpersonal experiences.

Personal Influence

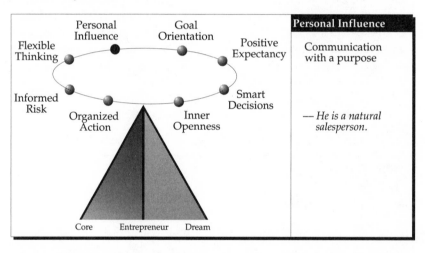

A great idea? Sure that your plan or approach is just what the doctor ordered for your company? Okay, that's terrific, but what are you going to do with that idea? If you can't get the rest of the team, or management, to accept it, then it isn't going to help matters any. Personal Influence is being able to give someone a message with a lot of meaning. Personal Influence is communication with a purpose. It is communication where you adapt your style so that the audience hears you. You use their language and understand their needs so you get the point across.

No man knows what he can do till he tries. —Publius Syrus

Personal Influence is the way you speak and the way you listen; it's the way you dress and the language of your body; it's technological adaptedness and how well you get along with other people. Personal Influence is all the ways you give expression to your wishes and sway other people to your cause.

Personal Influence is person-to-person communication, whether you have an audience of one or one thousand. Personal Influence is still personal, whether you are communicating in a face-to-face meeting or on the Internet. Technology has actually *increased* the need for Personal Influence in your core career, as you now have to communicate your passion and your meaning using new and perhaps alien media.

On the job with . . . Personal Influence

He is a natural salesperson. He seems to really connect with people, no matter who they are.

Peter is a super salesman, but he's not even *in* sales. Peter is an accountant with a midsize service business. Yet he is convincing, he communicates, he persuades. Peter is a team member as well as a team leader who is able to gain consensus from his group so that they devise and implement solid recommendations. How does he do it? "I talk to people, I talk to everybody. Not that I'm doing all the talking, you see. I listen. I listen to what they say, how they say it, and sometimes to what they *don't* say. Once I understand everyone's opinion, I can usually achieve consensus."

Peter is demonstrating Personal Influence—the ability to communicate with a purpose.

 Personal Influence interacts with:

Inner Openness

A sales professional has a chance at a management job; it's something he has been working toward for years. His powerful Personal Influence skills have made him the top salesperson for three of the last five years, and as two less productive colleagues have already received promotions, he feels the job is in the bag. However, the management job requires a number of skill sets he's never heard of, including planning and organization. The sales pro comes in second, but because he has worked on his Inner Openness skills, he listens and *learns* where management feels he is lacking. Next time, and there is always a next time, his Personal Influence is going to be supported by strong Organized Action skills too.

Absolute truth is incompatible with an advanced state of society.
—*Joaquim Maria Machado de Assis*

Organized Action

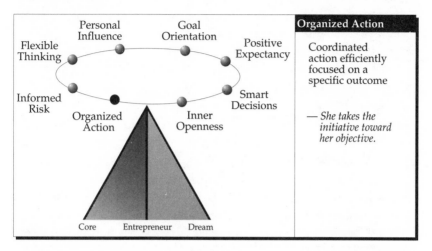

When you interview for a job, or talk about your work, you typically speak of your accomplishments—what you have done, what you can do. That's because all jobs require people to do things, to accomplish something. Getting things done is the lifeblood of every business, of every organization, and even of every human being.

You probably recognize people with Organized Action skills in your company. Isn't there someone you know with a reputation for getting things done? Someone who doesn't waste time or resources, who gets to the point and has a coherent plan of action to achieve the desired goal? That's Organized Action, and when you see it, you realize why it's so very important to you and to employers. Organized Action is how you get where you want to go.

On the job with . . . Organized Action

She takes the initiative toward her objective.

Susan knows how to get things done, and everyone knows it. She's always being asked to take on new responsibilities, to head up task forces, to transfer to other divisions. Susan is sociable and pleasant, but when she has something to complete, her office door is closed. She gets to the point very quickly when she's on the phone and doesn't waste much time. As a product development manager, her major devel-

---

I always do the first line well, but I have trouble with the others. —Molière

opment efforts have been on time—in a company where that is in short supply. "It's really a pleasure to watch her work," said one colleague. "She accomplishes more in a day than her peers sometimes do in a week." That's Organized Action—at work.

Organized Action interacts with:

Flexible Thinking

Organized Action, informed by your Flexible Thinking, helps you develop innovative plans, efficient methods, and new ways of looking at problems and their solutions.

The creativity of Flexible Thinking can suggest ways to make your actions more effective. You look for commonalities in the problems you face. You can generate methods that take less time and are more effective. Your Organized Action puts the raw input of Flexible Thinking into practical means of expression. And the result is—results!

Informed Risk

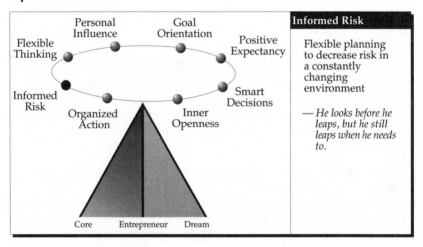

Used to be that you could live out your career in a big corporation so long as you didn't rock the boat. But the world has changed, and corporations can't do business the old way anymore. In the new world of work, where

One often contradicts an opinion when it is really only the tone in which it has been presented that is unsympathetic. —*Wilhelm Friedrich Nietzsche*

change is constant and nothing is certain, every business takes risks; consequently corporate America is desperate for people who can project some kind of order onto the anticipated but unknown future.

Informed Risk is a risk where you have considered the options, know your stuff, and stand ready to alter your direction as the situation changes. Informed Risk does not mean that you empty your piggy bank and buy lotto tickets—that's a bad risk. Informed Risk is action taken in the light of all probable outcomes, and in the awareness of all possibilities. Informed Risk allows you to be the innovator who is a catalyst of change.

Informed Risk is also understanding when the odds are against you, unlike the officers I read about in a history book about the Charge of the Light Brigade. These six hundred brave, daring soldiers rushed to certain death and destruction because their officers lacked the most elementary Informed Risk skills. They were forced by a bizarre sense of duty and honor to sacrifice their lives, not for a noble cause, not to save the lives of others, but because those in command lacked the ability to assess the risk and decide *not* to take that course of action. That is a powerful picture of *un*informed risk. Flexible planning in the light of Practical Know-how is key to your core-career buoyancy.

On the job with . . . Informed Risk

He looks before he leaps, but he still leaps when he needs to.

Ben is a navy pilot, or at least he was before working in the electronics industry. But you can hear the pilot as he describes his approach to his current work: "You have to rehearse in your mind emergency procedures so that when an emergency happens, you don't have to sit down and think about them, you just execute them. You always have to have a plan. If you have engine failure on takeoff, you have to know in your mind what you're going to do if it happens. It's the same here at work. I'm doing these enormously complicated projects, and if I'm going to meet my deadlines, it is absolutely critical to take chances, but at the same time to minimize my risks." Ben has thought about his options *before* the stuff hits the fan. He's already stacked the odds in his favor because Ben realizes risk is a fact of modern work life and consequently does everything he can to reduce and control that risk.

I do not believe in a fate that falls on men however they act; but I do believe in a fate that falls on them unless they act. —G. K. Chesterton

Informed Risk interacts with:

Smart Decisions

So, you took an Informed Risk and proposed an innovative and daring plan, one that challenges the status quo. Everything goes fine until you hit an unexpected setback. You watch as the world starts to crumble around you. But not for long. You are able to respond quickly to this near disaster. Since you studied the situation carefully and applied your Informed Risk to it before you implemented Plan A, you have contingency plans ready. You're flexible and open: You're not going to go down with this ship!

But implementing the new plan calls for some quick decisions. Not a snap decision you pull out of thin air, but a really Smart Decision, which is based upon your practical business know-how and experience. You check out available alternatives, add them to what you already know, and decide to jump to Plan X, a mixture of several backup plans.

The daring of Informed Risk sometimes doesn't immediately result in success, but by standing ready with the savvy decisiveness of Smart Decisions you increase the odds in your favor.

Flexible Thinking

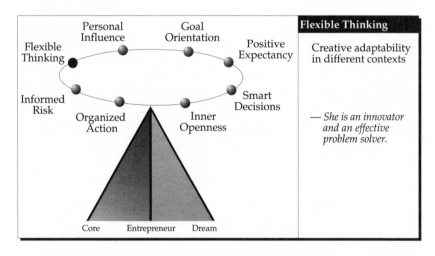

A man's to know his limitations. —Dirty Harry

Flexible Thinking is smart people connecting the dots. It is recognizing that a problem exists, identifying the root causes, and then generating multiple solutions. If you have developed your Flexible Thinking abilities, you are inquisitive and curious, eager to tackle a challenging problem and develop unique solutions. You love to learn new things, to explore and to create.

Flexible Thinking is curiosity and a love of learning. You realize that the world, and you, are changing rapidly. When you use your Flexible Thinking skills, you realize that the only way to stay buoyant is to stay current.

Perhaps most important, Flexible Thinking is your ability to solve problems *creatively*. Flexible problem-solving skills are at the root of what gets Knowledge Workers the rewards they do. Find a problem, understand how it is currently being addressed, and then find a new solution. Flexible Thinking is key to everything you do. Whether you apply it to your career planning or to your entire work life, developed Flexible Thinking skills will show you career pathways where once you saw only the thicket.

On the job with . . . Flexible Thinking

She is an innovator and an effective problem solver.

As the company's head of quality, Mary was given a daunting challenge: Find out why they were suddenly getting so many returns of defective merchandise. It was an enormous problem because it involved every aspect of the product, from the basic design through materials procurement, assembly, testing, packaging, sales, and customer operation and instructions.

Not only did Mary pull together multidisciplinary teams to tackle the job, but she immersed herself in every aspect of the product-development cycle. She built a few on the line; she called on customers; she went to her local electronics store and bought some of the merchandise. She even brought the products home, and installed and used them.

Using these different approaches allowed Mary and the team to identify several major problems. They came up with a short-term fix, which they implemented immediately, while another group started on the long-term solution. Her creative approach to identifying the problem, and solving it at several levels, produced a winning product.

The only difference between a rut and a grave is their dimensions. —Ellen Glasgow

Flexible Thinking interacts with:

Informed Risk

If you play the odds, you better understand the game. Informed Risk is based upon information, your analysis of existing alternatives, and the development of new options to pursue.

Where do you get these options and alternatives? How do you develop the ideas? Flexible Thinking can help you generate and discover exciting new plans and evaluate the environment so that you successfully place your bets. Flexible Thinking can make all of your risks informed ones.

Smart Decisions

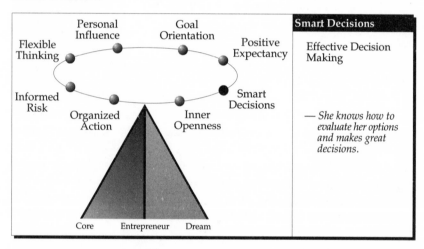

Smart Decisions combines your practical know-how with the confidence in your ability and judgment. Being decisive, making Smart Decisions, is the result.

Modern professionals, like corporations, *have* to be decisive. In a study of successful business executives, a team of researchers found that the successful ones were much less reluctant to make decisions in the absence of new information.[2] These executives didn't wait for all the data to be in before

We are both great men, but I have succeeded better in keeping it a profound secret than he has. —Bill Nye

they started to develop possible solutions. As the information became available, they would adapt their conclusions to embrace the new information. These buoyant people have recognized that all the information is *never* going to be in, no matter how long you wait, and it's best to start making decisions *now*. Buoyant careerists know that nothing moves forward without a decision being made, and decision making doesn't bother them.

All eight buoyancy behaviors interact with each other, but none more clearly than Smart Decisions. You could even define Smart Decisions as the result of the other seven behaviors interacting effectively:

> *Goal Orientations*
> *Inner Openness*
> *Flexible Thinking*
> *Personal Influence*   = *Smart Decisions*
> *Informed Risk*
> *Organized Action*
> *Positive Expectancy*

Smart Decisions then starts another cycle, because nothing happens after a Smart Decision until you take Organized Action. And then, like Washington crossing the Delaware, you are forging ahead while your competition sleeps. You are making Smart Decisions, moving ahead with your plans. Crossing the Delaware, you are getting closer to your goal. You see into your competitor's camp and understand what they are up to; it's not the first time you have engaged this particular enemy. You have plenty of practical experience, you know all about them. So, when the decisions you make are founded on real-world experience, because they are logical, practical, and have accounted for all the options, they are invariably Smart Decisions.

On the job with . . . Smart Decisions

She knows how to evaluate her options and makes great decisions.

Judy is a decision maker—you know, the kind of person who doesn't sit around and wait forever to make up her mind. She realizes that information has a certain shelf life and that decisiveness is critical to the success of her company.

Nothing great will ever be achieved without great men, and men are great only if they are determined to be so. —*Charles de Gaulle*

She told us a story about how she made a response—overnight—to a competitor's major pricing announcement. As the product-line manager she really knew her stuff. Knew the market, knew the customers, and knew her scrappy competitors. When the announcement happened, she was a bit surprised, but she wasn't ready to raise the surrender flag. Calling her staff together, they reviewed their knowledge of the market, and everyone made suggestions on how to combat the price cut effectively. The next day Judy decided on a strategy: Take the rest of her ad budget and hit the airwaves with a quality plus message. The best quality in the business, plus the best price. She undercut the competition, made price a nonissue, and hit home hard with a message that her company offered the best service. It turned out to be a very good, very smart, decision.

Judy didn't study this thing to death. She has been studying the market for years and knows it well. She combined this practical know-how with decisiveness to fight back, and win. She made a Smart Decision.

Smart Decisions interact with:

Organized Action

It was one thing for Washington to make the Smart Decision to cross the Delaware, but once the decision was made, *nothing happened*—until Organized Action plans were put into effect. Organized Action is the ability to take a decision such as "crossing the Delaware" and break it down into logical, doable steps. For example, Organized Action says that once you have a bridgehead on the other bank, you get the cooks and kitchen across so that the soldiers and horses can eat when they, too, make it across.

Organized Action is critical to the success of every endeavor, although unless it is based on Smart Decisions, all the Organized Action in the world won't take you where you want to go. Smart Decisions and Organized Action are balanced, interactive behaviors in your core-career buoyancy plan.

THE CHANGES IN YOUR HEAD

Career buoyancy is in your head and your soul, because career success is not just about how smart you are. It's about being a balanced person, and it's about controlling the direction of your life, with all its challenges and

It takes a great man to make a good listener. —Sir Arthur Helps

opportunities. Core-career buoyancy, and the eight critical behaviors, asks that you become whole, complete with the skills the new era demands of the people who receive a welcome in the new corporate America.

People fail in their careers when they are set in their ways. Such people have poorly developed buoyancy skills for the new world, they don't have a coherent game plan for their work lives, and they find it difficult to accept the reality of change. You do not want to fail and fall through one of those glass trapdoors into a working underclass.

You, just like a smart corporation, want to rightsize and retool for the modern world, and that's what the behavioral buoyancy circle is about. Each of the eight interactive behaviors is in great demand in all professions in all industries and each is learnable.

A little later in the book I am going to show you how to put these same behaviors to work in the totally different contexts of your dream and entrepreneurial careers. But right now let's integrate them into a core-career management program.

NOTES

1. S. E. Taylor, *Positive Illusions: Creative Self-deception and the Healthy Mind.* (New York: Basic Books, 1989).

2. S. Streufert and S. C. Struefert, *Behavior in the Complex Environment.* (Washington, D.C.:Winston, 1978).

To escape criticism—do nothing, say nothing, be nothing. —Elbert Hubbard

Chapter 6

Career Management in the Nineties and Beyond: A Core-Career Survival Kit for the New World of Work

I always admired poet Robert Frost's comment that by working faithfully eight hours a day for years, you'd eventually be rewarded by getting to work twelve hours a day. In the nineties there are two essential issues:

- Protecting your employability
- Protecting your rights to the fruits of your mind

Forget about corporate loyalty, because loyalty is a function of being appreciated. In a world where there are no long-term employment prospects for anyone and where business restructuring is destroying whole communities and classes of working people, we must move to create self-supporting professional structures around ourselves. We must shift the focus toward a more prudent loyalty: personal professional survival. It's already what other professionals around us are doing—in the last twelve months, 75 percent of chief executives have pursued alternate job opportunities.[1]

However, the more things change, the more they remain the same. In your core career there were three ageless ways of adding to your buoyancy:

1. Making money for the company.
2. Saving money for the company.
3. Saving time for the company.

Nothing can move a man who is paid by the hour; how sweet the flight of time seems to his calm mind. —Charles Dudley Warner

These same old pillars of wisdom still hold true in the new world of work.

PROTECTING YOUR EMPLOYABILITY

Forget about employment for life. There will likely be no more pretense about long-term employment relationships by 2005; by the end of the century we are likely to move to contractual employment for all, where the length of employment is clearly spelled out.

Many currently surviving executives desperately need to reevaluate their roles, because the specialist path that was an innate part of the hierarchical structures and career paths is now seen as narrow isolationist thinking. There is going to be a continuing major shakeout of the executive ranks as business cautiously rebuilds the entire corporate structure.

But there will be promotional opportunities and careers both into and within the irreducible corporate core. Those who succeed will be those who are most able to establish connectivity between the old world and the new, between the problems they identify and the solutions they can implement. To do this, you need an attitude of knowledge about your job, your company, your industry, and your boss.

An Attitude of Knowledge

STEP ONE

There is a cautionary tale about the Information Systems (I.S.) guy on some re-org committee who accurately identified that his entire department and function could be immediately outsourced. When the committee findings were reviewed and acted upon, the man nonetheless was caught completely unaware as he and his entire staff were eliminated from that company's new irreducible core.

You just cannot afford to stick your head in the sand and hope the sandman don't come get you—'cause he'll start in just about anywhere. Find out how your job fits into the department, and the department into the company's organizational structure. Even if you think you know the answers, *check*, because what's going on is that the very questions are getting reframed. The worst thing that could happen is that you wangle yourself a place on the nascent group who is tackling this very task.

The truth shall be told, though it kill. —*Timothy Thomas Fortune*

Our I.S. guy could have acted far more appropriately by (a) kicking his job-hunt plan into gear pretty damn quick; or (b) building a business plan that revolved around his department configured as a small "best in the world" supplier of the required services to the parent company. A well-thought-out proposal along these lines would have been given serious consideration; it would have been a brilliant public relations coup for the corporation, which now would have been viewed as a "people empow-erer" rather than a "people castrator."

STEP TWO

Become a student of your industrial biome and its cluster. For example, your industrial biome might be health care in the Service Brokers Cluster. If so, you will first strive to reach a rational understanding of how your *industry* is changing and functioning and then you will go on to develop the larger knowledge of the core cluster of which you are a part.

STEP THREE

Understand your employer's corporate objectives and their chosen course, and adjust your sheets accordingly. Knowing your employer's goals will show you how to steer a course that protects and enhances your core career.

STEP FOUR

Establish some connectivity between your employer's goals and your new work-life goals as you form and begin to implement them. This con-nectivity will allow you to recognize those special projects and activities where your interests and those of your employer most closely match. The result will be a more valuable relationship for both parties, and as value is added, so is commitment.

Become a World-Class Professional

From the new perspective of knowledge, get to know your job inside out. Start with your job description and match it with what you do day to day. If your responsibilities do not match the job description, either your com-petencies have outgrown the job or your function is becoming deskilled. Once you find out where you stand, you'll know what it will take to survive and stand out. Just as the corporate trend is to find "best in the world" mar-ket niches, yours is to develop your own world-class professionalism.

What is most honorable is also the safest. —Livy

You can then apply what you find to the changing picture of work and decide whether your current skills and responsibilities are fitting you for the kind of work you hope to be doing in a couple of years.

Identify those areas that you want to continue to build—either because they are currently weaknesses or because they are critical skills that should always be polished—then talk to your boss about them. The pitch (adapted to your situation and personality) will include phrases that echo the following:

- "I want to meet with you to make a recommitment to my job and to the company."
- "I really want to make a place for myself here, and to do that, I need to be the best I can be."
- "These are the skill sets I see as important in doing a stellar job, and I'd like to develop them by doing x, y, and z."
- "I'd also like to hear any suggestions you might have on skills I can work on that will help me be most valuable to the enterprise."

You must be prepared to react positively to the suggestions you get, and also be ready to bring up a single area of personal development for yourself. Don't couch your requests to grow in terms of "I wanna learn how to do so-and-so." It's better to say that such and such a skill would "improve your ability to ____," and that you could "pick it up by doing this job, or working on that project."

Once you have the direction and support of your boss, take concerted action. Then every couple of months, follow up with an informal meeting that confirms your progress. Implement this technique, and apart from improving professional competencies, you will have forged an image of yourself as someone who thinks, cares, and makes things happen.

Becoming a world-class professional with the work-life buoyancy it delivers necessitates that you:

1. Overlearn the basics. If you go back to the essentials of your profession right now, you may find basic skills you have forgotten. You may also discover that technology has changed some of those tenets and, in the process, the face of your job forever. It's best that you know this as soon as possible.

Shut up your mouth and chew the cud of understanding. —Congreve

2. Practice, polish, edit, and revise every critical function of your job. A good lawyer will never ask a question in court to which he doesn't already know the answer. The fourteen-year-old "overnight" tennis sensation has been practicing literally since birth. The mega-selling grunge band's members have been practicing half their lives. Many great fiction writers spent years in the press, advertising, or other nonfiction areas developing their craft.

Buoyant Knowledge Workers don't wait until the sales call to "just do it" or the night before the conference to work out what to say. They don't do as much as it takes to get by, they do *much more.*

3. Develop vital skills that allow you consistently to contribute *above* your rank and remuneration. This will position you for growth, enhance your marketability to others, and increase your usefulness to your current company.

4. Work with adjusted focus and passion. Australian tennis master Rod Laver talks about wiping "everything out of your mind but the ball." He says, never mind your opponent; forget about the weather; *just make the ball your obsession.*

However, bear in mind that twelve-hour days for the company year in and year out no longer warrant the sacrifice *unless* you have integrated your corporate zealousness with entrepreneurial and dream careers of your own. Striving toward one of these should simultaneously enhance your other career paths.

Knowing and Becoming Known

But becoming a world-class professional, and enjoying the work-life buoyancy that it brings, does not happen in a vacuum. As the poet John Donne said, "No man is an island unto himself." Success and buoyancy (the words are interchangeable) in the new world of work require allies and friends, and teachers and pupils.

Buoyancy starts at home, right where you work, with connectivity you establish first with your boss, peers, and colleagues and then in ever-widening circles of personal influence built, in part, on your mentor and acolyte relationships.

Understanding is the wealth of wealth. —W. G. Benham

Make Your Boss Your Ally

As long as you have a core career, you will have a boss. That person has a very profound influence over your ability to make a successful core career. And you will make a positive profound influence on him or her if you:

1. Understand what is needed and deliver it on time, and in the format your boss prefers. If it sometimes takes a little or a lot of extra effort, remember that you'll be working up a sweat and bonding with other like-minded core professionals.

2. Make it accurate and what is *requested* rather than what you can get away with or would like the project to be.

3. Share any credit you receive; eventually it comes back to you. Working well with others toward common ends displays traits of adjustedness, honesty, and agreeableness. Sharing credit is not only the right thing to do, it will also work as an advertisement of a person with good core skill sets and behaviors.

4. Communicate effectively, properly, honestly, and often. Be sure to customize your methods of communication to your audience:

• Use E-mail and other professional workplace technologies; they help define who you are in the new world of work.

• Write memos that carry a real-life signature and are delivered in person ("Here's a report on the questions you raised Friday"). This reminds your boss of *who you are.*

5. Be a reliable platoon member in thought, word, and action. Your boss is desperate to find people who'll stand at his back rather than snap at his heels.

6. Make your boss look good to others by *your* words and deeds.

7. Say thank you to your boss for either specific support on an endeavor or general encouragement.

8. Never assume a job is complete the day you hand it in. Revisions and adjustments are not to be regarded as criticism but as the ability to see more clearly now that the first phase has been completed. An important part of your professional adjustedness relates to your ability to revise, edit, recast, or otherwise change your work. Anything less than a wholehearted commitment to the spirit of teamwork and creativity innate to corporate life will unquestionably derail a career.

Gray skies are just clouds passing over. —Duke Ellington

9. Increase your practical know-how and connectivity skills by volunteering for interdepartment committees, or orphan projects that need to get done. If there is nothing going on that's suitable, get to work and come up with a project that justifies looking into. Also, you should join professional associations—as often as you can find them. These options will allow you to establish relationships outside of your normal sphere of influence.

On the other hand:

1. Be careful not to overcommit yourself willy-nilly. Instead, strive gradually to increase the amount of time you spend on tasks and projects that can in some practical way have an impact on your *whole* professional work life. This will become clearer as we address your entrepreneurial- and dream-career options.

2. Never display overt disloyalty. In other words, don't look at opportunities elsewhere in the company without having an agreement with your boss, or badmouth your employer or the products and services your employer provides.

3. If you get laid off, don't burn your bridges because of frustration and anger. Be prepared for what is likely to come to any one of us over the coming years.

4. If you do not build and maintain a wide base of professional contacts within and without the company, your communications with others outside your department can be misconstrued as bypassing the chain of command in some way. One of the keys to career buoyancy is to have a continually evolving job and web of relationships; don't allow yourself to be cut off from your future.

5. Never criticize your boss as a means to peer acceptance. It will invariably backfire and quite possibly cause your demise.

6. Don't become known as the prophet of gloom and doom in your company. Being the bearer of a constant stream of bad news or critical opinions will make others uncomfortable being around you—and isolation today is tantamount to professional suicide.

7. Forget everything you have ever heard about "squeaky wheels getting the grease." The tactic now is to take responsibility for identifying

---

This is the best day the world has ever seen. Tomorrow will be better.
—R. A. Campbell

problems and turning them into actionable opportunities. Being a pest will just get you sprayed one way or another.

Finely tuned core skill sets will in many ways be the same skill sets you can use in establishing a profitable dream or entrepreneurial career—you will just be applying them in different contexts.

The Vacuum Theory of Power-Base Building

In my younger days, back when I had a real job in corporate America— when that first wave of technology was invading the workplace with desktop computers and fax machines—I took advantage of the confusion of the time to suggest, research, and write for my employer and colleagues what we called "An Idiot's Guide to Data Processing." This allowed me unlimited access to anyone I wanted for three months, and all the kudos that went with a project my employer subsequently used as a giveaway promotional piece to employers all over America.

I didn't make any money off it, but, it did me a helluva lot of good in my core career, it made me many great friends, and it gave me the confidence to go take a swing at a nonfiction how-to. The project I subsequently began resulted in the best-selling *Knock 'em Dead* series. Yes, volunteering is absolutely where it's at.

My friend Peter Erbe, the trainer, once called an extended volunteering program his vacuum theory. In the vacuum theory you look around your department/division/office to find all the important jobs that aren't getting done, then one by one you start sucking up all this extra responsibility that no one else wants. The result is enhanced mobility, a power base for future growth, and more current *connectivity.*

Increased sensitivity to the value of others, and your practical involvement with them, exposes you to opportunities. As a result you will more likely be able to move interdepartmentally within your organization, and to move away from outsourceable functions toward core functions. These activities will also not only improve your standing with immediate superiors, they will give you a greatly expanded circle of personal influence.

The man who says it cannot be done should not interrupt the man doing it.
—Chinese saying

Increase Your Practical Connectivity with Others

Anthropologist Desmond Morris pointed out in his seventies classic *The Naked Ape*, that both mankind and animals seem to have an innate need to differentiate themselves into small groupings with all the defensive and self-image protection mechanisms of the tribe. What this has led to is a workplace culture that encourages separatism, where we hear comments like "Salespeople are only order takers" or "Accountants are just bean counters." While one could say this is only a way of having a laugh in the trenches, the insidious side effect is that many people attempt to diminish the importance of others' jobs in order to enhance the importance of their own.

This is dangerous narrow-band thinking—probably the worst professional crime any of us will commit over the coming years, and one quite capable of derailing a core career as well as subsequently thwarting any of your dream or entrepreneurial attempts.

In the age of specialization there was no practical danger in specialist isolation; in fact most corporate cultures encouraged it. Today separation is a clear and present threat to your security *that only connectivity can check*.

Choosing a Mentor

As you develop your professional work life along the lines we recommend in *Beat the Odds*, your increased involvement in your immediate workplace and your professional future will permit you the opportunity for the mentor and acolyte relationships that have been part of the foundations of successful careers throughout the ages.

I recommend building your personal-influence circles outward. Start with building strong relationships with your immediate work group and boss; wider relationships within the company will follow. Concurrently with this drive you can be building personal-influence circles within your professional community through an involvement in professional associations.

These are not formal-reporting employer-employee relationships (although a mentor can be your boss), but rather the relationships that develop between people of all ages who share a common commitment to their work lives. This professional respect allows the seeds of mentor and acolyte relationships to flourish.

Mentor-Acolyte relationships work for both parties.

For the acolyte in the relationship, the benefits should be obvious.

Always expect the worst, and when it comes, make the best of it. —French saying

Having chosen a mentor wisely and well, you hope she will be there to guide you through the madness of a modern-day core career. You do not enter into such relationships hoping to be spoon-fed success, instead you anticipate more of the Zen-master relationship, where you are given useful directions and the occasional whack up the side of the head that helps you align the wisdom.

For the mentor in the relationship, the benefits are less obvious but equally valuable. The opportunity to make a difference for the good of the profession is important, as is the opportunity to stay in touch with the needs and concerns of motivated yet less experienced professionals in the field. The mentor also has the right to expect a quid pro quo, in terms of real work on a pet project. Mentoring also allows emotionally mature professionals with an entrepreneurial bent to identify potential colleagues for future endeavors, and if the mentor chooses well, he will be able to tap into a generational network other than his own.

Your pool of potential mentors is as big as your enthusiasm allows it to be. You find mentors lurking everywhere in the many web relationships you develop to enhance your core career; you can also replicate these webs for both your entrepreneurial and your dream career. The people with whom you develop mentor relationships should resonate with your carefully evaluated work-life goals.

I have been fortunate in sustaining a number of successful mentor and acolyte relationships over the years. Here is what I have distilled from these relationships:

• They're not meant to be like lovers; you are allowed to have more than one at a time. My core career these days is writing and publishing (hey, it used to be my dream career!), where I have benefited greatly from four mentors. These relationships came to maturity last year when their cumulative advice led to my getting a 3,000 percent raise—thanks, guys. But besides which, developing multiple mentors prevents you from overworking one of these philanthropic relationships.

• Although age has never been synonymous with wisdom, the standard advice on mentors has been to choose those several years older than yourself. Now, when the computer started to appear on the desktops of the corporate world around 1980, the people at the top of today's corporations were then already well into the management ranks. Many

A woman who strives to be like a man lacks ambition. —Anonymous

of these people have never adapted personally to the technology of the modern world. A national study by the Times Mirror Center for the People and the Press[2] indicates that there is a "clear generation gap with regard to computers and technology" with those over fifty years old. So choosing a mentor based mainly on whether he or she has gray hair and wears bifocals is not a smart move. Yes, you need someone with more experience and influence than you, but what you don't want is someone who looks right, but who in reality is just hanging on till the next technology cull, or the one after that. Mentorship isn't the age- or sex-related thing it once was; it's about well-adjustedness and subject-matter expertise. My core-career mentors are of both sexes, and half are younger than I am.

• If your mentor is also connected in an acolyte position with a senior, and that person is professionally active himself, you tap into a power network of enormous potential, both up and down the reporting chain. Over a period of time you will come to be no more than a couple of calls away from anyone or anything you need to know.

• If you choose prudently, you will develop a relationship with someone who is competent, respected, knowledgeable, flexible, and innovative. It's helpful if your mentor works at the same company as you—at least at the start of your relationship, because it allows far easier communication and helpful supervision.

• Look for mentors both within and without your areas of subject-matter expertise. Those within will have an immediate frame of reference for your questions. Those without will give you fresh perspectives and increase your practical understanding and connectivity skills as they share the metaphors of their occupational and industrial biomes.

• Don't rush these relationships. It's best if they develop naturally over a period of time. It is not as if you are applying for a job or offering one, and need a yes or no answer.

• There is a time when you somehow grow up from being an acolyte and become a mentor yourself: Your mentor retires, you lose your waistline, and suddenly, *voilà*, you are a top dog and suitable mentor material. Unfortunately in an age when development, learning, and Symbolic Analysis skills are the buzzwords of success, it is most prudent to maintain acolyte sensitivities throughout your work life.

The Wright brothers flew right through the smoke screen of impossibility.
—Charles F. Kettering

VIRTUAL MENTORS

Virtual mentors are okay as an additional resource, or until you can find the real thing. A virtual mentor can be anyone you respect but don't know personally. With virtual mentors you learn to have glorious dialogues with yourself, having first mentally placed that mentor's face and mind-set in front of you.

I have had a virtual mentor for years now. I've never met him and probably never will, but he wrote a book that deeply influenced me. His name is Guy Kawasaki, and he was once an evangelist for Apple computer. After he left Apple, he wrote a book about the birth and nurturing of the Macintosh computer called *The Macintosh Way*. While it was ostensibly a story about a computer company, I found it to be the single most enlightening source of advice on marketing for a growing business. I haven't made a marketing decision since without "talking" to Guy.

THE ACOLYTE-MENTOR BALANCE

It really is true that successful people in any given profession largely know everybody else. What many people don't realize, though, is that a lot of those relationships predate the success by years. Establishing mentor-and-acolyte webs are another fiber in your buoyancy web.

Just as I recommend the acolyte mentality as a professionally healthy survival tool, I also actively endorse your becoming a mentor yourself. Even if you are only a couple or three years into the game, there are now those coming up behind you who need help. Besides, maintaining supportive relationships with up-and-comers serves to develop your own project and people leadership skills.

The observation here is that the goal is *not* linear in the way things once were: Start off as an acolyte, graduate to mentor. Your goal nowadays is to establish *both* acolyte and mentor webs, and maintain them both throughout your work life. The relationships you develop will create an environment for lifelong learning and teaching, and the greater connectivity will help enhance your buoyancy.

Enjoy your ice cream while it's on your plate—that's my philosophy.
—Thornton Wilder

You Are Always Looking for a Better Job

You are always on the lookout for new opportunities. It is much more prudent to be able to say no to a job offer than to have never heard about it in the first place.

Always keep an ear to the ground for new work opportunities and position yourself so that others in your biome know of your existence and how to get hold of you. To succeed at your task, you need to keep your association activity, networks, and webs healthy and growing. Make sure you are active in at least one association that crosses industry biomes.

With this in mind, rebuild your resume from the ground up for the needs of the nineties; if you don't, it runs the risk of being largely irrelevant to the needs of modern employers. A resume that demonstrates your contributions in diverse environments gives strong circumstantial indications of subject-matter expertise and those desirable Symbolic Analytical skills.

Whenever you hear about an interesting job, check it out. You have nothing to lose, everything to gain, and no decision to make until someone sends you an offer letter. Stay abreast of the job market with the techniques you'll find in good job-hunting books like my *Knock 'em Dead* books, and the work of my personal favorites, Doug Richardson, Joyce Lane Kennedy, Dick Beatty, John Lucht, Marilyn Moats Kennedy, Bill Rodin, and Yana Parker.

In choosing job-hunting and career books, be suspicious of books that limit your knowledge of the author. Career publishing is a hot market right now, and unfortunately it has attracted a number of charlatans who are preying on the ignorance of the publishing and book-selling industries by putting some really quite dangerous advice in your unsuspecting hands. Read the credentials of your career authors, and, best of all, *get personal recommendations.*

It is not easy to integrate the new attitudes of knowledge and connectivity into your work life, but the rolling impact of technology in the workplace means that modern careers are going to require more active involvement than in the past. Unfortunately, protecting your employability in the new world of work is now an important issue for every working American.

A man's worth is no greater than the worth of his ambitions.
—Marcus Aurelius Antonius

PROTECTING YOUR RIGHTS TO THE FRUITS OF YOUR MIND

In this era of the Knowledge Worker, when a single idea can be worth millions of dollars, the new hot issue is intellectual copyright, or who owns the fruits of your mind. Understanding how to protect your rights to the fruits of your mind could mean the difference between life working in a high-rise salt mine and life at the beach.

Many years ago, before being published and becoming a best-selling career author, I worked for a big staffing company, for whom I twice offered my services to write a job-hunting book under the president's name, and twice was rejected. The book I had offered was eventually published under my own name and started a whole new career and life for me. Back in those days, when I had the idea for what became *Knock 'em Dead*, to offer the fruits of your mind to your employer was the sensible, teamlike, and ethical thing to do. But I don't think I would make that same selfless gesture in today's employment climate. There has come a time where the modern professional will want to consider if a particular idea or solution should be offered up to the core employer of the moment. And having considered, you will want to protect the thoughts in your head, because just one of your ideas could be the answer to your American Dream.

By the year 2000 maybe 50 percent of our workforce will be employed outside the once traditional professional career. The American worker is therefore entering new and uncharted territory. With intellectual copyrights worth millions, you can bet corporate America is not going to wave you or your ideas on their merry way. To be fair to yourself, and to give your employer his fair due, you need to understand what the law of the land has determined to be fair and equitable treatment for everyone. Once you understand who owns the ideas in your head and why, you won't "sell your birthright for a mess of pottage."

Could What You Create On Your Own Time Belong to Your Employer?

When making decisions about intellectual property rights, and who owns what, the court usually rules in favor of *the creator of the work product*. But although whoever creates a product is *usually* the rightful copyright owner, there's more to the story. The court must also decide whether the intellectual property created was within the "scope of employment."

So intellectual property ownership isn't always clear-cut. In fact some

---

He that despises small things shall fall by little and little. —Ecclesiastes 19:1

states are still engaged in a case-by-case tennis match, trying to decide which rights are the employer's and which are the employee's.

Season of Change

Luckily there is a shift sweeping through the country, away from the rights of corporations and employers to individuals' rights.

In attempting to define the changing workplace, the courts are narrowing the blanket privileges traditionally granted to employers. No longer can the company take all your intellectual property, only to replace you by the very technology you created. You and your employer (or your client, if you are a consultant or subcontractor) have a right and an obligation to protect your intellectual property rights.

It is clear that the courts most often protect the creator of the work product, whether you happen to be an independent contractor or an employee; however, most states give more rights to the entrepreneur.

The Devil Is in the Details

To get a better idea of how this all works in relation to you in your real world of work, I am going to take you through a sequence of landmark intellectual copyright cases where employees sued employers for the rights to the fruits of their intellectual labor and vice versa. Together we'll come to understand how the ownership of ideas sometimes worth millions can hinge on the tiniest of details.

Let's look at a few examples of how the question of who owns what's in your head can vary depending on the circumstances.

WHO OWNS THE IDEAS IN DAVID'S HEAD?

David Miller worked for CP Chemicals as a senior laboratory chemist and, during his regular work hours, set up a customer-product specifications tracking system.[3] Then, at home and on his own time, David wrote a program for this system that computed highly complex mathematical functions and simplified the company's manual tasks, eliminating error. He never received overtime pay for the design or implementation of his new system, although he was paid by the hour. According to David and three other employees, the company had verbally agreed that David would main-

---

Ask, and it shall be given you; seek, and ye shall find; knock, and it shall be opened unto you. —Matthew 7:7

tain copyrights to the computer programs that he developed and that his company could use the designs as long as he remained an employee.

In June 1991 David was fired after he was arrested for smoking marijuana. Upon his termination David requested that the program he'd designed either be returned to him or that his employer pay him a license fee for its continued use. When the company refused to comply, David sued for copyright infringement.

David lost the lawsuit because he had failed to register his program for copyright. Based on the allowable evidence, the court ruled that the computer program was developed within the scope of his job to serve his employer. Though the facts were seemingly weighted heavily in favor of David Miller, the court's decision was based on David's failure to file for copyright. His mistake ended up costing him, and of course benefiting his former employer.

ARE THESE JEFF'S IDEAS?

Jeffrey Peiffer was a full-time employee of Avtec Systems, a government contractor that marketed space-related computer systems that were used in space-application satellites.

An employee of ten years who started as a work-study student, Jeffrey had a passion for both astronomy and programming. At home he developed a highly complex computer program related to satellites. When he demonstrated the program to the president of the company, he was awarded a five-thousand-dollar bonus. The company then used the program as a marketing tool to gain U.S. Air Force contracts.

Unlike David, Jeffrey retained the copyright for his entrepreneurial program, and eventually, in his spare time, he merged his efforts with those of another software company. Their first-year sales of the program generated almost $200,000, half of which went to Jeff. This collaboration angered Avtec, which then sued for copyright infringement.

The court had to decide whether Jeff, as an employee of Avtec, was acting within the scope of his employment with the company when he created the program, or whether he was simply engaging in a hobby outside of work.[4]

Whose property is it? If you answered that Jeffrey owned the computer programs he designed, you were correct. Jeffrey proved that he performed

---

We must not, in trying to think about how we can make a big difference, ignore the small daily differences we can make which, over time, add up to big differences that we often cannot foresee. —Marian Wright Edelman

the majority of the work during his nonworking hours and utilized his personal computer equipment, which he had purchased at his own expense. Avtec failed to present evidence that Jeffrey developed the program within the authorized work hours to serve the company. The court found that Jeffrey's work was created as a personal hobby and not to satisfy specific work obligations of his employer. Avtec Systems was therefore not allowed to claim either complete or joint ownership of the program.

Underlying both of these cases is the big issue: Does the court view me, in this particular context, as an employee or as an independent contractor?

REID'S RIGHTS

The just-mentioned issue was settled in the landmark Supreme Court case of sculptor Robert Reid, who sued for possession of the intellectual copyright of his work.

Reid was a sculptor in Washington, D.C. The Community for Creative Non-Violence (CCNV), an organization dedicated to eliminating homelessness, entered into an oral agreement with Reid for a sculpture display at a 1985 Christmas pageant that would dramatize the plight of the homeless. Reid worked in his Baltimore, Maryland, studio on the sculpture and periodically held meetings there with his client to assess the work's progress. He incorporated most of the organization members' suggestions during the creation process and accepted final payment when the work was delivered. The client, who never discussed copyright registration, then filed suit against Reid for possession of intellectual property rights.[5]

Reid was an independent contractor rather than an employee of CCNV, although his work was directed by CCNV and met their specifications. As a sculptor Reid engaged in a skilled occupation, supplied his own tools, worked in Baltimore at a separate studio of his own without daily supervision, was retained for a limited time span while in the process of the creation, had absolute autonomy to decide his daily hours and schedule, and could hire or pay any assistants necessary for the completion of the project. CCNV didn't engage in the business of sculptures, and they didn't plan to assign additional projects to Reid. CCNV paid Reid on a project basis in installments, as is often the case with independent contractors. They did not deduct payroll or Social Security taxes on Reid's compensation, did not give him em-

---

The man whose life is devoted to paperwork has lost the initiative. He is dealing with things that are brought to his notice, having ceased to notice anything for himself. He has been essentially defeated in his job. —C. Northcote Parkinson

ployee benefits, and did not contribute to unemployment insurance or workman's compensation funds.

Nonetheless, the Supreme Court ruled in favor of *joint ownership* of the sculpture on the basis of a provision of the U.S. Constitution that specifies *authors are the owners of their ideas.*[6]

The Copyright Act of 1976 provides that copyright ownership "vests initially in the author or authors of the work." Generally the author is the party who actually creates the work: the person who "translates an idea into a fixed, tangible expression." For example, you are the author if you view swans floating on crystal-blue lake, then go home with only the thought in mind and take out your watercolors, duplicating what you remember in a watercolor painting.

The law, however, specifies an exception to this rule for "works-made-for-hire"; it says that "the employer or another person for whom the work was prepared is considered the author" and therefore owns the copyright unless there is a written agreement to the contrary. For example, let's say that Charley, your next-door neighbor, asks you to walk down to the lake and paint him a vivid watercolor as the evening shadows start to fall across the water and the swans drift close to shore for shelter. You agree on a price of $150 for the painting, and then start to create. He is then the owner and legal author of your painting. The act also goes on to say that there are no "blanket work-made-for-hire" agreements. That means that for each individual work, according to the act, ownership must be clearly specified in writing.

In the case of *Reid* the Court determined that the statue was not a "work-made-for-hire" but rather a "work prepared by an employee" as defined by the Copyright Act of 1976. In fact Reid's lawsuit forced the Court to establish a clear understanding of the difference between employees and independent contractors. These criteria are now used by state courts and also by the IRS, State Unemployment Insurance Offices, Medicare, and Social Security Administration to determine whether an employer must provide benefits and pay withholding taxes.

Although the factors I've starred in the following box *generally* weigh more heavily than others in determining whether a party is an independent contractor or an employee, it's more complicated than that. Courts usually use a combination of them to make a decision, although any one of these factors alone can affect the outcome. Take the case of Cliff Aymes.

I just invent, then wait until man comes around to needing what I've invented.
—R. Buckminster Fuller

The Twelve-Factor Test

The comprehensive *Reid* twelve-factor test developed by the Supreme Court to distinguish an employee from an independent contractor is as follows (*note:* I've starred the points that are the most significant):[7]

1. The hiring party's right to control the way in which the product is developed*
2. The skill required to create the product
3. The source of the tools or utilities used
4. The location where the work is performed
5. The duration of the relationship between the parties
6. The capability of the hiring party to assign additional work to the hired party*
7. How long the work is performed
8. The mode of payment
9. The role of the hired party in engaging and compensating assistants
10. Whether the work is part of the hiring party's regular business*
11. Whether the hiring party generally provides employee benefits
12. The tax treatment afforded the hiring party*[8]

IS YOU IS OR IS YOU AIN'T MY EMPLOYEE?

Cliff Aymes was hired to work as a computer programmer. In his two-year employment with Island Recreational, Aymes was to create a series of programs. During that time his employer never paid payroll withholding taxes on Aymes's income. Instead he was paid a gross income and was provided with a Form 1099 (typically supplied to consultants and subcontractors) rather than a Form W-2 (typically given to employees).

He created a series of computer programs for his employer, which were used to maintain records of cash receipts, physical inventory, sales figures, purchase orders, merchandise transfers, and price changes. At no time did the company have Aymes sign a written agreement transferring ownership rights of the program.

Aymes always submitted invoices for payment, as an independent contractor typically would. After he left the company, he requested his wages

---

Soon after a hard decision something inevitably occurs to cause doubt. Holding steady against that doubt usually proves that decision. —R. I. Fitzhenry

and payment for the use of his program, but his request was denied. Both parties sued for copyright infringement.

Who do you think owns the program? The judge cited the decision in *Reid*, which distinguished between an employee and an independent contractor. In the *Aymes* case the most significant factor was the provision of employee benefits, such as health insurance and the tax treatment of the employee.[9] The employer's failure to extend benefits or to remit payroll taxes for Aymes was a significant factor in the court's decision that he was an independent contractor.

Also the judge noted that the employer was trying to have his cake and eat it too. Island Recreational benefited greatly from treating Aymes like an independent contractor. However, the company also wanted to claim full copyright of the program he had created.

Clifford Aymes won the case when the court noted that the employer should not in one context be able to claim him as an independent contractor and then, in another context, claim he was an employee in order to avoid a copyright-infringement lawsuit. Way to go, Cliff!

Who Owns the Entrepreneur's Work?

We are all independent contractors once we leave our nine-to-five jobs. In 1959 the Court defined the role of an entrepreneur in the epic words "No one sells or mortgages all the products of his brain to his employer by the mere fact of employment".[10]

Thus the Supreme Court has established five factors that help identify the bona fide independent contractor:[11]

1. Establishment in an independent business by offering services to the public. An independent business is usually marked by such elements as media advertising, a commercial telephone listing, and business cards, stationery, and bill heads; and by carrying business insurance and maintaining its own establishment.

2. A significant investment in the facilities. (Such items as hand tools and personal transportation are not considered significant.)

3. Assumption of the risk for profit or loss in providing services.

4. Freedom to establish own hours of work and to schedule own activities.

Decision is a sharp knife that cuts clean and straight; indecision, a dull one that hacks and tears and leaves ragged edges behind it. —Gordon Graham

5. No required attendance at meetings or training sessions; no required oral or written reports.

Our judges and courts seem to be leaning toward the side of entrepreneurial rights. For example, in Jeffrey Peiffer's lawsuit the court decided that an employer did not have the ownership rights to an employee's entrepreneurial intellectual property created outside his nine-to-five job.[12] The software was not intended for the employer, nor designed to fulfill work requirements, so the court ruled in favor of the entrepreneurial effort.

Sister Berta Hummel and God versus Mammon

Sister Berta devoted her life to God. While serving the Lord she also designed and mass-produced porcelain figures that generated a steady and significant income for the nunnery.

Soon after Sister Berta went to join her maker, her (biological) brothers pursued matters on a more temporal plane. They sued the convent for intellectual copyright infringement.

In this case the judge ruled that a drawing used to produce porcelain figurines created by a nun was her own intellectual property, despite convent support of all Sister Berta's activities.[13] Use of work time, premises, and assets of an employer did not constitute employer ownership despite the fact that the sister's extensive work hours paralleled a nine-to-five-and-then-some job.

Here again the lower court found that the employer does not own intellectual copyright unless the efforts of the copyright in question are covered in the job description. (We are still awaiting the highest Court's ruling on this one.)

When the employer does win in court, it generally reflects a miscarriage of justice. One of the reasons it happens is that in the changing workplace we often do not define "time of day" when work is produced. Employers may therefore own the works that are created outside regular working hours *if their creation falls within the employee's duties, regardless*

People are always blaming their circumstances for what they are. I don't believe in circumstances. The people who get on in this world are the people who get up and look for the circumstances they want, and if they can't find them, make them.
—George Bernard Shaw

of where the works were produced.[14] On the plus side, however, if that creation falls outside the scope of your regular job, you could be in for a pleasant surprise.

Overall, in copyright-infringement cases based on work product, the employee has had an advantage in the courts *as long as the work in contention is not part of the employee's day-to-day duties.* While employees can use their intellectual capabilities for their employer, employees can also use their talents in their spare time for their own entrepreneurial endeavors.

How to Avoid Uncertainty

As companies become leaner and meaner, it seems the courts are intent on protecting entrepreneurs. The benefits of this change can accrue to you so long as you look out for your own interests all along the way.

When you choose to share inspiration with an employer and client and that sharing falls outside of the employee-employer relationship, make sure to write an employment contract. *Note:* Work-made-for-hire agreements *"must precede the creation of the work."*[15] Works prepared by independent contractors and artists are not considered works made for hire, unless specifically ordered or commissioned.[16] Here are a few guidelines to follow:

- Make sure the agreement is signed prior to the creation of the work
- Specify each work that is being contracted separately
- Don't sign a blanket agreement that gives the employer a monopoly over your creative output
- Draft a sample bilateral contract for your entrepreneurial business or use a Blumberg form, which can be purchased at your local office supply store[17]
- Bill for services rendered and expenses[18]
- File a business license with the county—Blumberg Form X201
- Join a local chamber of commerce (you'll find a world of services offered there, including health and life insurance, banking, investment, retirement, and legal advice)
- Keep your entrepreneurial business separate from your nine-to-five job

A journey of a thousand miles begins with a single step. —Chinese saying

- Use your own tools and have a separate business phone line for incoming clients
- Don't give any one employer too much of your time
- Think of your intellectual property as billable product and don't work for free

Are You an Employee or an Independent Contractor?

If you are still confused about your status as an employee or independent contractor and want to be careful about separating that which belongs to an employer or client, answering the following questions for yourself will quickly clarify matters:

- Does my employer file a 1099 or a 1040 tax receipt?
- Do I have my own entrepreneurial business? Do I maintain my own establishment? Do I pay the rent and bills? Do I carry my own health or business insurance? Do I belong to a chamber of commerce? Have I filed a business certificate?
- Who assumes the risk for success or failure of the services I provide?
- When do I conduct my entrepreneurial business? During what hours of the day? For what purpose?
- Where did I perform my entrepreneurial work, at my home office or at my boss's office?
- If I work at home, do I keep the entrepreneurial and core work separate? What are my work hours for my core career? What are my work hours for my entrepreneurial career?
- How do I bill for my services—with an invoice, or do I collect a regular paycheck?
- Do I file a Schedule S tax return?
- Does my core employer provide health insurance, benefits, or pay unemployment insurance?
- Have I signed a work-for-hire agreement?
- Have I filed a copyright or patent application for the work I've created?

Acceptance of prevailing standards often means we have no standards of our own.
—Jean Toomer

In the future employment contracts need to address the changes in the workplace brought about by the massive corporate downsizing of the past decade. At the forefront of this change is the rights of the employee, employers, and independent contractors in regard to creative work product. Most vulnerable are contractors who perform creative work outside the once-traditional workplace. We can expect employment contracts of the future to define what the courts have been forced to determine: whether a hired party is an employee or an independent contractor.

A Beautiful Old-fashioned Loyalty

On January 3, 1995, *Newsday* ran a story about Bell Atlantic and its champion employee incentive program. It told of employee Tom Terry and how he took advantage of the new employee-incentive program. *Newsday* suggested that more and more companies would be relying on their employees to dream up the next great money maker. The article quoted Terry as saying he didn't submit his idea for money, which *Newsday* noted "is the attitude that company officials want to foster." And it's just as well. For the privilege of sharing his uniquely creative idea under the Champion program, he could "get the chance" to put one thousand dollars of his own money into it and, if it was successful, he could "make back ten times his investment." *Newsday* also noted that Terry's idea "has generated millions in revenues for his employer, Bell Atlantic."

The final words are left to a Bell executive, who states that the company is "looking for more gold" in ideas coming through the incentive program.

I merely tell this story in the spirit of "render unto Caesar that which is Caesar's, and keep for yourself the part that is rightfully yours." It's your life, and they are your decisions.

GRASPING THE NEW PHILOSOPHY

In the new world of work many will falter and fail, while others manage to maintain but still stagnate. Only the fortunate few will redefine their lives in terms that truly meet their personal vision of the American Dream.

Despite the odds, for those with ears to hear, there really are an infinite number of new pathways to the increasingly elusive American Dream, just so long as you take an honest look at where you stand. Once you

---

When the going gets tough, the tough get going. —Anonymous

know what you have to offer the new world of work, and by inference what you currently *don't* have to offer, you will know exactly where to start. You cannot reach for your dreams, with any hope of attaining them, without a firm foundation beneath you.

In the first part of this book I showed you the fundamental changes happening in the world today and how they are ravaging the odds of most Americans ever reaching their American dream. I exposed the danger of remaining enslaved to the workplace sensitivities of an earlier age, and to the beliefs and stereotypes that are outdated, irrelevant, and largely based on the discriminatory concepts of earlier times. Next we looked at how the best management consulting companies in the world are showing their corporate clients how to maximize profits by slashing millions of high-paying, previously secure jobs permanently from the payroll.

Smart professionals in smart companies are systematically disassembling whole companies on this advice, and rebuilding them again in more powerful and less labor-intensive structures than before. In response I showed you equally revolutionary ways in which to re-create a core-career buoyancy for yourself. In the process you have discovered the secrets for winning through to the relative safety of the ever-shrinking irreducible corporate core, with the hottest jobs and winning behavioral profiles for success in all of America's healthiest industries and jobs.

For some that would be enough, but for us this is just the stepping-off point on the adventure of your lifetime, and it all begins with a dream.

NOTES

1. Cornell University Center for Advanced Human Resource Studies.
2. Released in May 1994.
3. *Miller v. CP Chemicals, Inc.* 1992 U.S. Dist. 22020; C/A No. 3:91-2907-17.
4. *Avtec Systems, Inc. v. Jeffrey G. Peiffer.* 805 F. supp. 1312 (1992).
5. *Community for Creative Non-Violence v. Reid.* 490 U.S. 730; 109 S. Ct. 2166; 1989 U.S. 2727.
6. Article I, Section 8, of the United States Constitution advances the "Progress of Science and useful arts, by securing for limited times to authors and inventors the exclusive right to their respective writings and discoveries" for individuals and independent contractors alike.
7. Ibid.

The important thing is not to stop questioning. —Albert Einstein

8. The Copyright Act of 1976 did not define the terms *employee* and *employment*, leaving them to be defined by the courts. With Reid's lawsuit, the Supreme Court approached the issue of when an individual was an employee under the work-for-hire principle. "In determining whether a hired party is an employee under the general common law of agency, we consider the firing party's right to control the manner and means by which the product is accomplished. Among the other factors relevant to this inquiry are the skill required, the source of the instrumentalities and tools, the location of the work; the duration of the relationship between the parties, whether the hiring party has the right to assign additional projects to the hired party; the extent of the hired party's discretion over when and how long to work; the method of payment; the hired party's role in hiring and paying assistants; whether the work is part of the regular business of the hiring party; whether the hiring party is in business; the provision of employee benefits, and the tax treatment of the hired party." The Court further stressed that no one factor was used in determining whether a hired party was an "employee" or an "independent contractor."

9. *Clifford Scott Aymes v. Jonathan Bonelli.* 980 F.2d 857 (1992).

10. *Public Affairs Associates, Inc. v. Rickover.* 369 U.S. 111; 82 S. Ct. 580 (1962); 7 L. Ed. 2d 604.

11. Ibid.

12. *Avtec Systems, Inc. v. Jeffrey G. Peiffer.* 805 F. Supp. 1312 (1992).

13. *Schmid Brothers, Inc. v. W. Goebel Porzellanfabrik KG.* 589 F. Supp. 497 (1984).

14. *J. John Marshall v. Miles Laboratories, Inc.* 647 F. Supp. 1326 (1986).

15. *Playboy Enterprises, Inc. v. Dumas.* 840 F. Supp. 256 (1993); 831 F. Supp. 295 (1993). The court noted in this case that blanket work-made-for-hire agreements are a thing of the past.

16. *Schiller & Schmidt, Inc. v. Nordisco Corp.* 969 F.2d 410 (1992). The *Schiller & Schmidt* case made it clear that contracts are designed to protect people against false claims of oral agreements.

17. *Antonucci v. Stevens Dodge, Inc.* 73 Misc. 2d 173, 340 N.Y.S. 2d 979,982.

18. *George M. Jones Co. v. Canadian Nat. R. Co.*, D.C. Mich., 14 F.2d 852,855.

The turning point in the process of growing up is when you discover the core of strength within you that survives all hurt. —Max Lerner

Part Two

THE DREAM CAREER

▼

Chapter 7

The Alchemy
of Dreams

FOOTSTEPS OF A DREAM

People say to me all the time, "I've got a great book you should write." What they mean is, "I've got this idea that fascinates me, but I don't know where to go with it." People say to chefs, "There's never really been a restaurant that . . ." when what they should be saying is, "There's this mixture of cuisines and tastes that drive me wild, so perhaps it's time for me to start taking cooking classes."

If the projections are true that work lives are getting longer, then you have plenty of time to pursue any number of dreams. The alternative to pursuing your dreams in life is to deny yourself fulfillment, and a considerable measure of core-career buoyancy besides. Everything we will talk about in this part of the book will be woven into a web that simultaneously builds your core-career buoyancy with much-needed talents and behaviors.

Dreams die by the either-or voice that says no to protect the status quo. There is a plaque on my wall, right above my McDonald's fast-food-toys collection, that says, "Some people look at things and say why? I dream of things that never were and say why not. . . ."[1] The quotation is attributed to George Bernard Shaw, and I've never known if it was all he had to say on the topic, so I've finished it for years now in my own way. I add, *". . . so why not have a go? There is nothing to lose and everything to gain."*

It is time to go buy a box of art supplies and paint a nude after Wat-

---

If you think you can, you can. And if you think you can't, you're right.
—Mary Kay

teau; it's time to buy a trowel and become the plant doctor you have always dreamed of being. If owning a general store in a Maine resort town is your idea of heaven, take a trip and figure out how to start one up. If you dream of becoming a photographer, why don't you start shooting once a week? I'm not just talking about taking snapshots, I'm talking about planning and executing a shoot with the theme, location, and talent all determined with purpose and planning. *Why not have a go?*

In England, Paul and Lisa dream of owning a country pub (he's a gear specialist on the Grand Prix circuit, and she's also an automotive engineer). So this year, for vacation, they are subbing for a pub-owner friend they made in Devon while he stays at home and does some gardening. It wouldn't have happened unless they had gone out there and made it happen. While they're away, an American couple who own a bar in San Antonio are going to stay at their house. Next year for vacation Paul and Lisa are going to help run that bar in San Antonio during Cinco de Mayo.

There is nothing to lose by having a go. And there's everything to gain. If it's a writer you would be, pull out a sheet of paper and write down one word. Now cross it out, and write two more in its stead. That's it, you are writing, one word after another, one foot after another. It's maybe a fifty-year marathon, so there's no rush—except to take that first step. The trick is just to *start*, somehow, anyhow, to take that first nervous step that starts a chain of events with the potential to change your entire being by providing a practical means of fulfillment to your dreams.

Maybe you have a job, and it pays the bills and a bit besides. Does this make you a success? It depends to a large extent on what you sacrificed to get there and what the balance of your life outside this job is like.

By the time people reach forty, they are questioning to what degree their lives are living up to their dreams. This is when many people first face the possibility that where they are now in their careers is likely where they are going to be twenty years from now. Consequently I have never met a rational forty-year-old who didn't see the need for a little retooling in his or her life.

Erich Fromm, the psychologist, wrote, "One loves that for which one labors, and one labors for that which one loves." This observation is entirely in tune with the work-life philosophy of *Beat the Odds*, which is intended to help you find meaning and fulfillment in your work life as well as security. In the doing you will become a happier and more successful person. Understanding your dreams will help you become more buoyant,

---

No one can make you feel inferior without your consent. —Eleanor Roosevelt

and by developing activities that give a practical means of expression to those dreams you will win back some of the joy you lost when it came time to grow up and settle down into a single, straitjacketed career.

In the past you were meant to believe that a life sentence in the high-rise salt mines should be enough to fulfill anyone. You have been consistently told throughout your life that there simply isn't *time* for the foolishness of dreams. My contention is that the corporate needs for creativity, and the critical behaviors that allow creativity to occur, should make activities that develop these talents well regarded by employers, because the talents necessary for buoyancy at the corporate irreducible core are put to use in the pursuit of a dream career.

What constitutes a dream career? Whatever activity you want that gives meaning to your life. A dream career is just the development of that which allows you to achieve some long-held desire. For an unemployed single mother a dream career might be a secretarial job that provides desperately needed income and benefits. For the besieged middle manager it might be a bar in Tahiti with a state-of-the-art meeting room in the back. For you? Well, the choices are yours alone.

The only thing a dream career *should* be is fulfilling. Consider the case of Gutzon Borglum (now there's a name that had to make a success of itself), the sculptor who created Mount Rushmore. Borglum spent the last fourteen years of his life on the mountain. What vision to see the mountain like that, and what professional skills, and what practical business know-how he must have had to turn such a dream into reality!

When you give practical means of expression to a dream career, you are starting to live up to your potential. Who knows if you or I will be the Edison of a new age, or which of us will write the next great American novel that transfixes a generation, and who cares? What is important is that we are both *in the game*, living our lives and pursuing our dreams. I will show you that the means of achieving our two dreams, yours and mine, no matter how different they might appear on the surface, have far more in common than you ever thought possible.

Don't think for a moment that a dream career is a quick fix. It takes more than a couple of years to turn your dreams into reality. Dream careers don't bear fruit with the same speed or regularity with which promotions *used* to come in your core career.

The best ideas come from jokes. Make your thinking as funny as possible.
—David Oglivie

Sometimes building a dream career takes a lifetime, but in exchange you do get a life. For me and my dream of writing, it took twenty years just to get published, and another five to start making a living at it.[2] Achieving the dream is a quicker process for some than for others, but that is all right, because pursuing a dream will reshape your life for the better in how you spend your time in your corporate career, love life, friendships, and long-term professional associations. And the pursuit of your crazy dream will give your life meaning in its toughest hours.

If you stick with your dreams long enough, you will see them come alive. It's all in the weaving of what you've got into something you'd like to have. To pursue a dream career is to bring more balance into your life. It is a way to live in harmony with your needs by giving them a means of practical expression, and in the doing you are actively developing attitudes and behaviors that contribute immediately to your core-career buoyancy. There is a path that others have used that will help you make your dreams reality, while it increases your core-career security.

If this gets your blood tingling, it should, because here is another part of the work-life buoyancy puzzle about to be slotted into the whole. I am going to show you the behavioral connectivity between your core career and the successful achievement of a dream career. Each of the commonalities you find represents a major opportunity to bring your dreams that much closer to reality. When you find gaps between your dream and reality, don't turn them into chasms you could never cross; instead use the raw materials of your attitude of connectivity to build bridges from to-day's world to tomorrow's dreams. Look at the gaps you find as markers for your next Organized Action steps.

THE FIRST STEP OF THE LONG HAUL

Like objects in a car mirror, dream careers can be surprisingly closer than you think, which is not to say that they will result in untold wealth by the time of your next salary review. Your goal at the start of a dream career is to incorporate more of that which you love into your life. So in the early days at least, bringing more balance into your life will be the payback—that, and a more buoyant core career.

Take Carole, who dreams of running her own graphics business in

He who is firmly seated in authority soon learns to think security, and not progress, the highest lesson of statecraft. —James Russell Lowell

Cincinnati, and who is also doing something about it. Currently she is making time to teach herself some essential business software for administering such a business. Her subscription to the computer newsletter *Macworld*, which she took out last year when she finally kicked her butt into gear, led her directly to her current steps. In the fall of this year she is taking a long weekend from work and going to the annual graphics association convention. She may be the most timid new business owner there, but still she is doing it. Carole is *having a go*. She is not intimidated by setbacks, because it is all too much fun.

Each dream is different, yet every single one requires determination and passion. These two ingredients are essential, because it is the nature of most dream careers that they don't come easy. And they don't come fast; a dream has to be pursued with constancy.

Catching your dreams by building a dream career is *always* a marathon. It means putting one foot in front of the other with some regularity for years. Do it often enough and long enough, and you will be amazed at the ground you can travel and the dreams you can achieve. A marathon starts with a tiny step; your dream career starts in the same way. Maybe your small step is to take out a newsletter subscription, like Carole, or join an association. Everyone has the time to do that.

WAYS TO JUMP-START A DREAM CAREER

Life is too short to be lived on someone else's terms, with two weeks off each year for good behavior. People who work at their dreams, who give practical means of expression to their needs, learn to recognize opportunity when they see it, and over time develop the P.K.H. to take advantage of it. This is not luck. This is intelligently shortening the odds of success and achievement; some call it Yankee ingenuity, and others say it's the gods helping those who help themselves.

Here are six ideas to help you get a little more balance in your life, and get things moving along a career chain that will ultimately change your life for the better:

1. Find out what you love to do, and do it. If you look at the products-and-services chain that supplies your area of passion, what will

It is difficult to say what is impossible, for the dream of yesterday is the hope of today and the reality of tomorrow. —Robert H. Goddard

the results be? Well, there's one mad bicyclist who took to publishing a newsletter about his experiences as he rode around the highways and by-ways of America on a computer-equipped bicycle. Another biking enthusiast, who couldn't find good maps for his area, turned his experience creating one map for his own personal use into a nice little business creating bikers' maps for a regional publisher. Both these people looked at how they might make their passion more accessible to others; both are sharing ideas, opinions, and knowledge; and both are earning money and a greater measure of independence from doing something they love to do, something that isn't work to them at all.

2. Realize you don't have to be an expert to begin with. In fact it can be beneficial to be a bumbling novice. For instance it is arguable that Buckminster Fuller's entire fame rests on an uneducated question he asked during his early days in the navy: "Why are the bubbles in a boat's wake round?" This question led Fuller to invent the geodesic dome and other wonders. You will find that many breakthroughs are made by novices entering new fields out of curiosity who ask a lot of off-the-wall questions.

Shortly I'll tell you about a photographic klutz who became the co-inventor and patent holder of a hot photographic accessory. He's all the proof you'll ever need that anybody can do anything. With nothing more than a passionate interest in something and the eight critical buoyancy behaviors in place, you have what it takes to pursue any career of your dreams to a successful end.

3. The more you integrate your activities over the years, the more synergistic they will become. When you hit on an idea for a dream career, connect it to your core career. Ask yourself what core skills you might use to pursue this dream career.

Look for the connectivity, as did my friend Kristin. After a prestigious career in a Park Avenue law firm, she wanted to shift her core career from the defense to the prosecution, and specialize in spousal-abuse cases. Kristin decided she wanted to be a courtroom performer. Because of this it made all the sense in the world when I heard that she had recently taken up acting classes and was hoping for her first soap audition within the month. Way to go, Kristin. The reason this made all the sense in the world is—you guessed it—that acting lessons, fulfilling in and of themselves and a possible source of income, would also have a dramatically

---

Some folks can look so busy doing nothin' that they seem indispensable.
—Kin Hubbard

beneficial effect on her courtroom presence and performance. Smart woman, and I will not be surprised when I see her one day in Port Charles, stealing Luke from Laura.[3]

4. Dream your way to greatness. In your search for connectivity between your core-career experiences and your dream-career goals, a little daydreaming (or even night dreaming) can be helpful, because it helps you incubate ideas. With a little bit of work you can learn to "sleep on a problem" and come up with an answer in the morning.

Take that guy Elias Howe, who invented the sewing machine. The only thing wrong with his invention was that it didn't work. One night he had a dream about spear-carrying soldiers, only the soldiers' spears had little round holes just behind the tips. It was just an odd dream that stuck in his mind, until suddenly, eureka! *Voilà!* Bingo! I've got it! By putting the hole at the *pointy* end of the needle instead of at the blunt end—as had been the way with sewing needles since time immemorial— he turned his nonworking invention into a device that changed the world. It could be said that Howe was asleep when he did his best work.

5. Make believe and make real. Do everything you can to immerse yourself in your dream. You need to see, smell, touch, and feel it. You have to try it on for size and perhaps alter it to suit your needs. Look for associations and cyber communities to join, books to read, newsletters to subscribe to, and more. (You'll find sources for them all in the Resources section.)

6. Damn the torpedoes. If you have always listened to good advice, chances are that there are parts of your life being lived on someone else's agenda or in someone else's era. Are there some things you haven't done in your life because of limiting choices in the past? Well, you can hunker down and settle for less on someone else's terms, or you can spit on your hands and get to work on giving yourself more on your own terms. Sometimes you have to put good advice aside, and take an Informed Risk.

Sometimes you also have to put aside inner voices that say, "I'm scared of the unknown and unquantifiable. I'm scared of failing, because I've been brought up with a sense that failing is bad."

As you have already seen, failing and learning from the experience *feeds* your growth and buoyancy. If you wait until you are actually ready to start a dream career of any kind, you will wait until the snow is

---

All ambitions are lawful except those which climb upward on the miseries or credulities of mankind. —Joseph Conrad

dusting your funeral cortege. At some point you just gotta say, "Okay, lock and load, gang, 'cause here I come!"

Take William's sad case. William was a Wall Street guy working for the Soylent Green Investment Bank. William knew that, because he was now fifty, his days with the firm were numbered. This was something that no one could ever prove, it was just that at Soylent Green you never saw fifty-five-year-olds walking the halls.[4] His conclusion was that he had to examine other options before it was too late. So far, so good. But at a group session he was asked to conceive of alternate careers for himself, and he had extreme difficulty.

William said he knew everything about money—how it works, how to get it, and how to leverage it. He also knew everyone in town, but still he couldn't see a way out. When a struggling entrepreneur suggested he help her get a loan, he dismissed the opportunity without a second thought, seeing it only as something that accountants do. In the dismissing he showed his ignorance of what accountants do (as well as exclusionary thinking), and walked right past a legitimate, much-needed service for the millions of young businesses eager to grow. Would it have been the right opportunity for William? We'll never know, but we do know that William will never have the chance to find out because his thinking was so firmly stuck in the rut he wanted to escape from. He couldn't conceive of anything unless he had already done it and it had the same label that he was used to. Sometimes you just have to learn to say yes to discussing new ideas before it is too late.

ADVANCING IN THE DIRECTION OF YOUR DREAM

The old view had it that dreamers have no place in the world of big business. After all, we know that artists are impractical, disorderly, and emotional, right?[5] Maybe there is some truth to these biases and stereotypes. Michelangelo spent all those years alone, lying on his back painting the ceiling of the Sistine Chapel. More recently Mick Jagger and Axl Rose are pretty famous for their rebellious and raunchy natures. These guys certainly aren't corporate types; they have nothing in common with successful professionals you know—or they didn't until now anyway.

Our career-buoyancy research with dream careerists found some amazing and truly wonderful surprises about the *real* behavior of successful, buoyant dream careerists. Nothing like this has ever been considered, re-

---

A life spent in constant labor is a life wasted, save a man be such a fool as to regard a fulsome obituary notice as ample reward. —George Jean Nathan

searched, and suggested before, and the conclusions we can now draw about buoyant dream careerists I know are going to give you *a new lease on your dreams*. The path to your dream career parallels the path to core-career buoyancy. The journeys aren't the same, but both need the same behaviors to take you to your destination.

THE BUOYANCY OF DREAM CAREERISTS

Rather than rely on society's ingrained bias and stereotype, we asked many different types of already-buoyant dream careerists what it takes to achieve success in a dream career.[6] I believe this to be the first research-based work to be done on the subject.

Just what are the traits you need to be buoyant in a dream career? Some of the traits will confirm your suspicions; others will astonish you. And how do these traits compare with those core careerists need? I'll show you how these dream-career behaviors connect to core-career behaviors. It's a wonderful discovery that will launch your ship of dreams.

What behaviors does it take to make it as a buoyant dream careerist?

Goal Orientation

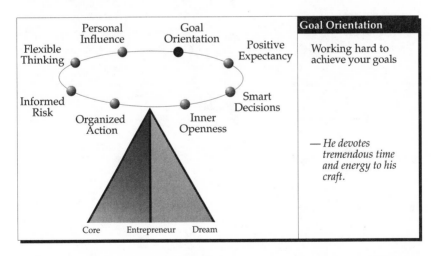

Authority without wisdom is like a heavy ax without an edge, fitter to bruise than polish. —Anne Bradstreet

All buoyant core careerists talk about Goal Orientation. Without it, they say, you end up sinking like a stone. The dream careerists in our research identified motivation as absolutely the most important thing they needed to be buoyant in their career.

Having the artistic talent, having the dream of that computer consultancy or the idea for the next big thing, isn't enough unless you have the drive to manifest your dreams.

DRIVING ONWARD

You need a goal to orient yourself and to give direction to your needs. You have to be able to say yes to the projects that help meet your goal and no to other projects that might be easier and thus more appealing to do but that aren't so important to your overall goals.

Pursuing Your Dream—Goal Orientation

The life of a dream careerist—in the case of yours truly, a working writer—consists of very long, tiring days, especially at deadline time. Days blend into nights and weekdays into weekends. There were times when I was writing *Beat the Odds* when I wanted to just stop, so I did. I took breaks. I had to, in order to keep being productive. But I never lost sight of the goal: to write the best book there ever was about careers.

Friends told me that throughout the process I had that gleam in my eye that I get when I'm absorbed in my work. In spite of the tremendous amount of time and energy that went into *Beat the Odds*, it also charged me up. It was Goal Orientation that kept me going, because I could see and taste and feel what *B.T.O.* was going to become.

The optimist proclaims that we live in the best of all possible worlds; and the pessimist fears this is true. —James Branch Cabell

Core Career

Dream Career

Goal Orientation—Resonance Between Your Dream Career and Your Core Career

The corporate world divides its inhabitants into doers, who are goal oriented and well rewarded, and ditherers, who are task oriented and poorly rewarded—you know, the people for whom the task always expands to use all of the allotted time. Your dream career will reward your behavior in the same way. When you are motivated to take any action toward a dream-career goal, your cause is advanced; when you dither, your momentum fails.

When you are not motivated by some well-defined dream-career goal, you are inactive and your dream-career path is stalled. Your Goal Orientation skills from your core job will keep your dream career advancing, or help jump-start it if you are stalled.

Positive Expectancy

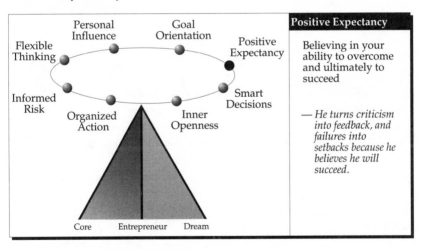

Positive Expectancy is the alchemy of dream-career buoyancy. It's the turning of lead into gold. It allows you to realize that *you* are not a failure when your creative work is rejected by an editor, agent, or a yet-to-be-adoring public. Maybe your work, this time, wasn't what people wanted

It is better to understand little than to misunderstand a lot. —Anatole France

or expected. Sure, you failed to get published or produced or exhibited or sold, and yes, there is a sting in a rejection. But that is the life of a dream careerist—a thousand no's for a single yes, and every no a valuable lesson in getting closer to yes; that's Positive Expectancy.

POSITIVE FOCUS

When people tell you they don't like your work, they are not saying that they don't like *you*. And when your work is rejected, you are not rejected. This is one of the secrets of dream-career buoyancy: If you expect to succeed, then you must experience what once might have been perceived as failures as simply setbacks. And a setback is an opportunity to get feedback so that you do ultimately reach your goal.

TRY, TRY AGAIN

Persistence, born of the belief in ultimate success, is a key trait of buoyant dream careerists. It's easy to see it in action when it comes to Positive Expectancy: When you fail, you don't roll over and play dead. Instead you approach the events with an "attitude of knowledge": What can be learned from the experience? Just how serious is the setback? You look at the negatives so that you can see how to turn them into positives, and you keep giving it a go, believing in your ability to overcome and ultimately to succeed.

Pursuing Your Dream—Positive Expectancy

Six weeks and hundreds of hours went into Dave's writing. He was focusing on the most important part of his new book. So when his editor called to say she had some feedback on this part of his manuscript, Dave looked forward to some good news. He didn't get it. "Not quite what I was expecting," she told him. Fifteen minutes later his vision of the manuscript was destroyed, completely obliterated. Fortunately his ego, though seriously injured, was still intact.

Dave took a lot of notes. He had a firm direction on which to base his revision. He knew that the book concept was still solid and strong, and that the fact that his editor had spent so much time reviewing his progress meant that she believed in his book too. With this detailed feedback in hand he was able to redo the section. Dave now figures that those six weeks weren't wasted and that he needed to get that first draft done so that he could discover the best path to take on the book. He turned criticism into feedback, and failure into success, because he believed in what he was doing and that he would succeed in the end.

Trust yourself. Think for yourself. Act for yourself. Speak for yourself. Be yourself. Imitation is suicide. —Marva Collins

Core Career

Dream Career

Positive Expectancy—Resonance Between Your Dream Career and Your Core Career

Core-career professionals are often up against huge obstacles in getting their ideas approved and projects moving. It always seems another signature is required, or there's some new delay or some disaster. Then, when things are sailing along, the new VP wants to dump the program and it's back to square one. Positive Expectancy keeps you going. Dream careerists, too, pay their bills with persistence. After sixty manuscript rejections, a poorly attended gallery opening, or people walking out of the bar as you play your signature boogie tune, you need to tap into your Positive Expectancy to keep yourself afloat.

Both careers require tremendous persistence to accomplish your objectives and vision. Both careers require you to envision your success in order to keep yourself going.

Inner Openness

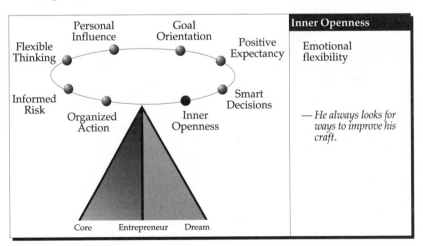

Inner Openness breaks down into three areas:

The world is divided into people who do things and people who get the credit. Try, if you can, to belong to the first class. There's far less competition. —Dwight Morrow

1. Self-awareness
2. Understanding others
3. Getting and giving feedback

SELF-AWARENESS

Self-awareness and understanding underlie all honest relationships with others. Self-awareness allows you to look at yourself and discover who you are—what you like, what you dislike, what things you are good at, and what you want out of your work life. After all, you define your own success—no one else does. Self-awareness also means you are aware how others perceive you, and how all your actions affect that awareness.

Inner Openness allows you to make peace with yourself and to honestly recognize all the faulty or inadequately defined behaviors that stand between you and your dream.

UNDERSTANDING OTHERS

Another aspect of Inner Openness is how you apply this self-awareness to other people. Inner Openness means that you are easy to work with and tolerant and that you respect the diversity of people with whom you journey. Inner Openness gives you an awareness of the needs common to all people, and allows you to be a true collaborator. Whether you're an author, an actor, or part of an artists' cooperative, your Inner Openness increases your opportunities for growth and creativity.

GETTING AND GIVING FEEDBACK

A writer I know complained, "Most of the people I show my work to send it back with comments like, 'I enjoyed it. Good work,' or with grammatical and spelling corrections, and with no substance." It is difficult to give good feedback because not only do you have to know your stuff but you have to know the other person. You have to pitch it in a way that the person can understand and accept.

Receiving feedback, on the other hand, is your brain telling your hand that it had better move off of the stove or get burned. Unsuccessful people have a tendency to react to negative feedback as criticism that needs a defense, while buoyant people are equally open to positive and negative feedback, because both offer the same opportunities for growth. Feedback gives you information about what is happening in the world around you, and how others respond to your interactions with the world whatever form the interactions take. Wouldn't you love to get feedback on your work of art, poem,

No one who has poured himself or herself into work has ever failed.
—Kim Woo-Cheng

song, or performance so that you can improve it? Feedback won't burn you and can't hurt you, *unless you ignore it.* When you are open to feedback and learn to channel it productively, your Inner Openness rewards you with increased tradecraft in the career of your dreams.

Pursuing Your Dream—Inner Openness

Temperamental artists? If you don't like it, tough? It wasn't that way with the dream careerists we spoke to, like this buoyant fine artist we met in our research:

"You have to believe in your own product. You also have to be able to interact with other people. I get along with people very well, and I also work with my customers. I'm completely open to suggestions. I don't have such an ego that when someone hires me to do something, I do it and then that's it, and if you don't like it, tough bananas. Some artists do. They feel that if you've seen their work and you've commissioned them to do something, then that's it. The input of people is important to me. If they're not happy with it, and my signature is on that painting, then they're not going to be enthusiastic about it when they show it to their guests. If they truly love the painting I've done for them, that gets me more customers, because their friends come over and see the work and then call me."

That's Inner Openness: the practical use of feedback to improve your dream career work.

 Core Career

Dream Career

Inner Openness—Resonance Between Your Dream Career and Your Core Career

Core careerists are involved in self-managed work teams, which require being open to suggestion and being able to work with people on a common goal. Inner Openness developed in a core career can pay off in your dream career—you develop the ability to turn suggestions that you may have considered to be rejection or criticism into productive feedback.

Other people and their opinions are just as much a part of a dream career as they are a core career.

If someone tells you he is going to make a "realistic decision," you immediately understand that he has resolved to do something bad. —Mary McCarthy

Personal Influence

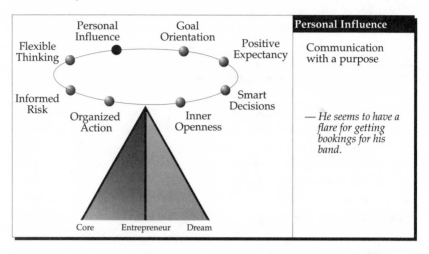

Sales is a core-career necessity, isn't it? It has nothing at all to do with a dream career, right? *Au contraire, mon cher!* Dream careerists told us that the abilities to sell and to position themselves in the market are both essential parts of their buoyancy.

COMMUNICATION FOR A REASON

I know a few people who simply love to talk. I'm not sure if it's the sound of their own voice that they enjoy hearing or whether they talk the way some people tap their fingers when they're nervous. Whatever it is, it is not communication with a purpose.

Communication *has* a purpose: to increase understanding, and in the case of Personal Influence, the communication purpose is to persuade, to change, and to enlighten someone else, all to benefit your own work-life buoyancy in some way.

YOUR WORK DOESN'T ALWAYS SPEAK FOR ITSELF

Buoyant dream careerists recognize that their work product—new surfboard, statue, poem, or macrame pot holder—makes a statement. They told us that their work has a message and that one of their goals is to make sure that that message is clearly communicated.

It takes a great deal of Personal Influence to convince someone to display,

The best way out is always through. —Robert Frost

distribute, or purchase their art. Sometimes just getting the shelf space or gallery space required the same amount of creative energy as the work itself.

Personal Influence gets your work the initial attention it needs to speak for itself—and sell itself!

Pursuing Your Dream—Personal Influence

Tim's core career is in fleet auto sales: always has been, probably always will be as far as he can tell. But Tim is one happy dude, because he is also pursuing his dream. Tim's band, Old Enough to Know Better, which is made up of middle-aged hippies like himself, is doing pretty well. It wasn't always the case. When they were starting out, they had a lot of time to practice, since no one was hiring them to play any gigs. In turning them down, one manager told them they didn't have a reputation. Tim decided to treat the band as he would a new territory at his job. He started to visit local bars, talk to the managers and get their ideas on what works, and look through the paper to figure out who was playing what. After a couple of months he understood what the market would support. The band added some new material and then produced a brief two-cut promotional cassette. Tim then pitched to his newfound customer base and got a break: a long-term gig as a resident backup band, which would give Old Enough to Know Better great experience and the ability to generate a following.

The effort Tim expended on marketing his band was not an easy thing to do, but it was necessary. By using his Personal Influence, he and his band are now on their way.

 Core Career

Dream Career

Personal Influence—Resonance Between Your Dream Career and Your Core Career

Core careerists must sell their plans, products, and ideas. Dream careerists must sell their creative wares, or perish. The formal approaches to sales and marketing learned in your core career will give you a real boost in your dream career. Creativity is of no value in a vacuum, but fortunately your core-career Personal Influence skills can make a tangible difference to your dream career, as they help you bring that work product of your dream career to a larger audience.

One chance is all you need. —Jesse Owens

Organized Action

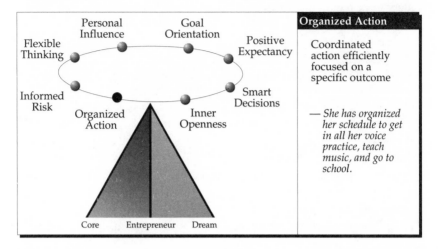

In your core career, Organized Action involves analysis, planning, and achievable milestone schedules, with each deadline reached by a hundred measured steps, each step a single action that can be completed in one day.

MAKING IT HAPPEN

Now, I know what it takes to get a book from my head to your local bookstore, so this critical behavior for dream career buoyancy wasn't much of a surprise to me. The steps are exactly the same as you would use in a core career. From the germ of an idea through the selling of the book off the bookshelves, every single step mirrors the simple common sense of professional project-management skills.

FOCUS, FOCUS, FOCUS

There's a nice analogy for Organized Action that one of our research subjects came up with. Steve, a rural Maine carpenter and furniture builder, likened Organized Action to a laser beam. Steve said that running around just doing things makes no sense. There's no power in that. Unfocused energy is like beams of light bouncing around in space—there's no power in all that energy.

Even if you are on the right track, you will get run over if you just sit there.
—*Will Rogers*

Unfocused Action

Take that same energy and organize all the beams toward something, and you have just created a very powerful tool. It has the power to get things done.

 Organized Action

That's Organized Action: energy with a purpose. A laser beam.

Pursuing Your Dream—Organized Action

Joanna's schedule is really busy. She teaches violin several days a week, plays in a regional orchestra, and supplements this with wedding and bar mitzvah work. She's also working on an advanced degree. "I'm really pretty disorganized," she told me. "So I provide structure for myself, which means I have to get things done." She first books her symphony practice and concert dates and puts them in her calendar. Next she checks out the college bulletin and chooses the two courses she needs to take. She tells the music studio then what days she's available to teach and books that time. Finally, when someone calls needing a violinist, whether in advance or as a last-minute stand-in, she checks to see if she's available and if she has the energy.

Study time and practice time usually come between teaching appointments. "I know it sounds like a lot, but most of my musician friends are this busy too. Most of the time it doesn't really feel like too much to do because I enjoy it all so much."

Joanna has developed procedures and methods to organize her time efficiently and to accomplish everything she needs to do. She makes things happen with Organized Action.

If at first you don't succeed, so much for skydiving. —Anonymous

Core Career

Dream Career

Organized Action—Resonance Between Your Dream Career and Your Core Career

Joanna reminded me of a really good corporate program manager who figures out the schedules for a product-development program, coordinates all the team members' actions, and makes sure that the whole process works smoothly, efficiently, and on time, thanks to adequate planning and momentum. Joanna, it turns out, was in program management once upon a time.

Informed Risk

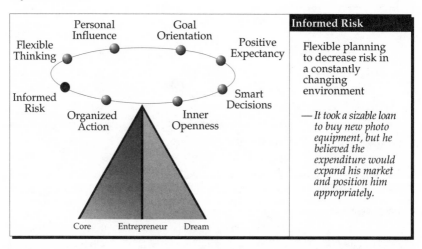

Dare to be different. Take an Informed Risk. Don't do it just to be different. Do it because it's the *right* thing to do, and because you understand the odds.

BEING DIFFERENT

Artists shouldn't have too much difficulty with this one, right? Perhaps the old stereotypes of the nonconformist artistic types aren't *totally*

The first hundred years are the hardest. —Wilson Mizner

wrong. Informed Risk allows the buoyant dream careerist to think and act differently, to compute the odds of success of the expected methods, and then to *not* go along with the common wisdom.

Informed Risk also allows you to follow the straight and narrow when that makes the most sense, when the odds favor the traditional course of action.

PACKING A BACKUP CHUTE

Buoyant dream careerists, when they dare to be different, don't go off half-cocked. They plan. They stay flexible. They pack a backup chute just in case their main chute—their Plan A—doesn't work out.

Flexible plans are essential to Informed Risk. Anyone can do something dumb, anyone can be different. By thinking through the consequences of your plans, and being ready with contingency plans, means that you are dramatically increasing the odds in your favor.

FEELING UNCOMFORTABLE

Informed Risk allows you to accept a certain amount of uncertainty in your life and your plans. The key word here is *informed*—where you know the odds, you know the context, and you know your own skills. Informed Risk asks you to take all that you know—about yourself, your craft, your market—and rate the options based on the information you have at that time.

Pursuing Your Dream—Informed Risk

Harry is a photographer and graphic artist. He loves his work, but he believed that his days were numbered if he stayed with existing techniques and customers. So he became interested in the new technology and its possibilities. Harry read about it, went to shows, talked to people, and worked out costs. Then he took the plunge with a sizable loan from the bank.

Harry used his bank loan to buy computer equipment that allowed him to digitize his darkroom. Friends and many of his colleagues thought he was nuts. But since he had already contacted some possible clients, Harry was able to start selling his new graphic capabilities pretty quickly. Except for one huge problem: he wasn't compatible with a new client's software! Disaster for someone else, but not for Harry. He had a backup plan—going to the computer store and getting a

---

I decided to box my way out of the ghetto. —Larry Holmes

loaner machine with the needed programs until the project was completed and he had won the business. Harry was able to gradually wean the client away from their in-house program and onto Harry's state-of-the-art system.

He lost money for about five months—which he had anticipated. But Harry knew that wouldn't last, and, in the sixth month Harry turned a profit. By the end of the year he had exceeded his previous year's income. But more importantly, he doesn't feel that his days are numbered anymore. Harry has what it takes— Informed Risk.

Core Career

Dream Career

Informed Risk—Resonance Between Your Dream Career and Your Core Career

Informed Risk in a dream career is identical to Informed Risk in your core career. They both involve understanding how the business end of the career works and consequently how everyone in a particular professional chain earns a paycheck. With a little P.K.H. the dream careerist can make an Informed Risk in targeting a particular aspect of his or her dream-career world for specific development. You'll try many different approaches over the years as you carve a niche for yourself; and as your P.K.H. increases, the accuracy of your Informed Risk improves accordingly.

New ways of expressing yourself in a dream career involve an element of uncertainty and risk, so the pursuit of a dream career will help you develop a talent for Informed Risk, which will help you to in turn achieve core-career buoyancy.

Defeat is not bitter unless you swallow it. —Joe Clark

Flexible Thinking

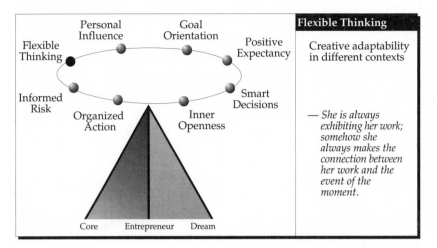

In a core career you hear Flexible Thinking talked about as problem-identification and -solution skills, symbolic-analysis skills, and analytical skills. In dream careers these same connectivity skills get referred to as "creativity." And in both parallel career paths, Flexible Thinking identifies new problems, opportunities, options, and angles and brings your unique perspective to bear.

ORIGINALITY

Good ideas, new ideas, and many ideas are an important part of Flexible Thinking. Indeed idea fluency in this context gets defined as creativity all the time. It is putting together existing forms and bits of information, and through your vision bringing into existence something new and different.

PROBLEM SOLVING

Flexible Thinking also embraces symbolic-analytical skills. Understanding your subject, framing the challenge, analyzing it, and then solving the problem on paper, with paints, or in a photograph, is part of a constant learning process. All art is an opportunity recognized and a response offered; art is a gift of vision given practical means of expression.

An optimist is a fellow who believes a house fly is looking for a way to get out.
—George Jean Nathan

CONSTANT LEARNING

Fish have to swim and birds have to fly, and you must always learn and grow if you are to stay buoyant. New techniques must be learned, and skills brought up to date. You must have a desire to learn, know, and discover, because a questioning mind is a flexible mind.

Here's what one of our buoyant careerists told us: "Creativity just enables you to get *into* the ball game. After that you have to have every little thing that everyone else has. You have to have the interpersonal skills and the adaptability, and you have to be easy to get along with." Creativity is nothing on its own; it requires the interaction of the eight critical traits in order to come into existence. This is what *Beat the Odds* is all about: the interaction of a single sequence of behaviors applied in different context to help you achieve your American Dream.

Pursuing Your Dream—Flexible Thinking

Rebecca worked days as a realtor and nights as a watercolorist. But the outlets for her paintings were pretty limited, so she had to expand her market somehow. As she was scanning the paper one day, she found an article about an upcoming show at the aquarium. "I know I'm not a biologist or oceanographer, but for some reason watercolors and an aquarium just seemed to be a natural together. Plus I was already working on some seascapes."

Rebecca decided to focus her efforts on the seascapes and then contacted the aquarium director. It didn't happen overnight, but after several meetings and explanations over the course of two months, Rebecca was exhibiting her paintings at a special aquarium event, and making sales.

Dream Career

Core Career

Flexible Thinking—Resonance Between Your Dream Career and Your Core Career

In your core career you struggle to come up with ideas and plenty of them (ideas and idea fluency). In this kind of career the prospect can be anything, but it will always be something that makes money for the company, saves money for the

---

I like work; it fascinates me. I can sit and look at it for hours. —Jerome K. Jerome

company, or saves time for the company (which is a double whammy, because it saves money and makes the time to earn more).

In your dream career you will use Flexible Thinking to benefit You, Inc. in exactly the same way. You will also use it to look at the world around you in new and different ways. Flexible Thinking is exactly what helped one dream-careerist jewelry designer come up with the multi-million-dollar mood-ring phenomenon.

The designer who first mounted these stones in ring settings, and allowed people to explore the changes based on their moods, was a dream careerist of exemplary Flexible Thinking skills. In a core career it's a new angle for an ad campaign; in a dream career it's a new angle for a photograph. In a core career it's the idea for a new service that increases revenue at little cost; in a dream career it's an idea for the next Hacky Sack, Pet Rock, or Hoola Hoop.

Ideas and idea fluency are always the same; it's the contexts that change. Flexible Thinking has resonance between your dream and your core career; listen, there's always a new idea.

Smart Decisions

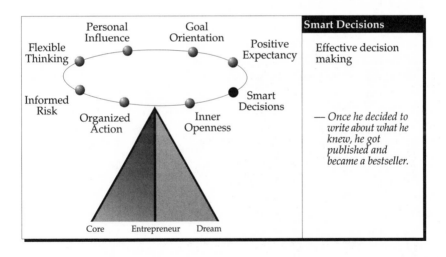

A lost but happy dream may shed its light upon our waking hours, and the whole day may be infected with the gloom of a dreary or sorrowful one; yet of neither may we be able to recover a trace. —Walter de la Mare

The benefits of Smart Decisions are earned. If you intend to become buoyant in your dream career, you must study the world in which this career occurs. Then you must pursue it with vigor and the attention to detail you apply to your core career.

As you take your dream career more seriously, your thirst for knowledge increases your practical know-how in your dream pursuit, to the point where you call the shots right on a regular basis, and you begin to feel like a member of the professional community in your new parallel career.

The ability to make Smart Decisions is earned over time by students serious about their passion. The benefits are directions and actions that work toward bringing a dream to life.

JUST SAY YES

You have to take the plunge sometime and just say yes. Just say yes to the invitation to exhibit a painting. Just say yes to fill in for the regular bass player. Just say yes to your dreams.

Just as your dreams seem to quickly fade away when you wake up in the morning, so, too, will your dream career fade away unless you jump right on it. A Smart Decision right now might be for you to buy a book related to attaining your dreams (see Resources). That's how a buoyant Dream Career starts, with the development of P.K.H.

Pursuing Your Dream—Smart Decisions

I first thought about being a writer when I was fifteen. Over the next twenty years I tried my hand at just about every kind of writing imaginable, from copywriting in the world of advertising to romantic fiction and beyond. I had no luck, as I then saw it. Then I read somewhere that you should write about what you know, and suddenly my decision became obvious: I would write about the workplace, jobs, and careers. That was one smart decision. I took what I had—fifteen years in human resource development—and used it as a bridge to get where I wanted to go—life as a writer.

Your reputation is only as good as what you did yesterday. —Traditional saying

Core Career

Dream Career

Smart Decisions—Resonance Between Your Dream Career and Your Core Career

Smart Decisions are built on firm foundations of common sense and practical know-how. Your core career will afford you many chances to exercise your Smart Decisions muscle, what with multiple projects, tight deadlines, and conflicting objectives screaming at you to be decisive.

Dream careers can greatly benefit from your core-career decisiveness. And although the context is different, decision making is decision making is decision making. By pushing you forward, the logical decision-making skills developed as a core careerist give your dream career a push forward too.

EVERYTHING THEY TOLD YOU IS WRONG

I mentioned two well-known artists earlier in this chapter: Mick Jagger and Michelangelo. Let's visit them again, only this time let's see how they stack up to the eight traits.

Think about old Mick Jagger for a moment. Some think that Mick is the most unbusinesslike person they could ever think of. Well, that's not quite right. Ever hear of the London School of Economics? If not, it's one of the world's most prestigious business-oriented schools. Do you know who attended the London School of Economics? Yes, our raunchy, crazy, ever lovin' Mick Jagger.

If you think about the Rolling Stones and read a bit about Mick, you realize that he is also a terrific businessman. He has a huge business enterprise that is enormously successful. He read the market just right. As you go through each of the eight dream-career buoyancy traits, you will recognize that Mick has them all, every last one, and all at a very high level.

A buoyant dream careerist needs these eight traits—and the stronger

Dreaming is an act of pure imagination, attesting in all men a creative power, which, if it were available in waking, would make every man a Dante or Shakespeare.
—H. F. Hedge

the traits, the greater the achievements are likely to be. How about someone whose career was in a different field, such as Michelangelo? Throw out your view of the solitary artist. Michelangelo wasn't a lone wolf. He had a huge creative enterprise going: teams of artists working under his direction preparing canvases and paints. He had a network of wealthy landowners to whom he sold his wares, so he did quite well for himself financially. In fact it's reported that Michelangelo spent his retirement on his estate in Tuscany.[7] In terms of buoyancy traits, Michelangelo is up there with the most buoyant of dream careerists.

So if you are an emerging dream careerist, especially in the arts, rid your mind of the societal biases and stereotypes you may have received about artists; they will do nothing to aid your buoyancy in any career, because, as we have finally proved, they aren't true!

CORE TO DREAM TO CORE AGAIN

Dream careerists and core careerists can form a mutual-admiration society. Core careerists can admire the Goal Orientation and Flexible Thinking of dream careerists. Dream careerists can ooh and ah over the Smart Decisions and Organized Action of core careerists. And they can hoist their glasses and toast each other's traits, happy in the knowledge that they are far more alike than they would ever have believed.

GETTING CLOSER TO YOUR DREAM

Dream-career success isn't a mystery anymore. There are eight behaviors that you need in order to succeed in any dream career, and they are the same critical eight behaviors necessary for buoyancy in your core career; they are just placed in a different context and given a different application. Doing well in your core career and developing core-career buoyancy traits is the best preparation for a buoyant dream career that I know of.

Have that budding dream careerist inside you take a look in the mirror. See that core careerist staring you in the face? You're looking right at a buoyant dream careerist in the making. The behaviors you need for your buoyant core career are the same ones you need to develop a buoyant dream career; and as you develop your new dream career, you will be enriching your core career. Your dreams can become real. You just have to reach for them.

If it is to be, it is up to me. —Anonymous

YES, YOU CAN

Yes, you can develop a dream career. It isn't an either-or proposition any-more. It isn't your core career *or* your dream career. Yes, you can have both, and pursuing one helps develop the other.

NOTES

1. The actual quotation by George Bernard Shaw reads, "You see things; and you say 'Why?' But I dream things that never were; and I say, 'Why not?' "
2. Of course I was doing it wrong for the first eighteen of the twenty years.
3. As of this writing, Kristin had an agent and an audition lined up.
4. This is something nobody talks about, but it happens all the time, and despite the law that prevents age discrimination, it will continue to happen with in-creasing frequency as the population ages.
5. These are some of the traits of the Artistic type in John Holland's domi-nant theory of vocational choices.
6. The upcoming blueprints in the next chapter talk about four particularly tough-to-succeed-in dream careers. However, these were not the only dream careers we examined in our research. We examined buoyant dream careerists in some twenty-five different dream careers. These twenty-five careers had been previously identified as "dream careers" in a separate study we conducted at a New York university in 1992.
7. A great book on Michelangelo is W. E. Wallace's *Michelangelo at San Lorenzo: The Genius as Entrepreneur.* Cambridge University Press, 1994.

There are those, I know, who will reply that the liberation of humanity, the freedom of man and mind, is nothing but a dream. They are right. It is. It is the American Dream.
—Archibald MacLeish

Chapter 8

Dream-Career Blueprints

REACHING FOR YOUR DREAMS

No matter what your dreams are, it will take focus and action to give them life. Dreams don't come easy. Many take years to achieve, and some of the most fulfilling take a lifetime. Nevertheless they are entirely within your grasp.

When you spend time and energy involved in a pursuit of your choice that's alien to your core-career job, you come back to your core career reenergized. As you find and follow your dreams with passion and Organized Action, you will become totally absorbed by them. Then, when it's time to get back to your core career, you'll approach it completely refreshed. When you pursue a dream career, you get to take a regular mental vacation from the stress of everyday work life.

It's really a pretty good deal: Find something you would love to spend some time doing—dancing, sailing, repairing old radios, or whatever turns you on—and learn to apply *essential* professional skills *you are already developing* in your career to these new personal goals. When you run two intelligently integrated parallel careers like this, you get the opportunity to apply important core-career buoyancy skills to goals of your own choosing, and to make those core-career skills so much better in the process. You will learn just as much from your passion as you will from the core-career training courses you are privileged to attend, and the benefit to your core-career buoyancy will be enhanced by the same amount.

If we did all the things we are capable of doing, we would literally astonish ourselves.
—Thomas Edison

Simply put, dreams and dream careers are just all-around good for you. The pursuit of a dream or two on a regular basis will fill a hole in your life. It is even possible to have a wildly meaningful dream career spanning many decades and never make a penny from it, because simply giving practical means of fulfillment to one or more of your needs is payback enough. Yet as a natural by-product of the process you

- Get time for yourself on your own terms
- Increase professional buoyancy in your core career
- Improve the odds of turning a dream into a dream *career*

So it makes sense to find something you love and get immersed in it as quickly and as often as you can. As you develop the P.K.H. in the workings of the industry that nurtures your dream, you will see that, as in your core-career work world, there are two essential functions to make a dream career economically viable: (a) **Research and Development** of goods, services, and people; and (b) **Sales and Marketing** of those goods, services, and people.

In the following illustrations of a handful of fascinating, though wildly different dream careers, although some of the jobs are very different, you will easily identify their commonalities in terms of core-career skills. The jobs may be different, but the skills and behaviors that lead to buoyancy and success are the same.

THE DREAM-CAREER BLUEPRINTS

It's shop class—a time to look under the hood at a handful of dream careers to see how dreams really get started. When we each have such highly personal dreams and needs to fulfill, it's a challenge to find illustrations that everyone holds in common. Now if, as the songwriters say, dreams don't come easy, what I needed was a handful of extremely tough-to-succeed-in dream careers that everyone would recognize. I wanted dream careers

- That are known to be fiercely competitive
- Where getting established takes a long time
- Where the rewards for those who make it can be substantial

The game is well worth the candle that may have to be burned far into the night. There is no feeling like the feeling of success. —*J. Paul Getty*

I also wanted examples that could be used by you as a metaphor for success for your own personal dream. I reasoned that since just about everything you see, touch, and hear was invented by someone, you've probably wondered if you too had it in you to become an inventor; that you have read books and at least once wondered what it would be like to try your hand at writing one; you have taken photographs and imagined the life of a Scavullo or a Liebowitz; and at one time you have wished you could paint a lover's face on the last leaf of fall.

Hence I chose to examine the working lives of inventors, writers, photographers, and artists. If you can take this handful of careers we have all dreamed about on at least one stormy night and can make connections between them and your own self-managed professionalism, you will learn how to give practical expression to your personal vision of the American Dream.

As I give you close-ups of how to start these four distinct dream careers you'll find each covers slightly different terrain. In the inventor's blueprint, we'll follow the true story of two successful inventors who spent three years developing and refining their invention, getting it patented, and taking it to market. In the writer's blueprint, I'll share with you the business side of writing, including how to identify good story ideas and potential markets for them and how to maintain a steady stream of income from writing. In the photographer's blueprint, rather than showing you how to click the shutter, I'll be showing you how to apply your core-career planning and organization skills to get photographs you can sell to *Look* magazine. In the artist's blueprint, I'll show you something Van Gogh would have given his other ear for: better ways of getting the artwork in front of a larger audience. In each blueprint you'll see the different aspects of research and development, and the selling and marketing that are necessary to make your dream a reality.

As you proceed from one blueprint to the next, look for the symmetry they share. Look for the behaviors and values that come into play, and look at what gets done and how it gets done. In each of these blueprints you are going to get a real practical look at some of the things it takes to make a dream come true—any dream, but especially yours.

Diamonds are nothing more than chunks of coal that stuck to their jobs.
—Malcolm Forbes

The Inventor's Blueprint

Edison said, "Invention is ten percent inspiration and ninety percent perspiration." As an accomplished inventor he realized early on that people who can create ideas are a dime a dozen. What really caused him to break out in a serious sweat was the hell he had to go through in order to get those ideas out of his head and into the hands of a larger audience.

Taking an idea from concept through the creation, patent, and sales process can be expensive and difficult. While there are no guarantees that you will profit from your invention, to increase the chances of doing so, you should follow this popular advice: *Find a market and serve it.* In other words, develop a product that you feel will serve a need.

We'll profile here the guys who invented Redout, a photographic accessory that solves the red-eye problem in photographs. Marty and Neil, the co-inventors of Redout, stumbled on the idea for their invention quite by accident.

Neil had bought his wife a camera for Christmas. They took some holiday pictures, but when the pictures came back from the lab, their beautiful daughters looked like they were possessed by demons. In fact all the subjects in the pictures had horrible cases of red-eye. The inventor-to-be took the camera back to the store to exchange it for another that didn't cause red-eye, but the salespeople only chuckled, "Oh, everybody has a problem with red-eye!" Inspired and challenged, he went home and, using his core-career expertise in video, created a solution to red-eye. By attempting to solve a problem for *himself,* he gave birth to an invention that would eventually solve the red-eye problem for millions of consumers.

Many people say, "I have a great idea!" or "I've invented the next pet rock," but they never *do* anything about it. The task seems so big that they don't know where to start. The Redout inventors found the best way to start was to just plunge in—into the research and development stage, that is.

RESEARCH AND DEVELOPMENT

The Patent Search. The Patent Office receives over 140,000 patent applications each year. So before investing money, time, and energy into developing an invention idea, it is wise to find out whether your product, or a similar one, has been patented and is already on the market.

If you don't know where you are going, you might end up where you are.
—Dr. Rod Gilbert

A preliminary patent search can be done at a business library, by mail, on-line, or in person at the Search Room of the Patent and Trademark Office in Arlington, Virginia. You should also check retail stores, catalogs, trade journals, magazines, and newspaper classifieds for any products similar to your invention. This can take time, but it is a great way of educating yourself about other inventions and developing your practical know-how about the business side of the inventor's art. Looking at other people's inventions can also give you ideas for improving your own idea.

Take Notes. You should maintain and keep in a safe place a chronological up-to-date notebook or diary of your product's development. This should include notes and diagrams of all you've done in regard to your invention. It doesn't hurt to have a friend back up your claims by serving as witness to the written records that you keep of your invention's progress. Ask that friend to sign your dated descriptions. This will provide an important paper trail if anyone ever questions your claim to being the inventor of a product. Keep all related receipts and paperwork too, for tax purposes.

Make a Prototype. Unfortunately it's not enough just to have the idea and to jot down a description or sketch a diagram. In order to sell your invention to the public, you must at least have a working model.

A prototype will aid you in your market research and make it easier to convince prospective investors that your product is viable. It does not have to be a full-scale model; its purpose is to allow others to see, touch, and feel your idea in a concrete form. Keep in mind that the materials you use on your prototype do not necessarily have to be the same as those you'll use in the finished product. For example, the Redout invention was originally constructed with kitchen foil and cardboard from a shoe box.

Never expect your first prototype to be the last. Chances are, you'll have to refine it over and over again. Redout, for example, went through twenty-five incarnations before it settled into its final form.

After the tinfoil and shoe-box prototypes were made to work properly (it took about two years), the inventors of Redout had an industrial-design engineer draw up the schematics for a model maker to make an engineering prototype.

The engineering prototype is used to test your invention, and from it a preproduction prototype is made. This prototype will help you determine

---

So of cheerfulness, or a good temper, the more it is spent, the more of it remains.
—Ralph Waldo Emerson

a mold, and the actual cost per unit, for manufacturing your invention. It will also help you figure out what other, unanticipated costs are involved and whether you have to do any redesigning to reduce your manufacturing expenses. If your budget is limited, it may be worthwhile to check into schools that offer an industrial-design curriculum. They might be able to put you in touch with an experienced professor or student who would be willing to do the work within the limitations of your budget.

By the way, when you discuss your idea with other people, be *cautious* about what you say. It is normal business practice *to ask for and receive nondisclosure statements or confidentiality agreements* (see Appendix 3). They essentially state that the signatories will not disclose the information to anyone else.

Patent Your Invention. Who legally owns what's in your head could be the difference between your never having to do another thing you didn't want to do for the rest of your life and relinquishing any rewards you might have earned from your invention. A patent protects your rights as an inventor so that no one can legally copy, use, make, or profit from your invention without you, too, profiting. Patents fall into three categories:

1. Plant—covers biotech, flowers, trees, vegetables, and so on
2. Design—covers the ornamental design of products
3. Utility—the most commonly issued patent, this covers the invention's function and design.

You file for a patent by applying to the United States Patent and Trademark Office, Washington, D.C. 20231. In the United States most patents are good for seventeen years from the date issued, but laws do vary from state to state as well as from country to country.

There are those who dismiss patents because a patent is not necessary to sell anything. Neither does it always prevent people from ripping you off.

However, a patent *is* your protection under the law that ensures that you reap the fruits of your intellectual copyright. There is a story I'd like to share, although I'm not allowed to tell you the real names of the players. Nevertheless, "Keith," a hairdresser, had this great idea for a fashion accessory. Lucky Keith—he fell in with some moneyed people, who got the product a direct-

Experience is not what happens to a man. It's what a man does with what happens to him. —Aldous Huxley

response TV spot. Keith is said to have made twenty million dollars—but already more than two million of that has gone to trying to stop other people from marketing this *unpatented* bauble from which Keith's competitors have, to date, earned an estimated eighty million dollars. If Keith had the protection of a good patent, he wouldn't be in this situation. So, to those people who say a patent doesn't protect you completely, I say that condoms don't stop AIDS one hundred percent of the time, but they certainly can decrease your risk.

Out of the hundreds of thousands of patent applications that are filed each year, only about half are actually granted. Obtaining a patent is not as cut and dried as you may think. A patent application takes between two and three years to be argued, and can cost several thousand dollars. It is because the process is so detailed that a patent stands out as the ultimate insurance in business ownership.

The way the patent process works, first of all, is that if your invention is the same as another existing patent, the Patent Office rules you out. Furthermore, the Patent Office can deny your application because, say, half of your invention is covered in the Smith patent while the other half is covered in the Jones patent.

It is often up to you to prove that your invention is different. The guys who invented Redout were initially denied all but three of their twenty-five claims in their original patent application, yet were eventually able to persuade the Patent Council to grant all but two of them.

There are other legitimate reasons why you could be prevented from obtaining a patent. There is a clause called the One-Year Publication Bar that states that you cannot file for a patent application if more than one year has passed since you started disclosing information in a public forum—for example, in a publication or trade show—or displaying or selling your product to the public. You have every right to sell, distribute, or display your product at any time—*just make sure you apply for your patent within 365 days from the first day that you do it.*

Another reason why you may be turned down is that you and someone else have applied for the same patent of the same invention at the same time. In that case the first inventor would be awarded the patent. Although it is rare that two inventors seek a patent for the same product at the same time, it can happen, as it did with Alexander Bell and Elisha

---

If it's true that you learn from adversity, then I must be the smartest S.O.B. in the world. —Gene Mauch

Gray for the telephone. The owner of one of the world's great inventions was decided according to when their patent applications were registered with the Patent Office—and in this instance both patents were filed the same day, just a few hours apart.

Other Ways of Protecting Your Invention Besides Having a Patent. If you cannot justify the patent process, it would be worth your while to file your idea with the U.S. Patent Office's Document Disclosure Program (U.S.P.T.O. Document Disclosure Program, 2011 Crystal Plaza 2, Room 1B03, Arlington, Virginia 22202). After they receive a description of your invention, they will date-stamp your documents and provide you with a registration number and a copy of your application. Your document will be kept in confidential files for two years. Although this is not an official patent and will not protect you against copycats, it is good evidence to have in case your claim to the invention is disputed.

Alternatively, perhaps copyrighting your idea would be possible. Copyrighting, which is the legal right to use the copyright symbol followed by the year of first publication and your name or abbreviation, lets others know that they cannot copy the material without your permission. It can be used in many fields, so it is worth investigating whether or not you can use one on your product. A copyright is inexpensive and offers legal protection by providing the "exclusive right to the publication, reproduction, revision, sale, etc. of a literary or artistic material." Contact the Registrar of Copyrights, Copyright Office, Library of Congress, James Madison Memorial Building, 101 Independence Avenue S.E., Washington, D.C. 20559, (202) 287-9100, for forms and information.

A trademark is a name, symbol, word, or device that distinguishes you from other products and also serves to protect you and represent your invention. It cannot be used by others; it is a potent advertising and marketing tool. In time the public will recognize it and associate it with your invention, and any other future products you devise. The letters ® and *S* that you often see on product packaging represent the registration of a trademark or service mark with the Patent and Trademark Office.™ or *SM* represent the impending registration of that product's trademark or service mark. This is another method you can use to protect your rights as the originator of an idea.[1]

There are two educations. One should teach us how to make a living and the other how to live. —John Truslow Adams

SALES AND MARKETING

The day that Redout got its patent, the inventors found that the phone didn't ring, and Fuji didn't come knocking at the door. It is a popular misconception that once a product is patented, it will sell itself. When you have the patent, *all* you have is a patent. When the Redout guys got the patent, what they thought was the end of the game was actually the beginning of the second half.

Beware of Invention Brokers and Invention Promotion Firms. Ninety-eight out of a hundred people will think you, as an inventor, are nuts; the other two will take you to the cleaners. This is especially true of invention brokers, the middlemen who purport to find buyers for inventors. A number of these brokers are unscrupulous and make money by *claiming* to promote and market your invention. They often advertise in classified sections of magazines, newspapers, radio, or television, and may even offer a toll-free number to call for information. Be wary of these wolves, or they will eat you alive!

Some brokers entice you in by offering to review your invention for free. This is just another sales tactic they use to reel you in. After they do their preliminary review, they go on to tell you that they need to do further research and that you need to pay them so much for this report and so much for that report. In reality none of these reports will benefit you or help with the marketing of your product. All they do is provide cash for the broker.

I heard so much about invention brokers that I decided to check them out personally. I told my sample invention broker that I had a great idea for an invention, and he told me that for eight hundred dollars he'd evaluate my invention. For $2,300 he would show me how to get a patent and would put my product in front of executives in one thousand of the country's biggest companies. That sounds great, if you don't know what it actually means. Let me translate.

When you give him $2,300, he will put your invention into a loosely bound folder that includes hundreds of other inventions, and he will mail it to someone at each of the Fortune 1,000 companies. But there's no guarantee that it's going to get read or acted upon. Invention brokers also participate in and promote invention fairs; the bad news is that the people who buy patents don't *go* to invention fairs. Most of the people

Every man believes that he has a greater possibility. —Ralph Waldo Emerson

who go to them are fellow inventors! That's certainly not going to help you sell your product to a company. As far as showing me how to get a patent, there is no way on earth to obtain a patent without a lawyer, so the other claim was bogus too, and I would have paid a portion of $2,300 to find out I had to hire an attorney. The broker wasn't going to do anything except take my money and put my invention in a folder. I said no, thank you.

Run from all the invention brokers and companies that claim to shop your invention to independent manufacturers but don't offer you proof that they will. Some firms may want to act as your exclusive marketing and licensing agent, but only after you agree to pay them a large up-front fee along with a portion of any royalties your invention may generate. This is a *red flag*.

Credible firms don't require high fees up front; instead they rely on the revenues they receive from the clients they've helped establish and market. After all my research on this book and my active involvement with inventors and inventions, I never found a single invention broker with a track record and credentials.

If you think you've found a straight-arrow broker, ask questions. Find out about the company's qualifications and the criteria it uses when evaluating inventions. Reputable firms will be happy to provide you with any information you request. Take the time to call the Better Business Bureau, attorney general, or any local consumer protection agency to see if any complaints have been filed against the broker you want to do business with. Get as many details as possible, and ask for references! Question the reputation of a firm that refuses to disclose information about its success rate and how many of their clients actually profited from their inventions.

When working with invention brokers or invention promotion firms, remember to get everything in writing, including the cost of all its services, before you sign on the dotted line. Use an attorney to review all contacts. The FTC provides a complimentary pamphlet entitled *Facts for Consumers: Invention Promotion Firms.* Call (202) 326-3268 to request a copy. It's worth the cost of the call.

Choose a Manufacturer and Distributor for Your Product. Once you've developed a preliminary prototype of your product and have taken the

---

All good things which exist are the fruits of originality. —John Stewart Mill

proper steps to protect your idea, you can start looking into its manufacturing and distribution.

Remember, you don't need patent approval to sell your product. If you have applied for a patent and want to go ahead and sell your invention, you should use the words "patent pending" on it while progressing through the patent-approval process.

There are several traditional methods of distributing your product:

• *A third party manufactures and distributes the invention and you receive a royalty for sales.* This typical licensing method requires the least financial and physical effort on behalf of the entrepreneur and is the least risky. The benefit is obvious, but it is often difficult to find a company willing to license your invention. There is no set royalty rate for licenses. They can vary, but the average tends to be approximately 5 percent of sales.

In order to find companies that would be interested in licensing your invention, go to the library and check the *Thomas Register of American Manufacturers.*

Unfortunately some companies do not accept unsolicited material because they are fearful of getting sued by outsiders who may claim the company stole their secrets. But that doesn't mean you shouldn't send them a letter explaining your interest in meeting with them. The problem with this approach is generally felt to be that unless you are properly protected and represented, a major manufacturer will stall you while trying to reengineer your product.

• *Use an OEM (Original Equipment Manufacturer).* This essentially means a third party manufactures the invention but you distribute it. When seeking a manufacturer to do this, keep in mind that in order to be profitable, manufacturing should not cost more than 25 percent of the retail price of the product.

• *You manufacture it, but someone else distributes it.* Shop around for the most cost-effective method of manufacturing your product.

• *Do it all yourself.* You manufacture your product and you distribute it. While this method is the most difficult, it is the most financially rewarding if the anticipated volume of your invention is minimal.

The habit of looking on the bright side of every event is worth more than a thousand pounds a year. —Samuel Johnson

Be aware that, in order to successfully market your idea on your own, you have to have money; sales, advertising, marketing, retail, direct response, and mail-order experience; knowledge of legal contracts and infringement laws; and so on. You must also have the time, and the willingness, to travel to display your merchandise at appropriate trade shows and other exhibitions. The biggest advantage to doing everything yourself, aside from the fact that you make the largest profit if the product is successful, is that you retain control of your product.

How Redout Was Marketed. The Redout inventors looked at all these options and didn't like the either-or choices presented. Instead they thought they'd use some tricks they'd learned from their core careers to raise cash.

Instead of using a single approach to bringing their product to market, the Redout inventors approached everyone they possibly could and exercised their options all at once. In so doing they maximized the odds for bringing their invention to market. If they said to their potential investors, "Gee, would you like to invest in this new product?" the investors could say yes or no. But if they also said, "We have a new product, and a lot of people are interested in investing in it" and could back up their statement, they would have a measure of leverage.

Such a philosophy can be summed up this way: getting to no. Most people talk about negotiating as the process of getting to yes and reaching an agreement. Well, if you're an inventor or creator, you're always on the back end of the train, and you have no control except when you're in a position to say no. It's only when you can say, "I don't want to do business with company A, because I'd rather do business with company B," that you are in control. The best way to reach the control of veto is create some *competition.*

Capital and Inventors. It takes serious money to bring a new product to market. Whom should you consider as sources of financing?

• *Family and Friends.* Neil and Marty didn't have that wealthy family member who could lend them money, and their friends lived just as close to the bone as they did, with kids to support and mortgages to pay.

So the question is, do corporate executives, provided they stay within the law, have responsibilities in their business activities other than to make as much money for their stockholders as possible? And my answer to that is, no they do not. —Milton Friedman

• *Bank loans.* Banks lend money to inventors about as often as they do to the homeless.

• *Venture Capital and Investment Banking Firms.* These companies are generally not regarded as good sources for individual investors; they specialize in corporate ventures and investments. However, Neil and Marty inspired great interest in six such companies with their pitch letter.

• *Professionals.* Lawyers and accountants can sometimes put you in touch with those who might be willing to provide the financing, or they might even be willing to provide the financing themselves. Neil and Marty contacted such professionals but they weren't interested.

• *Small Business Investment Companies (SBIC).* This organization is licensed by the SBA and is partially federally funded. Neil and Marty contacted them, but they said no.

• *State-government grants.* Many states are offering grants and capital for high-technology start-ups. Redout was low-tech and was being developed by two guys with six-packs in their spare time; thus it wasn't eligible for state funding.

• *Small Business Innovation Research (SBIR).* This agency dispenses a certain proportion of funds for individuals and independently owned companies with five hundred or fewer employees. Unfortunately our inventors didn't have luck here either.

With Redout so near to the retail shelves and yet so far, Marty and Neil were fresh out of money. They had their engineering prototype, but the next task at hand was to make molds at a price tag of between fifty and sixty thousand dollars! Industrial-design fees would amount to thirty thousand, and short-run manufacturing and other items would soak up an additional sixty thousand. They simply couldn't see how to produce their product.

By August 1994 they had progressed to owning two engineering prototypes (built to engineering specifications and manufactured by a professional model maker). They had also pitched Redout to some one hundred and forty prospects, including lawyers, accountants, wealthy individuals, and venture capitalists, as well as film, camera, and accessory companies. Still no go.

Man was made at the end of the week's work when God was tired. —Mark Twain

The Payoff. Two and a half years into the project they finally had a favorable audience with an influential attorney. It seemed all they had to do was test the new prototype, give it to the attorney, and start planning ways to spend the loot. Unfortunately the new prototype didn't seem to work as well as older models. It took them two months to identify and solve the problems and complete successful tests.

Then, in October 1994, they again sat down with the attorney, but this time he had six other lawyers with him. One week later they were on first-name terms with the head of an investment bank, and plans are now progressing to raise a million and a half dollars and to launch Redout on television nationally, in time for the 1995 red-eye holiday season, and that was just the first offer.

Our two dream careerists, the Redout partners, are ordinary suburban guys with families and mortgages and day jobs that take up sixty or seventy hours a week. As you have read, it took certain behaviors to achieve their dream and to take them from where they were—two guys with the latest pet rock—toward were they wanted to be: multimillionaires who could spend their time chasing bluefish and inventing other things.

THE BUOYANT INVENTOR

Redout started as a D.I.Y. solution to an irritating problem known to three hundred million red-eye-producing camera owners; it was a gizmo invented on the kitchen table. Exactly how far have the inventors come by behaving the way they have? What was the creative part of Redout? Was it the initial invention or everything that took place after that? When a tree falls alone in the woods, does it make a sound? Was it creativity as it is *traditionally* interpreted, or was it what *we* believe creativity to be—a result of the interactions between the eight critical behaviors we have identified in the *B.T.O.* research? Like buoyancy, creativity requires the interaction of all eight of the following critical behaviors at a developed level of performance:

   • **Goal Orientation.** Like many breadwinners, Neil and Marty desperately wanted to get rid of the mortgage millstone from around their necks; the longer they worked on Redout, the better it looked. Their goal orientation grew in relation to the effort they put into the project.

Not he is great who can alter matter, but he who can alter my state of mind.
—Ralph Waldo Emerson

• **Positive Expectancy.** Neil and Marty had both reached an acceptable level of success in their core careers, and they kept calling on this strength. They'd say to each other, "We're brilliant, so we know this is a great idea." They'd say, "Hey, we made mistakes in our core careers, corrected them, and won out." And they'd say, "There's no reason we can't apply the same skills to our new hobby." They believed they would succeed in this project *just as they had succeeded in other giant projects in their separate core careers.*

• **Smart Decisions/Practical Know-how.** Neither Neil nor Marty understood the world of inventing, or how to take an invention to market, but both knew that common sense and their core-career P.K.H. would lead them in the right direction. They'd face a problem and say, "What would we do at work if faced with a similar obstacle?" This feet-on-the-ground orientation invariably helped them make smart decisions.

• **Personal Influence.** The Redout partners understood that developing and selling any product or service was one ongoing communication exercise. Sometimes it manifested itself in their winning responses to Patent Office questions, sometimes it was the way one picked the other up when he was feeling down, and at other times it was the phone calls they made and the letters they mailed that eventually generated two fistfuls of high-powered suitors.

• **Organized Action.** One thing they'd both learned from their core-career experience was that nothing gets done without endless tiny steps taken with purpose. If there is anything that impressed those who saw Redout come to life, it was how Neil and Marty always had a next step in place, no matter what the obstacle.

• **Informed Risk.** Did Neil and Marty make mistakes along the way? Yes, but over the course of the project they were right more often than they were wrong. As we say, they looked before they leaped, but still leaped; they knew what they were looking for and they usually landed safely as a result.

• **Flexible Thinking and Inner Openness.** Constantly beset with design problems, and performance challenges of their prototypes, Neil and Marty found that their Flexible Thinking skills were continually being tested; they knew that many inventors gave up too soon, and this

---

The grand essentials of happiness are: something to do, something to love, and something to hope for. —Allan K. Chalmers

was confirmed one day in a camera store, when they were fitting Redout onto different camera bodies. Another customer got talking to them and said, "You know, I invented this two years ago, but I just couldn't get it to fit on all the different cameras."

This made a big impression on them. Here was a man who could have beaten them to the punch, but a problem had beaten him instead, and he'd given up. But they never gave up. It was always "okay that didn't work, let's look at the problem from a different perspective." And they'd say, "If we aren't getting the right answer, it just means we aren't asking the right question."

Independently and interactively, the eight behavioral traits they had developed in their separate core careers served them equally well in this dream-career project.

Redout was cardboard and tinfoil on the kitchen table. It is now protected by a full U.S. Patent. It exists as a registered-C corporation. Six camera and accessory companies, including Konica, Kodak, and Vivitar, have expressed serious interest in it, as have another six investment banks. The two partners have chosen one of these investment banks to raise the money and take the product directly to television. They have also structured the resulting company in a modern way and have outsourced almost all the necessary production and operational functions, including

- Design, manufacturing management, and quality control
- Financial management and legal representation
- Sales, advertising, and placement
- The front office

With no plant, people, or equipment beyond their two PCs, Neil and Marty created a product and a company with the ability to launch a new product on the national stage. They spent little personal money and did it in whatever spare time they could make. They took on the idea and the eight traits and brought a dream to life. I know. My name is Marty.

A tool is but the extension of a man's hand, and a machine is but a complex tool. And he that invents a machine augments the power of a man and the well-being of mankind. —Henry Ward Beecher

‖‖‖‖‖‖‖‖‖‖‖‖‖‖‖‖‖‖‖‖‖‖‖‖‖‖‖‖‖‖‖‖‖

US005337104A

United States Patent [19]

Smith et al.

[11]	**Patent Number:** **5,337,104**
[45]	**Date of Patent:** **Aug. 9, 1994**

[54] **APPARATUS AND METHOD FOR REDIRECTING CAMERA FLASH LIGHT SO AS TO AVOID RED-EYE**

[76] Inventors: **Neil D. Smith**, 159 Maple Ave., McCoy, N.Y. 11654; **Martin Yate**, 9 Central Park, McCoy, N.Y. 11654

[21] Appl. No.: **973,615**

[22] Filed: **Nov. 9, 1992**

[51] Int. Cl.^{5} G03B 15/03
[52] U.S. Cl. **354/149.11**
[58] Field of Search 362/16–18; 354/126, 141, 148, 149.1, 149.11

[56]   **References Cited**

U.S. PATENT DOCUMENTS

2,292,044	8/1940	Bucky	354/77
3,263,584	8/1966	Knus	354/126
3,369,467	2/1968	Land	354/126
3,747,488	7/1973	Bennett	354/126
3,821,764	6/1974	Shelton	354/126
3,925,320	4/1976	Blount	354/126
4,019,042	4/1977	Baliozian	354/126
4,078,170	3/1978	Sloop	362/16
4,085,436	4/1978	Weiss	354/126
4,121,232	10/1978	Jones	354/126
4,122,333	10/1978	Crouse	362/18
4,235,541	11/1980	Jamel	354/79
4,333,127	6/1982	Alkema et al.	362/17
4,690,531	9/1987	Hansen et al.	354/149.11
4,847,647	7/1989	Ueda	354/149.1
4,855,771	8/1989	Alligood et al.	354/149.11
4,893,139	1/1990	Alligood et al.	354/149.11
4,893,140	1/1990	Yamamoto et al.	344/149.11
4,897,680	1/1990	Lo	354/149.11
4,970,539	11/1990	Sasagaki et al.	354/149.1
5,050,044	9/1991	Shibayama	354/149.1

Primary Examiner—David M. Gray
Attorney, Agent, or Firm—Beveridge, DeGrandi, Weilacher & Young

[57]   **ABSTRACT**

An apparatus for redirecting beams of light emanating from the flash of a camera so as to avoid the creation of "red-eye" in a photograph. The apparatus redirects the beams of lights so as to be distanced even further from the central axis of the camera lens. To provide the full effect of the flash, the apparatus redirects the beams of light in a direction parallel to the original direction the light beams travel off from the flash and to the central axis of the lens. The apparatus includes a main body which forms an enclosure with an inlet and outlet opening and is attached to the camera such that the inlet opening is aligned with and covers the camera's flash. The main body includes at least two reflective surfaces for redirecting the flash beam from a first direction to a second direction and then from the second direction to a third direction exiting the main body. The device can be releasably mounted to existing flash cameras (including pop-out flash members). It can also be built into new compact cameras and act as a sliding lens cover and power switch. With the built-in design, the flash of the camera can be directed either vertically or to one side of the camera and a built-in light shifter with single reflective surface is provided to redirect the light parallel and far removed from the central axis of the lens.

25 Claims, 4 Drawing Sheets

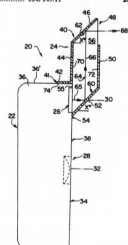

Excellence in any department can be attained only by the labor of a lifetime; it is not to be purchased at a lesser price. —Samuel Johnson

The Writer's Blueprint

Some people think a writer sits down at a typewriter and starts typing away. Three weeks later the writer puts the finishing touches on the 365-page manuscript and sends it off to become a best-seller and a TV movie-of-the-week. Maybe this happens to Danielle Steel, but it doesn't work that way for most writers.

It takes time, hard work, and determination to give birth to an article or a book, and then it takes time, hard work, and determination to sell the resulting product. And as buoyant writers know, writing *never* ends with the manuscript. Once you finish your piece, you have to get it *out there*, into the hands of the larger market. Which means you've got to focus your energy not only on writing but on marketing and selling your work as well. So let's look at the soft underbelly of another artsy field and see the behavior parallels between successful writers and successful core careerists. Again I'll break the blueprint down into two sections: (a) research and development; and (b) sales and marketing.

RESEARCH AND DEVELOPMENT

The Markets. Most everything you have ever read, from the free offer for that decoder ring on your cereal box to the novel or personal-development book on your nightstand, someone wrote and got paid for. Here are some of the markets that pay for the written word:

- Consumer and trade magazines
- Newspapers, both local and national
- Newsletters
- Directories
- Fiction and nonfiction publishers
- Corporate magazines, brochures, newsletters, and press releases
- Advertising agencies
- Radio, television, film, and theater
- Poetry publications
- Greeting cards
- Writing contests

Obviously it is much easier to get published in small-circulation poetry magazines for poets than it is to sell your script to Disney. Many of the

The fruit derived from labor is the sweetest of all pleasures. —Luc de Clapiers

world's great writers once worked at newspapers or wrote copy for ad agencies; there are even a couple that started by entering poetry competitions. The challenge for most yet-to-be-viable writers is finding not just the subjects that demand that you write about them but the publishers that will give you a deadline to do it under.

To find the latter, study the individual markets and their products. Come up with half a dozen specific examples in each field. For example, select trade magazines that would logically be the ones you'd subscribe to for your core-career buoyancy, and consumer magazines that would be those publications that you naturally accumulate or subscribe to as a result of your hobbies, personal interests, or dream career. Read a year's worth of issues for each magazine you're interested in and become familiar with the magazine's format, style, and subject matter.

Discover the Proper Presentation. Next always write to the editorial department at each publication, requesting "writers' guidelines" to learn what the submission policies are. Armed with this knowledge, you are now ready to pitch story ideas to your target magazines.

Whether you submit a finished article or a query letter suggesting an idea, you should follow the editorial style of the target publication and the writers' guidelines. This shows the editor that you've done your research and puts a positive spin on the working relationship you're, hopefully, about to begin.

Writing for magazines is a great place to launch your writing career. You find work, because there is such a wide variety of publications, both domestically and internationally, that rely on the efforts of freelance writers. And because the form is short and specific, it's a good skill teacher and subject-matter-expertise builder. There are *thousands* of magazines that are potential clients. For instance David, who is an educator with a young family, writes for parenting magazines and women's magazines that run parenting pieces. Peter, who's a technician and one day dreams of being a successful sci-fi writer, writes articles about new technology for computer publications and for general magazines that have technology or computing columns.

Even if your article ideas or manuscripts are turned down, if you act professionally and continue to pitch new ideas, you'll find that the rejection notes become more encouraging. Your persistence will eventually pay

Perfection is attained by slow degrees; it requires the hand of time. —Voltaire

off with your first assignment that could turn into . . . who knows what? A steady stream of work, or a column, and maybe eventually a book.

All Ideas Are Good, But Not All Are Marketable. In the universe of ideas some have greater marketing potential than others. You might have a wealth of information that you could turn into a fantastic article—but how many people do you suppose would be interested in "Thirty-Five Ways to Prepare Lima Beans"? The ideas that make the most salable articles are those that appeal to the biggest readership, because the bigger the interested public, the more numerous your writing outlets. You should also focus on an area or topic that you are passionate about. Your enthusiasm will come across and enrich your writing, and you'll enjoy the experience all the more and undoubtedly create a better piece in the bargain.

When you write about things you know nothing about, you're taking a big business risk. Your inexperience or lack of knowledge will probably show through in your work, which will look amateurish as a result. You may have a good idea, but it may not be marketable for you, at your current skill level, at this point in time. The old wisdom is still the best for marketing your ideas: *Write about what you know.*

So do as much research as possible about your field of expertise. For example I write about the workplace, careers, and personal development, because I know a lot about employment and buoyancy. Likewise a pathologist would have a head start in writing police-procedural thrillers. Work over time to become an authority. Study the available statistical data and the trends that are unfolding in publishing. This will help you pinpoint the areas of strong market potential. For instance books and magazines targeted to the minority population have done well in recent years. Other strong sellers include special-interest categories such as parenting, home improvement, self-help, cookbooks, and spiritual pieces.

By identifying the target market, or the portion of the population that is going to take an interest in your work, you should be able to figure out how to appeal to those readers. Do something to make your writing stand out. Develop a hook or angle that is innovative and different. Look at what the other writers do and find a hole, a weakness, a gap, then jump in with both feet and make it all yours. Go on-line, go to the library, go and study works on the topic. Find out how the competition is approaching the same subject, and go them one better; put *your* slant on it. Take ad-

All things excellent are as difficult as they are rare. —Benedict Spinoza

vantage of on-line computer services to search *Books in Print* and *Articles in Print* for the titles, authors, and publishers of every published book and article on your topic.

If you're stuck for ideas, look through books, newspapers, and magazines to find gaps: things the other authors and journalists aren't saying about the topics, or things that aren't being addressed. Make it your job to write about the topics that *sell.* This is exactly how I got my break as a writer. When I came on the scene, there wasn't much advice on careers and job hunting of the hand-to-hand-combat variety. No one was saying, "when this happens, this is why, and this is what you should do." So I found a niche that no one else was occupying.

Write On. Whether you're writing fiction or nonfiction, all writing really is is putting a story down on paper. You craft each sentence and move sections from here to there to change the flow of the story. It all comes down to sentence structure and the flow of sentences within a paragraph. This doesn't happen automatically, in the first draft, for any author I've ever met. Crafting a piece that's worthy of sending to an editor with your name on it takes many drafts and painstaking, ten-hours-a-day-at-the keyboard, backbreaking work, and then they hate it and you start over.

Which reminds me of something that happened recently. My youngest son's kindergarten teacher was talking to the class about books. Knowing that Jasper's dad was a writer, the teacher asked him, "What do we call a person who writes books?" And Jasper, my dutiful son, replied, "An editor."

When the teacher called to tell me what she thought was a funny story, I told her that Jasper was right. What writers really do is rewrite and rewrite. At last count the chapter you're reading now has gone through eight rewrites. This is why they say writers need rubber buns; but then again, writers are a group of people who know the value of sticking to the task at hand.

This leads us to something that many people call writer's block. I call it either laziness or bad planning. If, as a writer, you work on more than one project at a time, just as every modern-day professional does, you will never have writer's block; you'll be too *busy.* And the more ideas you have in development, the less chance you'll ever be unable to write. If you can't write anything on a particular subject that day, you simply move on to the

Aim at perfection in everything, though in most things it is unattainable. However, they who aim at it, and persevere, will come much nearer to it than those whose laziness and despondency make them give it up as unattainable. —Lord Chesterfield

next project and write on that instead. Develop enough projects to juggle, just as you do in your core-career work, and you'll never again experience writer's block. Writer's block is for bums.

Stirring around various projects at once also serves another purpose, which one writer describes as "throwing a lot of projects at the wall and seeing which ones stick." Some things will sell, and others won't. But you never know which is which until you've developed the ideas, and you're unlikely to sell much of anything with the one-at-a-time approach. One of the stumbling blocks beginning writers encounter is that they don't plan for project flow. They get one contract at a time and they do their best to fulfill it. Then, once that assignment is completed, they're back to square one and have to start from scratch again. There's no filling the hopper with ideas so that they can develop organically. If you learn to develop a number of ideas at once, you don't have as much hanging on one deal, and there is more continuity in the flow of work.

Naturally there will be times when you're under deadline and you sit down and can't write a word. In that case you can type out something like, "I can't write anything that makes any sense! I have a huge writing assignment to hand in by Friday, and I don't know where to start!" As one writer told us, "It doesn't matter what you write, just keep on writing." At your day job you may not want to make that call, but you have to, because it's part of the job. And if you didn't, you would decrease your buoyancy as an employee. The same is true of writing, or any other dream career; you have to take the rough with the smooth if you are to benefit from the fruits of your labor.

When you hit a brick wall, you have to realize that your words aren't sacrosanct. They haven't come down from Mount Ararat. Develop a healthy disrespect for them. Think of words as hammer and nails, and use them to nail a point home. Keep in mind that a lot of your writing is going to come out anyway, in rewrites and edits. If you accept that, you won't agonize as much over whether a word you're using is right or wrong. You can just leave a blank when you can't think of the perfect word, or do what I do: Write a silly word in its place. You can always go to a thesaurus later. The point of writing is to get the words down on paper and communicate a message to your readers. All the beauty and the poetry of the great writers comes from rewrites.

Many a man fails as an original thinker simply because his memory is too good.
—Wilhelm Friedrich Nietzsche

Tearing away and hacking out the deathless prose is difficult, partly because you're concerned about volume; you don't think you can write two hundred pages, let alone five hundred! I always compare writing to sculpting. You start off with a great pile of rock, your first draft, then gradually you chip away at it with a hammer and a chisel, and in the end you have Rodin's *The Thinker*. You have turned something that came out of your head into something that you can sell for money!

SALES AND MARKETING

Sales and marketing techniques vary from business to business, but overall the same sound principles hold true. In this part of the blueprint we are going to look at some of the tactics used in selling a book and establishing the book as a revenue stream.

Getting an Agent. If you're an unpublished author, it's tough to get a good literary agent, and many major publishing companies won't accept your manuscripts unless you're represented by an agent, so it's a catch-22 situation.

But that doesn't mean you can't get published. You *can* represent yourself. You just have to keep knocking on the publishing and agency doors until something opens a crack. Persistence on both fronts is the key.

If you do hire an agent, you are hiring both a salesperson to sell your intellectual copyright and a critic of your work. An agent for a writer is the same person as a salesperson for the company; it's a person whose job it is to sell the work product. He or she will also have you change your work, just as editors and publishers will do later, to make it salable. If you can't take direction, you will fail as a writer. If you can live with these professional facts of life, as you do in your core career, you greatly increase your odds of success using behaviors and attitudes you already use in that core career.

The best way to find an agent is to get hold of a copy of *Literary Marketplace* at your local library. It references agents according to their speciality in its yellow pages.

Agents typically receive 10 to 15 percent of any monies they generate for you. They earn their cut of your intellectual copyright because they know who's who in the world of publishing and therefore which editors and publishing houses will be most responsive to your work.

Send potential agents you track down a personalized query letter de-

Faultily faultless, icily regular, splendidly null, dead perfection; no more.
—*Alfred, Lord Tennyson*

scribing your work, why you feel your book will sell, and who will buy it. If the agent subsequently turns down the manuscript, you might get a rejection letter in the mail. Don't take it personally, just keep plugging away. If you don't hear anything, you might try contacting the agent personally to learn the status of your manuscript. Listen to what you are told, even if it hurts, and come back again with an improved product.

Like most other writers, when I finally got a book contract, I didn't understand a word of it. A literary agent or, if you don't have one, a literary lawyer, can help you figure out what it all means and what you are entitled to, including

- The kind of advance you'll get and when you'll receive it. Will enough of the money be received up front to enable you to pay the bills and expenses you might incur while writing the book?
- The type of royalty agreement you are entitled to for this kind of work, and if it should escalate once you've sold a specified number of books.
- If there is a special reserve set up against your royalties for returned books.
- The rights the publisher wants you to give up. For example, do they want all rights to the hardcover and to the paperback version of your book? Or do they want world rights, or just U.S., Canada, and Open market? (*Note:* Make sure you educate yourself as to all the rights you have as a writer, including the copyright law. The more control you have over your own work, the better.)
- The type of distribution and sales center the publisher has.
- The manuscript due date, and the release date of your book.
- What happens to the money you've been paid if the work is rejected upon completion.

Taking the Unsolicited Route. Like many working writers I didn't use an agent to sell my first book. No one would take me on, so I did it myself. My approach was that of the sedulous ape,[2] that is, I bought a book called *Writer's Market* (see "Resources") and did exactly as it advised. And it worked.

I recommend that you, too, go through every listing in *Writer's Market* and target as many publishing houses as you can. Send every publisher that could possibly be interested in your book a query letter (according to

---

Who will not suffer labor in this world, let him not be born. —John Florio

their submission guidelines) to introduce your idea. Some houses require that you enclose a SASE. Your job is to sell your idea to an editor who will in turn sell it to his or her publisher. If an editor or publisher responds by asking for a finished chapter, send it; if they ask for two chapters, then send them two. If they say that they accept simultaneous submissions, which means they understand you might be presenting your work to other publishers, you can tell them it is a simultaneous submission. You're not exactly creating leverage at this stage, but at least you're letting people know you have both oars in the water professionally. If a publisher only accepts exclusive submissions, pitch the idea anyway, along with everyone else you pitched to; you have nothing to lose. Is this ethical, you ask? Well, if you sold widgets for a living, what would you say to a potential new client who said, "I won't even talk to you about your widgets unless you promise not to sell them to anyone else?" *Do whatever it takes to make it happen.* In the real world of publishing, exclusive submissions are based only on existing relationships, and even then they aren't typical.

Don't overlook university presses; despite their abysmal advances it could be your path for getting into print. Besides, the big publishing houses regularly scan these for books to reprint and for potential writers.

Plugging Product. Ultimately any business can be defined by the shipping of the product or delivery of service. And while it's one thing to write a book, it's another to move that book off bookshelves. You can't expect publishers to do anything that you won't do for yourself; they have too many other books and writers to be concerned with. Publishers focus on the math: If they give you this much money for a book advance, that means they believe that without a lot of effort they can get that money back plus some profit. That's what they do: Their job is to bring a steady stream of books to members of the reading public who want to read something new.

So 95 percent of books remain in print for only about eleven months. Bookstores return unsold books as soon as possible in order to make room for newer titles. As an author you have to work hard at supporting your product in the marketplace over the first few years until it becomes an established brand name.

Many writers agree that getting your name into print, as tough as it may be, is easy compared with *keeping* your name in print. Selling your product *off* the shelves is the real creative challenge.

A man's best friends are his ten fingers. —Robert Collyer

Because I couldn't get any regular publicity when I was starting out, I wrote some articles myself under a pseudonym to get my name in print. My articles were about a book called *Knock 'em Dead* and its writer, Martin Yate, and about how much the two could help your job hunt. This was Flexible Thinking in action, and brought me some great publicity.

So let's look at some things a freshly published writer could do to stay in print and keep those royalties rolling in. As you read, think about how you could use these same proven techniques to promote any dream.

- Send complimentary copies out to book reviewers at magazines and newspapers.
- Carry a copy of your book with you wherever you go, so that you can show it off.
- Let everyone know about your book. Talk it up.
- Speak publicly on your topic wherever you have the opportunity, and if you get paid for it, so much the better.
- Pull out newsworthy pieces from your book and send them to magazine or newspaper editors, along with a short note that you're a published author of a book and that's where your article is from. Recycle excerpts as articles, providing you have the publisher's permission.
- Develop a regular column in a newspaper or magazine, to establish credentials and promote your work.
- Hire a freelance publicist to promote the product and to supplement the efforts of the publisher's in-house publicity department.
- Pitch yourself as a guest to local radio and television shows using your book as a publicity hook.
- Commit to promoting the product ceaselessly for twelve months. Keep your publisher informed of your publicity hits, and talk to your publisher about an updated and expanded version of your book.

TIPS FOR WRITERS

As an unpublished writer for twenty years I made plenty of mistakes; in the last ten years as a published writer I've begun to make smarter decisions about my writing. As we close out this writer's blueprint, I'd like to share some tips or ideas that I hashed out with two writer friends one night. Are these ideas really practical? Well, one of the writers has written over

Money is like a sixth sense, and you can't make use of the other five without it.
—*W. Somerset Maugham*

forty nonfiction books over the last ten years, the other has written thirty-plus adventure stories. Each of us have at least a successful series in print.

- Rework, rework, and rework.
- Network with other writers. Meet with other writers, and critique one another's work. Go to trade associations and meetings, and press some flesh.
- Whenever possible, read other people's work. This will inspire you, and improve your vocabulary and writing.
- Write like you talk. If you're looking for a writer's voice, use your natural voice. You're undoubtedly fluent, sincere, and exciting when you speak; capture that in print. It's important to develop your own writing style. And then adapt it, as appropriate.
- Try writing in different environments. Don't limit yourself to one place. If a book takes a thousand hours to write, it's nice to spread the time between different locations.
- Solicit input *only* from those who can influence the purchase of your work. Their opinions are the only ones that count.
- Worry about what will sell, not what might impress the local poets' society (unless of course you're writing poetry).
- Think, research, and outline before you write, but put words on paper every day regardless.
- Save what you've created but can't use on this project. You might need it later on for other work.
- Walk away from your work once in a while; take a break from it.
- As you're working on one project, think about other potential story ideas that might grow out of it. For example, perhaps you can build an article around a person you've interviewed or an interesting fact you've discovered. Keep track of your ideas by writing them down.
- Write every day.
- Carry 3" × 5" cards with you wherever you go; use them to jot down observations, facts, or story ideas that come to you on the fly.
- Subscribe to writers' magazines and newsletters.
- Keep an eye out for opportunities to promote your book. Any new newspaper or magazine or radio or television show you come across is a potential vehicle for publicizing your work.

It is only through labor and painful effort, by grim energy and resolute courage, that we move on to better things. —Theodore Roosevelt

- Don't plan to retire on the proceeds of your first book.
- Don't expect your book to finish itself. Writing takes vigilance and hard work.
- Relax and enjoy your writing; very few writers create perfect first drafts. If you get out a germ of an idea on the first pass, you are doing great.

THE BUOYANT WRITER

It is absolutely critical that you develop the eight buoyancy traits if you want a buoyant writing career. Before I got my first proposal accepted, I thought that editors and publishers were a dastardly lot who couldn't recognize talent or a good idea if it was shoved up their noses. It turns out that they have a good understanding of what it takes to write and, even more important, what it takes to publish books that readers will buy. Editors aren't just looking for a few good stories. They are looking for good people who can *get the job done professionally.*

What does it take to get the job done? You guessed it—eight critical behavioral traits, and most especially:

- **Flexible Thinking's** important, but not just for the creativity or the writing skills. Before you put pen to paper, or fingers to keyboard, you have a lot of thought research to do: investigating markets and outlets, checking out the competition and what the market wants. The Flexible Thinking a core careerist uses to develop a marketing plan is what you need to complete this critical step toward buoyancy as a writer.
- **Informed Risk** can help you to exploit an unexplored niche of the market, or to approach an old problem in a new way. The skepticism of some writers helps them see things in new ways and pushes them to express new and daring ideas.
- **Organized Action** is the only way that you can get the book written. With thousands of notes to juggle, countless drafts to rewrite, having to write proposals and query letters while writing the book, and keeping an eye on the schedule and deadlines all the while, you need Organized Action. *You can't just wing it.*
- **Smart Decisions** helps you select the right agent, sign the best contract you can, and choose the best projects to work on.

The safest way to double your money is to fold it over once and put it in your pocket.
—Kin Hubbard

• The rejection that is inherent in writing can quickly drain your **Goal Orientation** and your **Positive Expectancy**. But I didn't let this happen to me.

It's All About Determination

The book that came to be known as *Knock 'Em Dead* (its sales are currently at 2 million copies) was rejected by sixty-four different publishers! But one day I did receive the response I had been waiting for. It was from Bob Adams, Inc., who in those days published about ten books a year.[3] They offered me a one-hundred-dollar advance, perhaps the smallest in modern publishing, but that didn't matter to me. I had been turned down by publishers all across the country, and Bob Adams was offering me 100 percent more than anyone else had. Once I got the contract, I went to see a literary attorney in Manhattan, who looked at the contract and said, "Young man, it's not the best contract I've seen and it's not the worst, but it's your first one, and I suggest you accept it." I was happy just to be in print; I had beaten the odds, and once you're *in* print, life gets a lot easier. Ten years later the opportunity to publish this book cost the publisher hundreds of thousands of dollars.

So, even on the days when you feel you just can't face the computer, when you absolutely can't write a bloody word, you *have* to. You must. I wouldn't be surprised one day if writing was admitted to the Olympics as an endurance sport.

Am I this perfectly mentally healthy guy who is never down or who never makes a dumb decision? Sorry to say, I am not. But I *am* able to use these critical eight traits when I need to. I am able to go on with the show, because I know what I have to, what I must, and what I deep inside *want* to do, in order to maintain my dream-career buoyancy as a writer. Why am I successful as a writer? Well, from doing a lot of something, my writing skills and my confidence have definitely improved. Nevertheless I credit my entire success to the behaviors I developed in my core career—and you can too.

I'm tired of love, I'm still more tired of rhyme, but money gives me pleasure all the time. —Hilaire Belloc

The Photographer's Blueprint

We are surrounded by pictures in magazines, books, on billboards, the television, at the movies, and in the mall. Pictures make our hearts race and bring tears to our eyes, they can thrill us and disgust us; and sometimes they do these things simultaneously. Pictures make us want stuff, pictures make us strive to keep up with the Joneses.

Pictures impact life in powerful and subtle ways; that's why it's said that a picture is worth a thousand words. But you don't have to react to pictures; you can make them too. And if you work at it long enough, apart from the joy of creation you might even make a buck or two and taste a little more freedom, a little more happiness, a little more security.

Work at your craft diligently, with the same intensity you pursue your core career, and who knows? One day it might become your core career. One thing is certain: each of the pictures you see every day was framed and shot by someone—and that someone started off with a camera and an urge to take a single photograph.

As I said earlier, you must have a firm foundation from which to reach for the stars. Successful photographs are rarely accidents, and it's the same with successful photographers. Photography is fun, but developing it into a revenue stream and a reliable profession takes P.K.H.

The commercial outlets for photographers' work are so vast and diverse that you could write a book just on the different fields of photography where you can make money: advertising, aerial, architectural, art/academic, audio-visual, documentary, fashion, illustration, institutional, legal, military, motion picture/TV, photojournalism, portrait/wedding, school, scientific, special effects, still-life, tourism/travel, corporate, and on and on. But it's time now to get started on the path.

RESEARCH AND DEVELOPMENT

Your Portfolio. To sell himself, the photographer's main tool is his portfolio.

In the old days photographers used slide trays to display their work, and their clients viewed the slides through projectors. Nowadays the trend for initial presentations is to have a portfolio the size of a three-ring binder containing samples of work you may have had published—actual black-and-white and color photos, transparencies, and laminated tear

---

The merit of originality is not novelty, it is sincerity. The believing man is the original man; he believes for himself, not for another. —Thomas Carlyle

sheets. You will need at least three portfolios: one for yourself, one for your agent or rep, and one to circulate.

If your photographic aspirations include more than one of the recently listed markets, you would need custom portfolios for each particular market. In other words you present your work product to niche markets professionally, in much the same way that successful companies customize their products and services to better develop market share; you differentiate your art for its targeting by customizing its presentation and context.

By the way, the experts we spoke with agree that less is usually better, and you shouldn't put anything in your portfolio that you're not absolutely proud of.[4]

Also, different markets may well require a style of presentation suited to the particular medium. Professional photographers advise that your *editorial portfolio* contain tear sheets of the articles to accompany your work; your *advertising book* display transparencies and laminated tear sheets; and your *corporate portfolio* feature tear sheets, transparencies, or photos of actual work you've done in the corporate environment. Research your market and prospective customers' needs in order to identify the photographic challenges, limitations, and opportunities you will encounter.

It sounds like the photography business is very logical and orderly, and those who get their foot in the door have already developed a modicum of practical know-how. It also seems that there is a very straightforward way to present your art to the people for whom it is business, in a businesslike and professional way—and, as everyone knows, presentation is half the battle for true Personal Influence competency.

However, there are no written rules for presenting your portfolio; it is a matter for negotiation between you and your potential client. Everyone has his or her preferences, and some contacts may insist that you call them first before showing them your book. Some may ask you to drop off your portfolio on a particular day of the week and leave it there for a few days. The quickest way to find out the procedures for viewing portfolios is to call and ask for exactly that information.

After your portfolio has been reviewed and returned, don't forget to send a letter of thanks to the person who looked at your work. For your own records, you should keep track of all the people you submit your portfolio to,

---

He that is of the opinion money will be everything may well be suspected of doing everything for money. —Benjamin Franklin

what you left with them, what the status of the review is, what they would like to see in the future, and how they'd like it presented.

If your customers are not local, you have to go into the direct-mail business. Using regular post office delivery is risky for important stuff like portfolios, proposals, and contracts. As you've learned through experience in your core-career job, the best policy is to use tracking and ground-mail services.

Magazine Work. Magazines are an excellent market for photographers to break into because most publications use freelance photographers. But naturally, the more popular the magazine is, the more competitive it becomes, because it pays more. The smaller its circulation, the more accessible a magazine is to the newly working photographer.

Magazines list contacts on the masthead at the front of the book. You will usually want to contact either the picture editor, art director, or assistant art director. Sometimes even the editor-in-chief may be the appropriate contact; it varies from magazine to magazine.

Your Magazine Portfolio. Every magazine has its own style. Before you submit work to one, it is important that you study the magazine and pinpoint its photographic needs as well as its target market. An editor or art director might buy one of your shots or give you an assignment. When the latter happens, you should ask whether you will receive your day rate plus the space rate (where the amount paid varies depending on the published size and position of your work), or exactly what the magazine's payment policy is. You should also find out whether or not your photos will be reused in the future by the same magazine or show up in sister publications. If they are going to be reused, then you should request extra compensation.

Newspaper Work. Pick up your local daily paper, and you'll find that it uses photographs of everything imaginable. Traditionally a black-and-white market, newspapers now use more color photos as a result of an increased use of electronic imaging. Weekend editions are especially liberal in their use of color. Check out your Sunday newspaper for syndicated inserts; *Parade,* to name the most common, has a photo editor listed on its masthead.

Most newspapers have a particular photo department, staffed with its

It is better to create than to be learned. Creating is the true essence of life.
—Barthold Georg Niebuhr

own photo editors and photographers. But they do accept outside material, and once you get your foot in the door, it can open up greater opportunities. You get in with persistent, respectful inquiries to the right editors. With smaller newspapers, department heads are usually the people responsible for photographic selection.

Photographers tell us that the nature of newspaper photography means that most work is done on speculation. That means that there is no guarantee the paper will pay for or use your material. Although getting published in newspapers may provide positive recognition and is part of your professional growth, don't expect to get rich from selling shots to the *Daily Planet*. However, what this does provide is the stepping-stones of experience.

Weekly newspapers and tabloids are also good markets that use color much more frequently than dailies. Weeklies pay more than tabloids, but consider both if you want to build up your resume and pursue your passion.

Your Newspaper Portfolio. If you're approaching a newspaper, your portfolio should include photos that would supplement a newspaper's layout, including photos of news, sports, and entertainment events, as well as those of celebrities and political figures.

Ad Agency Work. Standards are high in advertising. Before a final advertising project is approved, it must pass through many hands, including those of the various art directors at both the ad agency and the client company, all of whom have a say in the decision making. That's why advertising pays great money to the most professional of photographers, and it explains why the field takes time to break into. Advertising agencies' rates vary depending on what media source is used, how much is being paid for ad space, who the audience is, and so on.

Effective ways of promoting your talents to ad agencies include marketing yourself in person with your portfolio, mailing pitch letters, and making follow-up phone calls. An ad agency is unlikely to use your existing work but might assign you a shoot.

Your Ad Agency Portfolio. To create an ad agency portfolio, study the various print advertisements that the particular ad company has created in order to get a feel for the agency's personality. Also, study all the types of ads there are for different product categories. This will give you ideas for photographing similar products in similar ways. Once you know technically

---

Only mediocrity can be trusted to be always at its best. —Max Beerbohm

how the published work gets that way and can replicate it, you will see your own style begin to emerge.

This sounds a lot like the way you can build new skills in your core career: Study and understand the area where you will apply yourself; work with, watch, and emulate competence in the field; practice, practice, practice.

Corporate Photography. The press, business magazines, printed sales literature, training materials, and annual reports: Sometimes the in-house public relations or communications departments of companies handle the editorial and photo aspects of these publications, but many companies hire outside contractors to do the work for them, some of whom usually have staff photographers and some of whom don't.

While corporate clients aren't at the top of the scale, they usually pay more than, say, publishing companies. So to locate potential corporate buyers, check marketing and communications directories (see Resources).

Your Corporate Photography Portfolio. Corporate photographers tell me that three-quarters of the job in this field entails solving problems with location, lighting, casting, and presentation. Usually it includes taking executives, office environments, and three people standing around a PC with a report. If you go after lucrative corporate work, your portfolio should reflect the kind of work you are seeking: people, interiors, three people around a PC with a report.

Public Relations Work. One of the broadest fields for your freelance photographic pursuits is public relations photography, which is widely used in print media. Public relations firms increasingly develop long-term relationships with outside photographers; some people say that more than 50 percent of the stories and photographs you see in print are P.R.-driven. The business of P.R. is to sell its promotional ideas, events, products, or celebrity news to the media.

Your P.R. Portfolio. Public relations firms want to see a portfolio that will help supplement the editorial coverage they are seeking for their clients. For example, they are interested in photographers who can do flattering portraits, candids, and still lifes. (Note that P.R. and corporate clients are essentially interested in the same things.)

I feel that the greatest reward for doing is the opportunity to do more.
—Jonas Salk

Book Publishing. The book field is an active and open market for the as-piring photographer. Over a thousand major publishing houses produce tens of thousands of new books annually. In recent years publishers, espe-cially paperback houses, have discovered that a visually appealing book will sell better. Here is an opportunity for front- and back-cover, as well as in-book, photographic commentary.

A photographer who is serious about cracking into the publishing busi-ness will break the market down into photographic subject-matter clus-ters—for example, outdoors and animals; or people—in the same way that the publishing industry segments itself. We can break the market down further into textbooks for the academic audience, and into paper-back and hardcover books for the trade audience.

The disadvantage of academic publishing is that neither the authors nor the photographers seem to get a decent reward for their effort. This means that the new freelance film slinger is also likely to get poor royalties and unfavorable work-for-hire agreements.

On the positive side, once you open the door, the sheer volume of text-book publishing can provide you with an opportunity for steady business. Once you have identified a cluster of publishers whose needs match your capabilities, you'll want to learn something called house style (although your compositional and artistic viewfinder is what makes your profes-sional work stand out). This is how the experts distill their buoyancy, and to me this phrase sounds like any corporate job description: The buoyant photographer is one who customizes his work to the customer's needs and who supplies the work product in a professional and timely manner.

Research books at the library and bookstore to help you identify your photographic-market clusters. Instructional and how-to books are boom-ing in every field, and photographs are an integral part of the how-to process. Cookbooks are great opportunities for still-life photographers. Trade books unfortunately provide little opportunity for photographers.

Send for catalogs of publishers that catch your eye, and approach both small and large publishers. Once you decide on a market cluster for your talents, send a query letter to the picture editor. In it say that you'd like to present your portfolio, list the work you have available, and include some sample slides. Like all other users of creative materi-als, publishers would rather do business with a few professionals than

---

Aim at the sun, and you may not reach it; but your arrow will fly far higher than if aimed at an object on a level with yourself. —*Joel Hawes*

scores of amateurs, so your initial objective is to demonstrate competence and reliability.

Authorities in the field recommend that you approach different publishers with ideas suitable to the medium and the specialty. If publishers believe your idea will sell, they'll offer you a contract to handle the photo assignment. And down the road you'll get called with plum assignments like this one, in which one of our research subjects was given an assignment to shoot pictures for a book on Miami, Florida. He was given the writer's rough draft and told to supply X shots for $Y. Eighteen years ago, when he started moonlighting, he was fortunate to be photographing the underside of sinks for plumbers' manuals, because it was a foot in the door.

Other Markets to Consider. Publishers of greeting cards, postcards, calendars, and posters are all looking for good professional photographers. All the big card companies such as Hallmark, American Greetings, and Gibson, have their own significant in-house capabilities, yet they constantly look outward for suppliers. These companies may also have separate divisions that specialize in items such as posters and calendars.

Catalogs. The American consumer is having an intense love affair with mail-order catalogs. In recent years sales from catalogs have skyrocketed, but be aware that competition for catalog photographers is *tough.*

To be a good catalog photographer and to earn real money at the trade, you must have a knack for production. Most catalog projects involve studio work: putting together sets and running hundreds of products through as if you were working on an assembly line. If you love catalog work, your portfolio will feature lots of clean, flattering still lifes.

Stock Agencies and Photographer's Representatives. Many photographers sell their work through stock agencies and enlist the help of a photography agent. Getting into a stock agency takes time. You have to show you are competent, reliable, trustworthy, and productive professionally before you're given a shot. Such a reputation, such a resume, and such credentials take time to build. However, the advantages to using stock agencies are that they

- Take care of part of your marketing program
- Negotiate on your behalf

Hitch your wagon to a star. —Ralph Waldo Emerson

- Recognize the potential of photos you may have overlooked
- Are able to reach more clients than you can

Make sure the stock agency satisfies your wants and desires as well. You want to be able to protect yourself from the rip-off artists that exist in every field. So before you sign on the dotted line, you should

- Get references from other photographers who have used or are currently using the agency.
- Contact trade associations that you belong to, such as ASMP (American Society of Media Professionals), APA (American Photographers of America), and PACA (Picture Agency Council of America), for information about specific stock agencies. By becoming a member of one or more professional associations, you can research not only who your clients are and what their standards are but also the industry norms.
- If you have to sign an exclusivity contract, limit its duration to a time period you can live with. If possible, ask for a special provision in the agreement stating that the contract will be renewed only if both parties notify each other of their desire to do so.
- Work out and understand the payment schedule.

Before you contact an agency, make sure you have an ample amount of slides to offer them—a minimum of a hundred. After signing on with an agency, you should continue to provide them with new work on a regular basis.

Besides using a stock agency, you can also have a photographer's agent or representative shop your photographs around for you. Reps are not for everybody, but they are another good marketing tool for a dream-careerist photographer; the agent becomes another salesperson working on productivity. The majority of photo reps are located in New York and Los Angeles. For further information on how to find them, you can contact SPAR, the Society of Photographer and Artist Representatives (see "Resources").

SALES AND MARKETING

Direct Mail. Direct mail is effective, but unless you control it, it can prove to be a very expensive marketing tool. A good direct-mail shot would fea-

---

No bird soars too high if he soars with his own wings. —William Blake ture one or more examples of your work, as well as information about how you can be contacted.

A photographer should consider having a few hundred mailers printed to send to potential customers three or four times a year. Naturally you'd want to update the pictures on your mailer so that potential customers don't receive the same pictures over and over again.

By purchasing mailing lists of company names and addresses from direct-marketing companies, or compiling your own lists, you can easily send your mailer to as many art directors as you'd like in whatever fields you choose.

In a direct-mail solicitation you should send a one-page cover letter with your mailer explaining what you have to offer and stating that you will follow up with a phone call in the near future. A direct-mail shot can be an effective tool to entice a much larger audience to look at your portfolio; it is also a marketing tool that lends itself to time-conscious dream careerists and entrepreneurs.

Magazines and Directories. Another marketing technique is to advertise in the creative industries' magazines and directories. The three major publications are: *American Showcase, Ad Week,* and the *Black Book.* They're all read by decision makers in corporations, publishers, ad agencies, and others in the business of hiring professional photographers.

Working on Speculation. Everyone in every creative field says never to work on spec, which is when you do a job for a client and agree to be paid at a later date—for example, once the work is accepted, or sometimes even published.

If you agree to take an assignment on spec, you leave yourself open to getting stiffed. You'll provide your time and effort and deliver the product, but your clients may change their minds, decide your work wasn't good enough, claim they never assigned you the job, or claim that they are not obligated to pay you.

"Never work on spec" sounds good in theory, but the fact is that I, and almost every working creative person I know, has done work on speculation. I didn't like doing it, but when I agreed to do it, it was because I needed either money or the experience, or both.

Pass world! I am the dreamer that remains; the man cut clear against the last horizon.
—Roy Campbell

THE ASSIGNMENT

Putting Together a Successful Shoot. When working out a quote for a photo shoot, you have to consider how long you'll be on location. Allow extra time for delays, bad weather, and travel. Other expenses directly related to the assignment may include the rental of special equipment as well as the costs of materials and processing.

You should discuss the specifics of what your clients want from you: how many prints, what type of prints, what dimensions, and whether they have any special preferences in regard to the finished product. Also find out if the clients provide a kill fee if they give you an assignment but then decide not to use your photos.

When you are starting out, taking a loss for the experience can be justifiable, but you should *always* know what your real costs are so that you can track how your activities are affecting your bottom line. Remember to calculate in your general overhead costs, such as rent, liability insurance, taxes, travel costs, equipment rental, printing charges, copying, assistants, and so on. To run a successful business, you have to charge enough to cover your costs and make a decent profit on top of these expenses. Earnings should be in the range of 25 to 40 percent of your billings. Don't shortchange yourself for fear of losing the sale; whatever you charge will be too much, but it is easier to negotiate downward than upward.

As you gain more experience and a good reputation in the industry, you will be able to increase your rates and watch your profits grow.

Staying on Top of a Shoot. If it hasn't happened yet, the day you get your first assignment you'll undoubtedly experience some roller-coaster emotions. Here's how you can boost your self-confidence:

- Make a list of all the things you are going to need for the shoot.
- Put together a storyboard that shows the shots and the sequence in which you're going to get them.
- Make sure your talent sign the necessary model releases.
- Prior to the shoot, make sure you have all your equipment, and check it to make sure everything is working.
- When you arrive at your destination and before you unpack,

Death comes to all But great achievements build a monument Which shall endure until the sun grows cold. —Georg Fabricius

inspect the location of the shoot carefully and quietly. Make any necessary changes on the set.

• Take enough supplies, and then some. Unless you're working in a major city, keep in mind that trying to find a professional photographic shop is comparable to trying to find a needle in a haystack.

• Make sure you have your method of transportation, hotel arrangements, and car-rental information all spelled out before you leave your studio.

• Handle all the specifics of your own travel arrangements if at all possible. Anyone who travels will tell you that the more control you have over travel arrangements, the better.

• Be involved in location scouting; after all, you are the image maker, and the location becomes part of your product.

• Acquire any necessary location permits and permissions.

• Have your props accessible so that they can be easily set up. If you're shooting for stock agencies and using props, remember to bring along tape, liquid paper, or paint to cover up brand names and logos so that they won't be seen in the close-up shots.

• Use a self-stick label on the leader of each roll to write down a number and other relevant information, including your name and address. In a compact notebook you can jot down what each numbered roll consists of. You should also include all f-stop/exposure stats for every exposure, but that often will be tough to do on location unless you have an assistant or the foresight to use a tape recorder.

If your core career has you involved in any way with business, sales, and training meetings, you will recognize the overwhelming similarities between what it takes for a photographic shoot to run smoothly and the practicalities of a seamless off-site meeting. If you have this core-career experience, it will help you in your photographic career; if you don't, the work experience in your dream career will carry back over and affect your core-career buoyancy with a new set of desirable Personal Influence skills.

Delivering Your Product. After you've picked up your work from the lab, you should take the time to look through it all. Make a primary set of the very best quality pictures from the lot, a secondary set of the good-quality

---

The very substance of the ambitious is merely the shadow of a dream.
—*William Shakespeare*

pictures, and a third set of the okay-quality pictures. Make sure *all* of your work is inserted into glassine envelopes. Then send your clients the slides or transparencies, preferably by messenger service.

In the professional photographic world your client may request the original transparencies. That's fine, *as long as you have duplicates.* Make sure you label your work for your clients so that they do not have to sec-ond-guess the content of the work. You should also provide your clients with any additional notes that relate to the assignment.

Keeping Track of Your Work. Buoyant photographers, like artists, writers, painters, and sculptors, need a well-organized professional office space. A good filing system is crucial and should provide you with easy access to your work. You should include such information as the date the roll was taken; where and for whom it was taken; who or what the subject was; and whether the film was black-and-white or color.

There Are Laws to Protect You. Get to know the industry you are selling into and the copyright laws; they are there to protect you. Unless you agree otherwise with a client, the copyright law states that a photographer owns the negatives from a shoot because they are not the finished product and are considered intermediate materials. Just like a manufacturer who sells you a product but not the mold that made it, you want to protect your molds (read: negatives) so that you can sell them again. Unless you are an employee or you sign a work-for-hire contract, you *own* the pho-tographs that you take.

You will sell rights to the buyer, at a price that is partly dependent on the usage of the photographs. There are different types of rights; get to know them, and use them accordingly:

- Onetime rights—leased on a onetime basis for a flat fee
- First rights—same as onetime, except that the buyer is paying for the first use
- Serial rights—the right to use the photograph in a periodical
- Exclusive rights—guarantees the buyer exclusive right to use the photo in a particular market or for a particular product; the photogra-pher may retain the right to other markets
- Promotion rights—allows the publisher to use the photo for

Obviously, the highest type of efficiency is that which can utilize existing material to the best advantage. —Jawaharlal Nehru

promotion of a publication in which the photo had appeared; usually means more money

• Work-for-hire—photographer surrenders all rights for active cost payment

• All rights—photographer sells or assigns all rights for a specific period of time, at which time print rights revert back to the photographer

THE BUOYANT PHOTOGRAPHER

It really isn't surprising that the business end of a dream career like this one has such a ring of familiarity to it, because your art is being sold into some aspect of the vibrant communications industry. It is therefore logical that the means of doing business, the relationships, as well as the behavioral values of those relationships, should closely resemble the core-career way of getting the job done. The same successful behaviors are recognized and lead to repeat business; the same professional shortcomings lead to the emptiness of dreams unfulfilled. In the business of the photographic world there are the same weave of the eight critical behaviors, especially:

• **Goal Orientation.** In the early days of your career the fact that you get the opportunity to publish your photos and receive some payment should be motivation enough. Do not choose your specialties based on their rates of pay; base your choices on your ability to generate the right photographic product for your client base. With exposure comes experience; with experience comes Practical Know-How; with Practical Know-How comes the ability to handle the more complex projects.

• **Personal Influence.** Your finished artwork may speak a thousand words or more, but it must speak to an audience, and only developed Personal Influence skills will get you there: with the phone calls you make, the letters you write, the portfolios you build, and the good humor and professional manners you display after the sixtieth rejection. It is these skills, along with the quality of your work, that will over time encourage people to beat a path to your door.

• **Organized Action.** Photography is a business that uses plant (a studio), equipment (cameras and gear), and people (the talent). You have to bring all these diverse elements together before you frame the first shot, and that requires Organized Action.

Loyal and efficient work in a great cause, even though it may not be immediately recognized, ultimately bears fruit. —Lord Lichfield

• **Inner Openness.** Turning your photography into money demands Inner Openness of a high order. In the real world, bringing your work to a larger audience invariably necessitates the presence of a client, who pays you to create a work that is suitable to his or her needs. It is this understanding and accommodation of your client's needs in harmony with your feelings that make the Inner Openness of the successful and buoyant photographer.

• **Positive Expectancy.** Your work will not achieve prominence, or even profitability, overnight. You know it might take years to make your mark, and until that starts to happen, it is your belief in yourself and your work that will see you through. When you believe in yourself, you get to hang in there long enough so that when opportunity finally does knock, both your artistic skill and your professional behaviors enable you to seize the opportunities with both hands. Until then enjoy your art for the joy it brings; the chase is just as much fun as making the win.

The Artist's Blueprint

"Business is cold, cruel, and base. Art is pure, clean, and above the world of commerce. Businesspeople are boring and ordinary, artists are interesting and exciting."

I believe the above statement to be about as accurate as the one about artists being uncontrollable wack-jobs. My observation of the rules for success in the new world of work is that business is unquestionably a high art form and that art is unquestionably one of the most cutthroat businesses around.

The buoyant core careerist will endeavor to inject the elegance and balance of art into all his or her professional dealings, just as buoyant artists will endeavor to inject the elegance and balance of professionalism into the business side of their dream career.

If you expect to make money with your art, you have to sell it—so the artists who make money are the ones who study the art of business.

RESEARCH AND DEVELOPMENT

Your Portfolio. Whether you're making a presentation to an art-gallery buyer, applying for an art grant, or meeting with an art collector, you

---

Action, to be effective, must be directed to clearly conceived ends.
—Jawaharlal Nehru

should have a current resume. Of course there will be those who won't care about seeing your resume, but there will be others who will agree to preview your work only after you've sent a resume or bio. Good professional practices in the art industry mirror good professional practices in the corporate world more than you might imagine.

However, whether you're eventually accepted or rejected by clients depends very much on whether or not your portfolio turns them on. Like a photographer's, an artist's portfolio is a case or book that holds samples of your work. It is your most important sales tool, so make sure you have your most exceptional artwork in it. Working artists recommend that you use one or more of the following in your portfolio:[5]

- Tearsheets (published samples of your work)
- Photographs of your work
- Slides and transparencies
- Color photocopies
- Original works

Remember to label your slides, transparencies, and so forth, and make extra copies of everything you have in your portfolio to leave with your prospective clients. All working artists have business cards, and many also have brochures that explain and position their work—in this, again, they are like their corporate counterparts. If you decide you have no choice but to physically carry your original work, make sure to wrap your pieces well, and of course handle the items carefully.

Choosing a Marketplace. Before you try to sell your work, do your market research. Go to the library and read trade publications, art magazines, directories, and the like; attend art association meetings, fund-raisers, and gallery receptions to find out as much as you can about where and how art crops up in your community. By doing this investigative work, you'll form a foundation of P.K.H. for your subsequent success.

To support their livelihood, most artists, at one time or another in their careers, do one or more of the following:

- Sell artwork by contracting with retail galleries, co-op galleries, rental galleries, or art shops

---

Ideas are the factors that lift civilization. They create revolutions. There is more dynamite in an idea than in many bombs. —John H. Vincent

- Exhibit at art shows, and arts & crafts fairs
- Accept commissions directly from clients who request specific work

It's up to you to decide which of these avenues you'd like to pursue.

Photographing Your Artwork. Whether you include an assortment of color or black-and-white photographs and transparencies in your portfolio, you should make sure the print quality is the best it can be, because their color and textural quality represent what you have to sell. And it is not copping out to hire a photographer; it's an additional expense, but it can be a worthwhile investment.

SALES AND MARKETING

Just as you need a paintbrush to paint a picture, you need a sale to pay for the paint. The artists who actually move ahead are the ones who understand and apply core-career sales, promotion, and marketing techniques to their body of work, to bring their work to that all-important larger audience.

Marketing Materials. Compile a mailing list of possible customers from your research that includes names, addresses, and phone numbers. You should include collectors, art critics, editors of art magazines, museum curators, galley owners, institutions, and so forth.

Some artists prefer to save time by leasing or buying general mailing lists directly from market research firms, galleries, or art organizations. Keep in mind that these lists cost about a hundred dollars for a thousand names, and they may not pinpoint your target market as well as you could have yourself, were you prepared to sweat out the details.

The collateral materials you develop to market your work product should be as professional as money allows. They may include the following:

- As many portfolios as needed to pursue your chosen markets
- Color brochures that show samples of artwork, quotes, exhibition information, and how you can be contacted; these brochures should be between one and four pages long
- Fliers that specify where you will be exhibiting or selling your work

The actions of men are the best interpreters of their thoughts. —John Locke

- Business cards
- An information sheet that lists prices of individual pieces as well as other pertinent facts about your art

Each potential catalog or flier must speak of the competency and professionalism of the artist; they are *not* artistic statements in and of themselves. Successful artists with cash flow may spend a great deal of money to have four-color catalogs published that feature pictures of the artist's work and personal data. The catalogs are then sent to contacts on a mailing list or sold individually for ten to thirty dollars each. Marketing materials of this nature cost up to thousands to produce.

Do not send original work through the mail. Instead send transparencies, photocopies, and photographs.

Galleries. Most galleries work on consignment, which means they take a commission from everything they sell. Commissions range from 30 to 50 percent, although some galleries may prefer buying artwork outright.

Locating an art gallery is relatively simple. You can look up addresses and phone numbers in the yellow pages, at your local library, or in the advertisements of national art publications, directories, or big-city gallery guides.

Don't concern yourself with getting into the biggest and best gallery in town. Remember what I say about job hunting: If the best jobs in town are at the ABC Bank, that's where the competition will be stiffest, so get your chops down with the *other* alphabet-soup bank: XYZ Co-operative. The same philosophy applies here. Small steps will get you where you want to go, so make a list of all the galleries that interest you, no matter what their size, then start cutting your teeth on the smaller ones.

If possible, visit the galleries on your list individually. While there, don't be afraid to talk to the staff to get some insights about the following:

- Whether or not they're accepting new material
- What their policies are for displaying work of new artists
- The name of the dealer or director
- Any brochures you can take home with you

The real Antichrist is he who turns the wine of an original idea into the water of mediocrity. —Eric Hoffer

It's also a good idea to attend some of the gallery's openings. This will give you an opportunity to meet the director of the gallery and perhaps even talk with him or her.

Don't expect to be able to visit a gallery with your artwork in hand and get an interview with the decision maker right then and there. Most gallery dealers work by appointment only. After identifying suitable galleries, contact them by telephone and request an appointment with the dealer for a viewing of your work. You may be told the gallery is not accepting new work at the moment but that you can send your resume and samples of your work. If you do that, you take the chance that your biography will be filed away and forgotten. But it's still a chance. Your goal of course is to get a personal appointment with the director. When you send your work, enclose a letter saying that you will follow up, and do so with notes, calls, and casual in-person visits every couple of months. Eventually that gallery will be accepting new work, and your follow-through will have positioned you as a professional. Again, this sounds a bit like the professional behavior you would use in a corporate marketing or sales job, or perhaps some of the techniques you would use on a job hunt.

At the initial meeting let your portfolio guide the conversation. When the interview is over, don't forget to leave behind a business card and other print pieces you may have put together.

The Art of Negotiation. Before you sign on with a gallery, there are several things you should clarify first:

- What kind of contract does the gallery want? Are they asking for exclusive representation; in other words do they want to be the only ones to represent you in a certain area or region? If so, can you still sell your work in places not covered in the contract? And if you do, is the gallery entitled to a commission?
- What is the commission structure? When do you get paid?
- Does the gallery offer opening shows or receptions to introduce new artists' work to the general public?
- Does the gallery offer their customers discounts or payment plans? This could affect your profit potential.
- Does the gallery advertise in newspapers, periodicals, or other media? Publicity is crucial to a gallery's success. You should supplement

---

Things won are done, joy's soul lies in the doing. —William Shakespeare the gallery's advertising with your own, by sending press releases to the media contacts on your mailing list. This is a much-overlooked technique, because it sometimes takes years to bear fruit. I have heard of artists pitching galleries and reviewers for years before they got their break.

• Does the gallery work in conjunction with other galleries or museums to help exhibit your art? The more exposure you get, the better it is for you.

• Do you have to pay for any related expenses, such as advertising, public relations, reception costs, and so on? Reputable galleries will not require that you pitch in any additional moneys for these items. The exception are co-op galleries (see below).

• What type of insurance does the gallery have? Will it cover the entire value of your artwork if it is damaged? If their insurance doesn't, then it is up to you to obtain the additional coverage.

• What happens if the gallery loses or misplaces an art piece? To prevent problems and keep track of your artwork the gallery has in its possession, you should develop your own tracking system. The wisest thing to do is to get a signed receipt for each piece you deliver to the gallery that acknowledges what you've given them.

• When and how your work will be returned to you if it is not sold?

Remember that all your contract specifics should be in *writing*. A verbal agreement or firm handshake is not enough. Also, read the contract very carefully before you sign it, and make sure you understand what the legal wording of the contract means.

Co-op Galleries. In a co-op gallery the exhibiting artists share in the ongoing responsibilities and expenses of that business. It's a good way to meet other artists and get involved in the business of art. In order for you to be part of the co-op, you have to be willing to help with the upkeep of the gallery, or pay a fee and have the maintenance duty waived. Before joining the co-op, speak to other artists to get feedback about the co-op. You will want to know such things as how much foot traffic there is and how many pieces they sell each month.

Usually co-ops pay their overhead expenses by charging initiation fees,

The vitality of thought is in adventure. Ideas won't keep. Something must be done about them. When the idea is new, its custodians have fervor, live for it, and if need be, die for it. —Alfred North Whitehead

monthly dues, and a commission on each piece of work sold. Usually the commission is not as high as that which a retail gallery might charge.

Booth Shows. For many artists, renting display booths and exhibiting at art shows may be the best way to go. Some artists prefer doing booth shows because it gives them local exposure, as well as an opportunity to get feedback and talk to people. But exhibiting yourself this way does require you to develop your communication skills (a.k.a. Personal Influence).

Before embarking on your first show, it's a good idea to go to other booth shows as a spectator and check out what other artists do with their displays and how they communicate and build rapport with their customers. Figure out what seems to work and what doesn't; take notes on what attracts the general public. Don't forget to bring the following:

• Tools and hardware to hang and display your artwork, including tape, staples, signs, change, business cards, pens, bags, brochures, tables, chairs, tarp, plastic sheets in case it rains, and so on.[6] Sometimes you can rent some of the necessary items from the booth sponsors, but find out for sure ahead of time what's available; don't take anything for granted.

• Enough inventory. Bring whatever you can transport and then some. Display assorted samples and differently priced pieces to appeal to various types of buyers.

If you don't get an immediate sale at a booth show, you should still encourage people to leave their names and addresses with you so that you can send them information about upcoming exhibitions. Compiling a mailing list is smart marketing because you can use this information in the future.

To get listings of local and regional booth shows, look through your local newspapers or obtain information from local art associations.

Retail Stores. If you've been to a mall recently, then chances are you came across a retail art shop. These establishments are a source of potential income for artists who are not solely concerned with the individual promotion you get with a gallery. Some of these art dealers handle work on consignment, while others buy on a wholesale basis.

Before doing business on consignment with an art shop, you'll want to visit the store and make sure it gets enough floor traffic. If the art just sits

An idea that is not dangerous is unworthy of being called an idea at all.
—*Elbert Hubbard*

there for months on end because there's a lack of clientele in the store, you'll only end up frustrated and broke. You should handle a business relationship with a retail store owner just as you would with a gallery owner (see page 227).

Commissions. If you're an artist who specializes in portraiture, working directly with clients on commission can prove to be a very profitable option. The client comes to you with a particular picture in mind, and you agree to do the work for a certain price. By advertising in local publications, and by word of mouth, you can develop a good client base.

However, usually customers who hire you to create a particular piece of work for them already have an idea in mind of what they want the completed project to look like. If they are disappointed in your finished work, you run the risk of not getting paid for it, so clarify exactly what the client wants from you before you start the project.

Museums. Deacons of artist development advise that you first contact smaller or local museums and approach them about sponsoring a show on your behalf. Museums are open to considering the work of new and aspiring artists, especially for the collective shows that regional museums sometimes sponsor, but you still have to work at getting considered in the first place.

Juried Art Competitions. Juried art competitions are usually held by local and national art groups, local civic organizations, or museums. To be included in these shows, you must pass preliminary judging by submitting slides or original artwork, along with the proper fee. Don't expect to make a lot of money from these competitions. If your project does win, you may receive a small monetary award, a ribbon, or exposure in a catalog. It is a great way to earn local notoriety, however, and get your name and work out into the public eye. Also, your awards go on your bio/resume and over time help build your credibility.

Public Art. Nowadays the majority of new government construction projects must set aside a certain amount of money for the purchase of public art. Contact local art commissions for appropriate submission procedures to get an idea about how you can submit your work for consideration. The money isn't always great, but again, it's an opportunity to build your resume and with it your experience and credibility in the art world.

Let us not be content to wait and see what will happen, but give us the determination to make the right things happen. —Peter Marshall

You can also contact local houses of worship, libraries, restaurants, movie theaters, and the like. Any public or community gathering place can be receptive to the properly presented query or proposal.

Private Art. While there are directories available that provide information about corporations that collect art, corporate-sponsored art collectors exclusively buy the work of recognized artists. However, if you want to become known to this market once you become established, using a slide registry is a cost-effective way to introduce your work for the corporate market.

Individuals or corporations interested in purchasing artwork may go through art registries to obtain information and sample slides of qualified artists. To register with these organizations, contact them directly or call the local art commission and get the name of a reputable slide registry. If you use a slide registry, make sure you consistently provide updated work.[7]

Associations. Local and national artist support groups and associations can provide you with a wealth of career advice, experience, and resource information. There's no shortage of groups to join, so see the "Resources" section at the back of the book.

THE BUOYANT ARTIST

Many artists want so badly to exhibit their work that they suffer from performance anxiety when they meet people such as curators, judges, and art dealers. They feel threatened and nervous, fall all over themselves, and ruin their chances.

Accept the fact that not everyone will fall in love with your work, and that that's okay. You're going to get rejections. But if you keep shopping your portfolio and keep promoting yourself, you'll eventually meet that person of influence who can introduce your work to that larger audience.

Living and working as an artist is not quite what many people imagine. Skill with a brush, or the ability to form a lump of clay into a thing of beauty, are necessary, but not sufficient, for artistic career buoyancy.

When I was talking to artists to put together this blueprint, many of them spoke of key traits and behaviors. They didn't use my terms of course, but they did talk about the traits in their own way. I found out from them that buoyant artists especially used the following traits:

Let every man be persuaded in his own mind. —Romans 14:5

- **Smart Decisions** need to be made when you sign a contract and decide on the commission structure and how the gallery will promote your work.
- **Inner Openness** allows you to hear what people are saying, especially when you don't necessarily like what they have to say.
- **Organized Action** provides the structure you need to get your creative work done while you are also pursuing outlets for your work.
- **Personal Influence** is key, since you aren't working alone in your studio or artist's garret. To be a *buoyant* artist requires that you talk to others, get out in the world, and market your wares.

Your studio can be a mess, and you can dress the part of the disorderly, impractical artist if you wish, but it's *organization* and *openness* that help you attain buoyancy in your career.

MAKING THE DREAMS REAL

So there are the four blueprints of dream careers we can all relate to with little effort—dreams that are difficult, but possible, to achieve. With fifty thousand books published in America every year, and a similar number of patents awarded, why shouldn't one of them be *yours*? In a world that believes a picture is worth a thousand words, why shouldn't some of the millions of paintings and photographs sold every year be created by *you*? The answer is that it *can* be your work that makes it to a greater public.

These peeks into the day-to-day world of inventors, writers, photographers, and artists are aimed at demystifying some of the so-called creative arts. You will recognize that these examples are dream careers that can be woven into an evening and weekend dream-career chain, which is how most successful dream careerists and entrepreneurs begin.

You might also have noticed that the stereotypical creative/artistic dream careers don't fit the stereotype one jot. This is the message: Everywhere people like you are applying their core-career skills and personal values, passion, and creativity to something that relates to their inner sense of happiness and their definition of something that gives meaning to their lives. Dream careers present the opportunity for connectivity be-

Man's fear of ideas is probably the greatest dike holding back human knowledge and happiness. —Morris Leopold Ernst

tween your dream career and the skills you use to develop core-career buoyancy. And now that you've read the blueprints, I think you might understand why it is that successful creative people don't rank creativity as their most important asset. The reason is this: Anyone can have ideas, but not everyone has the P.K.H. to turn those dreams into reality, and even fewer know what it takes to sell the work product at the end of the day.

So going after your dreams isn't as scary as you think—and you don't even have to go it alone. The two inventors (and yes, the Marty is me) got together because they were married men with children, living in the same community. They both liked blues music, sick humor, and occasional infusions of the blissful Hippocrene. As comrades they talked of their dreams and frustrations, and of paying off the mortgage. Then one day they said, "Hey, let's start doing something about this," and they started to come up with ideas for fun projects that had some potential for making money down the road. They took a selection of their personal dream careers and set out to pursue a number of them with entrepreneurial intent. They got going with the invention, and at the same time they started work on scripts, and they are still noodling with an idea for an antique-bicycle rental business in New York City's Central Park. They have made a hobby out of developing core-career skills, and after three years they are just starting to see the possibility of revenue. They started out with four very basic principles:

1. They needed something constructive to talk about over a barbecue besides the wives, the kids, and blues music.

2. They realized they were not going to get any closer to realizing their dreams, just by dreaming about them. They knew they had to wake up and take action so that they would make mistakes and learn from them.

3. They said, "We are as smart as anyone else our age and others are out there who are already doing it."

4. They had nothing to lose, everything to gain, and a damn good excuse for hanging out and not mowing the lawn.

A collaboration is possible with any dream career: Lennon and McCartney, Smith and Wesson, Delaney and Bonnie. It's a way of harnessing your talents with those of another, of building your skills and helping

There is no medicine to be found for a life that has fled. —*Ibycus*

each other work toward a better and more fulfilling life. And if most of your working life has been spent in the "never trust a soul" corporate world, you might find this approach to be immensely empowering.

WAKING UP FROM DREAMLAND

A dream career is a series of activities that are rewarding to you and that achieve some long-cherished wish. A dream career is anything you don't have but are prepared to work hard for.

For me it was to become a writer or an actor. For you? Well, those are your choices to make, but the excuses are dwindling because you are getting a real comprehensive look at the blueprint for how other successful and buoyant people go about building their American dreams.

It will take time, but it can be done.

It's quicker for some and longer for others; nevertheless it can be done, and I guarantee it is a whole ball of fun.

Pursuing a dream for a quarter of a century has shaped my life in how I have spent my time—in my corporate career, in my love life, my friendships, and my long-term professional associations. And the pursuit of my crazy dream has given my life a meaning in its toughest hours, as it does for anyone who dares to give their dreams a means of practical fulfillment.

Put a dream career to work for yourself; stick with your dreams long enough, and you will learn how easy they can become to achieve. It's all in the weaving of what you've got into something you'd like to have. You won't be alone; you will find dream careerists everywhere.

The pursuit of a dream career brings more balance into your life. It is a way to live in harmony with your needs by giving them a means of practical expression and therefore possible fulfillment. In its pursuit you develop the skills and behaviors that will contribute to your core-career buoyancy at the same time that they satisfy the other needs in your life.

It may be a stretch between where you are today and where you want to be tomorrow in your dream career. Just be sure that when you find distance between your dream and reality, you don't turn it into a chasm you could never cross. Instead use the raw materials in *B.T.O.* to build bridges from today's world to tomorrow's dreams.

There are two times in a man's life when he should not speculate: when he can't afford it, and when he can. —*Mark Twain*

NOTES

1. The *Trademark Register of the United States*, which you can find at your local library, will assure you that no one else owns it. A trademark attorney offered to do such a search for the Redout inventors; her price was $350. They walked to the library instead.

2. Apes learn by mimicking or copying. To do something in the manner of a "sedulous ape" is to learn by copying in a repetitive and apelike manner. Oy.

3. Now they are known as Adams Media, and publish and distribute one hundred books a year.

4. Your portfolio will be handled by many different hands, so use the best quality you can afford.

5. For more information about portfolios, see "The Photographer's Blueprint," page 211.

6. Which, except for the plastic sheets, is exactly what you would pull together for an off-site sales meeting, presentation, or conference.

7. The American Council of the Arts in New York City publishes the *Directory of Artists Slide Registries*, which lists all slide registries by state. You can also get registry information from your local library or art publications.

Boldness is a mask for fear, however great. —Lucan

Part Three

THE

ENTREPRENEURIAL

CAREER

▼

Chapter 9

The Ticking of the New Entrepreneurs

DO YOU HAVE WHAT IT TAKES TO STAND ALONE?

If you're wondering whether the average person, like you or me, really can be gainfully self-employed, consider this. A couple of centuries ago, when America was young, cottage industries were the rule rather than the exception. If you were a baker, you probably worked at home and sold baked goods to your neighbors. Consumers certainly didn't have the option then of buying Wonder Bread at the A & P. You were the only game in town. Blacksmiths, candlestick makers, doctors, and just about everyone else, similarly plied his or her trade at, or close to, home. Most people managed to make a living, and they did it without answering to a manager, foreman, or vice president. In the old days the community was boss. Plying a reliable trade to a steady supply of potential customers led to success most of the time for just about everybody in colonial America, and with today's technology the whole world can become your customer.

Now the time is ripe for many Americans to go back to their own independent ventures. Harsh economic conditions are pushing people away from offices and factories in search of alternatives to what is increasingly seen as a work-life treadmill. At the same time, new technology has allowed companies of one or two people to join and, when necessary, even compete with the rest of the corporate world.

With all professional ranks shrinking, companies coming to rely more

---

The substance of the eminent Socialist gentleman's speech is that making a profit is a sin, but it is my belief that the real sin is taking a loss. —Winston Churchill

on a contingent work force, and with the fastest-growing occupations in the economy offering low wages and little opportunity for advancement, many workers are still valiantly trying to land yet another job. Maybe, they tell themselves, it will last longer than the last one did. And maybe it will pay some of the bills.

But there's another growing segment of the population that has a new, or perhaps an old, dream of the independence that comes from self-employment. More than anything, you want to control your own destiny. You think maybe you can learn how to run a business; after all, you're willing to work hard to make a buck. And technology has reduced the once-staggering cost of business start-up to almost zilch. So it doesn't really matter that the banker down the street isn't your uncle or your best friend, because you're not aiming to buy that little four-million-dollar-a-year business. In fact technology has not only made it easier and cheaper to open a retail or office-based business, it has also made it possible to operate a one- or two-person business from your own home that once would have required the overhead of commercial space and employees.

There are incredibly successful home-based businesses in every category imaginable, with the obvious exception of retail businesses, which are usually excluded from residential areas. And if your only entrepreneurial dream has been to open a retail operation of some kind, a home-based business start-up still makes lots of sense: You can develop a home-based wholesale operation, which will give you a ring-side education in the business problems of retailers while you choose your moment. This in fact has always been the traditional boot-strapping route into retail.

A home-based business is the lowest-risk/highest-opportunity option for getting a little more control over your life. It is because of this risk ratio that as I talk about life and opportunities for the new entrepreneur I am largely thinking of them as home-based. Not that you couldn't put any of these endeavors into commercial space right away, it's just that you don't *have* to; technology has changed all that. Today you can start almost any business part-time and based out of your home.

So as I talk about different aspects of the entrepreneurial life open to you, think about those three square feet of free counter space you have in the kitchen—which is exactly where the global Laura Ashley retail conglomerate started. On old Ms. Ashley's kitchen table.

It is wonderful what strength of purpose and boldness and energy of will are roused by the assurance that we are doing our duty. —*Walter Scott*

You don't need an M.B.A. from Harvard to start a business either. In fact you don't even have to fit the traditional entrepreneurial mold: a Reagan-era whiz kid whose main inspiration in life is to build an internationally renowned corporation. Today you don't have to fit anyone's preconceived notions of success except your own.

Why the Entrepreneurial Market Is Booming

Thank God the recession is over! Since recovery from the last recession got underway in 1991, employment secured through temporary-help agencies has increased 61 percent, and of the 3 million jobs created in the last year, fully 90 percent have no future, or are part-time or temporary in nature.[1] The temporary-help industry is the darling of Wall Street at the moment, with almost every publicly traded company consistently turning in ever-higher numbers and profits for the shareholders.[2]

The corporate core has shrunk because more can be done with fewer people, and with a smaller payroll the crippling overhead of payroll, taxes, and bennies shrinks too. This doesn't necessarily mean that the work has disappeared, but that it just isn't always packaged in the form of a forty-hour-a-week job. As William Bridges says, "The real opportunities exist outside the job matrix rather than inside."[3]

In 1985, when the Bureau of Labor Statistics weighed in with its first survey of home-based businesses, it came up with 18.3 million as the number of home-based businesses in the country. In 1991 alone America created 1.3 million more. Now at least one-quarter of adult Americans are involved in home-based businesses, at least part-time.

The boom began about ten years ago because of the workplace technology revolution. By 1985 the new entrepreneurs were able to have computers, laser printers, fax machines, home photocopiers, modems, and so on. This equipment narrowed the gap between smaller start-up businesses and older established corporations. And these technological capabilities reduced the need for more employees as the new venture begins to grow.

Home Office Computing[4] looks at the entrepreneurial phenomenon as whole generations try to "regain some measure of control over their lives." The opportunities for part-time or full-time home-based businesses have never been better.

Occupation is the necessary basis of all enjoyment. —Leigh Hunt

Then What's the Problem?

Early career planning and outplacement encouraged the view of "stop core career, start entrepreneurial career on a dime" as an acceptable way to live, but it is not.

The failure rate of new businesses is staggering: 25 percent in the first two years[5] and over 60 percent by the five-year mark. We have had five years of stories about frustrated executives leaving corporate America to open up their own businesses or franchises. I believe that many such endeavors were doomed to fail from their inception because too many started them because they had *no other alternative*. And this has proven to be the case. They weren't prepared for the inevitable slamming of the door to the irreducible core, so a considerable number are catapulted unprepared into the full-time entrepreneurial world every month.

Many professionals are sinking valuable layoff pay into starting a business or buying a franchise because the only alternative is starting at the bottom in another profession. For many mature workers the entrepreneurial route is the only one that holds out any chance of maintaining their standard of living.

You can make a success of the full-time entrepreneurial life if you decide to jump into it at the deep end, and I'll give you some of the best tools available to help. But it is not what I recommend, if you have the choice. Developing a non-core-career-conflicting business on the side, in your personal time, is a much more sensible approach. You can nurture one from moonlighting through part-time to full-time, as your circumstances dictate. This way you develop your entrepreneurial skills with the minimum fiscal and professional risk, while polishing the same behaviors, in a different context, that you are developing for core-career buoyancy.

Who Is the New Entrepreneurial Life For?

For anyone who wants a little more autonomy, who is madder than hell with the way the changing world has screwed up the traditional career track, who's sick of living his or her life as a cipher, and who is determined not to go down with the boat.

The New Entrepreneurial Life is especially for everyone who recognizes that the shift to a contingent workforce is a sea change that has the capa-

---

He who rejects change is the architect of decay. The only human institution which rejects progress is the cemetery. —Harold Wilson

bility of destroying the unwary. Did you know that 50 percent of laid-off workers get to swallow pay cuts when they get new jobs, and 60 percent of this number get to swallow pay cuts that exceed *20 percent*? The New Entrepreneurial Life is for people who want to start building a little fiscal bulwark for themselves, and it's for the outsourced who are not willing to settle for 20 percent pay cuts while the people who made the layoff happen to get record-breaking bonuses.

The New Entrepreneurial Life has special appeal for all minorities, and that includes women. The October 1994 pay-parity figures show that the parity gap for men and women is narrowing in corporate America. It shows that for every dollar a man earns, a woman earns seventy-one cents. That's up a penny since last year, and up a lousy dime since 1963. At the current rate of parity-gap closing, it will be 2152 before men and women will both be earning a dollar!

Given these statistics thirty-two years after the Equal Pay Act, it is not surprising that women are fervent entrepreneurs. In fact, since 1960 the number of women entrepreneurs has grown 1100 percent. The surge of minorities into the entrepreneurial market is also not surprising when you know that all men and women of color and foreign birth experience discrimination in the traditional workplace. On the thirtieth anniversary of the Civil Rights Act, if your skin isn't white or if you talk with a foreign accent, you are still discriminated against in the workplace. It's a case of accent, ancestry, and appearance; if you look within the federal government, the folks who passed Title VII of the Civil Rights Act, you won't find too many foreign-born Americans past level GS-14. And it is no better in the private sector.

If you are a black woman, chances are you are just achieving parity with a white woman, but Hispanic women are still lagging; they make only fifty-four cents on the Caucasian man's dollar for the same work. Strangely, the lowest-level jobs are those that get closest to parity. The closer your wages are to the poverty line, the closer you are to pay parity. The better your job, and the more successful you become, the less likely you are to achieve pay parity anytime soon.

So if you are a man or woman of color, or of foreign birth, the odds are you have experienced institutionalized discrimination in the workplace and will quite possibly never realize your full financial worth in a corporate environment until halfway through the next century. If you are a woman of any race or are disabled, you have also been exposed to discrimination up

---

Occupation is the scythe of time. —Napoleon Bonaparte

through the highest levels of American business and politics. For any op-
pressed community, entrepreneurial endeavor is an important path upward.

What About Mature Professionals and Seniors?

A guy called Harlan Sanders started a business with his Social Security
check when he was sixty-five. Less than ten years later, when he sold out,
he was a multimillionaire from the fried-chicken franchise that still carries
his name and likeness. The woman who wrote *Little House on the Prairie*,
the legendary Laura Ingalls Wilder, didn't start writing until she was
sixty-five. Then there are the two retired dentists who built a great business appraising their colleagues' dental practices to sell those practices on
to the next generation. Their concept was successful enough to franchise,
but they decided it would only interfere with a very hectic vacation schedule, so they didn't do it. The New Entrepreneur doesn't allow business to
run life, the new entrepreneur uses his or her endeavors to *balance* life.
That's the New Entrepreneur for you: someone who has gotten control of
life, someone who has autonomy, someone who has gotten to no.

I met a seventy-four-year-old woman, Amanda, and her business partner, an elder sister of seventy-six, on a plane. I was on a business trip, and
they were off to spend, as they put it, "the ill-gotten gains of our enterprise." It seems that the younger sister had spent a number of years in real
estate and, a few years after retirement, sparked on a brilliant idea for her
generation. She had noticed, in her real estate years, that reliable plumbers,
electricians, and other contractors were well-nigh impossible to find, and
as two elderly women living together, they were naturally concerned about
the type of workers who would come to their home.

Then Amanda recognized that referring reliable contractors to mature
homeowners was functionally no different from putting eager home sellers in contact with anxious home buyers. So they started up a referral service, and while these two weren't getting wealthy by some people's
standards, they were able to studiously spend everything they made by
taking two or three vacations a year to all the places they had always
dreamed of going but could never before afford.

Back in the fifties an entrepreneur called Per saw the entrepreneurial
potential of the baby boom. He founded Kinder Care, and thirty years
later the corporation was happily grossing over a billion dollars a year. To-

---

There is nothing permanent except change. —Heraclitus

day the graying of the baby boomers is opening up exactly the same kind of entrepreneurial opportunities for senior services and products—and who better to envision a practical means of satisfying the needs of this generation than senior entrepreneurs themselves?

How to Get Started

An old man in a beautiful top hat and shabby overcoat strides from his chauffeured car, elbows through the crowd surging at the not-yet-opened department-store doors, and raps smartly on the glass with his cane. The door opens, and the old man angrily faces up to his son.

"I haven't been retired a month, and already the store isn't open on time!" he fumes.

"But, Father, we're doing a quarterly profit-and-loss to see how much money we made and how much stock we have and. . . ."

The old man cuts him off with a demand for needle, thread, and shoe box. After an assistant scurries back with the items, the old man turns to his son and says, "When I come to this country, I come with this coat on my back, and a needle, and a shoe box, and a thread. And I stand here on this block and look for customers as they come down the street, and ask to sew on their loose button before it falls off. Son, when I come to this country, I have a needle, a thread, and a shoe box. Now, open the damn doors. Everything else is profit."[6]

All it takes to start a business is a shoe box, a needle, and a thread, and the gumption to sell people something that they need. Where you take it from there is up to you, but all you will ever need to stay in business is that needle, shoe box, and thread, as long as you are prepared to sell. Now, let's open the damn doors.

Four Kinds of Entrepreneurs

You can try your hand at building any kind of business you want. But before we look at all the hottest opportunities and what it is that makes successful and buoyant entrepreneurs tick, I want to give you a quick rundown of the four different ways people make a living as entrepreneurs. I shall start with the Supernova Entrepreneurs, those captains of industry who conquer the world not because they are the most important but because the media has convinced many people that this is the only kind of person who makes

Things do not change, we do. —Henry David Thoreau

it as an entrepreneur. For some people this is the ideal route to the American Dream, but it is by no means the *only* path to entrepreneurial success. That can only be defined by you and your needs. The four types are

1. *The Supernova Traditional Entrepreneurs.* These guys want to get out of the garage, pronto. In fact they'd rather not *be* there in the first place. These people build multimillion-dollar companies and sometimes create whole industries in the process. They generate 90 percent of today's new jobs, and they deserve to be lauded.

2. *The Traditionalist Entrepreneurs.* These entrepreneurs tend to develop labor- and space-intensive businesses: retail of all kinds, plus all the products, services, and trades that are tied to our communities. If you talk to these folks, they'll tell you they just built jobs for themselves, meaning that they just looked around their community for a job that needed doing and would support them and just started doing it. Traditional entrepreneurs use this route as a means of expressing their need for a secure income and a life in a safe community where families can grow up together. They generate most of today's new jobs.

3. *The New Solo Entrepreneurs.* These entrepreneurs have mushroomed in a world rapidly becoming accustomed to specialized services. Soloists thrive everywhere with motivation, some technology, a place to work, and an attitude of knowledge.

4. *The Minimalists.* The Minimalists are building operational entities for themselves, but in ways that apply America's downsizing philosophies from the moment the growth starts. They are accomplishing their work with technology and a web of other Minimalist and Soloist entrepreneurs with complementary skill sets, rather than with a permanent cast of permanently payrolled employees.

My own company is very much like this. I have had up to fourteen people working on a specific project, but unlike the traditionalist entrepreneurs I don't have any of these people on my payroll. In fact I'd destroy some good working relationships if I ever proposed such a ridiculous idea.

Many Minimalists have no intention of becoming industrial giants. They have very clear alternative visions of a work life that don't include the management headaches of traditional and supernova entrepreneurs. The minimalists are burning a completely new path to the American

---

Life belongs to the living, and he who lives must be prepared for changes.
—*Johann Wolfgang von Goethe*

Dream by forging project alliances that pull a disparate group of solos (or other Minimalists) into a marketable whole for projects that need more than one pair of hands. In the coming years you will see enormous growth among Minimalist entrepreneurial endeavors.

How Much Time, Energy, and Money Should I Invest?

You can work full-time at your entrepreneurial endeavor, part-time, or you can start by moonlighting. If you are unemployed right now and you have the pockets, you could start a full-time business immediately. I don't recommend it, because I don't think you will make the best choices when you are under pressure and making the entrepreneurial decision under stress. You can do it that way, but a more prudent path might be to devote your days to the core-career job hunt and evenings to the entrepreneurial endeavor. This way you won't be putting all your eggs in one basket, and while you'll probably progress a little more slowly, you might advance more surely, over the long haul.

If, on the other hand, you are employed right now, the challenge is to develop your entrepreneurial talents and endeavors without jeopardizing what you have taken so long to build. The most sensible way to start is by moonlighting your dream and entrepreneurial careers.

THE MOONLIGHTING OPTION

Deborah had been casting around for something she could do to turn a buck outside of her draining core career as an internal auditor for an accounting firm. Then her grandpa died, and she inherited his watch-repairing tools because no one else wanted them. The tools languished in a box in her bedroom for six months, but Deborah took them out one day and found, as she puts it, the spirit of grandfather in her hands. She bought a how-to book, but almost instinctively she knew what the tools were and how to use them. The peace she gained from the quiet acoustics, the mechanical sounds of the watches, was so different from the hustle and bustle of her core career. By the time spring was sprung, she was haunting the flea markets and junk shops looking for old watches. By the end of that summer a dealer had her work on consignment and was also sending her watch- and clock-repair work.

After three years she is thinking about doing the shows as a dealer herself

---

The world hates change, yet it is the only thing that has brought progress.
—Charles F. Kettering

next year. They all happen on the weekends, and she can work it around her core-career job. Deborah has built a wonderfully fulfilling entrepreneurial career, complete with a whole new world of friends and colleagues. In three years she has also put away almost five hundred dollars a month toward a home down payment, when she was putting away nothing before.

Deborah's quietly pursued entrepreneurial endeavor has allowed her to shine in her core-career setting. She talks about the resonance between her two careers; they both require meticulous attention to detail and unhurried methodical work. Because the process has parallels, one activity seems to encourage her in the other. "Now," says Deborah, "when I do a company's books, I listen for things that aren't ticking right to my ear."

When you integrate parallel evening and weekend activities into a core-career-dominated work life, and work at making money with them, you are said to be moonlighting. It is the smoothest way to ease into the entrepreneurial life, and provides you with a smorgasbord of low-risk opportunities to get aquainted with the joys and terrors of making a buck for yourself.

This is an especially important option if you are on the brink of chucking it all in and climbing out of the corporate salt mine right into a full-time entrepreneurial quagmire. Jobs with futures are not as easy to come by as they once used to be, and getting a profitable business going takes a lot more than apparently two-thirds of America's beginning entrepreneurs think it does. Moonlighting allows you to determine your own future with a parallel endeavor of your choosing that is completely under your own control.

During an early Compuserve appearance I spoke to a woman who worked as a loan officer at a bank. She said she hated what she did at the bank but was locked into the banking world because of her age and family responsibilities; she couldn't think of a moonlighting career she'd have time for, yet she felt trapped at the bank. When she looked at it another way, she discovered that it was not what she did that she hated but what she did at the bank. What was really wrong was that the environment in which she worked was no longer satisfying her.

Her solution was to develop a moonlighting business that took advantage of her core-career skills. She started a business that helped people get home loans; she'd find the forms from the banks with the best deals, fill them out, and tell her clients what to say and how to behave. She isn't frantic at her work. Her moonlighting venture isn't anything that would support her full-

---

A person reveals his character by nothing so clearly as the joke he resents.
—G. C. Lichtenberg

time, or even part-time, but she feels just a bit more comfortable than before. She's still living frugally, but she's finally getting to put something away, and the pressure at work doesn't seem quite so bad either.

THE PART-TIME ENTREPRENEUR

With a moonlighting foundation to your entrepreneurial career, your whole work life becomes more flexible: Should circumstances dictate or opportunity beckon, you are positioned to move from the moonlighting option to becoming a part-time entrepreneur.

It happens like this. After moonlighting for a while, perhaps trying your hand at a couple of things, the business takes on an aura of success, and suddenly the option of making it a full-time gig looms real out of the mists. What do you do? Well, you act cautiously and secure the future with as little exposure as you can manage.

Remember, all companies are looking to cut costs and might welcome someone with your skills and experience who is doing a good job with only half the overhead. Maybe you are part of that not-insignificant number who could do that corporate job in half the time anyway. Similarly there are an increasing number of job-sharing opportunities arising where companies are actually looking for two people to share one job (it's both a talent-finding and a cost-saving measure).

If circumstances permit you should start your entrepreneurial career as a moonlighter. Then, if success increases and looks sustainable, you can often work part of the week on your entrepreneurial career and part of the time on your core job.

The part-time option is a particularly attractive option for good people who find themselves seemingly trapped in the lower levels of I.P.S./R.P.S. purgatory. You can structure your work hours to support coordinated entrepreneurial- and dream-career activities.

THE FULL-TIME ENTREPRENEUR

Beat the Odds is a very prudent book, which is why I recommend that anyone with the opportunity prepare carefully for full-time entrepeneurdom over a period of time. I suggest four distinct stepping-stones for the New Entrepreneur:

Mandatory First Phase: Full-time Core Careerist. Most things you need to know to be a successful businessperson you can learn at your job. The first

The quality of the imagination is to flow and not to freeze. —Ralph Waldo Emerson

thing to do, if you have the opportunity, is to overhaul your core career and get a core-career buoyancy plan in operation.

Mandatory Second Phase: Full-time Core Careerist, with Moonlighting Interests. Get your feet wet with those aspects of the business world you can't experience back at the company salt mine. You gain experience without threatening your core career.

Optional Third Phase: Part-time Entrepreneur and Part-time Core Careerist.[7] This step isn't possible for everyone, but it is for a lot of people. It's a step you take only when you have had enough experience of moonlighting to know what you are getting yourself into.

Fourth Phase: Full-time Entrepreneur. When time and experience tell you it's the right time to fully break out on your own.

Remember, it isn't an either-or world anymore; you don't have to be just a corporate professional or just an entrepreneur. You can be both, and you can be happily both for as long as it suits your needs.

It is time to jettison outmoded ideas of the entrepreneur as either a captain of industry or an aproned shopkeeper. The mass of New Entrepreneurs are home based, because in the new world of work it is suddenly possible. They like it just fine that way, until the business is such a success that they have to move into bigger quarters. So put full-time entrepreneurdom in its proper place on the entrepreneurial curve: at the far end when you are fully confident in your Practical Know-How.

What steps you take along the entrepreneurial path, and when and how you take them, are up to you. However, just knowing where the stepping-stones are could save you a soaking and get you safely to that place where your American dream lives.

It Starts with an Idea, But It Takes a Whole Lot More: What Makes an Entrepreneur Tick

How many businesses fail every year? What's the success rate for franchises? A whole mess of business start-ups may fail, but the only time that matters is when one of them belongs to *you.*

Every man has three characters—that which he exhibits, that which he has, and that which he thinks he has. —Alphonse Karr

And it takes more than a great idea to be a buoyant entrepreneur. What gives the successful entrepreneurs an edge is what's inside their heads. We checked it out pretty thoroughly, reading all the psychological and business literature. Didn't find too much of interest. Some people thought that family background was the most important factor in an entrepreneur's success, others said it was education.[8] While having a good education helps, and a healthy home environment certainly gives anyone a leg up, the challenge was to see what critical behaviors were shared between buoyant entrepreneurs and buoyant core careerists that could be important and relevant to your core-career buoyancy.

Our buoyancy research included all four types of modern entrepreneurs—Novas, Traditionalists, Minimalists, and Soloists—who in turn told us about other buoyant entrepreneurs they knew. We found out some really amazing things about the traits you need for entrepreneurial career buoyancy, things no one has ever talked about before. Let's take a good look at them.

THE PATH TO A BUOYANT ENTREPRENEURIAL CAREER

Goal Orientation

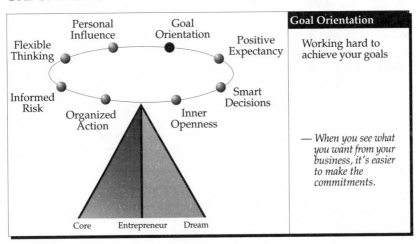

Entrepreneurs told us about many different traits that were necessary to be successful. But there were two things that kept on coming up again and again: Develop a vision for your company and stick with it no matter what.

All change is not growth; all movement is not forward. —Ellen Glasgow

KEEPING YOUR EYE ON THE BALL

Your vision is your personal blueprint for buoyancy. You have to know what you are driving toward, where you are heading, in order to get there.

Corporate planners call it a mission statement; you might call it the same. But whatever you call it, it is critical to your buoyancy. Your vision for your business is your North Star, guiding you through the wilderness. Keeping your eye on the ball lets you quickly evaluate opportunities as they present themselves. Does working for this client mean I am supporting my long-term goals, or not? If not, am I doing it for the cash flow? And if for cash flow, what technology and other expenditures will my company require to do the job? Should I really take out that loan for computer equipment?

Once you have the where and why of Goal Orientation worked out, you need to put some muscle into your career. It takes dedication, commitment, and a lot of hard work to then achieve your goals.

But be careful: Too much of a good thing—Goal Orientation—can wipe you out. After years of no vacations, no meaningful breaks, and no balance, a workaholic entrepreneur begins to lose drive and motivation, health and objectivity. Every buoyant entrepreneur finds a way to listen to the need for balance between the equally important needs for security, freedom, and happiness. You have to have the Inner Openness to know when you've had enough, to take a break and recharge your batteries, and to live and fight the battle anew another day.

On Your Own—Goal Orientation

Linda lives the good life. As a self-employed consultant Linda seems to have time to attend midday school functions for her active kids and she works out several afternoons each week. Her acquaintances figure she has it made. Easy Street.

But it isn't Easy Street now, nor has it ever been as long as she's been self-employed. Linda simply knows what she wants out of her work life and she is driven to achieve these goals. Her vision of her business includes the flexibility to see her kids at school, to be involved in their lives. The time she gives up to her family and personal health during the day is repaid during the 8:30 P.M.-to-midnight shift. That's when she does her marketing work—contact letters, brochures, and proposals get typed, revised, and copied.

Now in its fourth year Linda's consulting business is doing terrific. Her billings

---

What you are thunders so that I cannot hear what you say to the contrary.
—*Ralph Waldo Emerson*

have risen dramatically, she's added significantly to her client list, and she loves the work. Her intense motivation to achieve her personal vision isn't the same as strolling down Easy Street, but it is getting Linda to her destinations of security, autonomy, and fulfillment, and, as she puts it, "I've earned the right to take time out for my family."

Entrepreneurial Career

Core Career

Goal Orientation—Resonance Between Your Entrepreneurial Career and Your Core Career

The vision of an entrepreneur is a personal one. You create it. This personal vision is a powerful motivator, since it is *yours*. You can create a personal vision for your core career too. Your core career is for *you*, not for your employer. If you own your own core career, then you can develop your own powerful, personal, and motivating vision that embraces a parallel entrepreneurial career that uses the same talents.

Your core-career vision may be to acquire new skills, experience, or traits so that you develop and maintain career buoyancy, while your entrepreneurial vision is empowered by another set of goals—perhaps your financial independence—which use the same behaviors for achievement.

Positive Expectancy

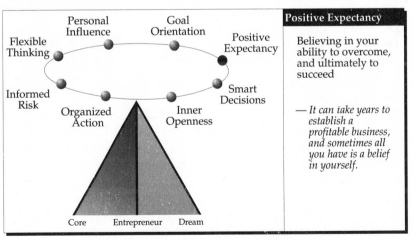

He that will not apply new remedies must expect new evils. —Francis Bacon

Entrepreneurs fail. They fail a lot. Why don't they take all of their failures and give up? Many of them do. Many of them go back to what they were doing before and give up on their dreams. The buoyant ones are the men and women who don't abandon ship when there is a sign of bad weather. They ride out the storm. No wonder entrepreneurs rated persistence and a positive attitude so highly. You have to believe that you will succeed, if not now, later. For now it sometimes has to be enough that you are on the road. Sometimes you will have to look hard to find a way to benefit from a bad experience, but the lesson is there. A buoyant entrepreneur reminds me of a terrier, a scrappy dog that, when it gets something stuck in its jaws, never lets it go. Persistent little bugger.

Entrepreneurs have to be persistent. They have to hold on to their beliefs, and not get shaken off by their competitors, clients, or banks. Buoyant entrepreneurs see the goal in front of them. They fantasize about what life will be like when . . . Because it is *their* vision of a life worth living, they will make almost any sacrifice to achieve it.

When they don't get that client they've worked so hard to get, they know that although it is a setback, it is only temporary. Smoke and mirrors, mere semantics here? No, definitely not! The goal of an entrepreneur is not to land a single account, not to get this one client. The goal is to achieve the vision for his or her business; it's the *big picture.* Envisioning the goal, entrepreneurs can slog through muck and mire to get there. And they do.

On Your Own—Positive Expectancy

I've heard many, many stories about persistent entrepreneurs—perseverance in the face of floods, fires, and lawsuits. One of these stories about Positive Expectancy comes from an entrepreneur our research team interviewed. Here's the craftsman's story:

"I'd been in business for about four years, struggling to get by, building a few houses, doing remodeling and roofing projects. Climbing onto a metal roof one morning, I lost my footing and fell about twenty feet to the ground. I guess I was lucky, because my back was okay and I didn't crack my head open. I broke both of my arms, though, and couldn't work for several months. In our financial condition that meant literally not surviving—not just the lack of income, but who was going to cut the wood we needed to heat ourselves through the Maine winter? Who

Character is what you are in the dark. —Dwight Moody

was going to finish the half-finished jobs? How would I pay the mills for the lumber already trucked to the building site?

"But I see things long-term. Maybe we'd be cold that winter, but I gradually started to feel that we would come out of this okay. I went into this business for a lot of reasons, a lot of really good reasons, and I knew that this was just one of those things that can happen to interrupt your life. So I figured out how to dial the phone with my arms in casts and began lining up some help to complete the biggest projects I had. Closed off some rooms of our house—then I really felt that we would survive.

"But what also got me through this was my neighbors and my assistant. Neighbors pitched in around the house, brought the wood in. Greg, my part-time assistant, brought in a friend and finished up the jobs I had. Paid off most of the longer-due bills. I hope something like this never happens to me again. But it did teach me two critical lessons: First, if you love what you do, you'll do whatever it takes to hold on to it. Second, watch your step!"

Persistence, Positive Expectancy, pulls you through the tough times that are part of any goal worth fighting for.

Entrepreneurial Career

Core Career

Positive Expectancy—Resonance Between Your Entrepreneurial Career and Your Core Career

"Sometimes it's just a test to see how much you're willing to fight. They just want to see if you really believe in what you're doing." This is how a core careerist described to us how she approached her presentations to the company president and how, sometimes, she would fail the test. The persistence of a buoyant entrepreneur is needed in many core-career situations. This persistence is born of belief and not of stubbornness; there's a big difference between those two traits. Anyone can be stubborn and obstinate, but that doesn't help you. What helps is belief in yourself and in what you are doing. That's what the company president is looking for: personal commitment. The story is exactly the same for the entrepreneur—simply replace *company president* with *client.*

The power which resides in him is new in nature, and none but he knows what that is which he can do nor does he know until he's tried. —Ralph Waldo Emerson

Inner Openness

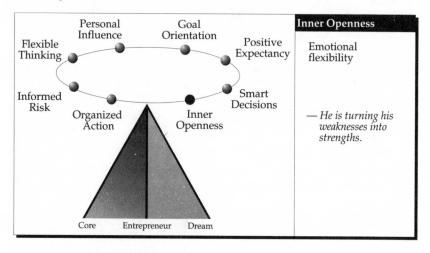

In a way Inner Openness is the trait that keeps you open for business. It is what keeps you open to feedback, open to options. Inner Openness provides you with the emotional flexibility and maturity to try new actions, consider new ideas, and develop new strategies.

Mistakes happen. You just can't get it right the first time every time. So what do you do with your mistakes? If you bury them under the carpet, you can feel good for a while. But then the same thing happens again.

Mistakes are useful, because they allow you to learn and to improve yourself. So turn a mistake into a learning opportunity; use it to figure out what went wrong and why. It helps to be able to say that you learned, not that you failed. You fail without Inner Openness.

COMPLEMENT YOURSELF

Be objective with yourself about what you can do and what you can't do. The problem an entrepreneur runs into is having to know how to do *everything.* From word processing to marketing, from sales to purchasing to finance, you are a business with all of its functions; you are the owner, chef, and bottle washer too.

You probably don't have skills in all of the areas you need, so you have to work with others to complement your skill set. You have to find these people and get along with them. Even in a tough economy I see the buoyant entre-

---

Common sense and nature will do a lot to make the pilgrimage of life not too difficult.
—*W. Somerset Maugham*

preneurs turning down opportunities because they can't stand working with a fellow entrepreneur. Or they phase out of a working relationship with a problem client, preferring to spend their energy and resources with a client they enjoy. Smart entrepreneurs do business with people who share certain values, who are honest and pleasant to work with, and who are self-aware.

We found out that entrepreneurs are not always the aggressive, brash businesspeople you hear about. That's because buoyant entrepreneurs have to listen to themselves and others, and work with others too. Being a decent work partner, a good collaborator, makes good business sense, and buoyant entrepreneurs realize the importance of Inner Openness.

On Your Own—Inner Openness

Imagine running your own whitewater-rafting company! One of our buoyant entrepreneurs does just that, and here's what he had to say about one of the reasons for his buoyancy: "I can honestly say that we've never had a big, knock-down, duke-'em-out fight. For four partners not to do that in seventeen years is pretty amazing. But we all did our share. The little things that went wrong or the disagreements that you have—you need to let those go, because you're looking at the big picture."

He and his partners were able to turn their business problems and personal differences into *feedback*. The falling out that so many partners have didn't happen to this business. They were all able to get along with one another, respect their different points of view, and discuss their differences. Inner Openness is the glue that holds this fun and successful company together.

 Entrepreneurial Career

Core Career

Inner Openness–Resonance Between Your Entrepreneurial Career and Your Core Career

The intense personal relationships business partners develop can benefit from the training you get in forming and maintaining relationships in your core career. It's amazing how many activities in a core career are group based. It takes a great deal of emotional flexibility to survive and prosper in that environment. It is also a great way to become more open and flexible for your entrepreneurial career.

Man's character is his fate. —Heraclitus

Personal Influence

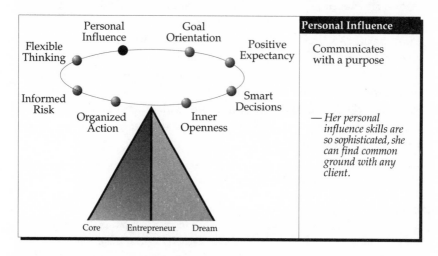

You can have the greatest ideas, but you still have to sell them to someone in order to pay the bills. So when you ask an entrepreneur what business he or she is in, the reply is often "Sales." Increasingly for modern entrepreneurs, the product sold to clients is *service.* And clients judge the worth of the service by how the service is delivered as well as by how it is presented. Personal Influence for entrepreneurs is the *getting* of business and the *keeping* of business.

One buoyant marketing consultant we talked with told us that "in our business, we sell trust, as you do with any consulting business. The first year, we established credibility, and let people know who we were. The second year, people really saw the work we did and liked it." He first sells his company's services through credibility, trust, and the personal relationships he forms with his clients.

How do you sell trust? And how do you maintain relationships? Personal Influence is the behavior that you use in building your relationships, to establish and maintain your business relationships over the years.

Common sense is instinct, and enough of it is genius. —*Josh Billings*

On Your Own—Personal Influence

The owner of a two-person computer-consulting firm talked to us about how she uses a form of Personal Influence—networking—in her business:

"Networking has been the most important element of marketing for us. Most of our business comes from networking and referrals from people we network with. Networking isn't something that just happens; it's something that you have to take a very planned approach toward. Not only do you want to network with individuals you work with as partners, you want to network with people who today might be your client and tomorrow might be your partner. You need to maintain those contacts that go back years and also maintain relationships that don't appear like they may pay off in the short term—because often they do in the long term.

"The networking avenue brings not only new projects to us but also people who might work with us on them. Joining associations helps a lot. Our large network gives us a better selection of people to do a project for a client. That combination of having access to many resources to choose from and finding the best person or team to work on a particular project affects our business positively."

Entrepreneurial Career

Core Career

Personal Influence—Resonance Between Your Entrepreneurial Career and Your Core Career

Go into any restaurant or small shop and you're bound to see a dollar bill taped to the wall. If you are an entrepreneur, or have ever been one, you know why that dollar bill is there: without sales there is no business. Core careerists, except for those in sales, can lose touch with *why* they are working, what their role in the company is. There's no dollar bill on their wall, and they forget how important it is to sell their products to consumers. They lose touch with the fact that the products of their company need an audience—and that they need to relate to that audience.

Pursuing an entrepreneurial career is a good way to understand the importance of Personal Influence—in sales, marketing, and making a buck through what you say and do. Both your core and your entrepreneurial careers will benefit as a result.

Common sense is compelled to make its way without the enthusiasm of anyone.
—Ed Howe

Organized Action

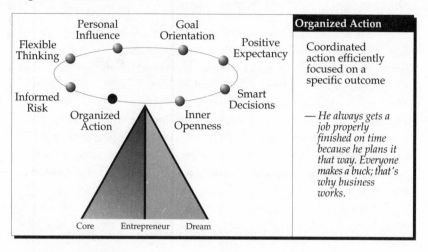

BEING EFFICIENT

Okay, I love to go to the post office to check my mailbox, buy a few stamps. But when it comes to meeting a deadline, I am extremely efficient. Buoyant entrepreneurs have to be able to focus their attention and energy on achieving their goals. Organized Action is critical to your profitability. If you are billing out by the hour, every trip to the post office is costing you money.

COMPLETING

Even worse, unorganized action may mean that the client's project is completed late or you end up missing something. If it is worth doing, it is worth completing. As an entrepreneur, you will have to make sure that the tasks you agree to undertake are actually completed. No loose ends, or no repeat business.

Organized Action pushes you to do what you need to do, as efficiently as possible, and completely as needed.

PRIORITIES

What business are you in? What is your vision of your company? It may sound pretty basic, and it is. It's basic and critical to your buoyancy as an entrepreneur.

He was one of those men who possess almost every gift, except the gift of the power to use them. —Charles Kingsley

If you know what business you are in, then you can prioritize your activities; your Organized Action plan will revolve around selling services today and positioning them to be bought tomorrow. Buoyant entrepreneurs always look at the benefits and the costs of every activity *as it relates to their long-term goals.* Organized Action is the essence of good time management; it's about what you do, when you do it, how you do it, and how long you spend doing it.

MANAGING YOUR TIME, EVALUATING WHAT WORKS

Time management has more to do with when you do things and how long you spend doing them. Organized Action adds an additional element: *should* you do things. One of our entrepreneurs used to put off cold calling prospective clients as long as possible, and would find ways to fill her time with other activities. The problem was, she wasn't getting anywhere. *"So I examined my marketing activities to find out what was working and what wasn't. I was surprised to see that cold calls weren't even all that effective. So, rather than feel bad about avoiding these calls, I realized that I needed to focus my efforts on my existing clients and get new clients through my professional associations and networks."* She was able to organize her business activities, to begin to say *no* to some activities and *yes* to some others. She evaluated each of her commitments and demands on her time to see how well they fit her business objectives. It was her start on the road to Organized Action.

On Your Own—Organized Action

The owner of a small product-design firm told us about one recent, huge assignment his company was given. "It was incredible: Revamp the entire product line. I'm talking about 225 or so S.K.U.'s (Stock Keeping Unit). And not a lot of time, since they were shooting to display the new designs at the August show. Even one of the big firms would have trouble with something of this scope.

"After my partner and I calmed down, we approached this like any other project, but were more careful. We devised a tight schedule that gave us some wiggle room, then made a list of needed materials and dates by which the client had to get us certain information, such as package copy. But we also got them to let us

---

If one advances confidently in the directions of his dreams, and endeavors to live the life which he has imagined, he will meet with a success unexpected in common hours.
—Henry David Thoreau

talk to their people, and their other vendors, directly. This way there was no lag time, and no missed communications. Every step, every milestone, we checked our progress against the schedule. When we were slipping, we tried to pull other work in closer. We brought in some other independent consultant to offload some of the work.

"Somehow the project was completed on time. And it was really good work. The client loved it. So did we. But I'll tell you, now I know what it's like to plan a battle or launch the space shuttle. What a project! We really needed to stay focused on this one. Thank goodness we did. And thank goodness for fax machines, modems, and overnight mail."

Organized Action is practical focus on getting things done. And that's what pays the bills.

Entrepreneurial Career

Core Career

Organized Action—Resonance Between Your Entrepreneurial Career and Your Core Career

The complex projects that core careerists have to deal with are an excellent way to develop Organized Action. You have to be efficient to meet aggressive schedules; you must be organized, and you have to know the way that things can and *do* get done. You also need to be able to focus on the job and not get distracted by a bunch of very interesting but irrelevant issues.

These core-career experiences are training opportunities for the rest of your work life, because it is Organized Action that brings your entrepreneurial dreams to life. Businesses don't start, structure, and maintain themselves; it takes your motivation and Organized Action to get that entrepreneurial endeavor ticking like clockwork.

All men of action are dreamers. —James G. Huneker

Informed Risk

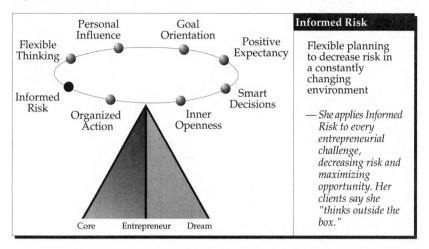

You're the boss! You cannot be the organizational yes man in your entrepreneurial career. You can implement your well-thought-out ideas and plans now, you can dare to be different, if that is what it takes to be effective.

Informed Risk is your wild card. The world may expect you to implement Plan A, but knowing the odds of success and failure, you decide that Plan B makes more sense. As you implement Plan B, the situation isn't quite what you expected and that could spell disaster. But for you, a career-buoyant entrepreneur, it's another day. Plan C is rolled out and wins the day.

Flexibility is a key element of Informed Risk, because it allows you to change your strategy as the game plays out. Taking an Informed Risk may present you with unexpected opportunities. And unexpected challenges. Keeping your eyes open, you take the plunge but stay alert. If the situation changes, you're ready for it.

Entrepreneurs not only spoke of the importance of Informed Risk for entrepreneurial buoyancy, they also said that uninformed risk was one of the chief causes of entrepreneurial *failure.* There needs to be a balance here between doing everything the same way all the time and doing things differently just for the sake of being different. There has to be sound reasoning to warrant any risk: and the goal of Informed Risk is to *reduce* that risk to a minimum.

If a man empties his purse into his head, no man can take it away from him. An investment in knowledge always pays the best interest. —Benjamin Franklin

On Your Own—Informed Risk

This was the second time around with the potential client. The last proposal was good, but the competition's was better. They gave Tina another shot at getting their business, but she knew that this would be it. And she knew that if she went head to head with the major players, she would lose again.

"It seemed clear. If I played by the rules, I'd lose. So instead of writing the typical proposal, the safe proposal that my competitor would write, I decided not to play by their rules. I did some initial work on the topic, a bit of quick research, then put it into a presentation on disk. When I went to the meeting, I said that I didn't have a proposal for them. What I had was some information and insights about their problem. No solutions, but they could be found. I could see the interest in their eyes. And the fear. Sort of like the 'nobody ever got fired for buying IBM' philosophy of years ago. I expected the interest, and I suspected the fear. That's when I took out my ace in the hole, a proposal outline with project steps, timing, and estimated expenses.

"That was it. They liked the new approach and felt I could 'think outside the box.' I combined stability, which they see as dependability, with flexibility."

Risky? Yes. But alert to her client's responses, and with flexible planning, she was ready for them. Tina's Informed Risk was a good bet.

Entrepreneurial Career

Core Career

Informed Risk–Resonance Between Your Entrepreneurial Career and Your Core Career

Entrepreneurs often get the chance to make their own rules and invent their own ways of doing things. They aren't limited by what others tell them; they aren't forced to do something because "that's the way we do things here." In the spirit of inquiry and Informed Risk, Thomas Edison declared, "There ain't no rules here; we're trying to *achieve* something." The Informed Risk you develop as an entrepreneur can also benefit many a stalled core career by injecting some life, daring, and difference into "the way we do things here."

He who opens a school door, closes a prison. —Victor Hugo

Flexible Thinking

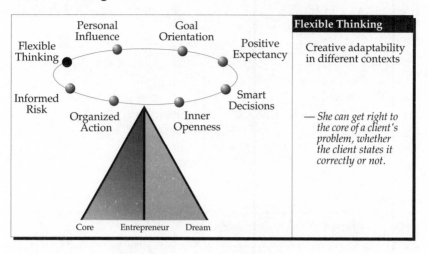

Because of stereotyping and bias we think of dream careerists as being the ones to talk about ideas and creativity, whereas we think of entrepreneurs as pragmatic types. However, our research showed that entrepreneurs value Flexible Thinking just as highly because mental flexibility helps them achieve their vision.

A GREAT IDEA

It takes more than a great idea to become a buoyant entrepreneur, but no entrepreneur becomes buoyant without great ideas. The ideas you have for your business will result from applying your Flexible Thinking skills. Your search for new markets and new clients taps deep into your Flexible Thinking. From the name of your company, to your presentation to a client, Flexible Thinking can set you apart from the pack. For many service-oriented or consulting entrepreneurs, Flexible Thinking is their product.

NEW PROBLEMS, NEW SOLUTIONS

I love to read the section of the paper that talks about patents and breakthroughs. Or the announcements of new businesses forming. It seems that people all over the world are discovering new problems that you and I have and that we need them to solve.

Education makes people easy to lead, but difficult to drive; easy to govern, but impossible to enslave. —Henry Peter Brougham

Recognizing opportunity is another key to becoming a buoyant entrepreneur. Flexible Thinking isn't just applied to creatively solving problems, it is also used to *find* problems.

Once a new problem is recognized, flexible thinkers are able to identify a new opportunity. They take this new problem and apply their attitudes of knowledge and connectivity to it to come up with a range of possible solutions. They aren't content with saying, "That's the way we do things around here." Buoyant entrepreneurs reject the status quo and invent. Flexible Thinking helps you find the silver lining in every cloud, the opportunities that others have ignored.

On Your Own—Flexible Thinking

Sharon is a great thinker, a creative thinker. Which is a good thing, because she is in a consulting business where ideas pay for the electric bill. She can get right to the core of a client's problem, whether the client states it correctly or not. She told us about one of her recent projects:

"This was supposed to be an easy one, a few days of billable time. This company wanted me to transfer their data from an old minicomputer to their new PC LAN system. No problem, I've done it before. But as I started the process, I immediately realized they hadn't thought out the new system. I could transfer all the data, but they wouldn't be able to access it without weeks of custom programming. Of course, quarterly reports were coming due, so I had to do something *fast*. I tried about a dozen ways of solving the problem before I called in a colleague, Chuck, to write a custom front-end for the new system. It took Chuck about three days before it was ready. By then the data were transferred, backup systems were in place, and I was ready to bring the client in.

They loved it! The department head had expected to see the same old hard-to-access stuff, only ported to a PC system. He was really shocked to see a truly easy-to-use system that was even customized to their reporting needs. In fact this one-shot deal turned into a long-term database-management contract for me, and for Chuck too."

Flexible Thinking—problem definition and inventive solutions—gets results.

The greatness of work is inside man. —Pope John II

Entrepreneurial Career

Core Career

Flexible Thinking—Resonance Between Your Entrepreneurial Career and Your Core Career

New ideas, inventions, and creative problem solving fuel the buoyancy of many entrepreneurs. Entrepreneurs need Flexible Thinking because it gives them the ability to come up with new solutions to new problems and new solutions to old problems. Flexible Thinking sets apart the buoyant entrepreneur through innovative ideas and ways of presenting information to his or her customers.

The Symbolic Analysis work of core careerists requires highly developed Flexible Thinking skills. The work of marketing analysts, product designers, engineers, corporate lawyers, salespeople, and others involves problem identification and solutions. Your core career offers endless opportunities to develop Flexible Thinking skills, and your entrepreneurial endeavors will polish them further.

Smart Decisions

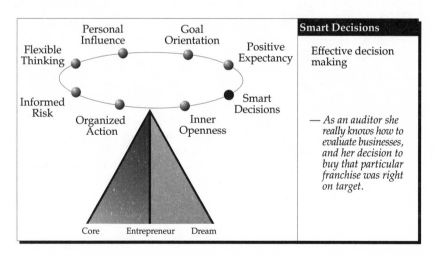

If you have built castles in the air, your work need not be lost; that is where they should be. Now put the foundations under them. —Henry David Thoreau

Time is money. Buoyant entrepreneurs live by this rule every day, so they have to make decisions, and more than anything they have to be the right decisions. Being decisive is a key to entrepreneurial buoyancy because it moves you forward toward your goal.

He who hesitates is lost. Every career calls for Smart Decisions, whether you realize it or not. I am a big believer in *planning*, but I also recognize that at some point you have to move off of the dime and make a decision. Not the kind of decision that makes itself, not the kind of decision that results from *not* deciding. Smart Decisions combines knowledge of how things work with the ability to commit to a direction.

"You have to know how things get done, you have to be able to call the shots right a majority of the time," one entrepreneur after another told us. This know-how isn't an academic textbook knowledge, it's a knowledge of how things work, what doesn't work, and why; it is wisdom acquired from experience. And it is this wisdom that we call P.K.H. When combined with the ability to weigh choices and make decisions, it becomes Smart Decisions. Practical know-how provides the facts that allow you to be decisive. P.K.H. is essential for anyone hoping to survive outside the core-career womb.

On Your Own—Smart Decisions

Making Smart Decisions doesn't always mean that you make the *right* decisions— although that would be preferred! As one career-buoyant entrepreneur told us, "I love to make decisions. I always enjoy being decisive because it moves me forward. Sure, I don't always make the best decisions in the world, but it gets me somewhere. Even a decision that turns out to be wrong can be a good decision because I learn from it. Making a decision is taking an action, and it's only by acting that you either learn from a mistake or you achieve your goal."

I feel like a fugitive from the law of averages. —Bill Mauldin

Entrepreneurial Career

Core Career

Smart Decisions—Resonance Between Your Entrepreneurial Career and Your Core Career

Smart Decisions are desperately needed in core careers, and this trait can be honed to a fine edge in your entrepreneurial career. The days of "I'll take a look at the committee report and get back to you next year" are pretty much over in corporate America. New corporate structures are pushing decision making down the hierarchy, closer to the action. Long-range planning is still crucial, but these plans now *support* decisiveness.

The types of decisions that are made by a core-career employer are made with an eye to the bottom line and the ultimate good of the corporation; as an entrepreneur of any scale these are now your identical concerns. So your core-career experiences in planning and decision making can help your appreciation of the concerns of every businessperson.

THE CHICKEN AND THE EGG

In our analysis of entrepreneurs we found an anomaly. It's not a trait, and it's not a behavior, but it is necessary for entrepreneurs. It's *money*. Adequate start-up funding was cited by a number of entrepreneurs. How much is enough? "More than you think," they all agreed. The lack of it was cited with equal force as a major cause of *failure* for entrepreneurs. This is why I recommend the moonlighting approach so strongly. It lets you test the waters, build cash flow, develop money-management skills, and learn what it costs to really run a business such as yours, without the actual expense. By running a home-based moonlighting business, you can keep your overhead minimal yet still have a history and a real basis from which to estimate.

The end of wisdom is to dream high enough to lose the dream in the seeking of it.
—William Faulkner

DO THEY SUCCEED BECAUSE OF LUCK?

It's important to know that I wasn't told that to be a buoyant entrepreneur you needed to be lucky, that you needed a break. Luck may enter into some specific situations, and a lucky break was mentioned by a few entrepreneurs as playing a role in landing a critical contract. However, there is an argument that being in the right place at the right time may not be luck; it may be the result of consciously doing the right things at the right time for the right reasons.[9]

Here's a story of one entrepreneur's 'luck': "It was really a bad year. I wasn't sure if I could pay the bills. And since I knew I couldn't pay all of them, I made piles: pay soon, pay next month, and try never to pay. It was not a good time in my life. That winter I got a call to do a proposal, a small one but one that was quite profitable. And then another proposal was accepted. The first lucky break was what I needed to get back on my feet."

It wasn't a lucky break, though. John had laid the groundwork for these projects by making calls, sending out proposals, and doing excellent work for other clients. That lucky call he got was due to the client's hearing about a job John did for a sister company. It was his own hard work, and good work, that provided the breaks. I guess John just needed to believe that luck had turned against him for a while, and now it was on his side. But I don't think it was luck at all.

YES, YOU CAN

Running your own business is something that you *can* do, although it isn't easy to become a buoyant entrepreneur. The good news is that as you develop buoyancy in your core career, you are taking the first steps toward entrepreneurial buoyancy.

And as you develop your entrepreneurial career, the experience you gather and the lessons you learn will boost your core career. Can you do it? *Yes, you can,* if you really want to.

Let us not say, Every man is the architect of his own fortune, but let us say, Every man is the architect of his own character. —George Dana Boardman

NOTES

1. *Trade Union Advisor.*

2. See *Staffing Industry Report* for all the insider scoop on staffing-firm investments and your professional future.

3. William Bridges, *Job Shift* (Addison-Wesley, Reading, Mass.: 1994).

4. Get it on the newsstand or subscribe, just so long as you get it. Full of usable information and sustaining stories. I've been a reader for ten years, ever since my business grew too big for my study and I moved out to a regular office.

5. Small Business Association.

6. God bless you, Gary A.

7. High-stress, high-burnout jobs are the easiest to turn into permanent part-time jobs because employers thereby lower turnover rate. However, all jobs are open to discussion. *Trade Union Advisor*, page 2, September 1994.

8. As you probably know, there has been a ton of research on entrepreneurs. Many different factors have been identified, such as your father's self-employment, education, and personal values. See R. D. Hisrich, "Entrepreneurship/Intrapreneurship," *American Psychologist* 45 (1990): 209–222.

9. With apologies to Guy Kawasaki, author of the phenomenal marketing text *The Macintosh Way.*

The best mental effort in the game of business is concentrated on the major problem of securing the consumer's dollar before the other fellow gets it. —Stuart Chase

Chapter 10

Going It Alone: Starting Your Own Business Enterprise

You have dreamed of owning your own business, you have thought what it would be like to have a life where you were in control; we all have.

Then all too often we say to ourselves, "No, I couldn't do that. I'm not one of those hard-driving captains of industry; I couldn't be like the people I read about in the business press." Maybe you're right, maybe you could never be like The Donald or Bill Gates; but then again, you don't have to be. Remember, these types of people are the Supernovas of the entrepreneurial world. They are just *one* of four profiles of the New Entrepreneur (Traditionalist, Supernova, Soloist, and Minimalist).

Every entrepreneur essentially starts in the same way, and very often in the same place: a great idea, a burning passion, and the kitchen table. When you trace the history of every successful entrepreneur back to his or her genesis, you will find that they all started at home, because it made sense.

Common sense still rules in the new world of work and in the considered actions of the New Entrepreneur; and today technology is allowing anyone with an entrepreneurial dream, guts, and P.K.H. to take the low-risk/high-opportunity shot.

In this chapter we'll cover hot entrepreneurial opportunities in all the hot industrial biomes. Yes, some of them will be food franchises and other retail businesses you couldn't run in your home, and yes, I'll talk a little about purchasing an existing business, but the prudence of the *B.T.O.* philosophy says you should be very careful about jumping in at the deep

---

Be not afraid of greatness: some are born great, some achieve greatness and some have greatness thrust upon 'em. —William Shakespeare

end without learning to swim in the shallow end first. And if you are like me and millions of other New Entrepreneurs, splashing about in the shallow end of industry and commerce from the safety of your own backyard pool could offer all the security, freedom, and happiness you are after.

In this chapter I am going to get your juices flowing with at least one example of a possible business for each of the hot industrial biomes we identified in the core-career section. So whatever industrial biome you currently work in, or whatever healthier biomes you are moving toward, read this chapter in light of how pursuing these and hundreds of other entrepreneurial ideas could lead your work life toward more personal independence and control.

HOME-BASED BUSINESSES

Who are these new home-based entrepreneurs? Are they like you? Yes. They are lawyers, financial planners, and insurance agents. They are also carpenters, painters, and gardeners. They are word processors, academic tutors, computer programmers, and the like. They work at home whenever possible, sometimes moonlighting in between other jobs. Forty-two percent of home-based workers are women, and the percentage has been steadily growing. Considering the way that women have been treated in the workplace, that's to be expected.

Although people of all ages and lifestyles are swelling the ranks of the self-employed, a great many are forty-something and married with children. They all make the quality of their lives an integral part of their business philosophy. They are not big risk takers, and they don't anticipate turning a five-million-dollar profit this year, yet they are confident in their ability to make a buck.

Having been through the corporate rat race, they wouldn't choose to return to it, even though the wrong circumstances pushed some of them into the entrepreneurial world. They may miss some things about corporate life—for instance receiving regular paychecks, having secretarial support, and watercooler socializing—and they may now have to handle some unpalatable tasks, such as office cleaning and taxes. But most home-based entrepreneurs are professionally and personally happier now than they were when they were employed by someone else.

They enjoy having more time to spend with their families, an increased

---

Work is love made visible. —Kahlil Gibran

measure of job security—if you own the company, it's much harder to get fired—more flexibility, the ability to work on interesting projects, and a newfound sense of independence. And often they're making more money than they were in the corporate world.

In general these entrepreneurs didn't take out loans, partly because of the difficulty of getting small-business loans and partly because of the relatively low start-up costs and minimal overhead of home-based businesses. The New Entrepreneurs are optimistic, multiskilled—in their past professional lives many of them worked for small companies, where they learned to handle a variety of tasks—self-motivated, independent, and (even if they don't start that way) they have learned to deal with the rejections—and outright failures—that come with a business venture.

Should You Do It?

Anyone can start a home-based business, provided community regulations are met. The question is, should you do it? Although working at home is a great option for some people, it doesn't fit everyone's style and personality.

Consider, first of all, whether or not you really need a boss. It's easy enough to say that you would love to work without somebody looking over your shoulder, cracking the whip, telling you how to organize your time, and even dictating what you wear. But if you worked for yourself at home, would you be able to lay down, and abide by, the rules you set for yourself? Do you have the self-discipline required to get up early each day (rain or shine), dress as though you were going to an outside office or to an appointment, manage your workload, and put in a full day—regardless of the temptations that might beckon? Would you be able to resist a crying baby, a sinkful of dishes, drop-by visits from neighbors and relatives, or anything else that might break your concentration?

How would you be able to function in the solitude and quiet of a home-based office? Do you currently enjoy watercooler chats, office parties, lunching with colleagues, and the company picnic as much as you do your work? Do you require social interaction, the feeling of being part of a team, and high-fives, or would you be able to work just as well—maybe even better—without them?

Could you work, eat, sleep, and unwind in the same space, or would

It is hard to fail, but it is worse never to have tried to succeed. —*Theodore Roosevelt*

you burn out in short order? Would you be able to draw a line between your work time and your personal life? These are all tough issues that never go away. I'm ten years into my own business. Five years ago I moved out of my home into a larger office space, but these challenges still raise their ugly heads every week, simply because I don't choose to work twenty miles away in some high-rise. My office is a hop, skip, and jump from my home, on the main street in my village.

Starting Up a Home-Based Venture

It all comes down to money, market, and what your community will allow you to do behind closed doors. Here are a few considerations you should always examine *before* beginning your venture.

THE HOME-BASED ZONE

Check your local zoning regulations before you open up shop in your home. You certainly don't want to find out you are in hot water with the community after the fact. For example many ordinances prohibit home-based businesses from hiring outside employees—which means, anyone who doesn't live in the house cannot work there. But even with strict zoning laws regarding home-based businesses, you yourself can usually work within their confines.

About 75 percent of all residential communities have laws that restrict or even prohibit home-based businesses. Running a business out of your home might interfere with the neighborhood by generating noise, traffic, parking problems, and so on. Some businesses, by their nature, cause more disruptions to the outside community than other businesses—for example, trying to run a recycling center in your backyard. Labor-intensive business, you'll find, will present the most problems while knowledge-based businesses, such as consulting, are safer and quieter. Be sensitive to how your business affects your neighbors; their complaints are more likely than anything else to buy you a cease-and-desist order from the community.

Many communities will look the other way as long as you don't advertise your business or use your street address for business purposes (arrange for a post office box instead). Other zoning boards simply have a blanket law prohibiting home-based businesses but won't enforce it unless they have a reason to.

I could never think well of a man's intellectual or moral character if he was habitually unfaithful to his appointments. —Nathaniel Emmons

As the number of home-based entrepreneurs grows, and as the number of telecommuters for large corporations increases, all cities and towns will become increasingly home-base friendly. Zoning laws to keep residential neighborhoods free of commerce have been completely undermined by technology and the telecommuting revolution. What was a clear line of demarcation is now a fuzzy smudge. Already many communities are staying away from enforcing existing zoning requirements for fear of what they might uncover.

TAXES

Check with an accountant to find out the tax consequences of starting your own business and what you need to do to take a home-office deduction. This is not a free-for-all tax dodge; the IRS is *very heavy handed* with home-based businesses. At your request the Internal Revenue Service will send you a free publication called *Tax Guide for Small Business*, No. 334. The phone number is 1-800-829-FORM. Also consider your insurance needs. For example you might have to add a rider to your homeowner's insurance policy to cover your office equipment, or to your car insurance if your vehicle is being used for deliveries or any other business purposes.

As you start up your business and it begins operation, keep careful records of all the money you spend on the business—for letterhead, business cards, advertisements, brochures, and so on—as these become tax-deductible operating expenses.

BUILD A PLAN

You will also want to create a written business plan for your new enterprise. I am not suggesting you have to have twenty pages of flow charts and breakevens, although that wouldn't hurt. You can begin a little more organically; after all, the goal is to motivate you, not to immobilize you with fear.

What I suggest is that you apply, "If you don't know where you are going, how will you know when you get there?" to your venture. The more clearly you can describe what you want, the greater your chance of reaching the goal. Start with who, what, why, where, when, and don't forget how.

Who. To whom will you provide the service or sell the product?

What. What product or service will you deliver, and what will you charge for it?

About the time you catch up with the Joneses, they refinance. —Anonymous

Why. Why do you want to sell this product or service, and why would others want to buy it?

Where. Where are you going to be doing business?

When. When are you going to start your business? Stick to that date.

How. How will you reach your customers?

Slowly create a full picture of your company and its services or products, start-up costs, marketing strategy, target customers, and completion. You don't have to be a corporate planner to formulate well-thought-out plans for your company. You do need to learn where you are headed, and you do need to develop an Organized Action plan to get there.

Hot Home-Based Businesses

Almost any hobby has the potential of paying for itself and turning a profit, and home-based entrepreneurs have turned just about everything imaginable—from selling home-grown produce, such as flowers, fruits, and herbs, to providing on-site makeovers for brides—into thriving businesses. Nothing—pet parties, weddings, supplying information to on-line computer services, or selling rabbit manure to farmers—is too zany. If you can imagine it, it has probably been done out of someone's bedroom on a moonlighting or part-time basis.

While the New Entrepreneurs have given almost everything a shot, the trends for hot home-based businesses closely, although not completely, parallel those hot industrial biomes where the core-career jobs are.

HEALTH CARE

Medical billing companies, which do particularly well when the economy is tight, serve hospitals, clinics, and doctors. They bill patients and insurance companies, which often have complex rules and procedures for filing claims. Medical transcriptionists translate doctor's and hospital's audiotapes into written reports for research and statistical purposes and to satisfy insurance companies' regulations. Medical transcriptionists need to know medical terminology and all aspects of the medical profession—inside and out.

FOOD SERVICE

There are a variety of ways for people who love cooking to make a living working out of their homes: catering kids' birthday parties and formal

---

The best helping hand I ever got was at the end of my arm. —Anonymous

affairs, selling baked goods such as breads or cookies, running a bed-and-breakfast, teaching specialty cooking classes, and more. Some caterers provide a range of services including food preparation, delivery, serving, and cleanup; others only cook the food. In either case it's important to have sufficient cooking equipment and to understand local health codes. Cities and states have rigid health ordinances concerning for-profit at-home cooking—so don't assume your cooking business is within the letter of the law until you have checked into it with your city or town's board of health.

PERSONAL SERVICES

Housecleaning, taking care of pets and houseplants, buying clothes, doing the laundry, and other personal chores are essential, yet people have less and less time to do such tasks. Many customers from two-income households are willing to pay others to take care of personal services in order to free up some much-needed time.

This makes Personal Services hot. Home-based companies in this field provide in-house child-safety inspections, launder diapers, iron clothes, give manicures and massages, take care of plants, house- and pet-sit, deliver newspapers, clean carpets, and offer a host of other person-to-person services. Home health aides, the fourth-fastest-growing job in the economy, are often home-based entrepreneurs. They provide nutritional guidance, housekeeping assistance, and companionship to senior citizens and others.

Child care in its many forms also provides opportunities. Many of these business owners—usually women—simultaneously provide care for their own young children. Having good references, a clean, comfortable, and child-safe home, the ability to maintain trusting relationships with clients, and the willingness to put in long, hard hours are all pluses. Getting licensed from the state you live in also gives you a competitive edge.

FINANCES

Two of the sure things in this world—taxes and bills—provide great entrepreneurial opportunities. Preparing taxes for companies and individuals is a seasonal and highly lucrative business that runs from January through April. However, collecting money from delinquent accounts is an evergreen business; the *Los Angeles Times* reported that even during a recession, a collection agencies' revenues increase by 20 percent.

Let others praise ancient times; I am glad I was born in these times. —Ovid

COMPUTERS

Not only will computers help you make your core, dream, or entrepreneurial career successful, they can also become the means of reaching your American dream in and of themselves.

If you own a computer and you know how to use it, you can easily put it to work for you as the basis of a money-making enterprise. For example, you might provide mailing lists to other companies. Mailing-list services use either public databases, such as the U.S. Census Information, or create their own lists from scratch. You have to be able to maintain, analyze, and manipulate the information to make it valuable to marketers, businesses, and fund-raisers, so powerful computers are essential. Computers can also form the basis of businesses that crunch numbers, desktop-publish, create mass mailings, and produce such documents as resumes and annual reports for individuals and companies.

You can also take advantage of the fact that many people still need some help getting up-to-speed with buying and using computers, and become a computer consultant. Or you can help individuals keep abreast of new hardware and software by acting as a computer trainer.

BUSINESS-TO-BUSINESS SERVICES

As corporations downsize, home-based businesses that provide secretarial services, executive recruiting, telephone sales, telephone answering, marketing, customer service, research support, and other business services are well positioned to pick up the slack. Writing and graphics services offer huge opportunities to creative dream careerists who seek to learn their craft on the way to becoming Mark Kostabi.

PUBLISHING

The publishing industry today encompasses specialty newsletters, magazines, newspapers, books, video, audio, CD-ROM, and software. If there is an industry undergoing an explosive revolution, this is it. Brides-to-be can find reference books devoted to wedding planning. Even swizzle-stick players can find a newsletter devoted to their passion, just as parents can find videotapes, audiotapes, CD-ROMs, and software that entertain and educate their three-year-olds. That means that if you publish it, you'll probably find an audience for it, especially if you have something to say on the hobby or collectibles front. And the advent of desktop publishing

---

Work is the greatest thing in the world, so we should always save some of it for tomorrow.
—Don Herold

and inexpensive high-quality printers have made it technically feasible for almost anyone to become a publisher. Other publishing-related, work-at-home opportunities that don't demand desktop-publishing skills include writing, editing, proofreading, public relations, and advertising. However, basic D.T.P. skills should be mastered by us all in the next few years; remember, the world's most admired marketing empire grew out of a humble newsletter.[1]

BIOTECHNOLOGY

Biotech companies are currently concentrating their attention on research and development of drug products used to combat the illnesses that plague our society. Which means if you have the education and experience as a chemist, biologist, or lab technician, you might want to consider consulting to corporations who want to take advantage of the newest developments in the industry. Producing a newsletter of biotech-related information might also be a viable option because companies and individuals are always thirsting for knowledge in this area. As more biotechnology products are developed and approved, there will be increased opportunities for entrepreneurs in sales, distribution, training, and other areas of information dissemination, and so on.

TELECOMMUNICATIONS

Computer knowledge, coupled with job experience in any large communications company, is a great background for entrepreneurial opportunities in this field. With craft and P.K.H. you can consult with companies that are interested in upgrading communications and cutting costs for video conferences, digital interactive services, cellular phone services, and other telecommunications services.

ENVIRONMENTAL

This is an area where employers are lining up ten deep for college graduates with state-of-the-art competencies in this booming technology, so you can expect the entrepreneurial activities to be just as exciting. The demand exists for ways to alleviate current environmental concerns, as well as create everyday products and supplies that are biodegradable and recyclable and free from harmful chemicals. The wave of the environmental

---

I studied the lives of great men and famous women, and I found that the men and women who get to the top were those who did the jobs they had in hand, with everything they had of energy and enthusiasm and hard work. —Harry S Truman

future is also flowing toward the management of water and air pollution, solid-waste removal, and hazardous-waste removal. Recycling continues to be enforced as a means of reducing the amount of trash in our landfills, and the government is always looking for businesses and product ideas to assist them in this area. Recycling is a young, vibrant, socially responsible industry with enormous potential. Of course because of this there will be competition. Writing a newsletter, column, or book on environmental issues is also a wonderful way of sharing your knowledge, educating people, and increasing worldwide awareness.

RETAIL

Entrepreneurial people with retail backgrounds can approach small or large organizations and act as independent purchasing agents for promotional items or business materials, or to research retail services that the companies may be in need of. Or they can become personal shoppers for individuals, buying gifts, groceries, furniture, and so on. Those with experience as interior decorators who have worked in retail can contract their services out to businesses that need an office makeover or families in need of decorating advice. Of course the most straightforward way to use your experience in retail is to open a retail outlet yourself.

INSURANCE

Insurance companies often use experienced homeworkers or independent contractors to type and investigate insurance claims, interview witnesses, or compile reports. All you need is a phone and a computer to set yourself up as a home-based freelance claims processor or claims adjuster. Independent insurance agents and consultants can serve as consultants to individuals, families, senior citizens, and baby boomers, advising them of their insurance options, including long-term health care.

LAW

If you're a lawyer, you can hang up a shingle and establish an office anywhere. You can even consult with corporations that need legal advice. If you're a paralegal, you can't offer legal advice, but you can market to individuals other legal services, such as name changes and wills. With legal costs skyrocketing, the low overhead of a home-based business in this industry can give you a distinct edge if you keep your prices under the competition's.

The things, good Lord, we pray for, give us the grace to work for.
—St. Thomas More

TRAVEL

If you're an experienced travel agent, or just a travel buff, you can become an information broker to those who are seeking information about all the details involved in traveling to different destinations. Maturing baby boomers love to travel, especially on cruise lines, which have become increasingly popular in recent years. Use your knowledge to become a one-person travel agency that perhaps caters to specific clientele such as corporate professionals, the physically impaired, or senior citizens.

MANUFACTURING/TRADE

Solo or Minimalist entrepreneurs may not have funds to compete with Microsoft, General Electric, or IBM. But there's an opportunity for those with a background in manufacturing and trade to distribute products, both domestically and internationally, that the big players produce. Another related avenue for profit is the import-export business. If you can navigate the laws that vary from country to country, and you're willing to travel frequently, then you can buy and sell electronics, computers, and other products with global market potential.

THE FRANCHISE OPTION

You don't have to go it alone as a home-based entrepreneur. Buying a franchise can give you the support of a big community.

Franchising is a commercial arrangement for marketing and distributing products and services. Franchisors offer franchisees—those who buy rights to operate franchises—proven strategies for making businesses work, and provide franchisees with a brand-name product or service. Because we're all a bit like Mikey (the kid on the cereal commercial who didn't like things he hadn't had before), the benefits of a trusted brand-name are considerable.

Because how you sell the hamburger can be just as important as the kind of burger you sell, the franchisor almost always provides training at the company's headquarters. The franchisor may also offer financial, organizational, training, management, sales, and marketing support. The fact that franchises are perhaps the cheapest way to buy yourself a management team may explain their appeal to first-time entrepreneurs.

Of all the properties which belong to honorable men, not one is so highly prized as that of character. —Henry Clay

There are three major types of home-based franchises that prospective franchisees can choose from:

1. Franchises that are structured specifically to be based and contained within the home, such as advertising, publishing, and finance companies.

2. Franchises that are primarily run from home but also involve going on-site to sell the products or provide the services, such as limousine rides, pet-sitting, or in-home care.

3. Franchises that, while based at home, also involve a mobile or temporary storefront, such as pizza carts, carpet-cleaning vans, and pre-school computer lessons that are taught at day-care centers.

A home-based franchise provides the benefits of working at home— more flexibility, greater control over your destiny, low overhead, and so on—along with the advantages that franchises offer—a brand name, financial help, training, and other support. Also, buying a franchise may be a good risk in that somebody else has already discovered, and, under the best of circumstances, fixed most of the problems; made and figured out a way to remedy or avoid most of the mistakes; ironed out the kinks; and so on. As a franchisee you don't have to reinvent the wheel. The wheel usually works fine as long as you follow the franchisor's instructions.

Home-based franchises of all types generally cost between $5,000 and $15,000, usually payable in portions, as compared with more traditional franchises, such as employment agencies, which start at $25,000, and those that can cost as much as several hundred thousand dollars, such as McDonald's. Buying a franchise gives you the right to operate under the franchise's name and use the franchise's trademark. The initial fee pays for opening costs, inventory, equipment, any necessary training, and so on. You will also pay a percentage of your revenue in royalty fees, between 2 and 8 percent of sales, as the cost of the corporate management structure.

Home-based franchises can grow just like any other business, but they are likely to grow more slowly than larger companies, especially if you begin with a moonlighting effort. If you choose to start a home-based franchise on a part-time basis, you should recognize that a franchisor who talks of financial rewards is invariably talking about the rewards that accrue from *full-time* efforts. So if you take advantage of the part-time flexi-

Learning without labor is lost; thought without learning is perilous. —Confucius

bility of a home-based franchise, you should adjust your expectations accordingly.

The home-based franchise concept with its part-time/full-time flexibility and low overhead increases your odds of success and can provide a smooth transition into the world of entrepreneurial effort. Even if you decide not to invest in a franchise, the research you do may spark an idea and prompt you to start your own business providing services similar to those offered by franchises worldwide.

Choosing a Franchise

First select a reputable franchise that matches your interests and skills. Second, remember that all franchises are not created equal. If they were, it would make sense simply to choose the one with the lowest franchise fee and be done with it. But the fact is you are hiring a management and consulting team as well as buying a brand name, and you are likely to get what you pay for. A cheaper franchise may not have the proven track record of a more expensive franchise.

To find out more, begin by reading the Uniform Franchise Offering Circular (U.F.O.C.). A U.F.O.C. is a legal document that franchisors must provide to potential franchisees at least ten days before buying a franchise. Ask for it up front. It covers details about the franchise agreement—what you get, what your responsibilities are, and so on, as well as financial information about the franchise.[2]

The F.T.C. rule covered in the U.F.O.C. mandates that the franchisor inform you of all the costs required to start and maintain the business, including hidden ones—so the fact that you need a three-thousand-dollar computer to run your business doesn't come as a shock after you've already laid down a large sum for the franchise fee. This is the time to find out whether you will have to buy any needed supplies directly from the franchisor or its suppliers, or whether you'll be allowed to shop around for the lowest costs. It's the little things, like having to buy all or certain of your supplies from the franchisor, that add up to hundreds of thousands of dollars over the years. The key is to be absolutely certain that you know how much money it will take to run the company and to be sure that you have enough capital to keep the company going until you turn a profit.

Common sense is very uncommon. —Horace Greeley

To find out if there have been any complaints against the franchisor, check with the Federal Trade Commission's Freedom of Information Act Office (6th and Pennsylvania Avenue, NW, Washington, D.C. 20850; file your request by letter); the Better Business Bureau; and the attorney general's office in the state where the franchisor operates. But be aware that the information you gain can be misleading or incomplete. While you will find out whether or not there have been any complaints filed, you won't know whether the complaints were justified. Also, not every person who has a grievance against a franchisor files a complaint, so just because there are no complaints on record doesn't mean that the franchisor has earned solid citizenship and scads of satisfied franchisees. It just means there are no complaints on record.

> A good overview of your rights is covered in a guide called *Franchising Business Opportunities Rule and Guide*. It is available free of charge, by mail or phone, through the Federal Trade Commission, Division of Marketing Practices, 6th Street and Pennsylvania Avenue, NW, Washington, D.C. 20580; (202) 326-3128.

Checking the Credit Ratings

Franchisors are also required to provide a financial statement and information about the background and experience of the key executives. Don't accept the biographies at face value; in my experience franchise biographies give new meaning to the term "specifically vague." You should also be given a rundown of the responsibilities you and the seller will have to each other, should you decide to purchase a franchise. But even though the F.T.C. rule mandates that the franchisor provide this information, it can be difficult to get all the straightforward information you want from the franchisor.

Since franchisors are legally prohibited from predicting how much money franchisees will earn, they will usually tell you that how well you do depends on how much effort you bring to the business, your sales ability, and the like. The FTC rule says that the franchisor must provide you with at least ten names, addresses, and telephone numbers of franchisees, and the franchisor usually refers you to those most successful in your region. Try to get the rest of the franchise list from the franchisor so that you can

---

A man never discloses his own character so clearly as when he describes another's.
—Jean Paul Richter

contact as many of the franchisees as possible; to get inside information, avoid being steered toward a few preselected model franchisees. Pay in-person visits to some of the franchisees so that you can see the franchises in operation, their daily chores, how the franchise responds to any problems that arise, and how adequately franchisees are trained and supported after the initial training. It's important to determine if the franchisees are still happy with their relationship with the franchisor two, four, or even ten years down the road.

Looking for Cracks

If you are checking out a franchise, chances are you'll get to meet all the big shots who might convince you of the merits of their franchises. Unfortunately you might not meet the person who will help you succeed or fail until it's too late. Once you become part of a franchise network, you will be assigned a representative (usually from Operations) whose job it is to help you succeed and who is available to you in-person and on the telephone to answer your questions and help you make the right decisions and take the right actions to ensure your franchise's success. The problem is that these people might be only 50 percent qualified to help you.

Time for a story: In my days as a headhunter many years ago, I joined a reputable employment franchisor as a part of the Operations staff. My job was to help new franchisees get established. Eventually I realized that I was one of two on the entire corporate staff who had successfully completed a recruitment assignment within the last twenty years. These employees were selling thirty or forty franchises a year—without any real-world understanding of the marketplace their franchisees would face every day. The current crop of executives were just franchise-industry professionals; they knew franchising but not the *business* they were selling. So:

- Obtain, in writing, the name and telephone number of the rep they would assign you.
- Interview that rep rigorously about his or her background and expertise. Check with other franchisees this person has or does work with.
- Do not buy a franchise if you cannot confirm your contact person.

Common sense is the knack of seeing things as they are, and doing things as they ought to be done. —Josh Billings

Then explore the franchise further by checking with trade associations and industry publications. Gauge the franchise's position in the industry. Is it a leader or a follower? Also, make a point of finding out all you can about any competitors. If there aren't any, then you have to wonder why nobody else is exploiting this line of service or products. Perhaps there isn't a big enough market for it or the concept isn't quite right. On the other hand, maybe nobody else has yet caught onto a great idea—if that's the case, then you're likely to have more competition than you bargained for all too soon. But that's just a part of business.

Also, you have to study your location. It's up to you to research the demographics—although the franchisor might help you conduct market research—to find out the sales potential in your area. The issue of territorial exclusivity is an important one: Find out whether you have exclusive rights to sell in your territory or whether other franchisees can operate on your turf as well. Unless exclusivity is specified, you can probably safely assume that you are getting involved in a free-for-all; this is a factor of varying importance that depends on the franchise industry you buy into. Other franchise owners will answer this question for you very quickly. And depending on which state you live in, you might have other rights related to franchise disclosure.

Evaluating the Facts

After thoroughly researching the franchises that interest you, compare the U.F.O.C.'s and all the information that you garner, noting the advantages, disadvantages, and risks of each franchise. Think about your preferences as well; are you genuinely enthusiastic about the industry you've selected? Considering the amount of time and effort operating a franchise requires, it's essential that you like what you're doing. Before you commit yourself, think about whether or not you really would be happy changing motor oil day in and day out. Being a business owner might sound great, but it is important that you know and enjoy what you are doing.

Many people without a background in a particular business use franchises as a way of switching careers, and that's certainly a valid way of breaking into a business and learning new skills. But going that route, as opposed to plying a trade that you already know, means relying heavily on the franchisor's training program and ongoing support—and you will

---

Character is not made in a crisis—it is only exhibited. —Robert Freeman

have to be especially sure that the franchisor is strong, and remains so over time, in these areas.

Since buying a franchise is gaining in popularity as an option for prospective business owners, a wealth of information is available to help you learn the ins-and-outs of franchises. Seek out franchise associations, and if your resources are limited, the library can help with suggestions on specific materials to access (see Resources).

Getting It in Writing

Once you have selected a franchise that seems like a good match for you, make sure that you get the franchisor's promises in writing as part of your contract. Be sure that the written agreement doesn't contradict anything you have been told. If you get into a dispute later on, it's what the contract says that will count.

You will want to have an attorney who is familiar with franchise law look over the agreement before you sign. You might also want to consult with an accountant to find out the tax ramifications of owning a franchise and to help you project costs and income. An attorney who specializes in franchise law can charge one thousand dollars and an accountant can cost another two hundred. However, any money you spend finding out that there is a problem with the contract before you sign on the dotted line is well spent—and it just might save you from disaster down the road.

Getting Funded

The tougher the economy, the more anxious franchisors are to get your business. Some franchisors—roughly 36 percent—are aggressively helping potential franchisees find money to fund their prospective business. The fact that franchises are seen to be better risks than other small businesses may help a potential franchisee get priority consideration with the Small Business Administration, which has loan money available. And sometimes the franchisor itself will finance a franchisee to buy a franchise.

To enlarge its pool of prospective franchisees, some franchisors have developed outreach programs to attract minorities, veterans, and the disabled. For instance Heavenly Hot Dogs, based in Cape Coral, Florida,

---

There is a strength of quiet endurance as significant of courage as the most daring feats of prowess. —Henry Theodore Tuckerman

launched a program to attract physically disabled people to their franchises. More than three thousand potential franchisees responded. And at least twenty-seven candidates bought Heavenly Dog franchises.

Heavenly Hot Dogs isn't the only franchiser to go this route. If you are a member of a recognized minority, or are challenged in some fashion, you might find special funding assistance available. It's a phone call that might make or save you millions.

The Road to Success

According to a Gallop poll, 94 percent of franchise owners consider their businesses to be either very or somewhat successful; the percentage is split pretty evenly between the two. The franchise industry itself always claims that 95 percent of franchises succeed. And a U.S. Small Business Administration 1978–88 study found that 62.2 percent of all new, *non*franchised businesses fail.

Unfortunately it's not true. The federal and state agencies that monitor franchises fail to track failure rates or termination of franchising agreements. Nor do they record changes in ownership, which routinely occur when times are tough or when franchise fees increase, thereby forcing franchisees to sell their businesses because they cannot afford to maintain them any longer.

In fact the latest research demonstrates conclusively that new franchises have a 33 percent, not a 5 percent failure ratio.[3]

And the comparison of franchises to other small-business-failure rates may not be accurate either: A recent National Federation of Independent Business poll revealed that independent retail businesses only have a failure rate of *27 percent* after three years.

So how successful is the average franchise? It depends on whose figures you want to believe. A more pertinent question is how successful can *your* franchise be? The franchise formula is generally a good one, *so long as you choose a franchisor wisely and use its resources well.*

Franchises in Healthy Economic Areas

It should come as no surprise, then, that the hottest franchises fall into many of the same categories as hot home-based businesses, which in turn

---

To endure is the first thing that a child ought to learn, and that which he will have the most need to know. —Jean Jacques Rousseau

mirror the hot occupational and industrial biomes we introduced in the core-career section. While I have specifically addressed home-based businesses and franchises in this section to date, you will find both home-based and commercially based franchises represented in the following areas.

PUBLISHING FRANCHISES

The latest desktop-publishing technology enables anyone to publish newsletters, books, magazines, and other printed materials. Publishing franchises can often have a low start-up-cost—beginning at under one thousand dollars—but have excellent money-making potential because of the new knowledge era. And with electronics you can service a global market.

Many publishing franchises are based on the traditional modern-newspaper model, in which the profit comes from advertising, and there is a publishing franchise to match just about anyone's fancy. Bingo aficionados have the Washington-based *Bingo Bugle*, which is a tabloid newspaper. Real estate buffs have Florida-based *Homes & Land Publishing*, a magazine that publishes ads and photographs of properties. Those who appreciate the virtues of television have the North Carolina-based *TV Times* and the Georgia-based *TV-Travel*, which contain TV listings and ads for local businesses. Then there are franchises that publish reference guides on planning a wedding, deciding which products to buy, managing a business, and more.

BIOTECHNOLOGY FRANCHISES

There are few biotechnology franchises today, but expect an increase in the near future. One, the Environmental Biotech Franchise, in Florida, offers a business-to-business program that provides environmental solutions using the latest, chemically safe solutions. Another, Bio-Care, Inc., from California, offers a lucrative concept that caters to restaurants and other food service establishments: its primary business involves the unclogging of drain lines in an environmentally safe manner by using live microorganisms to eat through the built-up grime, hair, and other materials in the pipes.

COMPUTER FRANCHISES

Computer-related franchises typically provide business services to other companies. For example, Maryland-based General Business Services, Inc., offers computer services to its business clients in conjunction with profes-

---

Endurance is patience concentrated. —*Thomas Carlyle*

sional business counseling, record-keeping systems, tax preparation, and the like.

Computer hardware and software consulting, and automated business services such as financial planning and management counseling, all have their franchise-success stories. Executrain in Georgia offers hundreds of courses to businesspeople who want to learn current computer applications. New Horizons Computer Learning Center in California trains businesses and individuals on computer applications. Another crossover franchise that connects kids to computers is California's Futurekids, which introduces children between three and twelve years old to computers.

BUSINESS-TO-BUSINESS SERVICES FRANCHISES

These franchises include those that provide services to other business owners or managers, including financial and computer services. American Advertising Distributors (Arizona) and Money Mailer (California) are among the various franchises that offer advertising services. Tri-Mark, Inc., based in Delaware, is one company that offers direct-mail services. Answering Specialists from South Carolina is an example of a franchise that provides office-support services. Ohio's ProForma, Inc., sells business products to businesses, and the Taylor Review from North Carolina provides personnel-screening services. Signs Now hails from Alabama and makes custom-made signs for businesses. And the list of other business services that franchises provide to corporate clients and businesses is almost endless. By the way, before these franchisors started selling their franchises, they had a successful business in the field. And before that they had a dream, and some place in a house or apartment that they called an office. That was where they built the dream.

PERSONAL SERVICES FRANCHISES

There are a vast array of housecleaning franchises in this category that are highly profitable. Businesses like Molly Maid in Michigan, the Maid Brigade in Georgia, or the Maid's International in Nebraska are just a few of the franchises capitalizing on the growth of the residential cleaning market. There's also franchises that specialize in pet care, chimney cleaning, decorating, home improvement, lawn care, and gift-giving and gift-sending.

And that's just part of the market. The fact that there are 40 million women in the workforce with children under twelve years of age is exciting

Each man's task is his life preserver. —*George B. Emerson*

news for child-related franchises, such as Tutor Time, day-care centers, nanny finders, child-fitness chains, and child-education centers. At the opposite side of the spectrum are franchisees who provide leisure-time activities, exercise programs, at-home nurse placement, housekeeping, and other services that are geared for the elderly. That the over-fifty American population is expected to nearly double in the next twenty years means good news for franchisees and other entrepreneurs who cater to this age market.

FINANCE FRANCHISES

These franchises offer financial planning, accounting, and tax reporting for individuals and small businesses. This will be a booming area in the years to come. I see an enormous potential especially for small-business accounting services. As a small businessman what I haven't found yet is an affordable corporate-finance heavyweight I can get to do my books, file my taxes, budget my year, help me raise cash, talk to the bank and my relatives, and the like.

HEALTH CARE FRANCHISES

Health care franchises provide a vast range of services and products, such as physical therapy, at-home care, optometry, dentistry, medical-personnel staffing, hearing aids, wheelchairs, and medical supplies.

Even people without a medical background can take advantage of the healthcare boom. However, because of strict health care industry regulations, franchisees often must have medical professionals on the payroll. Franchisors who operate under these sensible restrictions may help franchisees with finding and retaining qualified health care professionals. For example the Better Birth Foundation, a Georgia-based company, allows franchise owners to operate the business. But the owners must hire highly trained professionals to teach clients—in this case prospective parents—about birth, nutrition, exercise, health care, and parenting.

FOOD SERVICE FRANCHISES

Food service franchises come in three flavors:

1. *Mega Burgers.* Franchise fees six figures plus.
2. *Mega Burgers Lite.* Mega burgers stripped down to get under the $100,000 mark.
3. *Alternative Mega Burgers.* Other food service franchises.

Employment, which Galen calls "nature's physician," is so essential to human happiness that indolence is justly considered as the mother of misery. —Richard E. Burton

Mega Burgers. Buying a Burger King, McDonald's, Wendy's, or Roy Rogers' franchise in a prime location could cost half a million dollars or more. If you have that kind of money to invest, chances are you probably don't need to read this book.

Mega Burgers Lite. Fortunately there are other, more affordable ways to get into the food franchise business. Elementary schools, stadiums, hospitals, and airports can house minifranchises. Trucks, vans, and carts that are equipped with ovens, refrigerators, freezers, and the like, can sell such foods as hot dogs, pretzels, and ice cream. Drive-through-only restaurants are also lower-cost alternatives for mega-money food franchises.

Among those companies selling minifranchises to people who don't have a half million dollars to spare are Pizza Hut, Dunkin' Donuts, and Arby's. The smaller versions of their franchises are one-third to one-half the size of their larger restaurants, and they cost considerably less to run. Equipment costs, and land or leasing fees, are lower. Away from prime locations in major metropolitan areas, these restaurant franchises may face less competition and still be able to offer convenience and fast service. Still, minifranchises may not achieve the sales of a full-size franchise. Also, some franchisors, although not all, require that a franchisee own a full-scale store before launching scaled-down units. Established franchisees might then receive special financing and other incentives to open satellite stores in their territory.

Alternative Mega Burgers. There are many choices available to those who want to purchase a food service franchise and still have some change left over in their pockets. Fast-growing, but less costly franchises, such as Blimpie's Sandwiches from Georgia, Subway Sandwiches from Connecticut, and Fox's Pizza from Pennsylvania, offer the advantages of bigger franchises without the costly investment. These popular eateries are eat-in or take-out establishments, and also offer the added benefit of home delivery to their customers. They require an initial investment of $30,000 to $100,000. Leasing, rather than buying, the necessary equipment for these franchises may even save you more money.

TELECOMMUNICATIONS FRANCHISES

Comm World in Colorado is a retail establishment and franchise that sells and services an array of telecommunications equipment to businesses

---

Still achieving, still pursuing, learn to labor and to wait.
—Henry Wadsworth Longfellow

and individuals. National Tele-Communications in New Jersey bases its success on providing the industry with experienced consultants who specialize in long-distance telecommunication services and help clients figure out ways to reduce carrier costs. This is not currently a booming area for home-based franchises, yet because of the prohibitive start-up costs and the voracious competition of big business, expect to see big developments in the coming years.

ENVIRONMENTAL FRANCHISES

Green franchises are expected to do well as aging baby boomers continue to pay for services and products that promise to make their offspring's world a better place to live. More and more people are drinking bottled water and purchasing water-purification products because they feel the water that comes out of their faucets is tainted by toxins. Culligan International in Illinois appeals to this broad market by distributing water-conditioning products and bottled water. American Recycling Franchise Sales, Inc., from Illinois and Python's Recycling, Inc., based in Minnesota are franchise centers that specialize in the recycling of materials including metals, newspapers, and plastic. The Environmental Air Services International, Inc., in Waco, Texas, specializes in the testing, sampling, and removal of E.P.A.-classified materials for both residential and commercial customers. If you're interested in a retail-shop establishment that is earth friendly, SoapBerry Shop in Canada sells natural and biodegradable personal-care products to its clientele.

RETAIL FRANCHISES

Retail franchises are thriving because there are plenty of well-off, two-income families that have money to spend but little time to shop for themselves. Franchises like the Decorating Den in Maryland, whose reps make house calls and help homeowners make decorating decisions, seem to be thriving. Dial-a-Gift in Vermont offers the convenience of twenty-four-hour catalog shopping for all types of gift items. As employee theft exceeds nine billion dollars a year, North Carolina's Prove, a combined theft and customer-service franchise, watches employees to see both if they are doing a good job serving customers and if they are keeping their hands off the color televisions.

A sense of the value of time—that is, of the best way to divide one's time into one's various activities—is an essential preliminary to efficient work; it is the only method of avoiding hurry. —Arnold Bennett

INSURANCE FRANCHISES

With the aging population there will be an increased demand for insurance services franchises that specialize in offering one-stop-shopping insurance services for consumers. Expect to see growth in this industry.

Unfortunately natural disasters have taken their toll on insurance carriers as well as on the insured. Many insurance carriers now refuse to insure homeowners who live near or on the water. The Insurance Restoration Service franchise, from California, offers financial assistance to private owners who have had their properties damaged by natural and man-made disasters, including fires, and vandalism.

LAW/COMMUNICATION FRANCHISES

Unfortunately there are few legal franchises available to the public, except for writ-serving by Irving in New York. This franchise serves summonses and other legal papers to individuals who have to make court appearances. However, with the help of individual practitioners, some of the big personal-injury law firms are expanding by a number of means, including franchises, partnerships, and other associations.

TRAVEL FRANCHISES

There are a number of successful travel agencies nationwide that are franchised. Uniglobe Travel International, Inc., in Washington prides itself on being the largest travel agency in the world, while Travel Agents International, Inc., in Florida follows close behind. Cruise Holidays International, Inc., is a franchise that handles only cruises. Besides the initial investment, you have to consider the supplies you'll need to run your travel agency business, including computers, furniture, extensive telephone systems, and so on.

MANUFACTURING/TRADE FRANCHISES

You won't find any franchises in the manufacturing/trade industrial biome. Franchising is a business strategy for the distribution of goods and services at the retail level.[4] So, while you might buy a franchise that distributes mufflers, you'll find the company that manufactures the mufflers isn't franchised. In the same way, the hamburgers that you sell in your fast-food franchise aren't manufactured by you or the franchisor. You buy the beef from a manufacturer, and the franchisor gives you an approved list of manufacturers to ensure quality.

In the old world that is passing, in the new world that is coming, national efficiency has been and will be a controlling factor in national safety and welfare. —Gifford Pinchot

Buying an Existing Business

Buying an existing business is a risky proposition. It is a complex transaction, so plan on spending at least a year looking for and negotiating a deal. Also, don't look at this option as an instant cash career.

There are a couple of useful newsletters that cater to this business-service industry:

• The World Mergers and Acquisitions Network. (202) 628-7767. 717D St., NW, Washington DC 20004. $445 a year subscription.

• First List. Publisher Vision Quest, 655 Rockland Road, Ste. 103, Lake Bluff, IL 60044. $350 a year subscription.

As well as looking at the lists, you might wish to consult with a broker. A business broker is unlikely to cost you less than about eight thousand dollars; the fees you pay are based on 5 to 10 percent of the purchase price. This function is similar to that of a real estate agent, putting house buyer and seller together.

Additionally you should put the word out into legal, accounting, and banking communities. You can do this with a simple mass-mail shot to, say, fifty companies in each of these areas, then continue to expand this program over time as your search continues—just as you would with the direct-mail dimension of a professionally run job-hunting campaign.

Other sources for leads include the following:

• Business journals of all kinds list businesses for sale.

• Get to know other entrepreneurs in the field as part of your due diligence.

• Constantly review your expanding retrial of contents and information. A business doesn't need a For Sale sign on the door to be open to discussion.

• Get word out in the trade and industry associations, through your membership and involvement.

Examining a Possibility

Examining the ongoing short list of potential businesses and how to negotiate a deal is beyond the scope of the first edition of this book, although we will address it in further expanded editions of Beat the Odds, when we have a few more pages to spare. In the meantime I'll pass you into the very capable hands of Joseph Mancuso, head of the Entrepreneur's Institute and coauthor with Dougless D. Germann, Sr. of Buying a Business (For Very Little Cash) (Englewood Cliffs, N.J.: Prentice-Hall).

Every great advance in natural knowledge has involved the absolute rejection of authority. —Thomas Huxley

WHERE YOU GO FROM HERE

The goal of this part of the book has been to give you a glimpse of the oceans of entrepreneurial opportunity open to the thoroughly modern professional. At this changing of the eras there is clearly entrepreneurial opportunity in every healthy American industry. So your entrepreneurial activities can also take advantage of your professional/technical skills and knowledge base specific to your core career, by applying them in an entrepreneurial context within the same industrial or occupational biome.

Then of course there is the new approach of looking at your career in the larger frame of a half-century-plus work life. In this context there is always time to make significant changes in your life—it's just that the old cut-and-jump ways have been replaced with something infinitely more pliant, yet supportive, for the changing times. In an entrepreneurial career it is knowing that you can ease into it with the low-risk/high-opportunity approach of the home-based business. And that the type of business you subsequently build can have whatever structure is best for your American dream: Supernova, Traditionalist, Soloist, or Minimalist. Some people are connecting the dots, and because they have learned to look for similarities rather than differences, they are finding enormous windows of personal opportunity. You can seize the moment, too, when you integrate your personal work-life buoyancy plan.

NOTES

1. The Grateful Dead and Jimmy Buffet built marketing strategies that are the envy of all modern business, because they used techniques that bypassed the traditional means of communication.
2. To make it easier to understand the U.F.O.C., the Federal Trade Commission publishes an interpretive guide that explains the U.F.O.C. and franchise law, particularly the F.T.C. Rule 435—Disclosure Requirements and Disclosures Concerning Franchising and Business Opportunity Ventures—which was passed on December 21, 1978, and took effect on October 21, 1979.
3. "The Numbers Game," *Restaurant Business*, June 10, 1993, pp. 86 and 91.
4. According to Matthew Shay of the International Franchise Association.

Be nice to people on your way up because you'll meet them on your way down.
—Wilson Mizner

Part Four

BEATING THE ODDS

▼

Chapter 11

Designing Your
Personal Work-Life
Buoyancy Plan

There are few business travelers who don't know La Guardia Airport on Flushing Bay in New York. Fred Nickell and James May spent fifty-nine years of their combined work lives there helping the place run smoothly. They had less than a year to go before early retirement when tragedy struck. One foul night, a couple of years back, a jet failed to get safely off the ground and plunged into the bay. Fred and Jimmy were among the first on the scene, and in the darkness they plunged into filthy, contaminated water among burning jet fuel to save the passengers. It was a night of great daring and honor for two brave men, as the FAA recognized within a couple of months. So where's the tragedy? Fred and Jimmy were soon laid off, as part of a cost-cutting measure, only months before retirement after giving all those years to the airline and risking their lives. I have had Fred and Jimmy's photograph (from a *People* magazine article) on my wall throughout the writing of this book, because it seems to speak of the misplaced loyalty and sacrifice so many people make in their lives, trying to reach the American Dream.

There was perhaps a time when service and sacrifice meant something to a company. Unfortunately the time has passed, and the unwritten contract no longer exists. Instead people like you and I are doing everything we can to keep the corporate monster fed and satiated as best we can, knowing full well that one day it may be our turn to be the sacrifice. This is your only choice if you continue to live by one sequentially pursued career at a time. You have been told that as long as you find that one thing

Live so that you can at least get the benefit of the doubt. —Kin Hubbard

you love and do it, success will follow as a matter of course. This is not the same world your father grew up in, though, and the rules of that bygone time will only lead to dislocation and frustration for your dreams and your needs. You only go around once, as far as anyone has been able to prove, so make it work the best you can.

It seems to me that too much traditional career-planning literature reads like a search for the Holy Grail. Is the pursuit of the single perfect job, in a single perfect career, all it's cracked up to be? The facts of the matter are that, for most people, the standard of living has frozen or somewhat diminished; the work week has lengthened significantly; and our working lives have increased by ten, twenty, or more years, because we are living longer than we ever used to. Given these factors, is there any single pursuit in today's world that guarantees you security, freedom, and happiness for the next fifty-five years? I don't think so.

Far too many of us have sacrificed a life for a single career of drudgery only to find our careers destroyed, not out of malice but because of the changing times that we all have helped to bring about.

Our nation grew on the basis of its entrepreneurial spirit and willingness to try new things. George Washington was a farmer, surveyor, soldier, and politician. Thomas Jefferson, also a politician, had additional careers as a lawyer, architect, and author. Benjamin Franklin, again a lawyer and politician, added author, inventor, and military strategist to his accomplishments.

Then there's Buffet, Jimmy not Warren, one of the richest self-made men in America today. He learned his professional chops working for *Variety* in the early days when he couldn't make it as a performer. Later of course he parlayed his professional competence into a musical empire. Jimmy Buffet is now not only successful at writing, recording, and performing his music, but also at design, retail, and real estate. He is also a successful novelist.

Neither were these careers pursued *sequentially* by George, Tom, Ben, and Jimmy; they were pursued simultaneously by men with inquiring minds who recognized that *buoyancy in one profession frequently provides the tools necessary for buoyancy in another profession*. If there is one thing

---

When man learns to understand and control his own behavior as well as he is learning to understand and control the behavior of crop plants and domestic animals, he may be justified in believing that he has become civilized. —E. G. Stakman

these dead statesmen and the King of the Parrot Heads share, it is an unwillingness to pack their dreams away in the attic.

Though the old rules no longer all apply, and the world of work seems to be in an uproar, this doesn't mean you can't have a successful, rewarding, and fulfilling work life. All the dislocation caused by the changing way of conducting business is opening up a panorama of opportunity for everyone with the courage to stretch.

Throughout the book I have emphasized the point that "it's nothing personal, it's just business," and I've told stories about our leading corporations to illustrate it. My idea was not to vilify the leaders of these companies or the hundreds of thousands of good people who manage them (I know they will become my readers one day), but simply to get into everyone's head that *business is business*, and that your ability consistently to put food on your table and a roof over your head, and to build, nurture, and provide for a family, is also a matter of *business*. It's not emotion, unrequited loyalties, or misplaced ethical considerations. For you, too, it's business, and your work-life careers represent the product lines of your business (your individual careers, and career achievements, are the products you have to sell to the world); everything else is rocking-horse droppings.

Developing a properly integrated work life that will consistently support your needs for security, freedom, and happiness takes time, but must remain your consistent focus, whatever else is going on in your life.

To move forward along the lines of your Organized Action plan, you may have to step sideways once in a while, or even take a couple of steps back to take three forward. It could mean a cut in pay while you get things on the right track. At some stage contract or temporary work may be on your horizon. All these things are possible, but none of them have to mean that you are on a downward spiral, and none of them have to mean you have failed in life.

Taped to the top of my desk is a strip of paper—I've no idea where it originated—now coffee-stained and grungy, but still bearing pride of place, it reads:

> You've failed many times, although you may not remember. You fell down the first time you tried to walk. You almost drowned the first time you tried to swim, didn't you? Did you hit the ball the first time you swung at bat? Heavy hitters, the ones who hit the most home runs, also strike out a

---

Finite to fail, but infinite to venture. —*Emily Dickinson*

lot. R. H. Macy failed seven times before his store in New York caught on. English novelist John Creasey got 753 rejection slips before he published 564 books. Babe Ruth struck out 1,330 times, but he also hit 714 home runs. Don't worry about failure. Worry about the chances you miss when you don't even try.

Your immediate goal is to survive long enough doing some of the things right while you learn to do most of the things right enough to make a success. It is a case of surviving long enough to succeed. The first step to an integrated work life is surviving long enough in a healthy core career to develop the buoyancy skills necessary for success in the other parallel careers you develop.

There are those who have planned their currently successful core careers meticulously from the beginning, although I believe them to be in a minority. I suspect many of us end up with our current core careers by accident, or we became what those around us felt we should be or were capable of being, rather than what we ourselves dreamed of doing.

For example there are those college graduates who will drift into publishing because what the hell else do you do with an English major? Or the woman who drops out of school to put a husband through and who never gets a second shot because he replaces her with a trophy wife. Or the millions of others who take up a profession out of economic necessity or because society has conspired to limit their options because of gender, skin color, or accent.

Countless lives are shaped by such decisions, which aren't conscious decisions of the head and the heart of what would really be good for you, but are what others say is right for you.

Even if your career seems in good shape, the job you have today is insecure, because every job in the world today is insecure. For any prudent professional, now is the time to reevaluate your position and plan for the future. If we accept the studies, we are doubling the sum of our knowledge every ten years. Thus those special achievements from your past are sadly getting an ever-shorter shelf life, and this exponential growth of knowledge means that at least half of what we know at any given time is becoming obsolete. Which in turn means that successes that were a career's building blocks are inevitably becoming irrelevant.

Don't get caught asleep at the wheel. It's your career and you're driving,

When you cannot make up your mind which of two unevenly balanced courses of action you should take—choose the bolder. —W. J. Slim

and that means looking forward, backward, and in the mirror, and changing lanes when necessary. I'm talking about using where you are now to get to wherever it is you want to go. I'm talking about making smoother segues to a better life.

A STABLE WORK-LIFE FOUNDATION

Jobs that provide a source of steady money to put the food of your choice on the table and the roof of your choosing over your head aren't getting any easier to find. The good jobs are scarcer, the bad jobs are multiplying like fleas, and the average jobs are disappearing completely. Some jobs are much better than others; some aspects of most industries are booming, while others are dying, or blindly disemboweling themselves. This is not a time to be caught in the wrong place. Your immediate goal is to establish a core career in an area with the maximum stability (stable in that the demand for these types of people is seen to be significant and growing) and flexibility (flexible in that the majority of technical, professional, and behavioral skills in one job will apply to another in-demand job).

To do that, you must be objective about the kind of job you have, which falls into one of the following three categories:

> In-Person Services (I.P.S.)
> Routine Production Services (R.P.S.)
> Symbolic Analyst (also known as Knowledge Worker)

Don't fool yourself. Not all white-collar jobs are Symbolic Analytical jobs. Remember the ever-so-professional lawyers we spoke about earlier who, when you strip away the glitz, are actually doing routine production work.

An objective look will tell you how your employer is classifying the type of work you do. Once you face the facts by improving your skills, changing your job, or changing your core career, you can begin to build an integrated work life that is based on a firm foundation. Don't think for a moment that having abused a core career you can simply move onto fresh pastures in the entrepreneurial- and dream-career worlds. Long-term work-life buoyancy depends on buoyant behaviors, and the behaviors that lead to success and buoyancy *are the same* whatever career path you follow and in every field of endeavor.

Who bravely dares must sometimes risk a fall. —Tobias G. Smollett

CAREER SELF-MANAGEMENT

In the old days companies promised long-term employment. Now what is being promised by the most aware employers is not employment but employability. Corporate-sponsored career self-management is in its infancy, with the picture being painted by cutting-edge companies such as Apple, Chevron, and Pac-Tel. Such companies see career self-management programs not as employee benefits but as a necessity. As one H.R. manager told us, the velocity of change required for business success is accelerating, and "as we can't always go outside for expertise, we have to look inside for people with current skill sets." This sounds like the irreducible core. Providing a way for its employees to assess their skills and direction is enlightened self-interest for a growing number of companies.

It is symptomatic of the age that all these corporate-sponsored programs strive to get employees to take responsibility for their own careers. John Hancock, Hewlett-Packard, and Intel, among others, stress that they are there to help an employee develop a career and give it a sense of direction but that the pursuit of that career is exclusively the responsibility of the employee.

By the way, it seems that sometimes when these programs are offered as an employee benefit, they are the calm before the storm and are just another sign that you'd better have your bags packed and ready to go.

However, in most cases it's not that the company set out to dump you; it's just that the world is changing, and everyone gets caught. You can't hide your head in the sand about these changes. Every company in every industry is going through a metamorphosis, and the goal is not to reinvent the corporation for your benefit. The goal is to reinvent the corporation for its own health and flexibility, and the less draining personnel overhead it has, the healthier and more flexible the corporation will be. The typical American corporation in the new world of work wants to get rid of you, and people like you. It most certainly does not want to be responsible for your long-term employment.

The message is plain and simple: You must take responsibility for yourself and the buoyancy of your work life. You are the only person who can be relied upon to take care of you. You are the captain of your ship.

If I distilled this book into a To Do list, it might be:

Busy souls have no time to be busybodies. —Austin O'Malley

1. Become self-aware
   - Assess who you are.

2. Join your new career universe
   - What's happening with jobs like yours?
   - How is your industry changing?

3. Explore the new world
   - Investigate hot jobs.
   - Check out buoyant industrial biomes.

4. Diagnose your work-life buoyancy plan
   - Can you make it happen?
   - So, what challenges do you face?
   - What do you have to take you where you want to go?
   - What must you develop to take you where you want to go?

5. Decide on a direction
   - What direction(s) will satisfy your needs for security, freedom, and happiness?
   - Decide how to enhance your buoyancy.

6. Get your act in gear
   - Organize, plan, and *act* to enhance your work-life buoyancy.

7. Stay on your toes
   - Constantly monitor yourself and your career world.

1. Become Self-Aware

You must be self-aware if you hope to succeed. A young man came up to me after a bookstore appearance in Manhattan; he was a nice guy with a fairly distinct speech impediment. As his current job wasn't going too well, he thought he'd like to have a go at some of the money in voice-over work for commercials. Real buoyancy requires real objectivity, and unfortunately for this young man, he wasn't facing the facts.

If you aren't brutally honest with yourself about where you are now, you will set out on the journey to where you want to be with two strikes

Whoever admits that he is too busy to improve his methods has acknowledged himself to be at the end of his rope. And that is always the saddest predicament which anyone can get into. —J. Ogden Armour

against you. As Stan Katz and Amy Liu elegantly defined it in their book *Success Trap*:

> Tempting as it is to believe that we can command our own destinies, each of us possesses a unique blend of strengths and weaknesses, opportunities or limitations, none of which cannot be altered by using the right product or changing philosophies. Denying this basic fact to sustain the fantasy of unlimited possibility is like walking on thin ice. There's a chance you will make it all the way across, but you have no way of knowing or controlling whether you'll arrive safely.

If you are honest with yourself, you cannot accept the myth of unlimited possibility. Given your particular physical, intellectual, and emotional makeup, there are certain paths open to you and there are certain paths not open to you, and there are some that are inevitably going to disappoint. *The more accurate your self-perception, the more logical your chosen path is likely to be.* With self-awareness you'll know where you want to go, and, just as importantly, you will know where you have to start from in order to get there.

What's Important to You? Rightsizing Your Work Life

Self-awareness is also about learning what's important to the most important person in the world. It's about getting a grip on those intensely personal sliding scales of "nice to have" and "gotta have" that give us the values we ultimately live by.

But our values are shaped and altered by the passing of time. Just think how different you are today from the way you were just a few years ago. Maybe then you were just starting your professional life, trying to establish your own values, and perhaps now you are an established professional complete with an ever-increasing circle of dependents and obligations. Whoever and wherever you may be in life, it would be a good idea to sit down for an hour or two one day soon and ask yourself some serious questions about what you want the rest of your work life to be like.

THE SELF-AWARENESS QUESTIONNAIRE

How do you know where you stand? You start by asking some good questions, and taking the time to give thoughtful, honest answers.

The great happiness of life, I find, after all, to consist in the regular discharge of some mechanical duty. —Johann von Schiller

Critical Buoyancy Skills. How do your circle of buoyancy behaviors measure up? Measure up to what, you may very well ask. Picture a career-buoyant person you know well and use that person as your yardstick. So, compared with, say, Jean—your choice for the human yardstick—do you need to work on your Flexible Thinking skills? Does the behavior need development, is it okay, or is it an area of strength?

Now, you may be self-aware and truly understand yourself, but just the same, *check yourself out with other people*—people who know you *in the workplace*. Tell them about the buoyancy traits and have them compare you with the ideal candidate. Now, what have you learned about yourself?

Personal-Skills Assessment. You need skills to be buoyant. Step 1 is to generate a list of skills you think you have. List any and every skill you can think of. Also list the skills you *don't* have. Drawing a blank? Think about people in different careers and their skill sets. List their skills as well. Here's where traditional career theories can help.[1] Segmenting of work can be used to construct a pretty good list of skills areas, such as the following:

> Oral communication
> Public speaking
> Written communication
> Technical writing
> Supervision
> Leadership
> Training
> Team member
> Team leader
> Planning
> Decision making
> Idea generation
> Generating alternatives
> Problem identification
> Problem solving
> Classification
> Mathematical
> Mechanical

It is not enough to be busy; so are the ants. The question is: What are we busy about?
—Henry David Thoreau

Spatial
Verbal reasoning
Oral comprehension
Written comprehension
Manual/Repair
Financial

Step 2 for skill assessment is to rate your level of expertise. Try this simple system:

- Expert—could teach someone the skill
- Adequate—perform the skill well
- Needs work—can do it, but not well
- None—can't do it

Now that you've determined your skills levels, figure out what you do with this new knowledge. How do you apply it?

Professional Interests. It's important to figure out your interests. What do you like to do? When you're at work, what tasks naturally interest you? What makes you happiest at work? Is it solving a problem, figuring out new solutions, working with others? Do you jump at a chance to work on a new product-development team, or do you enjoy designing a new customer-service process? Find out where your joy is at work.

Lifestyle Issues and Your Job. How much effort and time are you able, and willing, to devote to your work? How strong is your need to be at home? Do you have to travel? What kind of work environment are you looking for, and what type of lifestyle do you want to lead? Figure out what you prefer in terms of the following:

- The hours you keep: Do you only want to work part-time? Banker's hours? Are you willing to put in overtime, or your weekend time?
- The commute: How far are you willing to travel to reach your place of employment?
- Work environment and surroundings: Do you like to work alone or in a group? Do you like a formal or a casual work atmosphere?

A really busy person never knows how much he weighs. —Ed Howe

- Employer flexibility: Would a flexible work schedule enhance your ability to live a fulfilled life?
- Vacation and time off: In education you get large blocks of time off, but the pay might not be as good as on Wall Street, where you may only get two weeks a year. Where is the balance that will satisfy your needs and long-term goals?

You only get one life to live. How happy that life is will be determined in part by how productively you manage your time. When you have looked objectively at the lifestyle issues affecting your life, you can incorporate those needs into an integrated work-life plan. Maybe you can't just stop traveling on company business today, but if you hate travel, addressing the issue squarely will give you the opportunity to reinvent your work life logically in a fashion that eliminates travel.

Assessing Your Preferences. Rightsizing your work life means first reevaluating yourself so that you may act on the basis of current judgment rather than habit or hand-me-down ideals. So, based on what you've learned from the previous questions, answer the following. (There are no wrong answers.)

- Write a one-paragraph description of yourself as you were when you entered your profession, and another that shows where you are now.
- Write a third paragraph that highlights the differences.
- For a period of one week keep an activity log that covers not only the workday's appointments but also any other activity you are engaged in. Identify your attitude going into the activity and also your attitude after it is over.
- Continue the previous exercise for all your personal-time activities. You might be surprised at how you spend your time.
- Recall real-world experiences and your reactions to working with others versus working solo, and to supervision, authority, and power.
- What gets you energized? When do you feel full of juice and full of life?
- What do you like most about your profession, and why?
- What do you like least about your profession, and why?
- What were you doing the last few times you felt calm, centered, and content?

The busy have no time for tears. —Lord Byron

- Make a list of five more professions that could answer your needs.

- Recall occasions when you've been under stress, and the different ways in which you have experienced risk. What were your reactions and feelings to those situations?

- What levels of competitiveness are comfortable for you, and why?

- When have you felt the most respected and most valued for your efforts?

- What does autonomy mean to you? Describe it to yourself, and write it down in two sentences.

- What is fulfillment to you? Describe it to yourself, and write it down in two sentences.

- Where is your current job taking you? What can you do to make it more secure? What are your options?

- Identify your professional experience, talents, and behaviors that you feel are transferable to other jobs.

- Look at the types of problems you have faced, solutions you've developed, and their consequences.

- For what activities have you received special recognition?

- What have been your most rewarding professional projects?

- What have been your most rewarding professional relationships? Why was the relationship rewarding? What special behaviors or characteristics have you admired about the people with whom you have worked?

- Write down the number of jobs you have had. Write down your reason for leaving each of these jobs and your reasons for starting each subsequent job. What does this tell you about yourself? (Job changes or core-career shifts should never be made for the sake of a few bucks but for reasons that make sense in terms of your whole life and goals.)

- If I was going to fire you, why would I be doing it? What are your weaknesses?

- Is your job growing in scope, or is it getting easier? What does this tell you? That you are working harder doesn't necessarily mean that your job has become more complex; it may mean that the means of judging productivity in a simplified environment has improved.

- Where and how would you most like to make a contribution?

Who makes quick use of the moment is a genius of prudence. —Johann Kaspar Lavater

- Where are you most competent? What behaviors are you going to have to work on? What's the plan?
- What are global workplace trends and industry-specific revolutions doing to your current and/or desired profession?
- What is it that you do that is most in demand? What is it that you could do better, and who might pay you to do it?
- Sketch out your current work-life plan. Can it be improved? Where is it heading? What security will this path provide? How will it widen your experience and increase the depth of your P.K.H.? How will it differentiate your skills from the state they're in today? How will your current path increase your professional flexibility? Or will it further isolate you from the mainstream?
- How do you want to spend the rest of your work life? I don't mean what anyone else thinks you should do, but rather what *you* want to do. Remember, it doesn't have to be one thing anymore. There's real choice in the new world of work.

Trips Out Travel

Trips Out Travel in Berkeley, California, has been my favorite travel agency for twenty years. Wherever you want to go, whatever you want to do, they'll make it happen for you. All you have to do is say, "Gee, I'd like to go backpacking in Nepal," or, "I want to go bar-hopping in the islands," and Trips Out will show you a way to make it happen. But *you* have to come up with the direction. With dreams you can go anywhere you'd like, without them you stay wherever you are.

- What are your alternative professional core careers? (If you are completely lost, a good place to start is by reading a book you can find at the library called *Occupational Outlook Handbook* [see Resources]. It describes in exhaustive detail some 250 occupations.)
- If you were to start a home-based business, what are some of the options for the type of company it might be? (Come up with six.) Where would you start?
- What might your dream careers be? List a few. What are some of the things you've always wanted to have a go at? Name anything you want, as long as it isn't what you are doing now.

What we hope ever to do with ease, we must learn first to do with diligence.
—*Samuel Johnson*

•   What are your time commitments? Are they really commitments or are they "employer-pressure" time?

•   What is the relative health of your professional core-career
biome? Are you well connected within it? What are you going to do to
clarify your understanding of your biome and to improve your professional connectivity?

•   Where might you start?

This is not a pop quiz. You will doubtless want to come back to these
questions over a period of weeks as you evaluate your work life and your
dreams in the harsh light of the new world of work.

Every corporation that hopes to survive in the new world of work must
reinvent itself following an often wrenching self-reappraisal. The task is
no easier for you, but the rewards are enormous: security, freedom, and
happiness as they combine to give you work-life buoyancy. No one else
but you can make you spend the time to look at yourself and the realities
of your career so closely, and no one but you, and perhaps your loved
ones, will suffer if you don't.

2. Join Your New Career Universe

All jobs are changing. Some are obsolete and disappearing, others are being simplified and deskilled, many are being automated or exported; no
jobs are safer today than they were yesterday. Ask yourself what is happening to jobs like yours in other companies. And ask yourself how your job
is changing to keep pace.

It might not be just your job or company that is changing, it might be
your entire industry. When jobs, companies, and industries restructure
themselves, those who keep themselves in the dark will be the losers. Instead use your attitude of connectivity to map the new career universe.

Join associations, unions, clubs, and societies connected with all your
work-life interests. Associations have local chapter meetings, networking
meetings, newsletters, and educational opportunities. They track job
openings and salaries. They promote the profession and sometimes help
to elevate its status. As a member you also get to mingle with people with
whom you have common bonds: your shared commitment to professional competence and your employability.

*The successful people are the ones who can think up things for the rest of the world to
keep busy at. —Don Marquis*

Then look at your own current job situation. How supportive is your present employer of your career development? No one is about to say that he or she doesn't believe in people and development, so you have to do some digging to find out the truth. Compared with other companies, does yours value your department's contributions or your own function? Do they encourage lateral transfers? Where are the opportunities to learn, to grow, and to develop? Will your company reimburse you for college courses? Are volunteers for short-term team assignments encouraged, and how are volunteers supported and rewarded?

You must become part of your career universe to achieve buoyancy in the new world of work. That means knowing what is happening with your job and others like it, as a result of workplace restructuring; and it means applying that same attitude of knowledge to the workings of your employer and your entire industrial biome. This is all going to be easier said than done unless you become part of your professional communities through association and volunteer work and get connected to all the people who make up your profession. Once you are connected and active, all of this information will fall naturally into your lap.

3. Explore the New World

Core-career jobs are defined in ways that are different from the old days. All core-career jobs changed to reflect the changing needs of the corporation. These changes have been so sweeping that everyone working today is being affected by them. The only intelligent response is the attitude of connectivity, which will keep you abreast of the changes in the new world of work as they happen.

Exploring the new world of work and the opportunities it holds for you should then come as a natural step to your personal reevaluation. Whether or not you feel your core job and career are safe, professional prudence demands that you examine your options constantly . . . just as your employer does to remain buoyant.

Cast back to the "Where The Jobs Are" chapter and browse through all the biomes again. Hopefully you are already developing a whole cartload of behaviors, sensitivities, and work competencies desirable in the biome you are currently employed in.

Everyone thinks of changing the world, but no one thinks of changing himself.
—Leo Tolstoi

In developing these buoyancy behaviors, you are developing Symbolic Analytical skills, and giving yourself a *passport to jobs in vastly different environments from the one where you are now.* The critical behaviors increase your mobility, and whenever you do that, you increase your entire work-life buoyancy.

There is always a learning curve when you start something new, and sometimes it's tough to crawl again when you were used to flying. But we all face suddenly having to start something new over the coming years. And when you take the long view, the fifty-year work-life view, maybe there *is* time to be made for starting over. So investigating hot jobs, companies, and industries should become just another dimension of your professional connectedness.

So when you explore core-career opportunities again in Chapter 4, look at it afresh, with the eyes of someone who really might have to make a big change one day. It's much easier to explore your options while the heat is off.

4. Diagnose Your Work-Life Buoyancy Plan

The quality of your life is dictated by the quality of your work life, because you spend the majority of your waking hours making a living. Now, it used to be you could just find the kind of work to which you were temperamentally suited and then, over the years and a gradually evolving series of job titles, you could meander into a graceful retirement. Corporate America has replaced this benign paternalism with an attitude of "paddle your own canoe, Jack!"

This is where the circle of buoyancy behaviors comes into play again. If you can no longer trade corporate loyalty for personal security, you must take care of your own security, and that means developing your employability. The research shows that a set of eight learnable behaviors open the door to employability in your core career, and then to buoyancy in every one of your alternate career paths.

Throughout *B.T.O.* I have shown you how these eight complementary behaviors impact your everyday work life. Now I'll show you how you can use the following behaviors:

> Goal Orientation
> —*Working hard to achieve your goals*
>
> Positive Expectancy
> —*Believing in your ability to overcome, and ultimately to succeed*

Change alone is eternal, perpetual, immortal. —Arthur Schopenhauer

Personal Influence
—*Communication with a purpose*

Organized Action
—*Coordinated action efficiently focused on a specific outcome*

Informed Risk
—*Flexible planning to decrease risk in a constantly changing*
environment

Inner Openness
—*Emotional flexibility*

Flexible Thinking
—*Creative adaptability in different contexts*

Smart Decisions
—*Effective decision making*

This new approach to buoyancy is appealing because you don't have to be a superstar to succeed; rather, you have to be a person with a balanced complement of eight behaviors (Principle 1). Each of these behaviors is interactive, and the more you develop one, the greater your power in the other behaviors becomes (Principle 2). The success principles are rounded out with Principle 3, which says that who you become as a person, and how you feel about yourself, will be defined by your behaviors, and how, in turn, the very judgmental world of work will react to you in response to your behavior.

Now you can apply these success principles and the circle of buoyancy behaviors to a multiple, parallel-career philosophy, where each career path uses and develops the same behaviors as the others. This has got to be the best-kept secret around: *So long as you see clearly where you stand today, you can move from anywhere you are in life to anywhere in life you want to be.* When you know where you stand, it doesn't matter how far away the horizon is, because you can learn the measured steps that will take you there.

It gets better. Our behavioral research showed that buoyant core, entrepreneurial, and dream careerists all agreed that while all eight of the behaviors were critical to buoyancy in each of the career paths, each path

---

We emphasize that we believe in change because we were born of it, we have lived by it, we prospered and grew great by it. So the status quo has never been our god, and we ask no one else to bow down before it. —Carl T. Rowan

had *five dominant behaviors* (in that the top five traits were found to be the *most* critical to achieving success in a particular career path) and the *top three* positions in each category revealed traits that were identical:

- Goal Orientation
- Positive Expectancy
- Personal Influence

However, the fourth and fifth behaviors varied according to the career context. Here's the breakdown, which lists the most important for each career path:

Core Career	Dream Career	Entrepreneurial Career
Goal Orientation	**Positive Expectancy**	**Goal Orientation**
Positive Expectancy	**Goal Orientation**	**Positive Expectancy**
Personal Influence	**Personal Influence**	**Personal Influence**
Inner Openness	**Inner Openness**	**Smart Decisions**
Flexible Thinking	**Organized Action**	**Informed Risk**
Organized Action	*Flexible Thinking*	*Organized Action*
Smart Decisions	*Smart Decisions*	*Inner Openness*
Informed Risk	*Informed Risk*	*Flexible Thinking*

These similarities and differences will help you tailor your behavioral development program to your personal goals, as the following examples show.

CORE CAREERISTS ADAPT AND SOLVE PROBLEMS

Core careerists build their eight critical traits around the three behaviors that lead all three career path rankings:

- Goal Orientation
- Positive Expectancy
- Personal Influence

and then build on them with:

Few will have the greatness to bend history itself; but each of us can change a small portion of events, and in the total of all those acts will be written the history of this generation. —Robert F. Kennedy

- Flexible Thinking
- Inner Openness

In a core career the targets for your development of Flexible Thinking are:

- Problem-Identification Skills
- Opportunity-Identification Skills
- Solution Skills

Flexible Thinking includes the generation of new ideas as well as just a whole lot of ideas. Core careerists have to be able to identify important problems to solve, because they aren't always given the problem. Or when they are told to fix a certain situation, they may need the flexibility to back up one step and figure out if this is really the problem or if it's just a symptom of the real problem.

You need Inner Openness to understand what you are good at, and what areas you must improve to stay current, competitive, and employable. You need Inner Openness to constantly adapt to the environment. The contract between employer and employee has changed, just as the world has changed, and continues to change. Core careerists who close themselves off to the ever-increasing velocity of change will not survive.

DREAM CAREERISTS HAVE TO ACT AND REMAIN OPEN

Dream careerists build their critical eight traits around the same three behaviors as core careerists:

- Goal Orientation
- Positive Expectancy
- Personal Influence

and then build on them with

- Organized Action
- Inner Openness

Organized Action allows the dream careerist to get things done in the most efficient manner possible, a key trait considering the demands on

In a progressive country change is constant . . . change . . . is inevitable.
—Benjamin Disraeli

their time and, often, the unstructured nature of their work. Inner Openness lets the dream careerist objectively view his work, and see where his strengths are—as well as those areas where improvement is necessary. Dream careerists do not operate in a vacuum; they know that when it comes to market demands, the opinions of others *matter*.

Inner Openness, Change, and the New World

Tom is forty-eight years old and has worked for the same company for thirty years. He is also angry, hurt, and confused. For thirty years Tom did what the company told him to do. They wanted him to learn how to repair returned products, and he learned. They wanted him to focus his knowledge in one niche area, and he obeyed. Tom made pretty good money doing what the company told him to do.

But the company changed, and the unwritten employment contract changed too. Tom was demoted in a cutback. He still had a job, but now he also had a longer commute by about an hour. Then he was told that they didn't need his skills anymore and that he could look for another job in the company.

Tom panicked. "For thirty years I learned this stuff, the lifeblood of this company, and now they say they don't need me!" He was angry too. Tom believed that the company owed it to him to find him a job, at his old pay rate, close to home. And they did, at least morally and ethically. But legally the company owed him nothing at this point, and since the new CEO was a lawyer, they were legally going to dump Tom.

Tom was isolated in thirty years of security, and his mind had become closed to the unthinkable, despite the storm clouds.

ENTREPRENEURS NEED TO BE DECISIVE

Entrepreneurs build their critical eight around the same three behaviors:

- Goal Orientation
- Positive Expectancy
- Personal Influence

and then build on them with

- Smart Decisions
- Informed Risk

Weep not that the world changes—did it keep a stable, changeless state, it were a cause indeed to weep. —William Cullen Bryant

Time is money. Buoyant entrepreneurs live by this rule every day, so they have to make decisions, and more than anything, these have to be Smart Decisions. Decisiveness is *not* impulsiveness. When you do something impulsively, you are doing something irrationally, without thinking through the consequences. Smart Decisions allow you to weigh your alternatives quickly and decide among previously considered actions.

For an entrepreneur, Informed Risk may mean that if you see a better way of doing it, you don't have to ask permission, but you do have to understand the odds to diminish your risk in a constantly changing environment. As an entrepreneur you aren't bound by the rules and regulations of the corporation, because you are the corporation, you are the one who has to make it work.

Remember, when you develop one of the critical eight traits anywhere, and for any reason, the enhanced skill competencies will immediately pay you back in other areas of your life. The beautiful part of all this is that everything you do in pursuit of your independence and dreams will help your core-career buoyancy, because you become a more valuable employee, while at the same time reducing your dependence on core-career employers by building skills that will help your alternate careers blossom.

THERE ARE DIFFERENCES IN LEVEL

You need all eight traits for career buoyancy, no matter whether you are pursuing a core, dream, or entrepreneurial career. Depending on the career application and your personal competencies, it may be best for you to polish your skills, one before another, but nevertheless you need them *all* in good measure. If you don't, you fail. That's Principle #1 in action.

IT'S ALL A MATTER OF BALANCE

Now what does all this mean for your core-career buoyancy, and your parallel career paths, in the larger context of your work-life buoyancy?

Do you remember when you first learned how to ride a bike or drive a car? It took all of your attention. You couldn't look around you, talk to anyone, or think about anything else. You were totally absorbed in not falling off the bike or crashing into oncoming traffic. That's why you are still here.

It's the same with career and work-life buoyancy. When you start a new job or switch careers, it seems that you are totally focused on the new aspects of your work life. Absorbed and focused. That's the way it should be, too, because it means you are increasing your chances of survival.

He that waits upon fortune is never sure of a dinner. —*Benjamin Franklin*

At some point, though, you can ride well. You can look around as you pedal. You can talk to people you whiz by on the street. You can even take your hand off the handlebars, for a second at first, then longer and longer. You've mastered it; congratulations! But by mastering riding a bicycle, you have just freed yourself up to do other things.

The same thing happens to careers. As your dream becomes an entrepreneurial career and the entrepreneurial career stabilizes into your core career, you have come full circle. It's time, then, to dream once more and begin the cycle again. Get your core career running on all eight cylinders first; after all, the foundation of a good attack is a properly prepared defensive strategy. Then pay attention to the personal-development programs you deem most important to the weaving of your unique work-life web, because suddenly it's more than an impossible dream.

5. Decide on a Direction

As you formulate options for the future, you will probably find that while things aren't perfect, neither are you boiling in the devil's cauldron. You'll know what you are capable of doing, what you enjoy doing, and what people are likely to pay you to do. You will also increase your work-life buoyancy as you start to develop entrepreneurial- and/or dream-career pursuits. The trick is to connect *where you are* with *where you want to get to* so that you have a path to pursue; some paths may be longer than others, but all paths have been walked before, using exactly the techniques we have discussed throughout *Beat the Odds*.

THE CORE-CAREER FOUNDATION

Your first move must be to protect and preserve what you have now: your professional core career. Within your core career look for ways to maximize your security, freedom, and happiness. A job that once fulfilled some or all of these needs may no longer do so, but the response isn't simply to switch jobs or careers. The order of play is really quite simple. Whatever is out of whack, correct. If it is skills, implement a program to improve them. If the problem is the job and not the career, then change the job.

If it is the career rather than the job, pursue your investigations of other healthy careers within your biome, or consider segueing to another biome. This can be a difficult decision, but better to start moving toward the future today than to languish in a deadened core career tomorrow.

A threefold cord is not quickly broken—Ecclesiastes 4:12

When you really seem stuck and completely unable to escape the clutches of a no-longer-hospitable career track, there are always a couple of escape hatches. Jobs in sales abound in all industries and have provided one foot in the door and another on the ladder of success for countless people segueing or starting over in a new field.

Another little-known escape hatch from an inappropriate core career is the franchise option; almost every industry supports a franchise base. With this option you can move to a franchisor within your industry, and develop an entirely new body of franchising knowledge. With that you can then move to other franchising companies in other biomes, and then, if you wish, from those franchising companies to nonfranchised companies in the targeted industrial biome. Your franchising exposure will also give you some valuable experience in the trials and tribulations of running a small business.

Or perhaps you are on the lower levels of a labor-intensive industry, working as an In-Person Server, and perhaps your circumstances mean you really are stuck. You still have choices. Companies in your industry may be rightsizing management. Your industry may be one where the need is for people management and some big operations are getting rid of levels of higher management and creating opportunities at the lower levels. You could move to a company that is rightsizing its management and thus better your career.

Or perhaps you are lucky and judgment tells you to sit tight, hone your skills, and head for the reducing corporate core while you develop your entrepreneurial- and dream-career options. *Whatever your situation, you can improve your buoyancy.* And no matter what your entrepreneurial- or dream-career possibilities might be, you already have a number of the most important assets with which to chase them down. You will also know what you will have to work on, and the resources you'll need to start the job.

Your job is to face where you really stand with your core career and place this knowledge in the context of where that puts you in a half-century-plus work life. The bare-faced reality of your circumstances may sometimes come as a shock, but it will also prompt some immediate short-term goals. Goals are stepping-stones; they determine the action steps you must take to progress along your chosen pathway.

If you hope to achieve core-career and work-life buoyancy, you must

---

A man can fail many times, but he isn't a failure until he begins to blame somebody else.
—*John Burroughs*

have firm foundations in place. For example you cannot expect great odds for success from launching an entrepreneurial career if you have never been able to keep a steady job.

Setting a direction for your dreams means first giving your work life a firm foundation, with a core-career that fulfills your needs for security. Again, this could include any or all of the following:

- Understand your company and become a part of your industry.
- Develop critical buoyancy behaviors as your own analysis dictates.
- Change jobs within your biome to be better positioned for the irreducible core with a healthier company.
- Switch your job or career to a healthier biome or one that might be more in tune with your other work-life goals.

Fulfillment of these essential needs for security must come *first* in your work life. Then, as soon as you have begun Organized Action on your work-life foundation, you can start working toward fulfilling your other work-life needs for freedom and happiness.

6. Get Your Act in Gear

Inertia-breaker Tony Robbins wrote in *Awaken the Giant Within*:

> Many people go through life putting off their joy and fulfillment. To them, goal setting means that "someday" after they achieve something, only then will they be able to enjoy life to the fullest. The truth is that if we decide to be happy now, we'll automatically achieve more. While goals provide a magnificent direction and a way to focus, we must constantly strive to live each day to its fullest, squeezing all the joy we can out of each moment. Instead of measuring your success and failure in life by your ability to achieve an individualized and specific goal, remember that the direction we're heading is more important than individual results. If we continue to head in the right direction, we may not only achieve the goals we're pursuing but a lot more![2]

It isn't enough to just enhance your core career, although that is your most important first step. So long as you are dependent on one source of

---

A failure is a man who has blundered but is not able to cash in the experience.
—*Elbert Hubbard*

income, you will never be free to actualize your dreams. Instead your dreams will be on hold while you fulfill the dreams of management and the investors. Do you want what's left of the illusion of job security, or do you want to achieve your *dreams*?

It is time to start living up to your dreams instead of living for your no-longer-reliable core-career income. And don't say you haven't got time, because time is the only thing you do have—maybe fifty years of it. Start investing your time and money in *your* future. Just because office technology can follow you anywhere doesn't mean you have to sacrifice all your waking hours to your core job; while you are working ten hours more a week and your productivity has risen 25 percent in the last twenty years, your real income has fallen 20 percent.[3] It is time to get real about your work life and your future. *You don't have to surrender every night and every weekend and every vacation to the career carrot-on-a-stick when the odds are that you won't get the carrot and you will get the stick.*

The moment has come to reapportion your time and energies so that all your good efforts are supportive of your needs and the long-term well-being of You, Inc.

Am I saying work less diligently for your core-career employer? Certainly not. I am saying work *smarter.* Integrate your core-career sacrifices so that they are additionally supportive of your dream career and/or entrepreneurial careers.

INVESTING IN TODAY AND TOMORROW

Here are a couple of ways to integrate your core career more effectively with the rest of your work life.

At the irreducible core, American corporations are looking for people who can manage themselves and their work (project management), who can manage people (people management), and who can handle the fiscal responsibilities of those projects and people. Any expertise gained in any of these areas, especially those self-management skills inherent in project management, will only serve to enhance your employability and thereby your core-career buoyancy.

These kinds of experiences will also be of use in your successful dream and entrepreneurial activities. In other words, as you strive toward enhanced core employability by developing desirable competencies such as these, all your efforts will in turn benefit your parallel careers, and your

A man is a worker. If he is not that, he is nothing. —Joseph Conrad

overall work-life buoyancy. Instead of helping your employer but not yourself, now everyone can benefit.

Project Management. This is where you are responsible for bringing a project in, having possibly been responsible for its genesis too. This is great core-career experience. It also builds experience and skills in an area that will have a direct beneficial impact on your dream and entrepreneurial endeavors, in which "bringing the project in" is what it all boils down to.

Project-management experience is a great way to develop the following traits:

- Organized Action
- Informed Risk
- Smart Decisions

People Management. The skill of supervising and managing people, much harder to come by in this day and age, is also valuable to your other endeavors in the way it prepares you for the coordination of human resources toward a specific end. Practical experience will show you that even the most seemingly solitary entrepreneurial and dream careers require in reality considerable people-management skills.

People management can help you develop your:

- Inner Openness
- Personal Influence

Fiscal Management. The hardest management experience to come by, this is an experience that would benefit any entrepreneur or dream careerist. If you can't get, or aren't prepared for, this type of responsibility, maybe this is one of those courses you should take. Not only will it benefit your parallel careers, it will also have an overall positive impact on your personal fiscal health.

Fiscal management often exercises this buoyancy trait:

- Flexible Thinking

Then there is what I call move management. It's tough to make a core career work, to know where you are going and how you are going to get

---

Genius is one percent inspiration and ninety-nine percent perspiration.
—Thomas Edison

there, especially in times as turbulent as these. But here's a question that 95 percent of people I speak to haven't considered:

What is your next job after this job and this company? What role does this next job play in a long-term work-life plan? I don't mean just that if you are a junior programmer now, your next job will be that of a senior programmer. I want you to understand how your decision on your next career move impacts your life needs for security, freedom, and happiness. Learn to look beyond this job, around the bend, and over the hill. Then, when the unforeseen throws you a career curveball, you'll have options with which to deal with the crisis.

7. Stay on Your Toes

You are nearing the end, but you can't put this book down and go back to business as usual; in the stormy new world of work you have to keep your weather eyes open. As a prudent modern professional you have to monitor yourself and your career world constantly:

- Make it a point to learn how your company works, and why it is changing.
- Get to know your industry, all the players, and all their parts.
- Become part of as many professional networks as is practical—at least one for each career path.
- Look for opportunities that allow you to develop your circle of buoyancy behaviors, both within your core career and outside it.
- Set up a home-based office to pursue your dreams.
- Take a step toward your dream every day.

Twenty-first-Century Career Management

We are living through a technological revolution that affects every aspect of our lives, with the eradication of millions of jobs and the export of millions more. Massive unemployment, career annihilation, and systematic restructuring of the nature of work downward in quality, security, and reward is spreading throughout every neighborhood in the nation. Faced with as many careers in a work life as we used to face jobs, Americans are experiencing a loss of the right to the American Dream, and with it a massive confusion.

One must not always think so much about what one should do, but rather what one should be. —Meister Eckart

In the last five years entry-level wages have declined 2.6 percent, while for college graduates average entry-level wages have declined over 6 percent.[4] The largest group of working Americans are justifiably uneasy about their own standing and fearful of their futures. Between now and 2005 we will create twenty-five million jobs, twenty-four million of them in the service biomes; and all but a small percentage will be low-wage, restricted-opportunity, or, worse than that, temporary.

I can't define success for you, but we both know it isn't one of the millions of McJobs clouding the horizon, so if you are seriously concerned about your economic survival, you must restructure and retool, the same way that our employers are doing with such vigor. Just as American corporations have turned themselves inside out and reinvented themselves in totally new forms to maintain maximum financial viability, you need to restructure the balance of your work life for that same maximum financial viability.

When you look at your core career in the context of a fifty-year-plus work life, where there is no longer any promise of lifetime employment, you may be a little less willing to sacrifice your best years in return for the stick. The more time you take back for yourself and your life, the more time you will have to invest in your future, the more opportunities for success will come your way, and the more fulfilling your life will be.

Webs and Chains

I believe you want a life that is financially secure for you and your loved ones; I believe you want enough autonomy and independence to enjoy your life; and I believe you want as much of this time to be as happy and fulfilling as you can make it. In *Beat the Odds* I classified these needs as

- Security
- Freedom
- Happiness

No longer are these needs for security, freedom, and happiness exclusively satisfied by a core career. The only way to meet these needs is to first give them a practical means of expression with a coordinated web of activities, each specifically pursued to satisfy one or more of your needs.

Fortune is the rod of the weak, and the staff of the brave. —James Russell Lowell

Your needs for security, freedom, and happiness are given means of expression through

- core
- entrepreneurial
- dream

careers. In turn the circle of buoyancy behaviors:

- Goal Orientation
- Positive Expectancy
- Smart Decisions
- Personal Influence
- Organized Action
- Informed Risk
- Flexible Thinking
- Inner Openness

will help you fulfill all of your needs in each of your career paths.

These are the essential materials for weaving a work-life web that supports your needs—but nothing is cut and dried. There is nothing as simple as either-or. Over the balance of your work life you have ample opportunity to try any number of dream, entrepreneurial, and core careers as your needs change with the unfolding of your life. It's okay to think you'll be a basket weaver one year and a photographer the next. In the new world of work you are not derogatively labeled a dilettante for trying your hand at different roles as part of an intelligently pursued work-life buoyancy plan. Such a work life would of course have a firm core-career foundation:

- Growth core-career job in a healthy industry with both vertical and horizontal flexibility
- Employment with a corporation that supports your long-term employability if it cannot support your long-term employment
- The availability of work that develops the critical eight behaviors that bring you closer to your American dream

---

A weak mind is like a microscope, which magnifies trifling things but cannot receive great ones. —Lord Chesterfield.

With a balanced core career, any dream or entrepreneurial endeavor that follows will resonate with your core career because:

- It will take advantage of core developed behaviors that are equally critical to your entrepreneurial and dream careers.
- The further development of those critical core behaviors in your parallel careers will repay your employers by your increased effectiveness and motivation.
- Over time those behaviors will multiply your chances of success in each of your separately pursued parallel careers.

But What About the Nature of Dreams and Needs?

Earlier we noted that needs demand fulfillment, but that once a need has been met, it has a sneaky way of changing and manifesting itself in other ways. So it was not surprising when our research noted that successful dream careerists weren't necessarily satisfied with their dream careers. Sound surprising that people making their living in ways they have always dreamed of should be in any way dissatisfied? My friend Nick, the photographer once said, "When I was a kid, I had this great hobby, photography. Now I've got a great business, but I don't have a hobby anymore." In twenty years he had progressed from being a young man with a dream and no autonomy, to a still-young man with a successful and stable way of life supported by his dream. In the twenty-year process of developing that dream into an additional source of entrepreneurial income and then into his solid core-career means of making a living, Nick had exhausted some of the joy he got from his passion.

As needs emerge and are met, those needs are, in the natural order of things, replaced with other needs, other dreams. It is simply human nature.

Such a problem you should have, right? Here's how dreams and needs fit into the *Beat the Odds* strategy: The goal of any seriously pursued dream career is to explode it, to take it from a dream to a fiscally sustaining entrepreneurial venture and perhaps ultimately to turn it into your core career. When you explode a dream career in this way, do not be surprised if you find yourself hatching up new dream schemes; *it's the result of having given practical means of fulfillment to your needs.* When this hap-

An education isn't how much you have committed to memory, or even how much you know. It's being able to differentiate between what you do know and what you don't.
—*Anatole France*

pens, your subconscious starts saying, "Hey, this ain't so tough, what do you want to try next?"

Fulfill one dream, just once, and you can do it a second time; fulfill a second dream, and you know you can do it a million times. As long as you use the calendar rather than the clock to measure your progress, you will find yourself exceeding your wildest work-life dreams.

With a *moonlighting* approach to seriously pursued entrepreneurial and dream-career ideas, you can create and stumble and learn as you earn, all with minimum risk and maximum opportunity. That's why I call *Beat the Odds* a prudent book.

For Joan, who works in human resources at a Georgia university, there were two options she pursued: one that advanced her entrepreneurial career and one that advanced her dream career. To work closer to her dream of becoming a playwright, she worked on her Personal Influence skills and wrote every manual she could convince her organization they needed. The university got superlative work, she enhanced her core-career buoyancy, and she got paid to develop critical dream-career writing skills.

Secondly she knew that not many people make a living as a playwright, so she added another string to her entrepreneurial bow. In a training-mad world where almost any speaker off his respirator gets one thousand dollars an engagement, she gradually became an active speaker in all her parallel professional communities. When she finally went out on her own full-time, it was her speaking and manual-writing skills she'd developed in her core career that for years supplemented her playwright's meager royalties.

In both instances she did what was in the very best interests of her employer, which was to develop her skills and worth to the company. She put effort into jobs that otherwise weren't going to get done, and everyone won. She was simultaneously increasing her employability and her grasp on her dreams, just as she was lessening the corporate grip on her overall work-life buoyancy, by developing other, more direct sources of income. *Beat the Odds* is a win-win solution for anyone concerned with the challenges of the new workplace.

Four Thoughts to Get You Going

1. *If you start a moonlighting activity, you are going to be far from alone.* Over the last decade America has generated an average of a million

---

Always do right; this will gratify some people and astonish the rest. —Mark Twain

new home-based businesses every year. In 1994 the number approached two million, and with the advent of technology far more of these companies are seen to be surviving than in the seventies, when last the numbers were crunched. The latest numbers tell us that up to 70 percent of new home-based businesses flourish after three years.

2. You will have to set goals and make plans, and stay focused on them, just as you do in your core career. As you do this, remember what the venerable Joe Mancuso says: "Few entrepreneurs are risk takers; they tend to set realistic and achievable goals. And when they do take risks, they're usually calculated risks that depend more on personal skills than chance."[5]

3. A sound entrepreneurial moonlighting venture will be based on needs that someone, somewhere, must be willing to pay for. That means a well-researched market. The needs of the outsourced corporation, the needs of your community, the needs of your time in history, and the needs of your planet will provide the source of many small fortunes over the coming years. Your goal is not to reinvent the wheel but to find a better or more convenient way of fixing it when it squeaks. Modularity is the key; you are not an entire industry, you are a cog within it that helps the larger entity move smoothly.

4. Moonlighting comes down to these simple steps:

- Find a need
- Get clients
- Do something for those clients
- Get paid
- Do something for those clients again
- Show a profit

Selective Influence Replacement

People who lead happy, buoyant lives are often referred to as inner-directed or self-referred; they are fully conscious of their needs and have the means of practical expression in action. They are careful about with whom they mix and to whose opinions they listen. They have goals and a pathway lined with positive influences designed to energize the pursuit of their dream. *Whenever a negative or no-longer-relevant influence is faced, it is selectively replaced with a positive influence.*

Negative influences manifest themselves as thoughts, opinions, behaviors,

---

As knowledge increases, wonder deepens. —Charles Morgan

environments, and people. For maximum work-life buoyancy you should selectively replace all the negative influences in your life with positive influences.

If you currently work in the back office of a bank and dream of being an actress but spend most of your free time in nightclubs, you would replace a nightclub influence with a drama-class influence, membership in a semipro troupe, and tickets to the theater. If you had kids in school and were having trouble with cash flow, you might replace a scotch-on-the-rocks with the influence of a personal financial-management course and a serious look at a home-based family business.

The selective influences you choose? That's up to you entirely—you, and what you want your work life to look like in the future. Just take a long, cool look at where you are today and where you want to be five, ten, and twenty years from now. If it is obvious that your current path is not going to guarantee your arrival, you will see where it is necessary systematically to replace no-longer-productive

- Thoughts
- Opinions
- Behaviors
- Environments
- People

Replace bad influences with good, narrow focus with panoramic vision, negative thoughts with positive thoughts, inaction with action, and a victim attitude with that of a victor. The victim points the finger of blame ever outward but fails to see that all the other fingers point right back at himself. No matter what may have happened in the past, you now have the tools and the P.K.H. to set a buoyant course in your work life—one that will maximize your opportunity for security, freedom, and happiness. Believe that you can gain a measure of control over your destiny.

Who Needs Snow to Sleigh?

No matter how well planned your buoyancy web, you can expect setbacks in a fifty-year work life; that's why you build a web, to support you in that event. As the late, great Malcolm Forbes said, "No job worth doing is with-

A man sits as many risks as he runs. —Henry David Thoreau

out its frustrations." Buoyant careerists, armed with the tools we have discussed in *B.T.O.*, are prepared to weather any storm and come back stronger than before. This is because they only experience frustrations and setbacks between themselves and their goals; they rarely, if ever, experience failure.

Experiencing adverse weather conditions in your career as frustrations and setbacks allows you to take a breath, gather yourself together, and say, "Okay, I did great to get this far. Let's look at the things that got me here, and if they're still relevant, do more of them." After that, tackle the things that need changing. Viewed with an attitude of Practical Know-how, setbacks are opportunities to learn how things work. P.K.H. allows you to look at what isn't working, understand why, and fix it.

When you have developed self-respect, the sixtieth publisher who fails to recognize the beauty of your great American novel simply becomes another minor irritant in your timetable for success and fulfillment. It becomes simply a nuisance, because there are a thousand publishers out there, and you are one rejection closer than you were before to the one who will say yes.

It's the same attitude that has one job hunter giving up when there is nothing in the want ads while another is getting multiple offers because he understands how every failure brings him closer to success, how every setback primes him for the leap forward, and how every frustration brings his dreams closer to fruition.

When you accept adverse circumstances as signposts on a fifty-year journey instead of as failures, your mind will automatically start seeking new directions for the fulfillment of its needs. Setbacks are gifts that show you what's not working right and what has to be tinkered with and fixed. Setbacks are just nature's way of flagging work-life buoyancy problems. Every setback gives you new direction and motivation to start moving again, because the odds of success have just increased. Every obstacle you encounter in the length of a long work life can bring you nearer to your goals, because it is by both good and bad experience that you nurture buoyancy. Each setback provides new experience and new information and offers the potential for moving forward along an ever-more-fruitful path.

Stumbling at a fence every now and then is par for the course, and it is when you stumble that you have to learn to believe in yourself, because you are an instrument with the capacity to change your environment. Re-

Do not attempt to do a thing unless you are sure of yourself; but do not relinquish it simply because someone else is not sure of you. —Stewart E. White

member *Cool Runnings*? It was a movie based on the story of the Jamaican Olympic bobsled team, and when you think of Jamaica and the winter Olympics, you know that this is a case of fact being stranger than fiction. What this true story tells is best explained by Christian, one of the real-life Jamaican winter Olympians: "I think it's possible, regardless of circumstances, to achieve things."

When you conjure up the image of a bobsled in full flight, you see a speeding bullet that has developed so much force and momentum that nothing can stop it. When you develop momentum in your careers, its forward thrust will carry you through the occasional work-life squalls. When you employ an attitude of momentum, you understand that action, no matter how small the action step, is the key to progress.

An attitude of momentum doesn't say you must gear yourself to someone else's concept of success, because someone else doesn't have to pay your bills or live your life. An attitude of momentum says that temporary setbacks will ultimately improve your chances of success, so you continue to take actions with positive expectancy and build momentum. The more actions you take, the quicker you build momentum and resemble that bobsled in full flight.

We wouldn't have had Gary Larsen's *Far Side* if he hadn't used his vacation time to build momentum in his dream career. He spent a week's vacation in San Francisco trying to get someone at the *Chronicle* to look at his work. And when he left without getting in to see anybody, he left his portfolio behind and went back to work, only to be laid off. But within days he received a call from the *San Francisco Chronicle* that changed his life for the better and that of millions of *Far Side* fans from around the world. If Gary Larsen hadn't invested his life in his dreams, he would never have developed the momentum that eventually triggered his success.

Whatever it takes, never stop pursuing your goals; you'll lose momentum and never recognize just how close you were to the realization of your very own American dream.

An Old Friend We Share in Common

Anyone who knows me would tell you that I am a constant whirlwind of productive mayhem. I'm a guy who really likes to make things happen, and I like to be around people who make things happen. Yet I can tell you

---

Common sense is genius in homespun. —Alfred North Whitehead

Momentum Builders

- Don't waste time trying to win over nonbelievers; life is too short. Spend your time looking for one true believer.
- Start with moonlighting to gradually build your experience, your business savvy, and your cash reserves. Build momentum in your dream and entrepreneurial careers in a gradual and orderly fashion.
- You must want security, freedom, and happiness enough to work hard for their attainment; achieving the American Dream requires you to put yourself on the line for that dream and stick with the program for as long as it takes.
- Make a list of your dreams, make a list of your needs, and develop goals that will give a means of practical expression for those dreams and a means of practical fulfillment of your needs.
- Watch the calendar, not the clock, because the mills of success grind exceedingly slowly. Success and buoyancy sneak up gradually over time, so you must position yourself for the long term. As long as you are alive, you will need a means of support, and how well your work-life web supports you will dictate your standard of living.
- To create a buoyant work life, you must look forward to setbacks as a means to your growth. Remember that the only people who never make mistakes are the people who never do anything.
- It is hardest at the beginning and gets easier once you get going. It all starts with:
  - A dream of what you want to achieve.
  - A set of deadlines, to check yourself by along the way.
  - And a To Do list of steps small enough so that one can be done every day.
- It is never too early and it is never too late to take control of your work life.
- Build a work-life plan that contains five- and ten-year goals, then break them down into yearly benchmarks, and never ever stop. Far too many people give up when they are only inches from achieving their goals. And as our research shows, people who really achieve things in life agree that whatever happens, *you should never stop short of your goals*. Never stop believing in your dream, and you'll never lose momentum.

Be happy while you're living, for you're a long time dead. —Scottish saying

about a time in my professional core-career life, during a period of respectable professional success, when I was so desperately unhappy that I hated going to work in the morning and did little more than hang on grimly, accepting mere existence as the best that could be hoped for. It soured my whole life, but it was a year before I faced up to who the real problem was: a friend you and I hold in common.

There I was, with a career and kids on the way, a ramshackle Victorian house, and membership in the local yacht club; I was in my thirties, the quintessential yuppie, driving to work crying every day. I was crying because I hated my job and everything I had worked for. Security, a little freedom, and the happiness that would bring all seemed to be within my grasp, and *you simply don't quit under these circumstances*, although I *hated my job*. It was a clear either-or choice: Either I buckled down and got on with the job, reaping success and the hell that went with it, or I quit and lost fifteen years' professional investment toward those goals. All around me people said, "Why start over when it's going so well? Everyone else seems to manage; why can't you?" Besides, there wasn't much I could do with what I'd become; I was a specialist in a specialized industry with the respect of my professional peers, but outside of that small work world of people, who knew my value? To the outside world I was a zero; how the hell could I walk away? The arguments went on for a year, with never an answer.

Yet in reality none of these self-imposed traps were what stopped me from making the job and career changes that I obviously had to make if my life was to be worth living. *Ageless Procrastination* was what stopped me, and is what will stop you if you can't recognize him when he casts his spell over you.

Building work-life buoyancy takes time, and if you don't start today in some small way, you are never going to start, because tomorrow never comes. Ever. Procrastination always comes as your wise old friend, looking out for what's best for you. His arguments are lawyer-tight, so you always listen, but Procrastination breathes a miasmic mist that hypnotizes you and conceals his true nature—he's not your friend at all, he's the greatest enemy of your life. If you make Procrastination your friend, the two of you will sit together and watch your life go by.

What face does your procrastination wear? What is stopping you from weaving your own supportive work-life web? You could be out of work and in dire financial straits and still procrastinate, because now procrasti-

---

Calm self-confidence is as far from conceit as the desire to earn a decent living is remote from greed. —Channing Pollock

nation tells you that you're hopeless anyway, a victim without blame or hope of control. This moves the story off to what things would be like if only circumstances were different. Procrastination can cripple your self-esteem, unless you act now.

The professional face Procrastination wears says there isn't time right now; there will be one day, but right now I gotta get the project finished, get a promotion, ask for that raise. I'm really busy and really focused, and I know that I'll never make it if I stop concentrating and start questioning my motives and wasting time on other stuff. Once I've got a lock on all these things here, I'll get right on with it, but first I have to achieve perfection.

Then there are your parents, and friends, and lovers, and everyone you've known longest in life, who have you nicely classified and stereotyped; they know and are comfortable with who you are now, because you are all pretty much alike. People who spend all their time with others who are pretty much like themselves are not going to get any encouragement to change, because to do so is to question the validity of the status quo.

Procrastination tells you there's not enough money to risk changing anything right now and that anything other than holding onto the way you're doing is altogether too dangerous to contemplate. Procrastination tells you that because the wages haven't been great of late, neither are you, so it's best just to hang in there. What happens when your grip slips and those glass trap doors yawn open beneath you?

You spend most of your waking hours tied up with your professional life. So much of what you see yourself to be is entwined with a professional identity. If you were to change your career, you would become an ex-whatever-it-is with no perceived value or identity. It's that stinking either-or thinking Procrastination is using on you again. One of his favorite gambits is telling you that things have to be one way or the other and that you have to be just one type of person or another; if you are going to be successful, you have to stick with one thing. You've grown up thinking it's an either-or world, and wily old Procrastination reckons you'll never recognize your limiting thinking.

Sometimes Procrastination will tell you that you don't know where you're going, so you might as well carry on doing nothing until you work it out; meanwhile let's hang with the guys. What guys? The guys who are hangin' out 'cause they don't know what to do either; Procrastination has them in a hammer lock too. Hangin' out with guys who keep their heads

---

Education is a progressive discovery of our ignorance. —Will Durant

in the sand like ostriches means you are dealing with a group who are very sensitive about looking ridiculous, and consequently get dissed very easily; they find the best defense is a good offense and neatly demean everyone unlike themselves for starters.

Procrastination will make movies just for you to watch—gripping, terrifying movies that star you, suffering humiliating rejection, crushing failure, and excruciating emotional pain. As soon as you start to build a contingency plan that makes you feel better, Procrastination pulls your attention away to another riveting horror classic. It could focus on your not-so-perfect educational background (join the club), the unknown job market, your age, and a hundred other concerns: Your family and friends may not understand, you will be frightened of the unknown, things aren't so bad as they could be right now, and you are not ready yet—you will be soon, but not yet. The excuses for letting your life be less than it can be go on and on.

No matter the face your procrastination wears, the result is the same. You end up paralyzed with cold, raw fear if you do anything but what you are doing now, when, instead, you could be opening up your life to realize your fondest imaginings of the American Dream.

All Procrastination ever gives you is excuses. He puts them all together, end-to-end, and they spell just one word: *b-u-l-l-s-h-i-n-e*. It's time to kick your act into gear. You only get one life, and it's later than you think. Please don't waste your time waiting for better things to just happen. Don't accept the status quo as the best that life has to offer.

You are already breaking the logjam by considering new approaches to new problems. You've taken a first step, and that is all it takes: just one step one day, the next day another step, and one day at a time. Start with the little things. Look in the Resources section and find a book to read; apply for membership in an association; get out your pencil or paintbrush, and just by doing so, you will have begun to paint a new picture for your work life.

You have the choice to stay in this job or get another one. You have the choice to change this core career or keep it. You have the choice to pursue an entrepreneurial or dream career, or to pursue both, or to pursue neither. You have the choice to be happy or to be sad. You have the choice to be rich or to be poor. *You have all the choices in the world.*

If you have been honest with yourself about where you stand, *Beat the Odds* can become a blueprint for the implementation of your work-life dreams, whatever they may be.

Character is a victory, not a gift. —Anonymous

Making Lemonade

When you get out there and work toward a buoyant work life in an intelligent fashion, you will come to success. But you cannot expect to come to success immediately; buoyancy is earned with time, effort, and practical know-how.

You will experience setbacks in your work life as you implement a *B.T.O.* philosophy, and it's times like these that you need to remember that Vanderbilt wouldn't back Westinghouse, calling him a fool, but Westinghouse carried on. Edison experienced 1,800 abortive attempts to develop the electric light bulb, and the Lord only knows how many more when it came to the rest of his illustrious career. When Buffington got his patents for a steel-framed skyscraper, the wise men of the day said the metal's expansion and contraction with the changing seasons would crack all the plaster off the walls.

At times like these you have to face what might stall you, and develop your tactics appropriately. You must look at what you have done well, and do more of it. Make improvements in the areas needed, and come back again for another shot and another until the setback dragons can't take your persistence anymore, and you push through to success and *your* vision of the American Dream.

When you can see where you stand, what better use is there of the one life you have than to give your dreams a practical means of expression and, perchance, fulfillment? There is none. So, instead of leading a life where underachievement is the best you can expect, let *Beat the Odds* empower you with everything you'll need to succeed in an Age of Great Opportunities.

NOTES

1. Like those of John Holland.
2. Anthony Robbins, *Awaken the Giant Within.* (New York: Fireside, 1991), page 286.
3. Labor Research Association.
4. Economic Policy Institute, 1993.
5. Joseph Mancuso is president of the Center for Entrepreneurial Management in New York and arguably the country's leading authority on the growth and management of small businesses.

Characters do not change. Opinions alter, but characters are only developed.
—Benjamin Disraeli

Appendix 1

Learning to Stay Abreast of Change: The Education Options

As all jobs become more complex, a good educational foundation is going to be more important than ever. In fact the Labor Department told us that a college degree will net you a half-million-dollar advantage over a nondegreed peer by the end of a half-century work life.

While the future is rosier for those who pursue a good education and then maintain an attitude of knowledge, it isn't going to be easy for either group. The degreed and credentialed professional workers will find themselves chasing fewer jobs with ever-escalating skill levels. The less well informed will find themselves confined to a lower working class with few ways out, as all the while more qualified people are being pushed down from above to compete for their jobs. Many of those currently gripping the lowest rung of the ladder or just straining to get a hand hold are going to lose their grip from the pressure of more qualified people being pushed down the economic work ladder in search of employment. These least fortunate will slip through a glass trapdoor into a Stygian Underclass.

So the need to reeducate yourself is not just about getting the degree you forgot, or getting another, better one. It is about staying abreast of occupational changes and coming up to speed on needed talents and behaviors. Catching up with change and then learning to stay abreast of it is going to figure in all our lives.

Education is for education's sake, the educators tell us, and our common sense says it is to help us get a decent-paying job, but there are other options.

Education is a social process . . . Education is growth . . . Education is not a preparation for life; education is life itself. —John Dewey

You don't have to use local centers of learning just to get a degree, or even to keep up to speed for work. You can use them to increase your work-life buoyancy by developing valuable entrepreneurial- and dream-career skills. As an entrepreneur without an accounting background I would be well advised to take some evening or weekend accounting courses, and I could benefit from any imaging course for my dream career (photography).

To satisfy these divergent needs of the adult in the world of education today, we have divided this section into two parts. In the first part we will talk about colleges, financing, and choosing specialties; and in the second part we'll look at how to get the best out of local institutions in order to enhance odd core-career skills and to build the skill sets you will need to improve your odds of success in your dream and entrepreneurial careers.

A NEW DEGREE, A NEW ME

A growing number of professionals are unhappy with their work and dream of trying new careers or fields. For many of us, career change becomes even more intimidating when it requires going back to college to learn a new discipline.

Whatever your age or experience, the fears about going back to college are similar: How do I get started? What if I can't remember how to study? What if I discover I don't like a subject or a professor? I work full-time; how can I fit college into my schedule? How do I pay for college? How do I juggle two careers at once? What if employers won't hire me after I graduate?

Going back to college, especially in midlife, may make you feel as though you are biting off more than you can chew. Yet the number of nontraditional, older students returning for either their first or second degree may surprise you. Today over 50 percent of the students registered for classes in the United States are at least twenty-five years old, and that percentage is growing every year, so you won't be the only older person on campus anymore.

Although rerouting your career into a healthier biome and increasing your income potential are probably your primary goals, starting over has other benefits as well.

1. Finding a job more easily than before is one advantage if you focus on a hot occupational/industrial biome. College graduates usually

Dost thou love life? Then do not squander time, for that is the stuff life is made of.
—Benjamin Franklin

have better career opportunities, more interesting work, and, as I noted earlier, can make about half a million more over their work lives than their nondegreed peer.

2. A second benefit is skill development. Say you're interested in computer programming, paralegal work, accounting, or becoming a nurse. While attending school you may balk at taking general education courses, but by concentrating in specific areas you can enhance those behaviors necessary for the ever-fluctuating career marketplace of the nineties.

3. Personal development is a third benefit of retraining. College provides the opportunities to develop your intellectual, artistic, and entrepreneurial skills. It's a time to take advantage of special-interest groups and to develop dream-career skills. Going back through college again can be intimidating ("I just can't learn like I used to"), but you will find that gradually, sometimes almost imperceivably, these "learning skills" will return and that you will develop both personally and professionally *regardless of your age.*

With a college education behind you, you will be able to communicate more effectively about a broad array of subjects, ranging from psychology to earth science. And you'll form a deeper comprehension of the connectivity of our world. If you already have a college degree, you'll gain similar benefits by getting an advanced degree.

4. But let's face it, the best reason for going back to school is that college is fun! There's nothing more thrilling than learning new things. The arts, great works of literature, painting, sculpture, dance, theater, music, and so on are like distant planets waiting to be explored. Returning to college opens doors, both metaphysically and in everyday life.

5. By combining these four benefits you get a refresher course in symbolic analysis, that all-embracing skill set so much in demand with all employees, and so important for the successful development of your entrepreneurial and dream careers.

DECIDING WHICH COLLEGE PROGRAM IS RIGHT FOR YOU

If you've made up your mind that recareering is something you need or want to do, the first question to ask is, "Which college should I attend?" Colleges are rated nationally and regionally. Your best bet is to make sure that the college or university you plan to attend is regionally and nationally accredited. This will allow for easy transfer of credits from your previ-

Fortune is ever seen accompanying industry. —Oliver Goldsmith ous degree work, and regional accreditation will increase recognition by potential employers.

The second question to ask about a potential school is, What services does the placement office offer? In other words, for my $XX,000, how prepared and committed are these people to getting me a job at the end?

American colleges vary widely in their ability and commitment to your success in the real world. So, if you ask and get fobbed off with all that early-twentieth-century pap about "education for education's sake," remember why you are visiting in the first place: to recareer.

The services your school offers should range from career counselors, resume and placement services, and computers, to both regional and national job listings, and so on. Make sure you find out how many companies recruit on campus every year and the placement rate of both graduating students and alumni. In today's marketplace, where the average four-year college education costs either the student or our government $88,000, "knowledge for knowledge's sake" is only for the independently wealthy.

If a college isn't willing to provide enough services to help you in your effort to recareer, give your business to a school that is! Much of American academia is dragging its feet in commitment to the practicalities of modern work life. As a rule of thumb, the more the placement or career-planning office tells you in specifics, the more committed they are.

Here's a listing of the job opportunities that are available to you upon completion of a bachelor's degree:

Industry Biomes and Corresponding Job Opportunities	
• Accounting	International Accountant, Tax Accountant Auditor (both Financial and Operations), Environmental Accountant, Forensic Accountant, International Tax, Audit Accountant.
• Biotechnology	Molecular Biologist, Organic Chemist, Computational Chemist, Ecologist, Geneticist, Biochemist, Nuclear Medicine Technologist, Protein Chemist, Occupational Chemist.

Failures are divided into two classes—those who thought and never did, and those who did and never thought. —John Charles Salak

• Computers	Software Developer, Computer Systems Analyst, Computer Programmer, Consultant, Information Services (I. S.) Manager, Network Administrator, Database Manager, Software Developer, Systems Integrator, Systems Management Specialist, Systems Analyst, Computer Consultant, Information Systems Analyst, Information Systems Specialist, Peripheral Equipment Operator.
• Engineering	Civil Engineer, Computer Scientist, Electrical Engineer, Electronics Engineer, Chemical Engineer, Mechanical Engineer, Biomedical Engineer.
• Environment	Environmental Manager, Environmental Engineer, Ecotourism, Environmental Law, Public Relations Professional (for energy companies and other firms that impact on the ecology), Waste-Management Expert, Environmental Scientist Specialist/Ecopreneur, Green Marketing Manager, Ecological Scientist/Biologist/Earth Scientist, Fund-raiser, Environmental Lawyer, Environmental Educator and Communicator, Recreation Wildlife and Natural Resource Manager, Geographical Information Systems Specialist, Toxicologist, Air-Quality Specialist, Recycling Coordinator, Environmental Specialist.
• Federal Government and Defense	Technician, Repairer, Communications and Intelligence Specialist, Officer in Administrative Services, Medical and Dental Specialist, Aircraft Pilot, Infantry Officer, Program and Project Manager.
• Finance	Investment Professional, Environmental Accountant, Forensic Accountant, International Tax, Audit Accountant, Financial Planner, Currency Trader, Financial Service Sales Rep, Auditor, Loan-Workout Specialist, Securities and Financial Services Representative.
• Food Service	Restaurant-Site Selector, Training Manager, Convention Services Manager, Front Office Manager, Food and Beverage Manager

Education is that which discloses to the wise and disguises from the foolish their lack of understanding.—Ambrose Bierce

• Foreign Trade	Specialists in all aspects of Global Trade, Import-Export, Sales/Purchasing, and Marketing Management.
• Health Care	Medical Assistant, Radiological Technologist, Medical Record Technician, Physical Therapist, Medical Secretary, Occupational Therapist, Physical Therapist, Surgical Technologist, Podiatrist, Dispensing Optician, Nurse Practitioner, Integrated-Care Deliverer, Nurse Anesthetist, Home Health Nurse, Family Physician, Geneticist, General Surgeon, Adult and Child Psychiatrist, Health Service Manager, Podiatrist. *Physicians:* Internist, Geriatric, and Preventive Medicine. *Dentistry:* Orthodontist, Oral and Maxio-Facial Surgeon, Pediatric Dentistry, Prosthodontics. *Nursing:* Intensive Care, Medical-Surgical, Rehabilitation and Geriatric-Care Specialist, Health Designer/Architect, Home Health Care Specialist, Managed-Health-Care Manager, Radiological Technologist, EEG Technologist, Respiratory Therapist, Registered Nurse, Licensed Practical Nurse, Recreational Therapist, Nursing Aide, Psychiatric Aide.
• Human Resources	Training Manager; Alternative-Dispute-Resolution Practitioner; Diversity Manager; Labor Relations, Benefits, and Compensations Manager; Director of Training; Employee Assistance Program Manager; Human Resources Manager; Employment Interviewer; Specialists in Human Resources, Corporate Training, Pensions, Union Negotiations, and Drug, Gerontology, and Day Care Programs.
• Insurance	Actuary, Underwriter.
• Law	Intellectual Property Manager, Paralegal, Lawyer, Judge, Litigator, Environmental Lawyer, International Lawyer, Specialist in Tax Law and Elder Law, Bankruptcy Attorney, Employment Attorney, Ombudsman.

Everything comes to him who hustles while he waits. —Thomas Edison

• Manufacturing/Trade	Chief Information Officer, Quality Control Manager, Manufacturing Engineer, Statistical Control Specialist.
• Marketing	Market Researcher, International Marketer, Information Specialist, Fifty-Plus Marketer, Home Entertainment Marketer.
• Media/Communication	Corporate Public Relations Director; Technical and Production Specialists at Radio and Television Stations, Newspapers, Magazines, and Newsletters. *Publishing:* Electronic Publishing Specialist, Database Manager, Technical Writer, Technically Trained Personnel (including Engineers, Systems Analysts, Technicians).
• Nonprofit Organizations	Member Services Director; Fund-raising/Planned-Giving Manager; Manager in Skilled Sales, Marketing, or Public Relations.
• Public Relations	Public Relations Specialist, Publicity Writer.
• Retail	Merchandise Manager, Sales Associate, Manager of Mall Marketing and Promotion, Cashier, Retail Sales Worker.
• Sales/Marketing	Industrial and Technical Sales—particularly Pharmaceutical and Medical Equipment Sales, Service Sales Representative.
• Social Services	Social Worker, Human Services Worker, Adult Education Teacher, Counselor, Social Welfare Service Aide.
• State & Local Government	Government Chief Executive and Legislator; Tax Examiner; Urban and Regional Planner; Judge, Magistrate, and other Judicial Workers; Police Officer; Firefighter; Wastewater Treatment Plant Operator.
• Telecommunications	Corporate Communications Manager, Sales Representative, Systems Analyst, Regulatory Compliance Administrator, Telecommunications Manager, Wireless Specialist.

Fortune is a great deceiver. She sells very dear the things she seems to give us.
—Vincent Voiture

| • Travel | Aircraft Pilot, Travel Agent, Flight Attendant, Aircraft Mechanic, Hotel Manager, Reservation and Transportation Ticket Agent, Travel Clerk. |
| • Miscellaneous Careers | Artist, Inventor, Musician, Photographer, Writer. |

YOUR TIME COMMITMENTS

Unfortunately the overwhelming amount of choices, including whether you'll attend day, evening, or weekend classes on a full- or part-time basis, drives away many potential students. Don't get discouraged. Deciding is a lot simpler than it looks.

A four-year college degree will require you to complete about 120 credits. One credit equals an hour of class time each week on the semester system. There are two semesters per year. Most classes are three credit hours. For example a three-credit course might require class attendance Monday, Wednesday, and Friday for an hour each day. Some night classes meet only once a week for three hours in a marathon session. There are also three-credit courses that meet twice a week, for an hour and a half each time.

A course load of twelve credits or more is considered a full-time schedule. Your schedule for evening part-time study should be filled with no more than six to nine credits. That's two or three classes per semester. You can figure twelve to eighteen hours of homework with such a class load, so be careful if you're working a forty-hour week. This will mean you've allocated fifty-eight to sixty-seven hours of your week.

If you want to attend classes on a full-time basis, the total hours per week spent in earning your degree will average between thirty-six and fifty-four. You can take between four and six classes per semester to graduate in four years. Figure on twelve to eighteen hours of classroom instruction, with twenty-four to thirty-six hours of assigned homework outside of class for that course load.

Colleges usually try to meet the needs of working people. So if the idea of becoming a full-time student is appealing but impracticable, consider the following six alternatives:

Education is too important to be left solely to the educators. —Francis Keppel

1. Evening classes—the traditional method to recareer and earn degrees entirely by part-time study.

2. Weekend classes—marathon all-day class sessions on the weekends allow students to work at a job forty hours a week while earning their degrees; total time spent is about the same as any conventional full-time study.

3. Cooperative work-study—students gain valuable career experience and earn a large part of college costs while working their way through college with an employer who tailors the work hours to an adapted educational schedule.

4. Correspondence coursework—permits at-home independent study but provides more structure and teacher guidance than in completely independent study programs.

5. Day classes—the traditional method of getting a degree by attending class during the day on a full or part-time basis.

6. Life-experience credit—students earn credit that they can apply toward a degree through tests that evaluate work experience, prior learning, or independent study.

7. On-line courses—course work is assigned and completed via a computer network while in the comfort of your own home.

ALTERNATIVES TO THE FOUR-YEAR DEGREE

If you're planning to change careers, but don't want to spend four years doing so, an associate degree, which takes two years, may be right for you. Associate programs are offered by most four-year and community colleges. They comprise a variety of programs that are a relatively inexpensive and effective way to learn a new profession or enhance skills in an existing one. Here are just a few of the programs offered:

Associate Degrees	
• Accountant's assistant	• Draftsman
• Bookkeeper	• Electronics technician
• Business administration aide	• EMT (emergency medical technician) paramedic
• Computer operator	• Health care technician
• Dental assistant	• Lawyer's assistant
• Dental hygienist	• Medical record technician

Freedom is not worth having if it does not connote freedom to err.
—Mahatma Gandhi

- Nurse's assistant
- Occupational therapy assistant
- Paralegal
- Physical therapy assistant
- Physician's assistant
- Radiation therapy technologist
- Real estate agent
- Receptionist
- Respiratory therapy technician
- Salesperson
- Secretary, legal, medical, or business
- Stenographer
- Surgical technician
- Surveyor
- Ultrasound technician
- Word-processing specialist
- X-ray technician
- Junior programmer

Once you have decided on a possible major and schedule, and selected a few colleges in your area that sound interesting, you will have to request more information from the institutions. Colleges and universities will gladly send you general information about the school without charge so call them or write them a letter. If you are interested in a detailed course book, it will cost between two and three dollars.

GETTING THE INFORMATION YOU NEED

Use the literature to narrow down your choices. Then call the admissions offices at each school that makes the cut to find out if they offer a schedule that fits your needs. They can give you the name of an admissions counselor for new students who will be able to answer any questions you may have about starting out or returning to school. Start off by introducing yourself:

"Hello, my name is Karen and I'm interested in what programs your college/university might offer to adult students. I work full-time and need to take evening or weekend classes. Can you explain the different programs to me?" When they describe a program that sounds interesting to you, say, "I'd like to discuss your evening programs in more detail and take a tour of the campus. When is the best time to schedule a visit?"

Depending on the school, an interview may or may not be required for admission. Either way an interview can be a great opportunity to get additional, firsthand information. So after you have arranged your trip, make a list of questions pertinent to your real-world needs and restrictions. Bring them with you, and don't be shy about asking anything you need clarified; most colleges and universities are staffed with friendly professionals who are eager to help. *But do not ever let admissions answer questions about career planning and placement;* get that from the proverbial horse's mouth.

Genius begins great works; labor alone finishes them. —Joseph Joubert

HOW DO I PAY FOR IT?

The financial aid office should be one of your stops on a tour of the college, or one of your first phone calls. You will be surprised by the amount of financial help that is available. Our nation spends an estimated $100 billion for education annually, and the Fed subsidizes $39.7 billion of that. Ask the financial aid office for the brochure, "Financing Your Education: A Guide to Scholarships and Financial Aid." It explains the different types of financial aid available.

Also, call the Federal Student Aid Information Center at 1-800-333-INFO. They will send you, "The Student Guide: Financial Aid from the U.S. Department of Education" and "Five Federal Financial Aid Programs." These booklets give you important information, including helpful phone numbers and addresses.

Scholarships and Grants

There are need- and merit-based scholarships and grants. Scholarships are usually based on your academic grade-point average, while grants are usually based on financial need. There are also special programs for minority students, as well as federally based college study programs.

Unless absolutely necessary, *don't borrow.* For those people who don't want to spend the rest of their life indebted, the general thinking is to get money that you don't have to repay.

Here are a few of the grants and scholarships available:

Federal Financial Aid		
Pell Grants	SEOG (Supplemental Educational Opportunity Grants)	CWS (College Work Study)
For undergraduates only	For undergraduates only	For undergraduates and graduates
Grant—no repayment	Grant—no repayment	Provides jobs on or off campus
Maximum award depends on program funding	For students with exceptional financial need—priority given to Pell Grant recipients	

A man's life is interesting primarily when he has failed—I well know. For it's a sign that he tried to surpass himself. —Georges Clemenceau

Maximum for 1995–96— $2,340	Maximum award—$4,000, depending in part on funds available at each school	Amount earned can't exceed need
Must apply no later than May 1, 1995–96	Schools set deadlines for applying	Schools set deadlines for applying
Students receive payment by submitting Student Aid Report (SAR) to school by deadline—paid directly or school account is credited	Students paid directly or school account is credited	Undergraduates paid by the hour; graduates paid by salary or by the hour; all students paid at least monthly

Perkins Loans	Stafford Loans (Formally Guaranteed Student Loans)	PLUS/SLS Loans (Supplemental Loans for Students)
Interest rate—5%	For new borrowers—8% interest rate for the first 4 years of repayment, 10% thereafter	Variable interest rates
For undergraduates and graduates	For undergraduates and graduates	PLUS-parents borrow for children; SLS: for all student borrowers
Maximum awards vary, depending in part on year in school	Maximum awards vary, depending in part on year in school	Up to $4,000 a year to a maximum of $20,000
School makes the loan, and sets its own deadlines for applying	Lender (bank, credit union, etc.) makes the loan. No deadline for applying, but students should apply as soon as possible	Lender (bank, credit union etc.) makes the loan. No deadline for applying, but parents/students should apply as soon as possible
Students must sign a promissory note agreeing to repay	Students must sign a promissory note agreeing to repay	Borrowers must sign a promissory note agreeing to repay

Genius is an infinite capacity for taking life by the scruff of the neck.
—Christopher Quill

The school and the U.S. Department of Education will collect from students who default	The lender and the guarantee agency will collect from students who default	The lender and the guarantee agency will collect from students who default
Under certain conditions, loan may be deferred or repayment canceled	Under certain conditions, loan may be deferred; Loan repayment can be canceled only for total and permanent disability or death	Deferments: PLUS–limited, apply to principal only; SLS—same as Stafford, but apply to principal only
		Repayment cancellation: only for total and permanent disability or death

From *The Student Guide to Financial Aid from the U. S. Department of Education.*

Here's the financial-aid-application process: Pick up a Financial Aid Form (FAF) and any paperwork you need at the financial aid office of your local college or call 1-800-433-3243 for a form. There's a minimal fee (under twenty dollars) for filing. For special financial needs the fee can be waived. Once you're accepted at a college, talk to the financial aid office about your options.

Submit all your forms early to the address on the form or to the college. Apply as soon after January 1st as possible, as some awards are given away on a first-come-first-served basis until the money runs out. You'll need a copy of your 1040 tax return to complete the information.

When the FAF filing process is complete, you'll receive, in about six weeks, a form from the College Scholarship Service (CSS). You then send this form to your college financial aid office where your awards will be calculated and processed. The college will then send you an award letter itemizing the different amounts you can expect to receive that semester as well as the total for the year.

Great discoveries and improvements invariably involve the cooperation of many minds. I may be given credit for having blazed the trail but when I look at the subsequent developments I feel the credit is due to others rather than to myself. —Alexander Graham Bell

Working Your Way Through College

College work-study programs are the new rage on campuses across the United States. They allow you to work and attend college at the same time. The programs are offered by most colleges and allow a student to complete a degree while gaining work experience and credits for working. The minimum pay is generally seven dollars per hour. Co-op programs are similar in nature, but offer a semester of work and then a semester of study. Talk to your financial aid officer to see if you're eligible, or go through the placement office to obtain a co-op work-study assignment. It's a good combination of the practical and the theoretical, and with the degree in hand you will have the practical equivalent of one to two years experience that you can expect to be reflected in your salary.

Seventeen Ways to Beat the Recareering Odds

You are not going to have enough time to work and go through college unless you maximize every moment. Effective time management can move mountains! Here are seventeen tips we compiled for adults who successfully recareer through school, to help you maximize the impact of your study hours. They're nothing flashy, but the people we spoke to swear by them.

1. *Silence is golden and make it so!* Turn off the TV set and the radio. There are some geniuses who can study Jung's theory of synchronicity while watching *Deep Space Nine*, but for most of us it's a distraction, and the media wins.

2. *Make a list of your study goals.* While we all make mental lists for ourselves, it's easier to plan your day on paper. As you complete each task on the list, cross it off. You gain a great sense of accomplishment from checking off tasks once they're completed. Put the most difficult tasks first on the list, because you'll have a better chance of getting them done. Carry your daily planner around with you at all times.

3. *Know when to communicate.* Come to an agreement with your housemates about when you can and can't be disturbed. Write down the rules—you can even have all parties sign a contract. Recareering through college is a major investment of your life and money, and you won't succeed without the cooperation of everyone in the household. Agree when it's okay to play the TV or radio in the house and who does what chores when. Study time needs to be regulated as well.

Happiness is not a destination. It is a method of life. —Burton Hills

4. *Return calls; don't make them or take them.* Set aside a time every day when you call everyone back. People will understand and admire your focus.

5. *Just say no.* Learn to say no when asked to do something while you're on the studying clock. While friends and family members usually don't mean any harm, they can be very distracting.

6. *Do not disturb.* Put a Do Not Disturb sign on your door when you're working. If you don't have a door, put it on the back of your chair.

7. *If.you have kids, use the campus day-care center.* Many campuses have day-care centers, which are staffed by students in elementary education or qualified community members. These facilities are usually free to students or are subsidized to keep the costs low. Your children will be within walking distance from you and in an excellent educational environment.

8. *Budget two hours' study time for every hour you spend in class.* If you are taking fifteen credit hours, plan to spend thirty hours a week studying. The maturity that comes with work experience can make the load a bit easier.

9. *Study during your best time of day.* It doesn't matter if you are a morning glory or an evening shade. Work when it's best for you, and if need be, challenge yourself to change for the better. Remember, many successful students and business people begin their day at five A.M., while the rest of the world is asleep.

10. *Take the big one on first.* Tackle the big problems and tasks when your energy is high. Never start with little jobs, because if you do, you will never get into the big jobs. Organize your study time most effectively by studying the most difficult or tedious subjects first, while you're fresh. The toughest subjects need our most creative attention. Besides, saving the best for last gives us something to look forward to.

11. *Change your schedule if need be.* If you find you are avoiding studying a certain subject, try a schedule change. Instead of studying in the evening, try getting up an hour earlier to study that subject. Once the task is out of the way, the rest of the day will be a breeze. If you encounter a pattern of task avoidance, review the context of the behavior; you might discover that one course is a potential trouble zone for you. So get some help from a professor, school counselor, or faculty advisor. You are not the first to face the problem, so there will be plenty of options to help you work through the block.

Great souls have wills; feeble ones have only wishes. —*Chinese saying*

12. *Avoid scheduling marathon study sessions.* Pulling all-nighters is a sign of the emotional immaturity and lack of organizational skills of a first-timer. When possible, study sessions should be short drills. Three-hour sessions are far more productive for most of us than eight- to twelve-hour sessions. There is a limit to our short-term memory's capacity—so develop the emotional maturity to recognize the signs of mental exhaustion, and adapt your study needs to your mental and physical capabilities.

13. *Use your off-time.* Most of us spend a lot of our day in lines or waiting. The bus doesn't arrive for a half hour, there are ten people ahead of you in line at the grocery store, and your doctor's office looks like a Howard Stern book signing. Although it may sound obsessive, add up how much of your day you're wasting and use that time to your advantage.

For example you can carry with you 3" x 5" index cards that contain class notes or information you need to memorize, or you can complete homework for another class. The point is, if you have a few extra minutes, you can find a way to spend them productively.

14. *Form alliances.* The first thing to do when you get into a new class is to form alliances. Some professors make this easier by passing around a class phone list, or by encouraging students to exchange phone numbers independently with other students. Write the numbers down in the front of your notebook for that class. This will enable you to get notes and homework assignments for missed classes. It will also allow you to form study groups. Studying for a difficult subject is much easier in a group, especially when you limit the group to no more than a handful of students. That way everyone has a chance to contribute.

15. *Use the library.* All libraries have desks and private study areas. The buildings are well lighted, and stacks of study materials are at your fingertips.

16. *Use a quiet, routine study area.* Your study area should be comfortable, well lighted, and above all quiet. Going to your study area should be like going to your office or studio. It is a place to read and think and learn, a place to create and achieve. Make it businesslike, but also comfortable and pleasant. This is where you plan your great campaigns.

17. *Complete one last task.* Yes, it's late and you have had a long day, but have you asked yourself if there is one more thing you can do? Think of something small. Little things add up over time and can eventually increase your overall endurance and effectiveness. Always try to do some little last thing today to get a jump start on tomorrow.

Happiness is not a reward—it is a consequence. Suffering is not a punishment—it is a result. —Robert Green Ingersoll

Appendix 2

When a Layoff Can Pay Off

A company that respects its severance responsibilities is one that will always be welcome in any community. And it is one that, by inference, will develop the invaluable reputation of reliability and responsibility in the fiercely competitive global marketplace.

Severance and out-placement packages are gradually becoming the norm, and it is now acceptable for you to inquire about such matters when you are considering employment with a company (but only *after* an offer has been formally placed on the table). In fact it is important to your career buoyancy that when you are making employment decisions, you evaluate career planning and out-placement assistance/policy along with the other benefits. An increasing number of employers are recognizing the importance of these considerations and are developing some almost-reasonable plans.

WHEN IT COULD BENEFIT YOU TO OFFER TO BE LAID OFF

There is, and will be, a window of opportunity for those people whose entrepreneurial preparedness allows them to seize the moment when the clouds of restructuring gather on their company horizon. Maybe there's a franchise you've been giving serious consideration to for a while now, or maybe that basement business is bursting the walls just from your moonlighting efforts. Either way, you might look at ways to leverage the policy to your specific needs.

What a good thing Adam had—when he said a good thing, he knew nobody had said it before.—Mark Twain

A company would always far rather have a resignation than a layoff; it's less damaging public-relations wise, and it's less costly. In the best of all possible worlds, the more money and higher up your title is, the better the company will appreciate an offer of early retirement, as this allows them to retire a high-level title and replace an expensive worker with technology and a cheaper worker. Given these circumstances, which are likely to come to most of us at some time in our careers, here are a couple of opportunities for negotiating and further customizing the plan to your needs.

If you have an entrepreneurial endeavor that's been carefully considered, perhaps you don't need the out-placement part of the plan, for which your employer typically spends about $1,500 for every $10,000 of salary you earn. So you can ask for the cash value to be applied somewhere else, or rendered to you in cash.

If you are very close to retirement, you could ask for the value of that part of the program you don't need to perhaps be applied toward additional years of service.

You will find timing to be *everything* in negotiating voluntary severance. Once the layoffs and the plan have been announced, the employer's flexibility necessarily decreases. If, however, you implement this advice intelligently and in a timely fashion, there is a good chance you can come out ahead and look like an all-around good guy for saving the hide of some less-prepared colleagues.

With good career planning, taking advantage of pending layoffs can be an opportunity for enhanced further relations. I know one human-resources professional who had a thriving technical-writing business on the side. She was able to leave not only with a sweetened severance package but also with her first client, whose business largely paid the bills for her first year in business. Smart girl.

Another professional saw the writing on the industry wall—that his was one of those areas likely to be outsourced. He thought and investigated and strategized, and when the clouds began to gather over his corporate horizon, he struck. He had put together a plan that had as its centerpiece the outsourcing of his entire department's functions, eliminating the need for himself and his entire staff. The beautiful part was that the proposal, itemizing cost savings and other competitive benefits, would be implemented by *him*.

Whatever necessity lays upon thee, endure: whatever she commands, do.
—Johann Wolfgang von Goethe

His team reinvented itself as a company with "best-in-the-world" abilities" within the niche environment. Smart boy.

There are also those occasions when a core careerist may recognize there is a "best in the world" entrepreneurial opportunity and, at the same time, a personal lack of business or entrepreneurial know-how. In this instance the careerist will plan personal-development and next-career moves to turn his or her identified weaknesses into strengths.

However, we must all be warned that the job you hate but have in the hand is not one to be summarily dumped, the way it might have been just a few short years ago. New jobs, and good jobs in new careers, are far from easy goals to achieve in this day and age, as are the rooting of successful entrepreneurial endeavors. For most of us this is first a time of important reappraisal and defensive actions that will help improve our long-term career buoyancy. For us the first job is to get a clear understanding of where the "irreducible core" within our companies is located, and then find out how the hell to get there.

Every man is the architect of his own fortune. —Sallust

Appendix 3

Law in a Box: Work-for-Hire and Nondisclosure Agreements

THE WORK-FOR-HIRE AGREEMENT

The work-for-hire agreement is an agreement in which one party hires another party to do something specific. As defined by the Copyright Act, it is:

> 1) a work prepared by an employee within the scope of his or her employment; or 2) a work specifically ordered or commissioned for use as a contribution to a collective work, as part of a motion picture or other audiovisual work, as a translation, as a supplementary work, as a compilation, as an instructional text, as a test, as answer material for a test, or as an atlas, if the parties expressly agree in a written instrument signed by them that the work shall be considered a work made for hire. [Blacks Law Dictionary]

There are certain types of commissioned works that are automatically treated as works-made-for-hire. These are

- Contributions to a collective work.
- Works specifically ordered or commissioned.
- Contributions to a movie or audiovisual work.
- Translations.
- Supplementary works. These include works that are somehow auxiliary to the main work, such as an illustration, a map or chart, editorial notes, a musical arrangement, a bibliography, a forward, or an index. These are considered supplementary only if they are subordinate to the main work.

When a man has no reason to trust himself, he trusts in luck. —Ed Howe

- Compilations. These include works that are created by collecting and assembling data or preexisting materials—for example an anthology or a hotel guide.
  - Instructional texts, such as a test, or answers to a test.
  - Atlases.

Work-for-hire contracts should include: the date the agreement is signed; the hiring party's name and address; the consultant's name and address; a statement of facts covering the specific work ordered or commissioned; the law (the Copyright Act); the dollar value or consideration for the work to be performed; a space for the hiring party's signature; and a space for the consultant's signature.

The first paragraph of the contract should state what both parties are agreeing to and the legal guidelines to which both parties are in agreement. The U.S. Copyright Act should also be stated. The consultant will assign (or relinquish) any and all rights, including copyright, of his or her work.

The next paragraph of the contract should specify ownership of the work- or works-made-for-hire. It should state who owns the specific work(s); the geographic location where these works are owned; the hiring parties' right to revise, modify, or edit the work(s); what the hiring party can do to exploit the work(s); who receives compensation from the exploitation of the work(s); and the name in which the copyright will be registered.

The last paragraph should explain the payment agreed upon for the work(s)-for-hire. A consultant who signs the agreement has agreed to be paid a onetime fee for a contribution to a specific work(s) and has relinquished all rights to any further payment, financial consideration, ownership, or copyright. These agreements are valid for the life of the work(s).

Sample Work-for-hire Agreement

Agreement dated as of this _____ day of _____, 1994, by and between (hiring party's name and address), and (consultant's name and address).

  The parties hereto hereby agree as follows:

When a true genius appears in this world you may know him by the sign that the dunces are all in confederacy against him. —Jonathan Swift

1) It is agreed that all of the results and proceeds of Consultant's services hereunder are works-for-hire within the meaning of the U.S. Copyright Act. If it is determined that the works are not or may not be considered works-made-for-hire, then Consultant hereby assigns to (hiring party) any and all rights, including copyright, Consultant may have with respect to the works.

2) The results and proceeds of Consultant's services hereunder, from inception of their creation, shall be entirely the property of (hiring party), in perpetuity, throughout the world, under copyright and otherwise, free of any claim whatsoever by Consultant. (Hiring party) shall have the right to (a) revise, modify, or otherwise alter and edit the works prepared hereunder as (hiring party), in his sole discretion, deems appropriate; (b) utilize and exploit the works prepared hereunder in any manner or media as (hiring party) determines in his sole discretion without additional compensation or obligation to Consultant; and (c) register the copyright in any works prepared hereunder in (hiring party's) name or in the name of his designee or assignee and to secure any and all renewals and extensions thereof and generally to exercise all worldwide rights afforded by the copyright laws of the world to copyright owners, without limitation or restriction.

3) In consideration of your services hereunder as well as the rights granted by Consultant, (hiring party) shall pay to Consultant (_____ dollars) per hour/project.

Please confirm that the foregoing is in accordance with your understanding.

_____

(hiring party's signature)

Accepted and Agreed:

_____

(consultant's signature)

NONDISCLOSURE AGREEMENT

The nondisclosure agreement is an agreement in which one party hires someone to perform a service and contractually requests that any part of the related business not be discussed with the outside world. Nondisclo-

---

He who can no longer pause to wonder and stand rapt in awe, is as good as dead; his eyes are closed. —Albert Einstein

sure agreements are used in preliminary discussions prior to one party entering into a contract with another party.

The agreement should include: the date the agreement is signed; the hiring party's name and address; the consultant's name and address; a statement of facts covering the specific work not to be discussed or disclosed outside the company; the law; a space for the hiring party's signature; and a space for the consultant's.

The first paragraph of the contract should specify: the work, products, patents, marketing, finances, contacts, customers, equipment, and other related matters to be included in the category of "not to be disclosed in discussions with anyone."

The second paragraph should specify the information not to be disclosed without prior written approval of the hiring party or the consultant.

The third paragraph is a disclaimer paragraph, for the protection of the consultant, where information specified in the contract was discussed because:

- The information was in the consultant's possession prior to the date the contract was signed or prior to the information being given to the consultant. (You should not have to hold in confidence company information that is publicly available or becomes publicly available by any other means.)
- The information was already in the public domain through no fault of the consultant's.
- The information was given to the consultant prior to the signing of this agreement and was disclosed by a third party who has the authorization to disclose the information.

The fourth paragraph is a termination clause, stating the limited time zone of the contract.

There should be spaces for signatures and acceptance of the agreement. A consultant who signs the agreement has agreed to not speak of any information specified as company private to anyone during the duration of the agreement.

He who has imagination without learning has wings and no feet. —Joseph Joubert

Sample Nondisclosure Agreement

I would like to freely discuss the possibility of our business relationship that may involve disclosure of information about and discussions regarding products, patents, marketing, finances, contracts, equipment, and other related company private matters (the Information) without the fear of release or disclosure of the Information and related discussions to any other persons or entities. For that reason I would like to set forth our agreement regarding disclosure of the Information so that there is no misunderstanding.

You will not directly or indirectly, for yourself or on behalf of, or in conjunction with any other person, persons, firm, partnership, corporation, or company disclose to any person, persons, firms, partnership, corporation, any of the Information without my written prior approval.

The restrictions on the disclosure and use shall not apply to any Information, as the case may be, which you can show: (a) was in your possession prior to its receipt from me; (b) is, or hereafter becomes, part of the public domain through no fault of yours; or (c) is obtained by you from a third party who has the right to disclose the same.

In any event, the obligations assumed by you shall terminate three (3) years from the date of this Agreement, or in the event the exchange of Information is of a continuing nature, three (3) years from the date of the last disclosure made by me to you.

I may request in writing the return of any Information sent to you and shall return this Information in your possession within ten (10) days from the receipt of such request.

_____

(contracting party's signature)

Agreed and Accepted:

_____

(consultant's signature)

Where there's a will, there's a lawsuit. —Addison Mizner

Core Career Resource References

GENERAL DIRECTORIES

The Almanac of American Government Jobs and Careers
Ronald L. Krannich
and Caryl Rae Krannich
Impact Publications
9104-N Manassas Drive
Manassas Park, VA
22111-5211
(703)361-7300

The Almanac of International Jobs and Careers
Same as above

The American Almanac of Jobs and Salaries
John W. Wright
Avon Books
P.O. Box 767
Dreden, TN 38225
(800) 238-0658

American Business Information
5711 South 86th Circle
P.O. Box 27347
Omaha, NE 68127
(800) 316-7601

America's Fastest Growing Employers
Carter Smith
Bob Adams Inc.
260 Center Street
Holbrook, MA 02343
(800) 872-5627

American Society of Training and Development: Who's Who in Training and Development
1640 King Street, Box 1443
Alexandria, VA
22313-2043
(703) 683-8100

Best Jobs for the 1990s and into the 20th Century
Ronald L. Krannich

and Caryl Rae Krannich
Impact Publications
9104-N Manassas Drive
Manassas Park, VA
22111-5211
(703) 361-7300

The Black Resource Guide
Black Resource Guide, Inc.
501 Oneida Place, NW
Washington, DC 20111
(202) 291-4373

Business Information Sources
Lorna M. Daniels
CPFS
1485 Lower Ferry Road
Ewing, NJ 08616
(609) 883-1759

The Career Advisory Series: Advertising, Book Publishing, Business and Finance, Healthcare, Magazine Publishing, Marketing and Sales,

---

Where there's a will, there's a way. —English saying

Newspaper Publishing,
Public Relations, Radio
and Television, Travel
and Hospitality
Gale Research, Inc.
835 Penobscot Building
Detroit, MI 48226-4094
(800) 877-4253

Careers Encyclopedia
National Textbook
Craig T. Norback
4255 West Touhy Avenue
Lincolnwood, IL
60646-1975
(800) 323-4900

Contacts Influential:
Metro Business Directory
Contacts Influential
Market Research and
Development Services
5711 South 86 Circle
Omaha, NE 68127
(415) 431-1571

Corporate and Industry
Reports
R.R. Bowker/
Martindale-Hubbell
121 Chanlon Road
New Providence, NJ
07974

Corptech Directory of
Technology Companies
Corptech, Inc.
12 Alfred Street,
Suite 200
Woburn, MA
01801-9998
(617) 932-3939

Dictionary of
Occupational Titles
U.S. Department
of Labor
U.S. Government
Printing Office
Superintendent of
Documents
P.O. Box 371954
Pittsburgh, PA 15250-7954
(202) 512-1800

Directory of American
Research and Technology:
Organizations Active in
Product Development
for Business
R.R. Bowker/
Martindale-Hubbell
121 Chanlon Road
New Providence, NJ
07974
(908) 464-6800

Directory of Corporate
Affiliations
A. Reed Reference
Publishing Co.
121 Chanlon Road
New Providence, NJ
07974
(800) 323-6772

Directory of Leading
Private Companies,
National Register
Publishing Company
Macmillan Directory
Division
121 Chanlon Road
New Providence, NJ 07974
(800) 323-6772

Directory of Overseas
Summer Jobs
Emily Hatchwell
Peterson's Guides, Inc.
P.O. Box 2123
Princeton, NJ 08543
(800) 338-3282

Directory of Special
Libraries and Information
Centers
Gale Research, Inc.
835 Penobscot Building
Detroit, MI 48226-4096
(800) 877-4253

Encyclopedia of
Associations
Same as above

Encyclopedia of Business
Information Sources
Same as above

Encyclopedia of Careers
and Vocational Guidance
William Hopke
J. G. Ferguson Publishing
Company
200 W. Madison Street,
3rd Floor
Chicago, IL 60606
(312) 580-5480

GOE Enhanced
Marilyn Maze
MN Verndale
JIST Works, Inc.
720 N. Park Avenue
Indianapolis, IN
46202-3431
(800) 648-5478

Give a man a fish and you feed him for a day. Teach a man to fish and you feed him
for a lifetime. —Chinese saying

*Hoover's Handbook of
American Business*
Gary Hoover,
Alta Campbell, and
Patrick J. Spain
The Reference Press
6448 Highway 290E.,
Suite E-104
Austin, TX 78723
(800) 486-8666

*Hoover's Handbook of
Emerging Companies*
Patrick J. Spain, Alta
Campbell, and Alan Chai
Same as above

*Hoover's Handbook of
World Business*
Alan Chai, Alta Campbell,
and Patrick J. Spain
Same as above

*How to Reach Anyone
Who's Anyone*
Michael Levine
Price/Stern/Sloan
P.O. Box 506
East Rutherford, NJ 07073
(800) 631-8571

*How to Read a Financial
Report: Wringing Cash
Flow and Other Vital
Signs Out of the Numbers*
John A. Tracy, CPA
John Wiley & Sons
Business Law/General
Books Division
1 Wiley Drive
Somerset, NJ 08875
(800) 225-5945

*Information Industry
Directory*
Gale Research, Inc.
835 Penobscot Building
Detroit, MI 48226-4094
(800) 877-4253

*International Business
Travel and Relocation
Directory*
Same as above

*Job Hotlines USA, The
National Telephone
Directory of Employer
Joblines*
Career Communications
Inc.
298 Main Street
P.O. Box 169
Harleysville, PA 19438
(215) 256-3130

*Job Hunter's Sourcebook:
Where to Find
Employment Leads and
Other Job Search Resources*
Michelle LeCompte
Gale Research, Inc.
835 Penobscot Building
Detroit, MI 48226-4094
(800) 877-4253

*Job Seeker's Guide to
Private and Public
Companies*
Same as above

MacRae's Blue Book
Business Research
Publications, Inc.
65 Bleecker Street

New York, NY 10012
(800) 622-7237

*Minority Organizations:
A National Directory*
Garrett Park Press
Box 190
Garrett Park, MD 20896
(302) 946-2553

*National Directory of
Minority Owned Business
Firms*
Gale Research Inc.
835 Penobscot Building
Detroit, MI 48226-4094
(800) 877-4253

*National Directory of
Women Owned Business
Firms*
Same as above

The National Job Bank
Bob Adams, Inc.
260 Center Street
Holbrook, MA 02343
(800) 872-5627

*National Trade and
Professional Associations of
the United States and
Canada and Labor Unions*
Garrett Park Press
Box 190
Garrett Park, MD 20896
(301) 946-2553

Newsletters Directory
Gale Research, Inc.
835 Penobscot Building
Detroit, MI 48226-4094
(800) 877-4253

---

*God moves in a mysterious way, / His wonders to perform; / He plants his footsteps in
the sea, / And rides upon the storm. —William Cowper*

*Professional's Private
Sector Job Finder*
Planning/Communications
7215 Oak Avenue
River Forest, IL 60305
(708) 366-5200

*Standard & Poor's
Corporation Records*
25 Broadway
New York, NY 10004
(212) 208-8000

*Standard & Poor's
Industrial Index*
Same as above

*Standard & Poor's
Industry Surveys*
Same as above

*Standard & Poor's
Register of Corporations,
Directors and Executives*
Same as above

*Summer Employment
Directory of the
United States*
Pat Beusterien
Peterson's Guides, Inc.
P.O. Box 2123
Princeton, NJ 08543
(800) 338-3282

Top Professions
Nicholas Basta
Same as above

Value Line Investment Survey
Arnold Bernhard and Co.
220 E. 42nd Street
New York, NY 10017
(800) 833-0046

Ward's Business Directory
Information Access
Company
362 Lakeside Drive
Foster City, CA 94404
(415) 378-5000

MAGAZINES, NEWSPAPERS, AND JOURNALS

*The Best Small Companies
in America*
Forbes, Inc.
60 5th Avenue
New York, NY 10011
(212) 620-2200

The Inc. 500 Issue
The Goldhirsh Group
38 Commercial Wharf
Boston, MA 02110
(800) 234-0999

ON-LINE SERVICES

*America Online's Career
Center*
America Online
8619 Westwood Center
Drive
Vienna, VA 22182
(800) 827-6364

Business Resource Directory
GEnie
P.O. Box 6403
Rockville, MD 20849-6403
(800) 638-9636

*CSI National Career
Network*
Computer Search

International
Corporation (CSI)
8206 Greensboro Drive
Suite 660
McLean, VA 22102
(307) 749-1635

Career Design
Career Design Software
7900 East Princess Drive
Suite 1277
Scottsdale, AZ 85255
(800) 346-8007

*The Computer-Powered
Job Search System*
Drake Beam Morin
100 Park Avenue
New York, NY 10017
(800) 345-5627

*Corporate Jobs
Outlook, Inc.*
P.O. Drawer 100
Boerne, TX 78006
(210) 755-8810

*FOCIS (The Federal
Occupational and Career
Information System),
Version 4*
National Technical
Information Service
Dept. of Commerce
Springfield, VA 22161
(703) 487-4650

Job Ads USA Database
Militran, Inc.
P.O. Box 490
Southeastern, PA
19399
(215) 687-3900

He does not possess wealth that allows it to possess him. —Benjamin Franklin

JobHunter
Resumate
P.O. Box 7438
Ann Arbor, MI 48107
(800) 530-9310

Looking for Work
InterDigital, Inc.
742 Route 625
Hampton, NJ 08827
(908) 832-2463

P.D. News/Job Listings
Publications and
Communications, Inc.
12416 Hymeadow Drive
Austin, TX 78750
(800) 678-9724

*Standard & Poor's
On-Line Services*
Standard & Poor's
Corporation
25 Broadway
New York, NY 10004
(212) 208-8300

ASSOCIATIONS

*American Association of
Advertising Agencies*
666 Third Avenue
New York, NY
10017-4056
(212) 682-2500

*American Bankers
Association*
1120 Connecticut
Avenue, NW
Washington, DC
60601
(202) 663-5000

American Bar Association
750 North Lake
Shore Drive
Chicago, IL 60611
(312) 988-5000

*American Federation
of TV and Radio
Artists*
4340 E. West Highway
Bethesda, MD 20814
(410) 792-7707

*American Hospital
Association*
1 North Franklin,
27th floor
Chicago, IL 60606
(312) 422-3000

*American Institute of
Certified Public Accountants*
1211 Avenue of the
Americas
New York, NY 10036
(212) 596-6200

*Association of American
Publishers, Inc.*
71 Fifth Avenue
New York, NY 10003
(212) 255-0200

*Independent Insurance
Agents of America*
127 South Peyton Street
Alexandria, VA 22314
(703) 683-4422

*Industrial Biotechnology
Association*
1625 K Street, NW,
Suite 1100

Washington, DC 20006
(202) 857-0244

*Institute for Certification
of Computer Professionals*
2200 E. Devon Avenue,
Suite 268
Des Plaines, IL 60018
(708) 299-4227

*Inter-American Defense
Board*
2600 16th Street, NW
Washington, DC 20441
(202) 939-6600

*National Association
of Environmental
Professionals
(Environmental Biome)*
5165 MacArthur
Boulevard NW
Washington, DC
20016-3315
(800) 526-NAEP

*National Association of
Manufacturers*
1331 Pennsylvania
Avenue, NW,
Suite 1500N
Washington, DC 20004
(202) 637-3000

*National Association of
Personnel Consultants*
3133 Mt. Vernon Avenue
Alexandria, VA 22314
(703) 684-0180

*National Association of
Social Workers*
750 First Street, NE,

Patience is bitter, but its fruit is sweet. —Jean Jacques Rousseau

Suite 700
Washington, DC 20002
(202) 408-8600

*National Restaurant
Association*
1200 17th Street, NW
Washington, DC 20036
(202) 331-5900

*North American
Telecommunications
Association*
2000 M Street, NW,
Suite 550
Washington, DC 20036
(202) 296-9800

*Public Employees Roundtable
(Government Biome)*
P.O. Box 14270
Washington, DC
20044-4270
(202) 927-5000

*Public Relations Society
of America*
33 Irving Place, 3rd Floor
New York, NY 10003
(212) 995-2230

BOOKS

*The 40+ Job Hunting
Guide*
E. Patricia Birsner
Facts on File, Inc.
460 Park Avenue S
New York, NY 10016
(800) 322-8755

*The 100 Best Jobs for the
1990s and Beyond*
Carol Kleiman

Dearborn Financial
Publishing, Inc.
155 North Wacker Drive
Chicago, IL 60606
(800) 621-9621

101 Careers
Michael Harkavy
John Wiley & Sons, Inc.
1 Wiley Drive
Somerset, NJ 08875
(800) 225-5945

*A Young Person's Guide to
Getting and Keeping a Job*
J. Michael Farr
JIST Works
720 North Park Avenue
Indianapolis, IN 46202
(800) 648-5478

*After College: The Business
of Getting Jobs*
Jack Falvey
Williamson Publishing Co.
Box 185
Charlotte, VT 05445
(800) 234-8791

*America's 50 Fastest
Growing Jobs*
JIST Works, Inc.
720 North Park Avenue
Indianapolis, IN
46202-3431
(800) 648-5478

*The Best Companies
for Women*
Daila Zeitz and
Lorraine Dusky
Simon & Schuster
1230 Avenue of the
Americas

New York, NY 10020
(800) 223-2348

*Career Guide to America's
Top Industries*
JIST Works, Inc.
720 North Park Avenue
Indianapolis, IN
46202-3431
(800) 648-5478

*Careers Checklists: 89
Proven Checklists to Help
You Plan Your Career
and Get Great Jobs*
Arlene S. Hirsch
VGM Publishing Group
4255 West Touhy Avenue
Lincolnwood, IL
60646-1975
(800)323-4900

*Change Your Job, Change
Your Life*
Ronald L. Krannich
Impact Publications
9104-N Manassas Drive
Manassas Park, VA
22111-5211
(703) 361-7300

*College Majors and
Careers: A Resource Guide
for Effective Life Planning*
Paul Phifer
Garrett Park Press
Box 190
Garrett Park, MD 20896
(301) 946-2553

*The Complete Guide to
Public Employment*
Ronald L. Krannich and
Caryl Rae Krannich

Happiness is the harvest of a quiet eye. —Austin O'Malley

Impact Publications
9104-N Manassas Drive
Manassas Park, VA
22111-5211
(703) 361-7300

*Cover Letters That Knock
'Em Dead*
Martin Yate
Bob Adams Inc.
260 Center Street
Holbrook, MA
02343
(800) 872-5627

*Discover the Best Jobs
for You!*
Ronald L. Krannich
and Caryl Rae
Krannich
Impact Publications
9104-N Manassas Drive
Manassas Park, VA
22111-5211
(703) 361-7300

*Discover What You're
Best At*
Barry and Linda Gale
Simon & Schuster
1230 Avenue of the
Americas
New York, NY
10020
(800) 223-2348

Effective Networking
Venda Raye-Johnson
Crisp Publications
1200 Hamilton Court
Menlo Park, CA
94025-9600
(800) 442-7477

*Electronic Job Search
Revolution*
Joyce Lain Kennedy and
Thomas J. Morrow
John Wiley & Sons, Inc.
1 Wiley Drive
Somerset, NJ 08875
(800) 225-5945

*Electronic Resume
Revolution*
Same as above

Find a Federal Job Fast!
Ronald L. Krannich and
Caryl Rae Krannich
Impact Publications
9104-N Manassas Drive
Manassas Park, VA
22111-5211
(703) 361-7300

The Five Minute Interview
R. H. Beatty
John Wiley and Sons, Inc.
1 Wiley Drive
Somerset, NJ 08875
(800) 225-5945

Get a Better Job!
Ed. Rushlow
Peterson's Guides, Inc.
P.O. Box 2123
Princeton, NJ 08543
(800) 338-3282

*The Government Job
Finder*
Daniel Lauber
Planning/Communications
7215 Oak Street
River Forest, IL 60305
(708) 366-5200

*Graduation to the
9–5 World*
Jerry Bouchard
Impact Publications
9104-N Manassas Drive
Manassas Park, VA
22111-5211
(703) 361-7300

*Great Connections: Small
Talk and Networking for
Businesspeople*
Anne Baber and
Lynne Waymon
Same as above

*Guerrilla Tactics in the
New Job Market*
Tom Jackson
Bantam Books
2451 South Wolf Road
Des Plains, IL 60018
(800) 323-9872

The Hidden Job Market
Peterson's Guides, Inc.
P.O. Box 2123
Princeton, NJ 08543-2123
(800) 338-3282

Hiring The Best
Martin Yate
Bob Adams Inc.
260 Center Street
Holbrook, MA 02343
(800) 872-5627

*How to Locate Jobs and
Land Interviews*
Albert L. French
The Career Press, Inc.
180 5th Avenue
P.O. Box 34

He who is firm in will molds the world to himself. —Johann Wolfgang von Goethe

Hawthorne, NJ 07507
(800) 227-3371

*How to Make $1000 a
Minute: Negotiating
Salaries and Raises*
Jack Chapman
Ten Speed Press
P.O. Box 7123
Berkeley, CA 94707
(800) 841-2665

How to Work a Room
Susan Roane
Little Brown Company
Warner Books
200 West Street
Waltham, MA 02154
(800) 759-0190

How You Really Get Hired
John L. LaFevre
Macmillian Publishing
Simon & Schuster
201 W. 103rd Avenue
Indianapolis, IN 46290
(800) 428-5331

*If You Don't Know
Where You're Going,
You'll Probably End Up
Somewhere Else*
David P. Campbell
Argus Communications
Tabar Publishing
P.O. Box 7000
200 E. Bethany
Allen, TX 75002
(800) 527-4748

International Careers
Arthur H. Bell
Bob Adams, Inc.
260 Center Street

Holbrook, MA 02343
(800) 872-5627

*International Careers:
An Insider's Guide*
David Win
Williamson Publishing Co.
P. O. Box 185
Charlottesville, VT
05445
(800) 234-8791

International Jobs
Eric Kocher
Addison-Wesley
Publishing Co., Inc.
1 Jacob Way
Reading, MA 01867
(800) 447-2226

Is Your "Net" Working?
Anne Boe and Bettie B.
Youngs
John Wiley and Sons, Inc.
1 Wiley Drive
Somerset, NJ 08875
(800) 225-5945

Job Hunting After 50
Samuel N. Ray
John Wiley & Sons, Inc.
1 Wiley Drive
Somerset, NJ 08875
(800) 225-5945

*Job-Hunting Tips for the
So-Called Handicapped
or People Who Have
Disabilities. A Supplement
to What Color Is Your
Parachute.*
Richard Nelson Bolles
Ten Speed Press
Box 7123

Berkeley, CA 94707
(800) 841-2665

*Job Power: The Young
People's Job Finding Guide*
Bernard Haldane,
Jean Haldane, and
Lowell Martin
Acropolis Books, Ltd.
2311 Calvert Street NW
Washington, DC 20008
(800) 451-7771

*The Job Search Companion:
The Organizer for Job
Seekers*
Ellen J. Wallach and
Peter Arnold
The Harvard Common
Press
535 Albany Street
Boston, MA 02118
(617) 423-5803

Job Search Education
Martin Kimeldorf
Educational Design, Inc.
345 Hudson Street
New York, NY
10014-4502
(212) 255-7900

*Job Strategies for People
with Disabilities*
Melanie Astaire Witt
Peterson's Guides, Inc.
Box 2123
Princeton, NJ 08543-2123
(800) 338-3282

*Jobs for English Majors
and Other Smart People*
John L. Munschauer
Same as above

He's no failure. He's not dead yet. —*William Lloyd George*

*Jobs for People who Love
Travel*
Ronald L. Krannich
and Caryl Rae Krannich
Impact Publications
9104-N Manassas Drive
Manassas Park, VA
22111-5211
(703) 361-7300

*John Molloy's New Dress
for Success*
John T. Molloy
Little Brown Company
Warner Books
200 West Street
Waltham, MA 02154
(800) 759-0190

*Joyce Lain Kennedy's
Career Book*
Joyce Lain Kennedy
Co-authored by Darryl
Laramore
VGM Publishing Group
4255 West Touhy Avenue
Lincolnwood, IL
60646-1975
(800) 323-4900

*Knock 'Em Dead: The
Ultimate Job Seeker's
Handbook*
Martin Yate
Bob Adams Inc.
260 Center Street
Holbrook, MA 02343
(800) 872-5627

Liberal Arts Jobs
Bradley Jay Nadler

Peterson's Guides, Inc.
Box 2123
Princeton, NJ 08543-2123
(800) 338-3282

*The New Network Your Way
to Job and Career Success*
Ronald L. Krannich and
Caryl Rae Krannich
Impact Publications
9104-N Manassas Drive
Manassas Park, VA
22111-5211
(703) 361-7300

*The New Quick Job
Hunting Map*
Richard N. Bolles
Ten Speed Press
P.O. Box 7123
Berkeley, CA 94707
(800) 841-2665

The Nonprofit's Job Finder
Daniel Lauber
Planning/Communications
7215 Oak Avenue
River Forest, IL 60305
(703) 366-5200

*Not Just Another Job:
How to Invent a Career
That Works for You—
Now and in the Future*
Tom Jackson
Times Books
Random House, Inc.
400 Hahn Road
Westminister, MD
21157
(800) 726-0600

*Profitable Careers in
Nonprofit*
William Lewis and
Carol Milano
John Wiley & Sons, Inc.
1 Wiley Drive
Somerset, NJ 08875
(800) 225-5945

Put Your Degree to Work
Marcia R. Fox
W. W. Norton & Co., Inc.
National Book Company
800 Keystone
Industrial Park
Scranton, PA
18512-4601
(800) 233-4830

*Resumes That Knock
'Em Dead*
Martin Yate
Bob Adams Inc.
260 Center Street
Holbrook, MA 02343
(800) 872-5627

Salary Success
Ronald L. Krannich
and Caryl Rae
Krannich
Impact Publication
9104-N Manassas Drive
Manassas Park, VA
22111-5211
(703) 361-7300

Skills for Success
Adele Sheele
Ballantine Books
Random House, Inc.

---

*I am only one, But still I am one. I cannot do everything, But still I can do something;
And because I cannot do everything I will not refuse to do the something that I can do.
—Edward Everett*

201 E. 50th Street
New York, NY 10022
(800) 726-0600

*Stop Postponing the Rest
of Your Life*
Paul Stevens
Ten Speed Press
P.O. Box 7123
Berkeley, CA 94707
(800) 841-2665

*Summer Opportunities for
Kids and Teenagers*
Peterson's Guides, Inc.
Box 2123
Princeton, NJ 08543-2123
(800) 338-3282

The Three Boxes of Life
Robert G. Wegmann
Ten Speed Press
P.O. Box 7123
Berkeley, CA 94707
(800) 841-2665

*Training for Life: A
Practical Guide to Career
and Life Planning*
Fred J. Hecklinger and
Bernadette M. Curtin
Kendell/Hunt Publishing
4050 Westmark Drive
Dubuque, IA 52004
(800) 228-0810

*The Truth About You:
Discover What You Should
Be Doing with Your Life*
Arthur F. Miller and
Ralph T. Mattson
Ten Speed Press
Box 7123

Berkeley, CA 94707
(800) 841-2665

U.S. Industrial Outlook
JIST Works, Inc.
720 North Park Avenue
Indianapolis, IN
46202-3431
(800) 648-5478

*What Color Is Your
Parachute?*
Richard Nelson Bolles
Ten Speed Press
P.O. Box 7123
Berkeley, CA 94707
(800) 841-2665

*What's Next? Career
Strategies After 35*
Jack Falvey
Williamson Publishing Co.
P.O. Box 185
Charlottesville, VT
05445
(800) 234-8791

*Where Do I Go from
Here with My Life?*
John C. Crystal and
Richard N. Bolles
Ten Speed Press
P.O. Box 7123
Berkeley, CA 94707
(800) 841-2665

*Wishcraft: How to Get
What You Really Want*
Barbara Sher
Ballantine Books
Random House, Inc.
201 E. 50th Street
New York, NY 10022
(800) 726-0600

Who's Hiring Who
Richard Lathrop
Ten Speed Press
P.O. Box 7123
Berkeley, CA 94707
(800) 841-2665

*The Woman's Dress for
Success Book*
John T. Molloy
Little Brown Co.
Warner Books
200 West Street
Waltham, MA 02154
(800) 759-0190

*Work in the New Economy:
Careers and Job Seeking
into the 21st Century*
Robert Wegmann,
Robert Chapman, and
Miriam Johnson
JIST Works, Inc.
720 North Park Avenue
Indianapolis, IN
46202-3431
(800) 648-5478

The Work of Nations
Robert B. Reich
Vintage Books
Random House, Inc.
400 Hahn Road
Westminister, MD 21157
(800) 726-0600

*Write Into a Job: Resumes
and More*
Martin Kimeldorf
Meridian Education
Corporation
236 E. Front Street
Bloomington, IL 61701
(800) 727-5507

I do not like work even when someone else does it. —Mark Twain

Dream Career
Resource References

GENERAL DIRECTORIES

American Showcase
915 Broadway,14th Floor
New York, NY 10010
(212) 673-6600

Artist's & Graphic Designer's Market
Mary Cox
Writer's Digest Books
1507 Dana Avenue
Cincinnati, OH 45207
(800) 829-0963

Audio Video Marketplace
R.R. Bowker
A. Reed Reference
Publishing Co.
121 Chanlon Road
New Providence, NJ 07974
(908) 464-6800

CMJ Directory
Kathryn Krassner
11 Middle Neck Road,
Suite 400
Great Neck, NY
11021-2301
(516) 466-6000

Creative Black Book
Black Book Marketing, Inc.
866 Third Avenue
New York, NY 10022
(212) 702-9700

Creative Illustration Book
Same as above

Directory of Editorial Resources
EEI
66 Canal Center Plaza,
Suite 200
Alexandria, VA
22314-5507
(703) 683-0683

The Directory of Illustration and Design
RSVP
P.O. Box 314
Brooklyn, NY 11205
(718) 857-9267

Directory of Testing Labs
American Society of
Testing and Materials
(ASTM)
1916 Race Street
Philadelphia, PA 19103
(215) 299-5585

Dramatist's Sourcebook
Gillian Richards and
Linda MacColl
Theatre Communications
Group, Inc.
355 Lexington Avenue
New York, NY 10017
(212) 697-5230

Encyclopedia of Associations
Gale Research Co.
835 Penobscot Building
Detroit, MI
48226-4094
(800) 877-4253

Originality is nothing but judicious imitation. —Voltaire

Fine Art Index
International Art
Reference
938 North Honore
Chicago, IL 60622
(312) 335-8219

*Graphic Artists
Guild's Directory of
Illustration*
Serbin Communications
511 Olive Street
Santa Barbara, CA
93101
(805) 963-0439

Green Book
AG Editions
41 Union Square, #523
New York, NY 10003
(212) 929-0959

Guide to Literary Agents
Kirsten Holm
Writer's Digest Books
1507 Dana Avenue
Cincinnati, OH 45207
(800) 289-0963

*How to Write Irresistible
Query Letters*
Lisa Collier Cool
Same as above

*The Insider's Guide to
Book Editors, Publishers &
Literary Agents*
Jeff Herman
Prima Publishing
Box 1260
Rocklin, CA
95677-1260
(916) 632-4400

*International Directory
of Little Magazines &
Small Presses*
Len Fulton
Dustbooks
P.O. Box 100
Paradise, CA 95967
(800) 477-6110

*Literary Market Place
and International
Literary Market Place*
R. R. Bowker
A. Reed Reference
Publishing Co.
121 Chanlon Road
New Providence, NJ 07974
(908) 464-6800

Madison Avenue Handbook
Peter Glenn Publications
42 W. 38th Street
New York, NY 10018
(212) 869-2020

Music Business Directory
Ray McGinnis
P.O. Box 120675
Nashville, TN 37212
(615) 255-1068

*O'Dwyer's Directory of
Public Relations Firms*
J.R. O'Dwyer
Company, Inc.
271 Madison Avenue
New York, NY 10016
(212) 679-2471

Photographer's Market
Michael Willins
Writer's Digest Books
1507 Dana Avenue

Cincinnati, OH 45207
(800) 289-0963

Songwriter's Market
Cindy Laufenberg
Same as above

*Standard Directory of
Advertising Agencies*
National Register
Publishing
A. Reed Reference Co.
121 Chanlon Road
New Providence, NJ
07974
(908) 464-6800

*Standard Rate and Data
Service (SRDS)*
3004 Glenview Road
Wilmette, IL 60091
(708) 256-6067

The Stock Workbook
Scott & Daughters
Publishing, Inc.
940 North Highland
Avenue, Suite A
Los Angeles, CA 90038
(213) 856-0008

*Texas Music Industry
Directory*
Texas Music Office
Office of the
Governor
P.O. Box 13246
Austin, TX 78711
(512) 463-6666

Writer's Market
Mark Garvey
Writer's Digest Books

Will is character in action. —William McDougall

1507 Dana Avenue
Cincinnati, OH 45207
(800) 289-0963

The Yellow Pages of Rock
The Album Network
120 North Victory Road
Burbank, CA 91502
(818) 955-4000

MAGAZINES, NEWSPAPERS, AND JOURNALS

ASMP Bulletin
14 Washington Road,
Suite 502
Princeton Junction, NJ
08550-1033
(609) 799-8300

Advertising Age
Crain Communications
740 North Rush Street
Chicago, IL 60611
(312) 649-5200

Adweek
Adweek Magazines
1515 Broadway
New York, NY 10036
(212) 536-5336

The Album Network
120 North Victory
Boulevard
Burbank, CA 91502
(818) 955-4000

*American Journalism
Review*
8701 Adelphi Road
Adelphi, MD 20783
(301) 431-4771

American Photo
1633 Broadway,
43rd Floor
New York, NY 10019
(212) 767-6000

*American Songwriter
Magazine*
121 17th Avenue S.
Nashville, TN 37203
(615) 244-6065

Amusement Business
Billboard Publications, Inc.
P.O. Box 24970
Nashville, TN 37202
(615) 321-4290

Art Business News
Advanstar
Communications Inc.
131 West First Street
Duluth, MN 55802
(800) 346-0085

Art Calendar
P.O. Box 199
Upper Fairmont, MD
21867
(800) 597-5988

Art Direction
10 East 39th Street,
6th Floor
New York, NY
10016-0199
(212) 889-6500

Art in America
Brant Publications, Inc.
575 Broadway
New York, NY 10012
(212) 941-2800

The Artist's Magazine
F&W Publications, Inc.
1507 Dana Avenue
Cincinnati, OH
45207
(513) 531-2222

Artnews
Artnews Associates
48 West 38th Street
New York, NY 10018
(212) 398-1690

Artweek
12 South First Street,
Suite 520
San Jose, CA 95113
(800) 733-2916

Billboard
1515 Broadway
New York, NY 10036
(212) 536-5055

Cash Box Magazine
6464 Sunset Boulevard,
Suite 605
Hollywood, CA
90028
(213) 464-8241

CMJ New Music Report
11 Middle Neck Road,
Suite 400
Great Neck, NY
11021-2301
(516) 466-6000

Communication Arts
Box 10300
410 Sherman Avenue
Palo Alto, CA 94303
(415) 326-6040

Our greatest weariness comes from work not done. —Eric Hoffer

Daily Variety
Daily Variety
Ltd./Cahners
Publishing Co.
5700 Wilshire Boulevard
Los Angeles, CA 90036
(213) 857-6600

Decor
Commerce Publishing Co.
330 North 4th Street
St. Louis, MO 63102
(314) 421-5445

Dramatist's Guild
Quarterly
234 West 44th Street
New York, NY 10036
(212) 398-9366

Editor & Publisher
The Editor & Publisher Co.
11 West 19th Street
New York, NY 10011
(212) 675-4380

Folio
Cowles Business Media
P.O. Box 4949
911 Hope Street
Stamford, CT
06907-0949
(203) 358-9900

Gavin Report
140 Second Street
San Francisco,CA 94105
(415) 495-1990

Giftware News
Talcott Communications
Corp.
350 Fifth Avenue

New York, NY 10118
(212) 629-0800

Greetings Magazine
MacKay Publishing Corp.
307 5th Avenue,
16th Floor
New York, NY 10016
(212) 679-6677

Guilfoyle Report
AG Editions
41 Union Square, #523
New York, NY 10003
(212) 929-0959

Hits Magazine
14958 Ventura Boulevard
Sherman Oaks, CA 91403
(818) 501-7900

Horn Book Magazine
11 Beacon Street,
Suite 1000
Boston, MA 02108
(617) 227-1555

How
F&W Publications, Inc.
1507 Dana Avenue
Cincinnati, OH 45207
(513) 531-2222

Industrial Photography
PTN Publishing
445 Broad Hollow Road
Melville, NY 11747
(516) 845-2700

Music Connection
Magazine
6640 Sunset Boulevard
Hollywood, CA 90028
(213) 462-5772

Music Row Magazine
Music Row Publications,
Inc.
1231 17th Avenue South
Nashville, TN 37212
(614) 321-3617

Outdoor Photographer
Werner Publishing
12121 Wilshire
Boulevard, Suite 1220
Los Angeles, CA 90025
(310) 820-1500

Party & Paper Retailer
4 Ward Corp.
70 New Canaan Avenue
Norwalk, CT 06850
(203) 845-8020

The Performing Songwriter
P.O. Box 158159
Nashville, TN 37215
(800) 883-7664

Petersen's Photographic
Magazine
6420 Wilshire Boulevard
Los Angeles, CA
90048-5515
(213) 782-2200

Photo District News
1515 Broadway
New York, NY 10036
(212) 536-5222

Photo Marketing
Photo Marketing
Association, Intl.
3000 Picture Place
Jackson, MI 49201-8853
(800) 762-9287

Our progress as a nation can be no swifter than our progress in education.
—John F. Kennedy

The Photo Review
301 Hill Avenue
Langhorne, PA
19047-2819
(215) 757-8921

Photoletter
Photosource International
Pine Lake Farm
Osceola, WI 54020
(715) 248-3800

Poets & Writers
72 Spring Street
New York, NY 10012
(212) 226-3586

Print
RC Publications
104 Fifth Avenue
New York, NY 10011
(800) 222-2654

Professional Photographer
Professional Photography
Professional Photographers
of America, Inc.
57 Forsythe St. NW,
Suite 1600
Atlanta, GA 30303
(800) 742-7468

Public Domain Report
P.O. Box 3102
Margate, NJ 08402
(800) 827-9401

Publishers Weekly
Bowker Magazine Group
Cahners Publishing Co.
249 W. 17th Street
New York, NY 10011
(212) 645-0067

Radio and Records
1930 Century Park West
Los Angeles, CA 90067
(310) 553-4330

The Rangefinder
1312 Lincoln Boulevard
Santa Monica, CA
90401
(310) 451-8506

Science Fiction Chronicle
P.O. Box 022730
Brooklyn, NY 11202-0056
(718) 643-9011

Shutterbug
Patch Communications
5211 South Washington
Avenue
Titusville, FL 32780
(800) 376-2237
(800) 677-5212

*Songwriter Products,
Ideas and Necessities*
NSP Music Publishing
345 Sprucewood Road
Lake Mary, FL
32746-5917
(407) 321-3702

Southwest Art
CBH Publishing
5444 Westheimer,
Suite 1440
Houston, TX 77056
(713) 850-0990

Step-by-Step Graphics
Dynamic Graphics, Inc.
6000 North Forest
Park Drive

Peoria, IL 61614
(800) 255-8800

Taking Stock
Jim Pickerell
110 Frederick Avenue,
Suite A
Rockville, MD 20850
(301) 251-0720

Upper & Lower Case
International Typeface
Corp.
866 Second Avenue
New York, NY 10017
(212) 371-0699

The Writer
120 Boylston Street
Boston, MA 02116
(617) 423-3157

Writer's Digest
1507 Dana Avenue
Cincinnati, OH 45207
(800) 289-0963

ASSOCIATIONS

*Advertising Photographers
of America*
27 West 20th Street,
Room 601
New York, NY 10011
(212) 807-0399

*American Book Producers
Association*
160 Fifth Avenue,
Suite 625
New York, NY
10010-7000
(212) 645-2368

Patience and time do more than strength or passion. —Jean de La Fontaine

American Book Publishers Association
Same as above

American Center for Design
233 East Ontario,
Suite 500
Chicago, IL 60611
(312) 787-2018

American Council of Independent Laboratories (ACIL)
1629 K Street, NW
Suite 400
Washington, DC 20006
(202) 887-5872

American Medical Writer's Association
9650 Rockville Pike
Bethesda, MD
20814-3998
(301) 493-0003

American Music Center, Inc.
30 West 26th Street,
Suite 1001
New York, NY
10010-2011
(212) 366-5260

American Musicians Union, Inc.
8 Tobin Court
Dumont, NJ 07628
(201) 384-5378

American Society of Artists, Inc.
P.O.Box 1326

Palatine, IL 60078
(312) 751-2500

American Society of Composers, Authors And Publishers (ASCAP)
1 Lincoln Plaza
New York, NY 10023
(212) 621-6000

American Society of Journalists and Authors
1501 Broadway,
Suite 302
New York, NY 10036
(212) 997-0947

American Society of Media Photographers
14 Washington Road,
Suite 502
Princeton Junction, NJ
08550-1033
(609) 799-8300

American Women Composers, Inc.
Dept. of Music
George Washington
University
Washington, DC 20052
(202) 994-6338

Art in General
79 Walker
New York, NY 10013
(212) 219-0473

Art Information Center
280 Broadway,
Suite 412
New York, NY 10007
(212) 227-0282

Arts Midwest
528 Hennepin Avenue,
Suite 310
Minneapolis, MN 55403
(612) 341-0755

Associated Writing Programs
International Letters Center
Tallwood House,
Mailstop 1E3
George Mason University
Fairfax, VA 22030
(703) 993-4301

Association for Visual Artists
1303 Hixon Pike
Chattanooga, TN 37405
(615) 265-4282

Association of Authors Representatives
10 Astor Place. 3rd Fl.
New York, NY 10003
(212) 353-3709

Association of Desk-Top Publishers
4507 30th Street,
Suite 800
San Diego, CA
92116-3245
(619) 563-9714

The Authors Guild
330 West 42nd Street
New York, NY 10036
(212) 563-5904

The Authors' League of America, Inc.
Same as above
(212) 564-8350

Originality is simply a pair of fresh eyes. —Thomas Wentworth Higginson

The Authors' Resource Center
4725 E. Sunrise Drive
Tucson, AZ 85718
(602) 325-4733

Broadcast Music, Inc. (BMI)
320 West 57th Street
New York, NY 10019
(212) 586-2000 and
8730 Sunset Boulevard
Los Angeles, CA 90069
(310) 659-9109

Coalition of Women's Art Organizations
123 East Beutel Road
Port Washington, WI 53074
(414) 284-4458

Composers' Guild
40 North 100 West
Box 586
Farmington, UT 84025
(801) 451-2275

Copywriter's Council of America, Freelance
7 Putter Lane
Linick Building
Middle Island, NY 11953-0102
(516) 924-8555

Creative Arts Guild
520 West Waugh Street
Dalton, GA 30720
(706) 278-0168

The Dramatists Guild
234 W. 44th Street
New York, NY 10036
(212) 398-9366

Editorial Freelancers' Association
71 W. 23rd Street, Suite 1504
New York, NY 10010
(212) 929-5400

Education Writers' Association
1001 Connecticut Avenue, NW, Suite 310
Washington, DC 20036
(202) 429-9680

The Friends of Photography
250 Fourth Street
San Francisco, CA 94103
(415) 495-7076

Gospel Music Association
7 Music Circle North
Nashville, TN 37203
(615) 242-0303

Graphic Artist's Guild
11 West 20th Street
New York, NY 10011-3704
(212) 463-7730

Independent Music Association
P.O. Box 609
Ringwood, NJ 07456
(201) 831-1317

Independent Musicians Co-Op
P.O. Box 571205
Murray, UT 84157
(801) 268-0174

International Bluegrass Music Association
207 East Second Street
Owensboro, KY 42303
(502) 684-9025

International Center for Photography
1130 Fifth Avenue
New York, NY 10128
(212) 860-1781

International League of Women Composers
Abilene Christian University
ACU Box 8274
Abilene, TX 79699
(915) 674-2044

International Television Association
6311 N. O'Connor Road, Suite 230
Irving, TX 75039
(214) 869-1112

International Women's Writing Guild
Box 810
Gracie Station
New York, NY 10028
(212) 737-7536

Lawyers for the Creative Arts
213 West Institute Place, Suite 411
Chicago, IL 60610
(800) 944-ARTS

Lincoln Arts
540 F Street
P.O. Box 1166

Patience is a minor form of despair, disguised as a virtue. —Ambrose Bierce

Lincoln, CA 95648
(916) 645-9713

Mystery Writers of
America
17 E. 47th Street,
6th Floor
New York, NY 10017
(212) 888-8171

NOVA (New Organization
for the Visual Arts)
4614 Prospect Avenue,
Suite 410
Cleveland, OH 44103
(216) 431-7500

National Academy of
Songwriters (NAS)
6381 Hollywood
Boulevard, Suite 780
Hollywood, CA 90028
(213) 463-7178

National Association of
Artists' Organizations
918 F Street, NW,
Suite 611
Washington, DC 20004
(202) 347-6350

National Association of
Composers/USA
Box 49652
Barrington Station
Los Angeles, CA 90049
(310) 541-8213

National Association of
Science Writers
Box 294
Greenlawn, NY 11740
(516) 757-5664

National Press
Photographer's Association
3200 Croasdaile Drive,
Suite 306
Durham, NC 27705
(800) 289-6772

National Traditional
Music Association, Inc.
P.O. 438
Walnut, IA 51577
(712) 784-3001

National Writer's
Association
1450 S. Havana, Suite 424
Aurora, CO 80012
(303) 751-7844

National Writer's Union
873 Broadway,
Room 203
New York, NY 10003
(212) 254-0279

New Dramatists
424 West 44th Street
New York, NY 10036
(212) 757-6960

New England Foundation
for the Arts
678 Massachusetts
Avenue, #801
Cambridge, MA 02139
(617) 492-2914

North American Nature
Photography Association
10200 West 44th
Avenue, #304
Wheat Ridge, CO 80033
(303) 422-8527

Organization of
Independent Artists
19 Hudson Street,
Suite 402
New York, NY 10013
(212) 219-9213

Photographic Art &
Science Foundation
111 Stratford Road
Des Plaines, IL
60016-2105
(708) 824-6855

Photographic Society of
America
3000 United Founders
Boulevard, Suite 103
Oklahoma City, OK 73112
(405) 843-1437

Picture Agency Council
of America
P.O. Box 308
Northfield, MN
55057-0308
(800) 457-7222

Poetry Society of America
15 Grammercy Park
New York, NY 10003
(212) 254-9628

Poets & Writers
72 Spring Street
New York, NY 10012
(212) 226-3586

Professional Photographers
of America
57 Forsyth Street, NW
Atlanta, GA 30303
(800) 742-7468

Show me a thoroughly satisfied man and I will show you a failure. —Thomas Edison

*Professional Women
Photographers*
Photographics Unlimited
17 West 17th Street,
4th Floor
New York, NY
10011-5510
(212) 289-6072

*Publication Services
Guild*
P.O. Box 19663
Atlanta, GA 30325
(404) 951-4721

*Recording Industry
Association of America*
1020 19th Street NW,
Suite 200
Washington, DC 20036
(202) 775-0101

*Romance Writers of
America*
13700 Veterans
Memorial Drive,
Suite 315
Houston, TX 77014
(713) 440-6885

*Science-Fiction Fantasy
Writers of America*
5 Winding Brook Drive,
Suite 1B
Guilderland, NY 12084
(518) 869-5361

*Society of American Travel
Writers*
4101 Lake Boon Trail
Suite 500
Raleigh, NC 27607
(919) 787-5181

*Society of Children's Book
Writers*
22736 Vanowen Street,
Suite 106
West Hills, CA 91307
(818) 888-8760

*Society of Photographer
and Artist Representatives,
Inc.*
60 East 42nd Street,
Suite 1166
New York, NY 10165
(212) 779-7464

*Society of Professional
Journalists*
16 S. Jackson
Greencastle, IN 46135
(317) 653-3333

*Society of Publication
Designers*
60 East 42nd Street,
Suite 721
New York, NY 10165
(212) 983-8585

*The Songwriter's Guild
of America*
276 Fifth Avenue,
Suite 306
New York, NY 10001
(212) 686-6820 and
6430 Sunset Boulevard,
Suite 1002
Hollywood, CA 90028
(213) 462-1108

*Volunteer Lawyers for
the Arts*
1 East 53rd Street,
6th Floor

New York, NY 10022
(212) 319-2787

*Wedding Photographers
International*
P.O. Box 2003
1312 Lincoln
Boulevard
Santa Monica, CA
90406
(310) 451-0090

*Women in
Communications*
3717 Columbia Pike,
Suite 310
Arlington, VA 22201
(703) 920-5555

Writer's Alliance
12 Skylark Lane
Stony Brook, NY
11790
(516) 751-7080

Writer's Connection
P.O. Box 24770
San Jose, CA 95154
(408) 445-3600

*Writer's Guild of America
(East)*
555 W. 57th Street
New York, NY
10019
(212) 767-7800

*Writer's Guild of
America (West)*
8955 Beverly Boulevard
West Hollywood, CA
90048
(310) 550-1000

Simplicity is the glory of expression. —Walt Whitman

BOOKS

Adventure Careers
Susan Angle and
Alex Hiam
The Career Press
180 5th Avenue
P.O. Box 34
Hawthorne, NJ 07507
(800) 227-3371

Attention: A&R
Teri Muench and Susan
Pomerantz
Alfred Publishing Co., Inc.
Box 10003
Van Nuys, CA
91410-0003
(818) 891-5999

*Beginning Songwriter's
Answer Book*
Paul Zollo
Writer's Digest Books
1507 Dana Avenue
Cincinnati, OH 45207
(800) 289-0963

*The Complete Guide to
Self Publishing*
Marilyn and Tom Ross
Same as above

Copyright Handbook
R.R. Bowker
A. Reed Reference
Publishing Co.
121 Chanlon Road
New Providence, NJ
07974
(908) 464-6800

*The Craft & Business of
Songwriting*
John Braheny
Writer's Digest Books
1507 Dana Avenue
Cincinnati, OH 45207
(800) 289-0963

*Guide to Travel Writing
& Photography*
Ann and Carl Purcell
Same as above

*How To Open Doors In
The Music Industry-
The Independent Way*
Frank Fara and
Patty Parker
Autumn Gold
Publishing
Starfield Press
10603 N. Hayden Road,
Suite 114
Scottsdale, AZ 85260
(602) 951-3115

*How to Pitch & Promote
Your Songs*
Fred Koller
Writer's Digest Books
1507 Dana Avenue
Cincinnati, OH 45207
(800) 289-0963

*How to Shoot Stock Photos
That Sell*
Michael Heron
Allworth Press
Distributed by Writer's
Digest Books
Same as above

*How to Write Irresistible
Query Letters*
Lisa Collier Cool
Same as above

*How You Can Make
$25,000 a Year with
Your Camera*
Larry Cribb
Same as above

*The Insider's Guide to
Book Editors, Publisher's
& Literary Agents*
Jeff Herman
Prima Communications,
Inc.
Box 1260
Rocklin, CA
95677-1260
(916) 632-4400

*Lighting Secrets for the
Professional Photographer*
Alan Brown, Tim
Grondin, and Joe Braun
Writer's Digest Books
1507 Dana Avenue
Cincinnati, OH 45207
(800) 289-0963

*Making Money Making
Music*
James Dearing
Same as above

*The Music Business
Handbook*
Jojo St. Mitchell
Amethyst Press
273 Chippewa Drive

---

*Sometimes men come by the name of genius in the same way that certain insects come
by the name of centipede—not because they have a hundred feet, but because most
people can't count above fourteen. —G. C. Lichtenberg*

Columbia, SC 29210-6508
(803) 750-5391

*Music Publishing: A
Songwriter's Guide*
Randy Poe
Writer's Digest Books
1507 Dana Avenue
Cincinnati, OH 45207
(800) 289-0963

The Perfect Portfolio
Henrietta Brackman
Watson-Guptill Publishing
1515 Broadway
New York, NY 10036
(212) 764-7300

*Playing For Pay: How to
Be a Working Musician*
James Gibson
Writer's Digest Books
1507 Dana Avenue
Cincinnati, OH 45207
(800) 289-0963

*Pricing Photography: The
Complete Guide to
Assignment & Stock Prices*
Michael Heron and
David MacTavish
Allworth Press
10 East 23rd Street
New York, NY 10010
(212) 777-8395

*Professional Photographer's
Guide to Shooting &
Selling Nature &
Wildlife Photos*
Jim Zuckerman
Writer's Digest Books
1507 Dana Avenue

Cincinnati, OH 45207
(800) 289-0963

*Professional Photographer's
Survival Guide*
Charles E. Rotkin
Same as above

Professional Writer's Guide
Sandy Whelchel
National Writer's Press
1450 South Havana,
Suite 424
Aurora, CO 80012
(303) 751-7844

*Recording Industry's
Sourcebook*
Michael Fuchs
Ascona Communications
3301 Barham Boulevard,
Suite 300
Los Angeles, CA 90068
(213) 874-5588

Sell & Resell Your Photos
Rohn Engh
Writer's Digest Books
1507 Dana Avenue
Cincinnati, OH 45207
(800) 289-0963

*Songwriter's Creative
Matrix*
Carl E. Bolte, Jr.
Holly Productions
800 Greenway Terrace
Kansas City, MO 64113
(816) 444-8884

*The Songwriter's Demo
Manual and Success Guide*
George Williams

Music Business Books
Tree by the River Publishing
Box 935
Dayton, NV 89403
(800) 487-6610

*The Songwriter's Market
Guide to Song & Demo
Submission Formats*
Cindy Laufenberg
Writer's Digest Books
1507 Dana Avenue
Cincinnati, OH 45207
(800) 289-0963

*Stock Photography: The
Complete Guide*
Ann and Carl Purcell
Same as above

Successful Songwriting
Carl E. Bolte, Jr.
Holly Productions
800 Greenway Terrace
Kansas City, MO 64113

*The Writer's Legal
Companion*
Brad Bunnin and
Peter Beren
Addison-Wesley
1 Jacob Way
Reading, MA 01867

*Writing Tools: Essential
Software for Anyone Who
Writes with a PC*
Hy Bender
Random House
Electronic Publishing
201 East 50 Street
New York, NY 10022
(800) 726-0600

Still achieving, still pursuing, learn to labor, and to wait.
—Henry Wadsworth Longfellow

Entrepreneurial Resource References

GENERAL DIRECTORIES

Business Organizations, Agencies, and Publications Directory
Donald P. Boyden and Robert Wilson
Gale Research, Inc.
Book Tower,
Department 77748
835 Penobscot Building
Detroit, MI
48226-4094
(800) 223-4253

Catalog of Federal Domestic Assistance
No. 922-016-00000-3
U.S. Government Printing Office
Superintendent of Documents
P.O. Box 371954
Pittsburgh, PA
15250-7954
(202) 512-1800

The Corporate Finance Sourcebook
A. Reed Reference Publishing Co.
121 Chanlon Road
New Providence, NJ 07974
(800) 323-6772

The Directory of Business Information Resources
Grey House Publishing
Pocket Knife Square
Lakeville, CT 06039
(800) 562-2139

Directory of Federal and State Business Assistance: A Guide for New and Growing Companies
No. PB88–101977
National Technical Information Service
U.S. Department of Commerce
5285 Port Royal Road
Springfield, VA 22161
(703) 487-4650

Directory of Franchise Business Opportunities
Franchise Business Opportunities Publishing Co.
1725 Washington Road, Suite 205
Pittsburgh, PA 15241
(412) 831-2522

Directory of Franchising Organizations
Pilot Industries, Inc.
103 Cooper Street
Babylon, NY 11702
(516) 422-2225

Directory of Special Programs for Minority Group Members: Career Information Services, Employment Skills Banks, Financial Aid Sources
Willis L. Johnson
Garrett Park Press
P.O. Box 190 C

People do not lack strength; they lack will. —Victor Hugo

Garrett Park, MD
20986-0190
(301) 946-2553

*Franchise Opportunities
Guide*
International Franchise
Association
P.O. Box 1502
Cranberry Township, PA
16066
(800) 543-1038

*Investigate Before Investing
Franchise Annual*
International Franchise
Association
P.O. Box 1502
Cranberry Township, PA
16066
(800) 543-1038

Lesko's Info-Power
Matthew Lesko
Information USA, Inc.
P.O. Box E
Kensington, MD 20895
(301) 424-4611
(301) 924-0438

Small Business Sourcebook
Charity Anne Dorgan
Gale Research, Inc.
Book Tower,
Department 77748
835 Penobscot Building
Detroit, MI 48226-4094
(800) 223-4253

Small Business Sourcebook
Kathleen E. Make
Gale Research Inc.

835 Penobscot Building
Detroit, MI 48226-4094
(800) 877-4253

Work-At-Home Sourcebook
Lynie Arden
Live Oak Publications
Box 339
Boulder, CO 80306
(303) 447-1087

*Worldwide Franchise
Directory*
Gale Research Inc.
835 Penobscot Building
Detroit, MI 48226-4094
(800) 877-4253

MAGAZINE, NEWSPAPERS, AND JOURNALS

AFA Quarterly
American Franchisee
Association
53 West Jackson, Suite 205
Chicago, IL 60604
(312) 431-0545

*Barbara Brabec's Self-
Employment Survival
Letter (bi-monthly)*
P.O. Box 2137
Naperville, IL 60567
(708) 717-4188

Business Franchise Guide
Commerce Clearing
House, Inc.
4025 West Peterson Avenue
Chicago, IL 60646
(800) 248-3248

Entrepreneur
2392 Morse Avenue
Irvine, CA 92714
(714) 261-2325

Home Office Computing
411 Lafayette
New York, NY
10003-9511
(212) 505-4220

*The Info Franchise
Newsletter*
Info Press
736 Center Street
Lewiston, NY 14092
(716) 754-4669

*National Home Business
Report*
Barbara Brabec
P.O. Box 2137
Naperville, IL 60567
(708) 717-0488

*Tax Guide for Small
Business*
Publication No. 334
Internal Revenue Service
(800) 829-3676

ON-LINE SERVICES

America Online
8619 Westwood Center
Drive
Vienna, VA 22182
(800) 227-6364

*Business Opportunities
Online*
65 First Avenue, Suite 202

When thought is too weak to be simply expressed, it's clear proof that it should be rejected.
—Luc de Clapiers

Atlantic Highlands, NJ
07716
(800) 872-8710

*CompuServe Information
Service*
5000 Arlington Centre
Boulevard
P.O. Box 20212
Columbus, OH 43220
(800) 848-8900

Data-Star
One Commerce Square
2005 Market Street,
Suite 1010
Philadelphia, PA 19103
(800) 221-7754

DELPHI
1030 Massachusetts
Avenue, 4th Floor
Cambridge, MA 02138
(800) 695-4005

*Dialog Information
Services, Inc.*
3460 Hillview Avenue
Palo Alto, CA 94304
(800)-334-2564

Dow Jones News/Retrieval
P.O. Box 300
Princeton, NJ
08543-0300
(800) 522-3567

Entrepreneurs Online
10550 Richmond
Avenue, Suite 125
Houston, TX 77042
(713) 784-8822

GEnie
401 N. Washington Street
Rockville, MD 20850
(800) 638-9636

Info-South
1500 Monz Avenue
Coral Cables, FL 33146
(800) 752-9567

Lexis/Nexis Guide Library
Mead Data Central, Inc.
9443 Springboro Pike
P.O. Box 933
Dayton, OH 45401-9964
(800) 227-4908

*Network Marketing
Solutions, Inc.*
756-F Walker Road
P.O. Box 945
Great Falls, VA 22066
(703) 759-7377

NewsNet
945 Haverford Road
Bryn Mawr, PA 19010
(800) 345-1301

Prodigy
Prodigy Services Company
445 Hamilton Avenue
White Plains, NY 10601
(800)-PRODIGY

SBA Online
U.S. Small Business
Administration
1441 L Street, NW
Washington, DC 20416
Electronic bulletin board
help line: (202) 205-6400

2400 bps line:
(800) 859-4636
9600 bps line:
(800) 697-4636

ASSOCIATIONS

*American Association of
Home Based Business*
P.O. Box 10023
Rockville, MD 20849
(202) 310-3130
(301) 963-9153

*American Franchisee
Association*
53 West Jackson, Suite 205
Chicago, IL 60604
312-431-0545

*American Management
Association*
135 West 50th Street
New York, NY 10020
(212) 586-8100

*American Marketing
Association*
250 S. Wacker Drive
Chicago, IL 60606
(312) 648-0536

*American Society of
Association Executives*
Information Central
1575 Eye Street, NW
Washington, DC 20005
(202) 626-2723

*American Woman's
Economic Development
Corp. (AWED)*

When we lose the right to be different, we lose the privilege to be free.
—Charles Evans Hughes

71 Vanderbilt Avenue,
3rd Floor, Suite 320
New York, NY 10169
(800) 222-2933
In New York:
(800) 442-2933

*Center for Entrepreneurial
Management, Inc.*
180 Varick Street,
Penthouse
New York, NY 10014
(212) 633-0060

*Center for Entrepreneurial
Studies*
Babson College
Forest Street
Babson Park, MA 02157
(617) 239-4420, x4332

*Center for
Entrepreneurship*
527 Zane Showker Hall
James Madison
University
Harrisonburg, VA
22807
(703) 568-3227

*Council of Better Business
Bureaus, Inc.*
4200 Wilson Boulevard,
Suite 800
Arlington, VA 22203
(703) 276-0100

*Council of Smaller
Entreprises*
200 Tower City Center
50 Public Square
Cleveland, OH 44113
(216) 621-3300

*Direct Marketing
Association*
11 West 42nd Street
New York, NY
10036-8096
(212) 768-7277

Foundation Center
79 Fifth Avenue
New York, NY 10003
(212) 620-4230

*Idea Exchange and
Promotional Services*
S. D. Warren Company
225 Franklin Street,
30th Floor
Boston, MA 02110
(617) 423-7300

*International Franchise
Association (main office)*
1350 New York Avenue,
N.W., Suite 900
Washington, DC
20005-4709
(800) 543-1038

*International Trade
Administration*
U.S. Department of
Commerce
14th Street and
Constitution Avenue, NW
Washington, DC 20230
(800) USA-TRADE

*Marketing Science
Institute*
1000 Massachusetts
Avenue
Cambridge, MA 01238
(617) 491-2060

MIT Enterprise Forum
Massachusetts Institute
of Technology
201 Vassar Street,
Room W59-219
Cambridge, MA 02139
(617) 253-0015

*National Association for
the Cottage Industry*
P.O. Box 14850
Chicago, IL 60614
(312) 472-8116

*National Association
of Home-Based
Businesses*
P.O. Box 30220
Baltimore, MD 21270
(410) 363-3698

*National Association of the
Self-Employed*
P.O. Box 612067
Dallas, TX
75261-2067
(800) 232-6273

*National Association of
Small Business Investment
Companies*
1199 North Fairfax Street,
Suite 200
Alexandria, VA 22314
(703) 683-1601

*National Association
of Women Business
Owners*
1377 K Street, NW,
Suite 631
Washington, DC 20005
(301) 608-2590

When you don't have an education, you've got to use your brains. —Anonymous

National Business Incubation Association
20 E. Circle Drive
Athens, OH 45701
(614) 593-4331

National Business League
5211 K. Street, NW
Washington, DC 20005
(202) 737-4430

National Federation of Independent Business (NFIB)
600 Maryland Avenue, SW, Suite 700
Washington, DC 20024
(800) 552-6342

National Small Business Association
1155 15th Street, NW
Washington, DC 20005
(202) 293-8830

National Small Business United (NSBU)
1155 15th Street, NW, Suite 710
Washington, DC 20005
(800) 541-5768

National Women's Economic Alliance
1440 New York Avenue, NW, Suite 300
Washington, DC 20005
(202) 393-5257

Promotional Product Association International
3125 Skyway Circle, N.

Irving, TX 75038
(214) 580-0404

Small Business Foundation of America
The Research Institute for Emerging Enterprises
1155 15th Street, NW
Washington, DC 20005
(202) 223-1103

U.S. Chamber of Commerce
1615 H Street, NW
Washington, DC 20062
(800) 638-6582

U.S. Department of Commerce
Business Assistance
Office of Business
Liaison, Room 5898-C
Washington, DC 20230
(202) 482-3176

U.S. Small Business Administration
409 Third Street, SW
Washington, DC 20416
(800) 827-5722

Women in Franchising
53 West Jackson
Boulevard, Suite 756
Chicago, IL 60604
(800) 222-4943

BOOKS

The 50 Best Low-Income, High-Profit Franchises
Robert Laurance Perry
Prentice Hall

15 Columbus Circle
New York, NY 10023
(800) 947-7700

Best Home Businesses for the '90s
Paul and Sarah Edwards
Communication
Creativity
425 Cedar Street
Buena Vista, CO 81211
(800) 331-8355

Big Ideas for Small Service Businesses: How to Successfully Advertise, Publicize, and Maximize Your Business or Professional Practice
Marilyn & Tom Ross
Same as above

Business Building Ideas for Franchises and Small Business
Med Serif
Pilot Industries, Inc.
103 Cooper Street
Babylon, NY 11702
(516) 422-2225

The Consultant's Kit
Jeffrey Lant
Communication
Creativity
425 Cedar Street
Buena Vista, CO 81211
(800) 331-8355

Decision Making for Small Business Management
Jerrald F. Young

I look on that man as happy, who, when there is a question of success, looks into his work for a reply. —*Ralph Waldo Emerson*

Krieger Publishing Co.
Box 9542
Melbourne, FL 32902
(407) 724-9542

*Develop a Profitable
Consulting Practice*
Howard L. Shenson
Communication Creativity
425 Cedar Street
Buena Vista, CO 81211
(800) 331-8355

*Evaluation and Buying a
Franchise*
James A. Meaney
Pilot Industries
103 Cooper Street
Babylon, NY 11702
(516) 422-2225

*FTC Franchising Rule:
The IFA Compliance Kit*
International Franchise
Association
P.O. Box 1502
Cranberry Township, PA
16036
(800) 543-1038

*Financial Security and
Independence Through A
Small Business Franchise*
Donald J. Scherer
Pilot Industries
103 Cooper Street
Babylon, NY 11702
(516) 422-2225

*Finding Your Niche . . .
Marketing Your
Professional Service*

Brad Brodsky and
Janet Geis
Communication
Creativity
425 Cedar Street
Buena Vista, CO 81211
(800) 331-8355

*Franchise Investigation: A
Contract Negotiation*
Harry Gross and
Robert S. Levy
Pilot Industries, Inc.
103 Cooper Street
Babylon, NY 11702
(516) 422-2225

*Franchise Law
Bibliography*
American Bar Association
750 North Lake Shore
Drive
Chicago, IL 60611
(312) 988-5000

The Franchise Option
Henward M. Debanks, III
and William Ginalski
International Franchise
Association
P.O. Box 1502
Cranberry Township, PA
16036
(800) 543-1038

*Franchises You Can Run
From Home*
Lynie Arden
John Wiley & Sons, Inc.
1 Wiley Drive
Somerset, NJ 08875
(800) 225-5945

Franchising
Gladys Glickman
Matthew Bender & Co.,
Inc.
1275 Broadway
Albany, NY 12201
(518) 487-3385

*Franchising Business
Opportunities Rule and
Guides*
Federal Trade Commission
Division of Marketing
Practices
6th Street and Pennsylvania
Avenue, NW
Washington, DC 20580
(202) 326-3128
(free)

*Franchising—The How-
to Book*
Lloyd Tarbutton
International Franchise
Association
P.O. Box 1502
Cranberry Township, PA
16036
(800) 543-1038

Franchising: The Inside Story
John Kinch
International Franchise
Association
P.O. Box 1502
Cranberry Township, PA
16036
(800) 543-1038

Franchising Opportunities
International Franchise
Association

---

*I pity the man who wants a coat so cheap that the man or woman who produces the
cloth will starve in the process. —Benjamin Harrison*

P.O. Box 1502
Cranberry Township, PA
16036
(800) 543-1038

The Freelancer's Career Book
Nicki Montaperto
Arco Publishing
Simon and Schuster
Reference Division
One Gulf and
Western Plaza
New York, NY 10023
(800) 858-7674

Government Giveaways
for Entrepreneurs
Matthew Lesko
Communication Creativity
425 Cedar Street
Buena Vista, CO 81211
(800) 331-8355

Handbook for Small
Business Advertising
Michael Anthony
Addison-Wesley
1 Jacob Way
Reading, MA 01867
(800) 447-2226

Home Business for Under
$5,000.00
Kennedy and Arden
Sun Features Inc.
Box 368-P
Cardiff, CA 92007
(619) 431-1660

The Home Office
Computing Handbook,
AT&T Edition

Editors of Home Office
Computing
Windcrest McGraw Hill,
Inc.
1331 Monterey Avenue
Blue Ridge Summit, PA
17294
(800) 822-8158

Homemade Money: The
Definitive Guide to Success
in a Home-based Business
Barbara Brabec
Communication
Creativity
425 Cedar Street
Buena Vista, CO 81211
(800) 331-8355

How to Be a Franchisor
Robert E. Kushell and
Carl E. Zwisler III
International Franchise
Association
P.O. Box 1502
Cranberry Township, PA
16066
(800) 543-1038

How to Become
Successfully Self-Employed
Brian R. Smith
Bob Adams, Inc.
260 Center Street
Holbrook, MA 02343
(800) 872-5627

How to Leave Your Job
and Buy a Business of
Your Own
C.D. Peterson
Consultants Bookstore

Templeton Road
Fitzwilliam, NH 03447
(603) 585-2200

How to Organize and
Operate a Small Business
Clifford M. Baumback
Prentice Hall
15 Columbus Circle
New York, NY 10023
(800) 947-7700

How to Prepare and
Process-Import Documents:
A Fully Illustrated Guide
Tyler G. Hicks
International Wealth
Success
Box 186
Merrick, NY 11566
(800) 323-0548

How to Prepare Effective
Business Program
Blueprints
David D. Seltz
Addison-Wesley
General Books Division
1 Jacob Way
Reading, MA 01867
(800) 447-2226

How to Run Your Own
Home Business
Coralee Smith Kern and
Tammara Hoffman
Wolfgram
VGM Publishing Group
4255 West Touhy Avenue
Lincolnwood, IL
60646-1975
(800) 323-4900

If a man should happen to reach perfection in this world, he would have to die imme-
diately to enjoy himself. —Josh Billings

How to Select a Franchise
Robert McIntosh
International Franchise
Association
P.O. Box 1502
Cranberry Township, PA
16066
(800) 543-1038

*How to Set Your Fees
and Get Them*
Kate Kelly
Communication Creativity
425 Cedar Street
Buena Vista, CO 81211
(800) 331-8355

*How to Start and Operate
a Home-Based Word
Processing or Desktop
Publishing Business*
Michele Loftus
Bob Adams Inc.
260 Center Street
Holbrook, MA 02343
(800) 872-5627

*How You Can Buy A
Business without Overpaying*
Eugene Merfeld and
Gary L. Schine
The Career Press, Inc.
180 5th Avenue
P.O. Box 34
Hawthorne, NJ 07507
(800) 227-3371

*Insider's Guide to Small
Business Resources*
David E. Gumpert and
Jeffrey Timmons
Doubleday

666 Fifth Avenue
New York, NY 10103
(800) 223-6834

*Investigate Before
Investing: Guidance for
Prospective Franchisees*
International Franchise
Association
P.O. Box 1502
Cranberry Township, PA
16066
(800) 543-1038

Is Franchising for You?
Robert K. McIntosh
International Franchise
Association
P.O. Box 1502
Cranberry Township, PA
16066
(800) 543-1038

*Legal Aspects of Selling
and Buying*
Philip Zeidman
Shepard's McGraw-Hill,
Inc.
P.O. Box 35300
Colorado Springs, CO
80935-3530
(719) 488-3000

*Low Cost Market
Research: Guide for
Small Business*
Keith Gorton and
Isobel Carr
John Wiley & Sons, Ltd.
1 Wiley Drive
Somerset, NJ 08875
(800) 225-5945

Making It on Your Own
Sarah and Paul Edwards
Communication
Creativity
425 Cedar Street
Buena Vista, CO 81211
(800) 331-8355

*Making Money With Your
Computer at Home*
Same as above

*Marketing for the Home-
Based Business*
Jeffrey P. Davidson
Bob Adams, Inc.
260 Center Street
Holbrook, MA 02343
(800) 872-5627

*Marketing Planning
Strategies*
Craig S. Rice
The Dartnell Corp.
4660 Ravenswood Avenue
Chicago, IL 60640
(312) 561-4000

*Marketing Without a
Marketing Budget*
Craig S. Rice
Bob Adams, Inc.
260 Center Street
Holbrook, MA 02343
(800) 872-5627

*New Venture Creation:
A Guide to Small Business
Development*
Jeffrey A. Timmons
Richard D. Irwin, Inc.
1333 Burr Ridge Parkway

---

*If I am not for myself, who will be for me? And if I am only for myself, what am I?
And if not now—when?—Hillel*

Burr Ridge, IL 60521
(800) 634-3966

*Organizing Your Home
Office for Success: Expert
Strategies That Can
Work for You*
Plume
Penguin USA
P.O. Box 999
Bergenfield, NJ
07621
(800) 253-6476

*Out on Your Own: From
Corporate to Self-
Employment*
R. W. Bly and Blake G.
John Wiley and
Sons, Inc.
1 Wiley Drive
Somerset, NJ 08878
(800) 225-5945

*Own Your Own
Franchise: Everything
You Need to Know About
the Best Franchise
Opportunities in America*
Ray Bard and Sheila
Henderson
Addison-Wesley
1 Jacob Way
Reading, MA 01867
(800) 447-2226

The Perfect Business Plan
William R. Lasher
Doubleday
1540 Broadway
New York, NY 10036
(800) 323-9872

*Pilot's Question and
Answer Guide to Successful
Franchising*
Pilot Industries, Inc.
103 Cooper Street
Babylon, NY 11702
(516) 422-2225

Promotional Strategy
James F. Engel, Martin
R. Warshaw, and Thomas
C. Kinnear
Richard D. Irwin, Inc.
1333 Burr Ridge Parkway
Burr Ridge, IL 60521
(800) 634-3966

*Protecting Your
Franchising Trademark
and Trade Secrets*
Donald A. Kaul
International Franchise
Association
P.O. Box 1502
Cranberry Township, PA
16066
(800) 543-1038

*Running a One Person
Business*
Claude Whitmeyer,
Salli Rasberry, and
Michael Phillips
Ten Speed Press
P.O. Box 7123
Berkeley, CA 94707
(800) 841-2665

*Small Business
Management*
Nicholas C. Siropolis
Houghton Mifflin Co.

c/o College Order
Processing
Wayside Road
Burlington, MA 01803
(617) 351-5000

*Small Business Management
Fundamentals*
Dan Steinhoff and
John F. Burgess
McGraw-Hill, Inc.
1221 Avenue of the
Americas
New York, NY 10020
(800) 722-4726

*Small-Time Operator:
How to Start Your Own
Small Business, Keep Your
Books, Pay Your Taxes,
& Stay Out of Trouble*
Bernard Kamoroff, CPA
Communication
Creativity
425 Cedar Street
Buena Vista, CO 81211
(800) 331-8355

*Start Up: An
Entrepreneur's Guide
to Launching and
Managing a New Business*
William Stolze
The Career Press, Inc.
180 5th Avenue
P.O. Box 34
Hawthorne, NJ 07507
(800) 227-3371

Starting a Business After 50
Samuel Small
Pilot Industries, Inc.

Imagination is not a talent of some men but is the health of every man.
—Ralph Waldo Emerson

103 Cooper Street
Babylon, NY 11702
(516) 422-2225

Starting a Mini-Business:
A Guidebook for Seniors
Nancy Olsen
Fair Oaks Publishing
Company
941 Populus Place
Sunnyvale, CA 94086
(408) 732-1078

Starting Your Own
Business: Books,
Periodicals, Organizations,
Agencies and Courses to
Help You Get Started
Women's Career
Center, Inc.
Temple Building
706 East Avenue
Rochester, NY 14607
(716) 244-0750

Strategic Planning for the
Small Business
Craig S. Rice
Bob Adams, Inc.
260 Center Street
Holbrook, MA 02343
(800) 872-5627

Twenty-One Questions
International Franchise
Association
P.O. Box 1502
Cranberry Township, PA
16066
(800) 543-1038

The Unabashed Self-
Promoter's Guide
Jeffrey Lant
Communication Creativity
425 Cedar Street
Buena Vista, CO 81211
(800) 331-8355

Understanding Franchise
Contracts
David C. Hjelmselt
Pilot Industries, Inc.
103 Cooper Street
Babylon, NY 11702
(516) 422-2225

A Woman's Guide to
Her Own Franchised
Business
Anne Small
Pilot Industries, Inc.
103 Cooper Street
Babylon, NY 11702
(516) 422-2225

Working from Home
Paul and Sarah Edwards
Jeremy P. Tarcher
Putnam, Inc.
P.O. Box 506
East Rutherford, NJ
07073
(800) 788-6262

Working Solo
Terri Lonier
Communication
Creativity
425 Cedar Street
Buena Vista, CO 81211
(800) 331-8355

Imagination rules the world. —Napoleon Bonaparte

Index

ABOUT THE AUTHOR

MARTIN YATE is an international bestselling author and America's leading advocate for working professionals. His previous positions include Director of Training for Dunhill Personnel System, Inc., and Director of Personnel for Bell Industries Computer Memory Division. His other books include *Knock 'em Dead: The Ultimate Job-Seeker's Handbook, Hiring the Best, Resumes That Knock 'em Dead,* and *Cover Letters That Knock 'em Dead.*